LIVING IN THE TIMES OF THE SIGNS

Bible Prophecy for the 21st Century

David R. Barnhart

xulon
PRESS

Living In The Times Of The Signs
by David R. Barnhart

Printed in the United States of America

ISBN 978-1-60477-051-3

Unless otherwise indicated, Bible quotations are taken from the NEW AMERICAN STANDARD BIBLE®, Copyright © 1960, 1962, 1963, 1968, 1971, 1972, 1973, 1975, 1977, 1995 by The Lockman Foundation. Used by permission. www.Lockman.org.

www.xulonpress.com

DEDICATION

This book is dedicated to Mary, my love, joy and inspiration, as we enter our 50th year of marriage and ministry.

OTHER BOOKS BY DAVID R. BARNHART

The Church's Desperate Need for Revival
Israel, Land of Promise and Prophecy
Contending for the Faith

For information about
Abiding Word Ministries
or to receive
The Vine and Branches

contact

Abiding Word Ministries
P.O. Box 275
Canal Winchester, OH 43110

www.thevineandbranches.org.

CONTENTS

SECTION ONE
LIVING IN THE TIMES OF THE SIGNS

SECTION TWO
MILITANT ISLAM—A CLEAR AND PRESENT DANGER

SECTION THREE
GOD'S UNIQUE REVELATION OF PROPHECY

SECTION FOUR
THE LORD STILL SPEAKS TO HIS CHURCH

SECTION ONE

LIVING IN THE TIMES
OF THE SIGNS

Jesus Christ is coming back again! It is the blessed hope of the Church, the redeeming hope of Israel, the only hope for a tottering world.

Yes, Jesus Christ is coming again, and whether you believe it or not, you will someday have to face Him as your Savior or your Judge.

M. R. DeHaan

Today there are some 10,000 Israeli Jewish believers in Jesus. Worldwide, conservative estimates put the number around 100,000. Some believe the number is closer to 300,000. What a startling increase—and my father and I and my sons are part of those numbers, part of that dramatic trend. Jews are turning to Jesus in record numbers, and they are getting excited about His Second Coming.

Joel C. Rosenberg

LIVING IN THE TIMES OF THE SIGNS

INTRODUCTION

Jesus Christ is coming again! He is coming for His church. He is coming to judge the living and the dead. He is coming as King of kings and Lord of lords to reign for all eternity! The hope of all the saints rests on this foundational Christian doctrine.

Those living in the twenty-first century have witnessed more signs of the Lord's return than any other people in history; and no more significant sign has been fulfilled than the return of the Jews to the reestablished State of Israel. Other signs also point to the Lord's imminent return, such as an unprecedented increase in knowledge that has taken humanity from the horse and buggy age to space travel in the span of a century. Earthquakes and other natural catastrophes are occurring with increased intensity. Crime, violence and lawlessness, much of it produced by illicit drug trafficking, have brought fear not only to those living in our cities but also in rural areas as well. With every passing year, our culture is becoming more decadent, as is clearly demonstrated by Hollywood and the media.

Today there is a depraved form of apostasy within the church that even dares to question and deny Christ's divine atonement. A great falling away from the faith is taking place, as Christians forsake their spiritual heritage. Throughout America and other Western nations, church structures, large and small, are being turned into commercial establishments or sold to non-Christian religions.

The United States has sanctioned and legitimized moral depravity. The legalization of abortion has caused the deaths of more than fifty million unborn babies since 1973. The acceptance of sodomy, promiscuity and same-sex marriages threaten to destroy the family structure that has been the strength of our nation since its founding. If God did not spare Israel for such infractions, you can be certain He will not spare America for the same grievous sins.

World War I was supposed to have been the war to end all wars, yet conflicts are erupting with increasing frequency from one end of the globe to the other. Even now respected national figures are suggesting we may be on the verge of World War III. As more nations acquire nuclear weapons, civilization faces the threat of a nuclear conflagration. Islamic terrorism has descended on the world like a plague. Once known only in the Middle East, terrorism now has major world powers running for cover. The terrorists have both the temerity and the capability to strike at the heart of the world's greatest powers.

Communist China, with its godless and humanistic form of government, has become a formidable competitor in the global economy. In 2006 the Chinese surprised the world when they successfully fired a missile into space and destroyed a satellite. The Chinese are pouring vast amounts of their resources into building sophisticated arms, naval ships and submarines. China has the largest army in the world. Its growing military complex and its ability to strike any nation on earth constitute a real threat to world peace.

While the breakup of the Soviet Union set Communism back on its heels, signs now point to the development of a political environment in Russia that resembles the days of the cold war. Once again

Russia is strengthening its military and projecting an increasingly hostile attitude toward the West.

Conditions in the Middle East continue to deteriorate. Terrorist organizations and hostile Islamic nations are making unprecedented threats against Israel. Iran is on the verge of becoming a nuclear power.

The magnitude of all these events and the speed at which they are unfolding should cause every Christian to carefully weigh the nearness of the Lord's coming. The words of Jesus to His disciples regarding His first coming may certainly be applied to us today: "Many prophets and righteous men desired to see what you see, and did not see it, and to hear what you hear, and did not hear it."[1] Truly we are living in the times of the signs.

JESUS WILL RETURN
TO THE MOUNT OF OLIVES

On the day of His ascension, Jesus and His disciples gathered on the Mount of Olives. As the disciples watched Jesus being lifted up into the clouds, two men in white clothing said to them: "Men of Galilee, why do you stand looking into the sky? This Jesus, who has been taken up from you into heaven, will come in just the same way as you have watched Him go into heaven."[2]

Zechariah foretold the day of the Lord's return: "In that day His feet will stand on the Mount of Olives...."[3] As Jesus literally ascended from the Mount of Olives, so also on a God-appointed day, He shall literally return to the Mount of Olives. Those who seek to spiritualize Christ's ascension and His coming again, saying that neither should be taken literally, are not accepting Scripture as it is written! The Bible says, "BEHOLD HE IS COMING WITH THE CLOUDS, and every eye will see Him, even those who pierced Him; and all the tribes of the earth will mourn over Him. So it is to be. Amen."[4]

THE CROSS AND THE CROWN

How may we be certain Jesus will personally and visibly return to earth? Because He said so! Not one of His promises will ever fail. The fact nearly 2000 years have passed since the Lord ascended does not mean the prophecies of Scripture were wrong, or anyone may justifiably question His literal return. Jesus often spoke about the day of His return. His coming is more certain than tomorrow's sunrise. Whether He is coming today or a thousand years from today, His coming is sure. It is the duty of Christians in every generation to be ready and watching for His appearing!

Even during the earliest days of the church, people mocked and raised doubts about the return of Jesus Christ, asking, "Where is the promise of His coming?" Peter answered them: "But do not let this one fact escape your notice, beloved, that with the Lord one day is like a thousand years, and a thousand years like one day. The Lord is not slow about His promise, as some count slowness, but is patient toward you, not wishing for any to perish but for all to come to repentance."[5]

The cross and the crown are forever connected. The message of Christ's return should never be proclaimed without connecting it to the loving heart of God, "who desires all men to be saved and to come to the knowledge of the truth."[6] The words "not wishing for any to perish" should be the motivation for all Christians to carry the message of God's redeeming love to a lost world. The cross of Christ bears witness to the truth that God desires neither the death nor the condemnation of anyone. Christ's return will be glorious for believers! The only people who need to dread His return are those who have willfully rejected Christ as Savior and Lord.

WATCHING AND WAITING

The Lord is not coming for a church that has prostituted herself to the world. He is coming for His holy and spotless bride, redeemed by His own precious blood. On that glorious day, the bride will be arrayed in "fine linen which is the righteous acts of the saints...

Blessed are those who are invited to the marriage supper of the Lamb."[7]

The time between Christ's ascension and His return is called the "church age" or the "age of grace." The New Testament refers to the entire church age as "the last days."[8] During the church age, Christians are directed to witness the gospel and gather in the harvest. While Jesus Christ is in heaven preparing a place for His bride, the church on earth needs to be preparing for the return of the Bridegroom. In every generation, the church should be eagerly watching, waiting and longing for His appearing.

Desiring that His church should not be taken by surprise, the Lord revealed various signs that will herald His coming. Because we do not know the exact day or hour of His return does not mean we should be ignorant or indifferent to those things He has chosen to make known. The Lord wants us to be alert, knowledgeable and ready. There are literally hundreds of prophecies regarding the first coming of Christ in the Old Testament. Every one of them was literally fulfilled. The Gospel writers detailed their fulfillment, offering chapter and verse as evidence. Therefore we may be confident all the promises of Christ's second coming will be literally fulfilled as well.

READY OR NOT,
THE LORD IS COMING

The history of the nominal church from Pentecost to the present hour is marred by many sinful practices. Certain epochs of church history are filled with violent acts. There were shameful times when portions of the church lauded heretics and persecuted the defenders of the true faith. There have been scandalous incidents, especially in the modern church, when trusted servants of God brought shame upon themselves and the church through perverse and immoral conduct.

The Roman Catholic Church in the United States is still reeling from thousands of allegations and charges against priests who molested children. It has paid out an estimated $2 billion in lawsuits filed against them over the last several decades; even now lawsuits against the Roman Catholic Church continue to mount. Several Catholic dioceses in America have had to file for bankruptcy protection.

Church history is also filled with noble deeds and acts of great faith, as men and women of God stood their ground during times of danger and persecution. Those saints who lived by faith (of whom the world was not worthy) chose death rather than shrink back from their loyalty to Christ.

John Wyclif and John Hus stood their ground against a corrupt and wicked church more than a hundred years before the Protestant Reformation. Luther, Calvin and Zwingli, whose voices neither emperor nor pope could silence, held high the cross during some of the darkest hours the church had ever known. John Knox, a Roman Catholic priest who after his conversion to Christ, led the Protestant Reformation in Scotland. Knox endured bitter persecution from Queen Mary and her supporters, yet the great Reformer's cry to God can still be heard today, "Give me Scotland or I die!" A new day dawned for the Body of Christ when the Protestant Reformers restored the great biblical doctrines—Grace alone, Faith alone and Scripture alone!

Down through the ages, thousands heard the call of the Holy Spirit to carry the gospel to the remotest parts of the earth and serve the Lord in poverty and obscurity. They sought no glory or fame for themselves, but only desired to do the will of the One who called them. Men and women like Hudson Taylor and Lottie Moon were among those who served the Lord with great faithfulness in China. Hudson Taylor once remarked, "If I had a thousand lives, I'd give them all for China."

One lone layman set the flames of revival burning in Norway in 1796 when he yielded his life to Jesus Christ. Hans Nielsen Hauge faced the fierce wrath of Lutheran clergy and government officials who controlled the state church of Norway, as he set out to preach Christ and call people to salvation. Because laymen were denied the right to preach in Norway, Hauge spent ten years in prison before being released in broken health. Yet when he died at age fifty-three, every Lutheran parish in Norway had been touched by his powerful ministry. The Hauge Movement was carried to Europe and America by thousands of Norwegian immigrants whose witness for Christ continues to this day.

UNIFIED PROPHECIES

Numerous passages that prophesied Christ's first coming also foretell His second coming. For example, Isaiah wrote:

> For a child will be born to us, a son will be given to us; and the government will rest on His shoulders; and His name will be called Wonderful Counselor, Mighty God, Eternal Father, Prince of Peace. There will be no end to the increase of His government or of peace, on the throne of David and over his kingdom, to establish it and to uphold it with justice and righteousness from then on and forevermore. The zeal of the Lord of hosts will accomplish this.[9]

The first portion of this prophecy describes Christ's first coming, while the remaining portion relates to His second coming.

In Nazareth's synagogue Jesus read from the scroll of Isaiah. It is no insignificant matter that He stopped reading in the middle of the passage.

> And He came to Nazareth, where He had been brought up; and as was His custom, He entered the synagogue on the Sabbath, and stood up to read. And the book of the prophet Isaiah was handed to Him. And He opened the book and found the place where it was written, "THE SPIRIT OF THE LORD IS UPON ME, BECAUSE HE ANOINTED ME TO PREACH THE GOSPEL TO THE POOR. HE HAS SENT ME TO PROCLAIM RELEASE TO THE CAPTIVES, AND RECOVERY OF SIGHT TO THE BLIND, TO SET FREE THOSE WHO ARE OPPRESSED, TO PROCLAIM THE FAVORABLE YEAR OF THE LORD."

Jesus closed the book and said, "Today this Scripture has been fulfilled in your hearing." He stopped reading in the middle of a verse because what followed concerned His second coming.[10] How can one embrace the literal fulfillment of verses dealing with the Lord's first coming, while ignoring or spiritualizing portions of the same passages that point to His second coming?

THE SILENCE OF THE CHURCH

There are church members who have never heard a sermon or attended a Bible study devoted to the second coming of Christ. Even some pastors have never undertaken an in-depth study of eschatology. There is no excuse for such gross neglect of this vital doctrine of the Word of God. Jesus chided the Pharisees, "Do you know how to discern the appearance of the sky, but cannot discern the signs of the times?"[11] A short while later, Jesus sat down with his disciples on the Mount of Olives and opened the Scriptures pertaining to His return.

At least thirty percent of the Bible is devoted to prophecy. That is a lot of Scripture to ignore. Some pastors do not preach sermons about Christ's second coming because they deem the subject too controversial; others keep their distance because they do not feel academically qualified to even broach the subject. Still others are fearful of being identified with date-setters or with those who promote controversial doctrines.

Perhaps no one has captured the need for Christians to embrace the whole counsel of God, including the second coming of Christ, as did the eminent theologian and preacher, R. A. Torrey. In his book *The Return of the Lord Jesus,* Dr. Torrey said:

> …The truth of the Lord's Second Coming is a truth of the very first importance. To many the doctrine of the Second Coming of Christ seems like an impractical doctrine. I once so regarded it. In my early ministry, one of my members came to me and asked if I would speak upon the Second Coming of Christ. I knew nothing about the doctrine and put him off, thinking to myself, "you will be a much older man than you are now before I speak upon a doctrine so impractical." But the day came when I found it was not only one of

the most precious but also one of the most practical doctrines in the whole Bible.

There have been four marked epochs in my Christian experience: first, when I came to know Jesus Christ as my personal Savior and my Lord; secondly, when I discovered that the Bible was indeed the inerrant Word of God, that its statements were absolutely reliable in every respect, and that everything any man needed to know was contained in this one Book; thirdly, when I learned that the baptism with the Holy Spirit was for the present day and claimed it for myself; and fourthly, when I came to see the truth concerning the Second Coming of Christ. The latter truth transformed my whole idea of life; it broke the power of the world and its ambition over me and filled my life with the most radiant optimism even under the most discouraging circumstances.[12]

The fact that so many teachers proffer their own misguided and unbiblical teachings regarding end-time events is reason enough for every pastor to seek a right understanding of the doctrine of the second coming of Christ and teach it to his people. Biblical prophecy should not be taught in order to satisfy people's curiosity about end-time events, but to prepare them for eternity and motivate them to enter the harvest field with a sense of urgency.

DIFFERING VIEWS ON ESCHATOLOGY

There are a variety of theological positions and opinions regarding the second coming of Christ. However, there are two basic positions that are held by the vast majority within the church; they are amillennialism and premillennialism. In addition there are a few who promote what is called postmillennialism. Each of these will be examined in this book. Interestingly, statements regarding the second coming in the Apostles' Creed and the Nicene Creed are confessed by persons who hold to any one of these positions. The Apostles' Creed simply declares "He ascended into heaven; and is seated on the right hand of God the Father Almighty; from where

He shall come to judge the living and the dead." The Nicene Creed adds to the above statement as follows: "And He shall come again *with glory* to judge both the living and the dead: *Whose kingdom shall have no end.*"[13]

God has set limits to man's understanding about future events, and we should never attempt to go beyond the revelation of the Word of God. The disciples of Jesus were with Him for three years; they listened to His teachings and witnessed His many miracles. Yet it was only after His resurrection that He sought to "explain to them the things concerning Himself in all the Scriptures."[14]

After the Lord had given a detailed description of the future to Daniel, the aging prophet did not understand and asked, "What will be the outcome of these events?" The Lord said to him, "Go your way, Daniel, for these words are concealed and sealed up until the end time."[15] Yet Jesus spoke of Daniel's prophecy regarding the future desecration of the Temple that will take place prior to His return.[16] The Holy Spirit continues to manifest biblical prophecies that were previously veiled.

Many questions and much mystery surround the books of Daniel and Revelation, as well as other prophetic writings. But our inability to comprehend the totality of biblical prophecies does not preclude us from studying them through the light of other portions of God's Word. The Lord gives to each believer the illumination of the Holy Spirit—"But when He, the Spirit of truth, comes, He will guide you into all the truth; for He will not speak on His own initiative, but whatever He hears, He will speak; *and He will disclose to you what is to come.*"[17]

As we move closer to the return of Christ and as prophetic events continue to unfold, our understanding of God's Word will be increased. For example, many commentaries and books on prophecy were written long before the nation of Israel was reestablished, in which the authors anticipated one day the Jews would return to the land of Israel. You and I, however, have been privileged to witness the fulfillment of this much heralded sign of the Lord's return. For them it was an event yet to be unfolded; for us it is prophecy fulfilled!

Near the conclusion of the Lord's unveiling of end-time events in the last book of the New Testament, He instructed John, "Do not seal up the words of the prophecy of this book, for the time is near."[18] God wants us to know about these prophetic events, so that we may be fully prepared to greet Him and motivated to carry out the mandate of the Great Commission.

ONE IN HOPE AND DOCTRINE

It is unfortunate differing theological positions on eschatology should cause division among Christians who otherwise hold to a high view of Scripture and the fundamental doctrines of the Bible. Christians have long held differing views regarding baptism, the Lord's Supper and a host of other foundational doctrines. However, truth is truth, no matter who affirms or denies it. For years most people believed the earth was flat. Those who held to the "flat earth" view, though intellectually restricted by their ignorance, were still able to function, regardless of their mistaken understanding. The Lord's Supper is what it is, not because of what various denominations or individuals confess it to be but in the reality of what Christ has declared it to be in His Word. Though none of us in this life will ever be able to comprehend the full meaning of the Lord's Supper, by faith we may partake of it and receive all its benefits and blessings.

Even a person with low mental ability can be saved. One does not need a doctorate in theology or be able to understand every nuance of doctrine in order to receive the free gift of salvation. Years ago I had the privilege to baptize a thirty-three-year-old man whose IQ was extremely low. Prior to his baptism, he joyfully sang "Jesus loves me, this I know, for the Bible tells me so." He did not understand the doctrine of redemption or know anything about the second coming of Christ, but he knew Jesus loved him, and he loved Jesus. According to the Bible, that is enough! In many respects, we are all like that man when it comes to possessing a complete understanding of God's revelation. Yet in His mercy God gifts us with His Word and His Holy Spirit, whereby He enables us, by faith, to lay hold of things that we cannot fully comprehend this side of heaven.

One day the Lord will impart His truth to us in all of its fullness. Paul wrote, "Now I know in part, but then I will know fully just as I also have been fully known."[19] In the meantime our hearts should not be hardened to believers who have a different understanding than our own regarding the second coming of Christ, when they, in fact, also affirm the fundamental doctrines of the Christian faith. All who truly profess Jesus Christ as Savior are our brothers and sisters in Christ. Paul said, "If I have the gift of prophecy, and know all mysteries and all knowledge; and if I have all faith, so as to remove mountains, but do not have love, I am nothing."[20] A perfect knowledge about the second coming of Christ will not get us to heaven, nor will the lack of it keep us from heaven.

DOCTRINES CONNECTED
TO THE RETURN OF CHRIST

The Bible directly connects numerous doctrines with the coming again of Jesus Christ. Without doubt, all doctrines have their fulfillment in Christ's promised return. His coming at the close of the age is the motivation for our faith and life on earth. Paul said to Timothy: "I solemnly charge you in the presence of God and of Christ Jesus, who is to judge the living and the dead, and by His appearing and His kingdom: preach the word...."[21] The Scriptures connect the Lord's Supper to Jesus' coming again: "For as often as you eat this bread and drink the cup, you proclaim the Lord's death until He comes."[22] The Bible urges us to faithfully carry out our respective ministries, based on the fact that the Lord is coming soon. "Let us hold fast the confession of our hope without wavering, for He who promised is faithful; and let us consider how to stimulate one another to love and good deeds, not forsaking our own assembling together, as is the habit of some, but encouraging one another; and all the more as you see the day drawing near."[23]

NO NEED FOR SPECULATION

The opening chapter of this book sets forth various views concerning eschatology. It will become clear, if it hasn't already, I believe the Bible is the inspired, infallible and inerrant Word of God, and I hold to the premillennial view of the Lord's return, including the pre-tribulation rapture of the church and the thousand-year reign of Christ on earth. My theological position is based on a literal interpretation of the Bible wherever that is possible. Passages that are clearly symbolic should be interpreted as such. In various portions of Scripture, symbolism is identified and explained. I agree with the long-established principle of interpretation: "When the plain sense makes good sense, seek no other sense."[24]

As you read this book, my desire is that you will see Jesus in all of His beauty and desire to walk in the light of His Word. My purpose is not to persuade you to accept every aspect of my understanding on all matters pertaining to the Lord's return. I have stated them; I stand on them with the deepest conviction, but I do not presume what is written here is the last word on end-time prophecy. It is the Lord who has the last Word, and one day He shall make all things known.

My purpose in writing this book is to enable Christians to better understand the prophetic passages of Scripture and apply them not only to current events but also to their daily lives. My hope is that believers will see the unity of the Scriptures as well as the centrality of the doctrine of Christ's return to the whole of the Bible's teachings. As one reads the Bible from Genesis through Revelation in the power of the Holy Spirit, there is an increasing awareness every word of Scripture is true and the words themselves are interconnected. One part of Scripture sheds light on yet another part. Words, names, numbers, events and geographical places in the Bible all have meaning, often prophetic meaning, and often multiple meanings which God wants us to know and understand.

The signs relating to Christ's return shall take place exactly as they were written. Prophecies that have been fulfilled, many of them in our lifetime, are there for us to see, if only we will open our eyes and our hearts. Prophecies concerning the return of the Jews to the land God gave to them as part of an eternal covenant are present-day realities. As events in the Middle East and around the globe continue to unfold, we need to examine them in the light of Scripture. Yet in the final analysis, we are not looking for signs but rather for the literal return of our Lord and Savior, Jesus Christ.

It is heartening to see people study as you are doing now, endeavoring to learn and grow in this important aspect of the Bible's teaching. This book was written especially for those who have not had much exposure to prophetic studies. Hopefully, undertaking this study will increase your desire to further examine the Scriptures.

It is my prayer that by considering various signs of the Lord's imminent return and comparing them with world and national occurrences your heart will be stirred with joyful anticipation of your own personal participation in that glorious event. May God grant you a sense of urgency to faithfully witness the gospel and remain true to His Word until He comes, or until He calls you to His heavenly home.

David R. Barnhart
August 2007

Chapter 1

BASICS OF BIBLICAL PROPHECY

Eschatology is a theological term meaning "a study of last things" relating to the return of Jesus Christ. There are three basic theological concepts in the study of eschatology—premillennialism, amillennialism and postmillennialism. Within each concept are several different methods of interpretation and, of course, several different opinions. Millennialism and/or premillennialism, also known as *chiliasm*, refer to the doctrine of the thousand-year reign of Christ. The word *millennial* is derived from a Latin root—*Mille*, meaning a thousand and *annus*, meaning a year.

Most mainline churches today espouse the amillennial method of prophetic interpretation, while evangelical and fundamentalist churches tend toward dispensational premillennialism. Not all pastors and members of evangelical and fundamentalist churches support the premillennial view, nor does everyone within mainline churches embrace the amillennial view.

Since most prophecy books, teaching tapes and seminars have a decided bent toward premillennialism, it may be surprising to learn that the majority of Christians hold to the amillennial view of eschatology, at least in theory. However, even though amillennialism is the official theological position of several mainline Protestant denominations as well as the Roman Catholic Church, the vast majority of members in these churches haven't a clue when it comes to understanding the basics about the doctrine of Christ's second coming. Those who attend churches where the premillennial view is embraced are usually more informed about the second coming than their counterparts in the mainline churches. Still there are numerous evangelical churches where the subject is rarely raised.

Rick Warren, in his best-selling book *The Purpose Driven Life*, suggested Christians need not bother to study about the second coming of Christ, since missions are more important. He described an incident when Jesus' disciples asked Him to tell them about prophecy. Warren put words in Jesus' mouth He never uttered and reached a conclusion totally foreign to what the Bible actually teaches about this topic.

> When the disciples wanted to talk about prophecy, Jesus quickly switched the conversation to evangelism. He wanted them to concentrate on their mission in the world. He said in essence, "The details of my return are none of your business. What is your business is the mission I've given you. Focus on that."[1]

Of course Jesus never said anything of the kind, nor did He intimate anything resembling what Warren has Jesus saying. Various Gospel accounts reveal that Jesus went into great detail explaining to His disciples many aspects concerning end-time events.

Teachings about the second coming of Christ are found in each of the four Gospels, in the Epistles and in the Book of Revelation. The fact every Christian should be engaged in witnessing the gospel is no excuse for neglecting this essential doctrine of the church. Unfortunately Rick Warren's attitude concerning the second coming of Christ is not uncharacteristic of the attitude held by many evangelical pastors today.

According to Paul there is no greater motivation in the world for witnessing the gospel than the realization Jesus Christ is coming again. He instructed Timothy, "I solemnly charge you in the presence of God and of Christ Jesus, who is to judge the living and the dead, and by His appearing and His Kingdom: preach the word...."[2]

Most mainline seminaries today offer little instruction in eschatology. They consider the subject as having little or no relevance in the daily lives of Christians. Consequently, pastors in these denominations tend to avoid prophetic texts or spin them with the denominational line. In my years of formal training at a mainline seminary, courses in eschatology were nonexistent. My professors never offered a study on Daniel, Ezekiel or Revelation. Courses dealing with the Major and Minor Prophets rarely included eschatological applications.

After completing seminary I was prompted by the Holy Spirit to search the Scriptures diligently on this vital subject. My counsel is that you do the same. Do not blindly support the prophetic views of your particular church, pastor or denomination until you have diligently examined the Word of God on this essential subject for yourself. Be like the Bereans who, after listening to the teachings of Paul, "...received the word with great eagerness, examining the Scriptures daily to see whether these things were so."[3]

HISTORICAL BACKGROUND

The writings of the early church fathers and assorted historical accounts offer ample evidence the early church held almost exclusively to the premillennial view of Christ's return. Christians interpreted biblical texts, including prophetic passages, in a literal sense or as they were written.

Throughout the New Testament era, there was a sense of expectation on the part of the early church concerning the Lord's literal and imminent return. Belief in this doctrine gave them motivation and hope! The writers of the New Testament frequently quoted prophecies from the Old Testament, understanding that if the prophecies concerning the person and work of Christ were literally fulfilled at His first coming, then prophecies relating to His second coming would also happen exactly as they had been described.

The amillennial view came on the scene in the late second and early third centuries. This view of eschatology was formed largely by Origen (185-254) and theologians in a school in Alexandria, Egypt, where it was taught that Scripture should not be interpreted literally but rather allegorically. Many of their biblical interpretations bordered on the bizarre, while some were outright heretical. Eventually amillennialism became the dominant view of the church, though there were always some within the church that espoused a more literal interpretation of Scripture.

Postmillennialism was advanced in the sixteenth century, but it never received much attention until the late eighteenth century. This view of eschatology is not widely held today because its basic premise is obviously flawed. Postmillennialism teaches Christianity will ultimately usher in a golden age of universal peace and goodwill before Christ returns. Postmillennialists believe the last thousand years of this present age will constitute the millennium. One is hard-pressed to look upon our world today and rationalize things are getting better.

PREMILLENNIALISM

A literal interpretation of the Old and New Testaments usually brings one to a premillennial understanding of end-time events. Premillennialism is based on the premise the Bible is the divinely inspired and inerrant Word of God, fully accurate in all of its teachings. Those holding to the premillennial view accept the biblical texts of prophecy literally, rather than attempting to allegorize them. Adherents of premillennialism employ what is called "a futurist approach" to biblical interpretation, believing end-time prophecies will be literally fulfilled in some future connection with the Lord's coming.

The life of Christ, the manner of His birth, death, resurrection and return were prophesied in precise detail throughout the Old Testament. On the day of His resurrection, Jesus met two disciples on the road to Emmaus and opened the Scriptures to them. "Then beginning with Moses and with all the prophets, He explained to them the things concerning Himself in all the Scriptures." They responded by saying, "Were not our hearts burning within us while He was speaking to us on the road, while He was explaining the Scriptures to us?"[4] The Lord could have showed them the scars on His hands, feet and side, but instead He brought them to faith in exactly the same way we are brought to faith, by beholding and believing the Scriptures.

The manner of Christ's death by crucifixion is described with amazing detail in Psalm 22, even though crucifixion would not be commonly practiced for several hundred years. Christ's reign on earth at the close of the age is described in Psalms 2, 72, 110, 118, 132 and a host of other passages in just this one book of the Bible.

Revelation and other writings of John and Paul unquestionably embraced the literal return of Jesus Christ and His thousand-year reign on earth. Numerous passages in the Old Testament describe conditions that will exist on earth under the rule of the King of Glory. The early church interpreted these and other prophetic writings in the New Testament literally. They also understood biblical passages containing symbolism, types and allegory should be interpreted accordingly.

John's disciple Polycarp, bishop of Smyrna (80-167), firmly held to a premillennial view of the second coming of Christ. Polycarp's disciple Papias, bishop of Hierapolis (80-163), likewise maintained the same view. Irenaeus, a student of Papias (140-202), also affirmed a premillennial view of the Lord's return. The fact that these four church fathers were linked to one another historically as well as theologically on this vital doctrine should not be glossed over.

In his book *Against Heresies,* Irenaeus stated:

Polycarp also was not only instructed by apostles, and conversed with many who had seen Christ, but was also, by apostles in Asia, appointed bishop of the Church in Smyrna, whom I also saw in my early youth, for he tarried [on earth] a very long time, and, when a very old man, gloriously and nobly suffering martyrdom, departed this life, having always taught the things which he had learned from the apostles, and which the church has handed down, and which alone are true."[5]

Other early church fathers who espoused the view of Christ's return and His millennial reign include: Clement of Rome (40-100), Ignatius (50-115), Justin Martyr (100-168), Tertulian (150-220), Hippolytus (160-240), and Cyprian (200-258).

Dispensational Premillennialism

Premillennialism experienced a revival in the nineteenth and twentieth centuries when it came to be called *Dispensational Premillennialism*. Chief among its proponents were John Nelson Darby of the Plymouth Brethren Church, and Congregationalist minister C. I. Scofield who wrote his widely used reference Bible. Dispensational premillennialism recognizes seven different epochs or dispensations in God's dealings with mankind. They are as follows:

- The first dispensation (Innocence) extended from the creation of Adam and Eve through their expulsion from the Garden of Eden.
- The second dispensation (Conscience) lasted from Cain to Noah and the flood.
- The third dispensation (Human Government) began with Noah following the flood to the Tower of Babel.
- The fourth dispensation (Promise) was from Abraham to the exodus.
- The fifth dispensation (Law) extended from Moses to the ascension of Christ.
- The sixth dispensation (Grace) began at Pentecost; it will end at the second coming of Christ.
- The seventh dispensation (Kingdom) will begin at the second coming of Christ and conclude with the final judgment.

Also critical in the teaching of dispensational premillennialism is the reestablishment of the nation of Israel as well as God's dealings with Israel and the Jews during the tribulation.

Dispensational premillennialism goes into greater detail about end-time events than did the millennialism espoused in the first and second centuries by the church fathers. Dispensational premillennialism lists the order of end-time events as follows:

- The Church Age (Pentecost to the Rapture of the Church).
- The Rapture of the Church (the resurrection and gathering of the saints).
- The Seven-years of tribulation when the antichrist shall rule the world. The second half of the tribulation is called the Great Tribulation. During this time the saints will appear before Christ in heaven to render an account of their stewardship. Finally the Marriage Supper of the Lamb takes place in heaven immediately prior to the return of Christ with His bride, the church.
- The Battle of Armageddon will take place at the time of the second coming of Christ. The Lord Himself will intervene and bring swift destruction on those who fight against Israel.
- The second coming of Christ in clouds of glory will bring an end to the rule of the antichrist; Satan will be bound for a thousand years; and the judgment of the nations will take place.
- The thousand-year reign of Christ from Jerusalem will bring peace and harmony to the whole earth. At the end of the thousand years, Satan will be loosed for a brief period and lead a rebellion against the Lord, but he and his forces will be defeated by Christ.
- The resurrection and judgment of the wicked will occur immediately following the millennial reign of Christ.
- The New Heaven, the New Earth and the New Jerusalem will be established; the Lord and His saints will be together for all eternity.

Premillennialism in the Lutheran Church

Even though amillennialism has been taught in the Lutheran church from the days of the Reformation to the present, highly respected Lutheran theologians embraced the millennial position in the nineteenth century. Chief among them was Joseph Seiss, a gifted theologian and author. George N. H. Peters, a pastor and theologian from Ohio, authored a 2100-page book *The Kingdom of Jesus Christ*, in which he championed the Lord's millennial kingdom. David Larson, professor at Trinity Evangelical Seminary in Deerfield, Illinois, stated: "Peters suffered much ecclesiastically for his stand, but exerted a broad and effective witness for truth."[6]

According to Dr. Francis Monseth, Dean of the Association Free Lutheran Seminary, theologians who broke ranks with the traditional Lutheran amillennialist position and adopted the premillennial view included: Revere F. Weidner, George H. Gerberding, Conrad E. Lindeberg, J. N. Kildahl and J. Michael Reu. Dr. Monseth cites other Lutheran pastors and theologians, associated with the Lutheran Bible Institute in Minneapolis and the Lutheran Evangelistic Movement, who also held to the premillennial view—Samuel Miller, A. W. Knock, Theodore Hax, Evald Conrad, J. O. Gisselquist and Arnold Stone.[7]

Premillennialism continued to grow even stronger in the twentieth century through the scholarship and influence of such respected men as Harry Ironside, Alva J. McClain, Charles Ryrie, J. Dwight Pentecost and John Walvoord, to name but a few.

AMILLENNIALISM

The letter "a" before millennial is Latin for "no." *Amillennial* literally means *no* millennium. Amillennialists believe there will be only one resurrection of both the wicked and the righteous at the coming of Christ; it will be followed by His judgment of all mankind. Then Christ will reign eternally with His saints in heaven.

The letter "a" in amillennialism could well represent the word *allegory,* because that word best describes the amillennialists' method of interpreting most biblical passages dealing with end-time events. Those who apply the allegorical approach to hundreds of Scripture passages relating to Christ's second coming must always conclude with the statement: "That's what the Bible says, but that is not what it means."

Amillennialists do not believe in the rapture of the church or the literal thousand-year reign of Christ on earth. They interpret references to the thousand years as the period of time between Pentecost and the second coming of Christ. Amillennialists believe Satan was bound at the cross, and he remains bound to this day.

Premillennialists argue that if we are now living in the millennium, which the Bible depicts as earth's most glorious time, how do the amillennialists account for the evil that continues to destroy so many lives? Considering the evil that presently exists in this fallen world, how could anyone believe that Satan is now bound from deceiving the nations? Why do so many Scriptures warn us of Satan's efforts to deceive and to destroy? Why would Peter caution us: "Your adversary, the devil, prowls around like a roaring lion, seeking someone to devour?"[8]

Amillennialists believe in "replacement theology," a belief that God is finished with the Jews. They assert that the church has replaced Israel in terms of God's promises, covenants and blessings. They see no connection concerning prophecies about the Jews returning to their homeland before the Lord returns and what is happening in Israel today. One of the most frequent criticisms amillennialists make against premillennialists is their support of Israel.

Liberal amillennialists hold to a low view of Scripture, questioning the divine inspiration of the Bible, while believing that all aspects of eschatology have no substance in fact. Most liberal amillennialists deny the miracles of Christ, His literal return at the end of the age, His virgin birth, His ascension and His literal resurrection. Furthermore, they question the existence of heaven and deny the existence of hell. If members of numerous mainline churches only knew what their pastors do *not* believe about Christ and the Bible, they would be appalled.

The Beginnings of Amillennialism

The allegorical approach used in the study of Revelation and other biblical works of prophecy was pioneered by Clement of Alexandria and Origen. Both expressed their doubts about the apostle John being the book's author, and they maintained the Book of Revelation was never intended to predict the future.

Augustine, bishop of Hippo (354-430), rejected the allegorical interpretation of Scripture that had gained popularity in the church through the influence of Origen and the Alexandrian school of theology. He sought to move the church back to a more credible exegesis of the biblical text, but Augustine retained the allegorical approach in matters of eschatology and the thousand-year reign of Christ.

Within the amillennialist camp are those who employ what is called "the preterist" approach. This concept of interpretation looks upon prophetic writings, such as Daniel and Revelation, as contemporary history rather than offering predictions about future events. Among the preterists are those who maintain the prophecies of Christ regarding end-time events were fulfilled with the destruction of the Temple in AD 70.

There are some amillennial adherents who hold to the historical approach regarding prophetic interpretations, teaching that some narratives describe future events in the context of history. Luther, for example, often applied the historical approach in his writings, believing end-time prophecies were being fulfilled in his day. He frequently spoke of the pope as being the antichrist, and suggested there would be a mass conversion of the Jews. The prevailing view at the time of the Reformation described the millennium as having begun with Emperor Constantine and having ended when the Turks invaded Europe.

John Walvoord said of the historical approach: "Its major difficulty is that its adherents have succumbed to the tendency to interpret the book [Revelation] as in some sense climaxing in their generation."[9] Walvoord added, "If the historical method is the correct one, it is clear until now that no one has found the key."[10]

More than any other person, Augustine established amillennialism as the church's official teaching; however, in his earlier years Augustine held to the premillennial view of the Lord's return. Luther, who was trained in the Augustinian theological approach, accepted the amillennial views of Augustine, as did most of the Reformers. At the time of the Reformation, so many other issues faced the Reformers that eschatology was given little attention.

The Second Coming and the Augsburg Confession

The doctrine of the second coming of Christ is affirmed in Article XVII of the Augsburg Confession. At the same time, it rejects "certain Jewish opinions which are even now making an appearance and which teach that, before the resurrection of the dead, saints and godly men will possess a worldly kingdom and annihilate all the godless."

Some Lutherans quote Article XVII in an attempt to disqualify any theological position other than amillennialism. But Article XVII can hardly be viewed as a condemnation of premillennialism for three reasons. First, Article XVII never fully defined what it meant by "a Jewish opinion," therefore interpretations regarding this vague definition of "a Jewish opinion" are subjective. Secondly, except for a few small sects, premillennialism was little promoted at the time of the Reformation. Thirdly, it seems unlikely the authors of the Augsburg Confession would have condemned the millennial teachings of the apostolic fathers.

Jews at the time of Christ did, in fact, believe God would one day send a messiah whose glory would exceed the reigns of David and Solomon. They further believed the messiah would come, not for any kind of redemptive purpose, but to liberate the Jewish people and establish an earthly kingdom. Jews living in the early part of the first century AD had no concept whatsoever of any type of messianic kingdom beyond this world. The concept of a liberating messiah had grown extremely popular because of the oppression of Rome.

Israel rejected Christ because He did not fulfill their messianic expectations. The prevailing Jewish concept of a messiah ruling over Israel was undoubtedly why John the Baptist sent messengers to Jesus asking, "Are you the One who is to come, or shall we look for another?" It may explain why the disciples were so confused immediately after the crucifixion of Christ and prior to the ascension when they asked Jesus: "Lord is it at this time You are restoring the kingdom to Israel?"[11]

It was not until after Pentecost that the disciples and the early church fathers began to comprehend exactly what the coming again of Christ and His millennial kingdom would mean not only to Israel and the church but to the whole world. As time went on, the Holy

Spirit opened their eyes to understand the teachings of Christ and the prophecies of the Old Testament that speak of end-time events and His coming.

Eventually the apostles and the early Christian fathers, thanks in large measure to the theological revelations of the apostle Paul, set aside their Jewish opinions not only about a messiah's on-going earthly kingdom, but also their belief that followers of Christ were expected to live under the law as well as under grace. Paul's expansive writings regarding both eschatology and the role of the law in a Christian's life are included in the Bible for good reason; they are God's revelation of truth to His church. In like manner, the Book of Revelation wedded Old and New Testament prophecies regarding Christ's return and brought the fullness of earlier revelations into one complete image.

Bishop Hanns Lilje, former head of the Lutheran World Federation and leader of the United Evangelical Lutheran Church in Germany, wrote a commentary on the Book of Revelation while he was imprisoned by the Nazis during World War II. Though an amillennialist himself, Lilje made some supportive statements regarding millennialism and/or chiliasm as they relate to Article XVII of the Augsburg Confession:

- The early church tended mainly in a chiliastic direction; therefore, it supported the doctrine of a reign of a thousand years. On the other hand, the Augsburg Confession rejected this view as a "Jewish doctrine."[12]
- A genuine chiliasm has been taught almost everywhere in the church, and has been held for centuries. In the early ages of the church, it was part of the true faith. So long as the church lived under the cross she held fast to this doctrine; the change took place when the church entered the sphere of public life under Constantine.[13]
- The modern rejection of chiliasm is usually based on dogmatic considerations, not on biblical exegis.[14]

While most Lutheran bodies embrace the amillennial view of the second coming of Christ, the Lutheran Brethren Church officially endorses the premillennial view. The Association of Free Lutheran Congregations leaves the study of eschatology as an open issue. The Lutheran Church-Missouri Synod and the Evangelical Lutheran Church in America are decidedly amillennial in their approach to eschatology, although some pastors in both church bodies hold to the premillennial view. The American Association of Lutheran Churches has within its ranks many pastors and church members who hold to the premillennial view; however, some of the church's leadership are attempting to influence the entire church body to reject premillennialism and embrace amillennialism.

There is nothing within the Lutheran confessions to prevent Lutherans from embracing either historical premillennialism or dispensational premillennialism, other than the subjective opinions of those who oppose these views. The substance of premillennialism is clearly in keeping with the hermeneutical principle set forth in the Lutheran confessions that Scripture interprets Scripture, and the Reformers' belief that Scripture should be interpreted literally wherever possible.

Luther's Literal Interpretation of Scripture

Martin Luther and other Reformers formulated most doctrines by interpreting Scripture literally. With the exception of eschatology, Luther nearly always interpreted Scripture literally. Carl Braaten, a theologian in the liberal Evangelical Lutheran Church in America (ELCA), admitted that Luther's inclination to interpret the biblical text literally was unambiguous. He said: "Luther held to the univocal sense of Scripture; basically he believed that its literal meaning is identical with its historical content. In other words, things happened exactly as they were written."[15]

Braaten went on to say the Bible is not accepted today [in the ELCA] with the same consideration as Luther's. He stated:

Today it is impossible to assume the literal historicity of all things recorded. What the biblical authors report is not accepted as a literal transcript of the actual course of events. Therefore, all critical scholars inquire behind the text and attempt to reconstruct the actual history that took place. In

Christology this has led to the endless debates on the relation between the historical Jesus and the Christ of apostolic faith and preaching....The Bible's thought world and its symbols and myths are felt to be utterly different from the modern ways of thinking. Therefore, Bultmann's call to demythologize the biblical concepts is an attempt to interpret the biblical message in terms that people today can understand without taking offense at the alien modes of thought one encounters in the Bible...For Christianity is not merely the ideas handed down from Scripture, but the life and action of Christ's people in the world.[16]

POSTMILLENNIALISM

The architect of postmillennial thought was Daniel Whitby (1638-1725). Whitby believed the church would blossom and flourish under the preaching of the gospel until the whole world would become Christianized.[17] Then Christ would return; the resurrection of the just and unjust would occur, as would the judgment of all men. Jonathan Edwards (1703-1758) was a postmillennialist. He believed the first Great Awakening was the start of the millennium. Postmillennialism and amillennialism essentially share the same teaching of a millennial kingdom without the King. Postmillennialists and amillennialists also share the belief that Israel has been replaced by the church, and modern Israel has nothing whatsoever to do with any prophecy concerning the Lord's return.

THE RAPTURE

The word *rapture* is derived from the Latin word *rapere;* it refers to believers being "caught up" to heaven as described in Paul's letter to the Thessalonians.[18] *Harpazo* is the Greek word used to describe the rapture. The concept of the rapture of believers is both stated and implied in several passages in the Gospels, the Epistles and Revelation. Scriptures relating to the rapture portray this event as being distinctly separate from the second coming of Christ. The apostle Paul clearly taught the rapture and the second coming of

Christ were two distinct events. To interpret his teachings otherwise, one must conclude that what Paul wrote is not what he meant.

According to the premillennial understanding of the Bible, the return of Jesus Christ will have two manifestations. On a God-appointed day and hour, Jesus shall come *for* His church before the judgments of God are poured out upon the earth. He will take His bride to His Father's House. The dead in Christ shall rise first, then we who are alive and remain shall be caught up in the clouds to meet the Lord in the air.[19] After the seven years of tribulation are completed, Jesus Christ shall return in the clouds *with* His church as both King and Judge.[20] Paul states in an altogether unambiguous way that Jesus will return "with all His saints."[21] How can He possibly return with His saints, if His saints are not already with Him?

The church is not mentioned after Revelation 4:1, until it again appears in Revelation 19. While God's judgments are being poured out upon the earth, the church will be safely gathered with the Lord in heaven.

Although certain prophetic signs will precede the second coming of Christ, no signs will be given relating to the rapture. Christ's return for His church may happen at any time; thus our mandate from Christ is to watch, wait and be ready for His appearing.

The first resurrection, which is the resurrection of the redeemed, will take place at the time of the rapture. Our Lord referred to the first resurrection as "the resurrection of the righteous."[22] A second resurrection of the unsaved will occur at the end of the millennial reign of Christ and immediately prior to the judgment before the Great White Throne. Jesus expounded on these two distinct resurrections: "Do not marvel at this; for an hour is coming, in which all who are in the tombs will hear His voice, and will come forth; those who did the good deeds to *a resurrection of life,* those who committed the evil deeds to *a resurrection of judgment.*"[23]

Paul described both the rapture and the nature of our resurrected bodies in his letter to the church in Corinth.[24] Believers will be clothed with the same resurrected body that was manifested by Christ at His resurrection. John also wrote: "Beloved, now we are children of God, and it has not appeared as yet what we will be. We know that when He appears, we will be like Him, because we will see Him just as He is."[25]

Most who hold to the premillennial view of eschatology believe the rapture will occur prior to the seven years of tribulation. Others place the rapture in the middle of the tribulation, while still others place it at the end of the tribulation. Thus premillinnialists further define their position concerning the rapture as being pre-tribulation, mid-tribulation or post-tribulation.

While nearly all amillennialists dismiss the rapture altogether, a few who embrace the preterist approach to eschatology insist the rapture occurred in AD 70 when the Christians fled Jerusalem in order to escape the destruction of the city. Of course they are referring to an allegorical rapture, which is really no rapture at all.

One of the principle reasons most premillennialists give for placing the rapture prior to the seven years of tribulation concerns the Bible's teaching that Christians will be spared from the wrath of God. Such a promise was given by the Lord to the church in Philadelphia: "Because you have kept the word of My perseverance, I also will keep you from the hour of testing, that hour which is about to come upon the whole world, to test those who dwell on the earth."[26] The preterists and amillennialists say this passage should be applied only to the church in Philadelphia. But in His letter Christ distinctly referred to it as a future event that not only involved the church in Philadelphia, but the whole world. Paul stated numerous times that believers would be rescued "from the wrath to come."[27] To claim, as the amillennialists do, that the wrath of God has already been poured out on the earth is in conflict with biblical passages that speak of God's wrath as a future event.

THE SEVEN-YEAR TRIBULATION

Seven years of tribulation will follow the rapture of the church. Both Daniel and the Book of Revelation divide the tribulation into two parts of three and one-half years each. Some commentators refer to the entire seven years as the *Great Tribulation*, while others refer to only the second half of the tribulation by that name. During this seven year period, God's wrath will be poured out upon the earth as described in Daniel, the Gospels, several of Paul's letters and Revelation. The antichrist will appear on the world stage, first in the role of a peacemaker and later as one who inflicts war and bloodshed upon the whole world. A unified world economy will be in place during the tribulation, as will a unified world religion. A religious figure called the false prophet will arise during this time to lead the unified world religion and promote the agenda of the antichrist. He will cause many to commit their allegiance to the antichrist. The antichrist will make a peace agreement with Israel, but after three and one-half years, he will annul the treaty and set up an abomination in the holy place (the Temple).[28]

During the tribulation the focus of the world will be on Israel. Jeremiah refers to this period as "the time of Jacob's distress," but he further states that Israel "will be saved from it."[29] At the same time, Israel will be attacked and two-thirds of the population will be destroyed.[30] Jews living in Israel who survive will embrace Jesus Christ as Savior and Lord. At the end of the tribulation, Christ will return with all His saints.

THE BATTLE OF ARMAGEDDON

The Battle of Armageddon will take place at the end of the tribulation and immediately prior to the Lord's return to earth with His church. At that time a coalition of nations will come against Israel, but the Lord will personally intervene to save Israel from her enemies.

Christ described the tribulation as a time "such as has not occurred since the beginning of creation."[31] He further described the purpose for His divine intervention: "Unless the Lord had shortened those days, no life would have been saved; but for the sake of the elect, whom He chose, He shortened the days."[32]

Armageddon is located on the former territory of the tribe of Issachar in the Jezreel Valley of Israel, about sixty miles north of Jerusalem. The ruins of the ancient Fortress of Megiddo are located on the western edge of the Plain of Armageddon. Some of the ruins may be traced to Canaanite times, while others date to the time of King Solomon and King Ahab. Megiddo was the scene of numerous battles in Old Testament times. Some battles were fought on the Plain of Armageddon as recently as 1917, 1948 and 1967. The future Battle of Armageddon is described in Revelation 16.

THE MILLENNIAL REIGN OF CHRIST

The only specific references to the thousand-year reign of Christ on earth are found in the twentieth chapter of Revelation; but the words "a thousand years" are used six times in that one chapter. In addition, there are an amazing number of verses in the Bible that offer detailed descriptions of Christ's reign on earth. Why would the Bible emphasize this event so often if it is only meant to be interpreted allegorically?

According to the Bible, Christ will rule over the nations from Jerusalem. He will be called the "Prince of Peace" because, at last, peace will be established over the whole earth.

> "Thus says the Lord, 'I will return to Zion and will dwell in the midst of Jerusalem. Then Jerusalem will be called the City of Truth, and the mountain of the Lord of Hosts will be called the Holy Mountain .... Old men and old women will again sit in the streets of Jerusalem, each man with his staff in his hand because of age. And the streets of the city will be filled with boys and girls playing in its streets.'"[33]

The redeemed of God will reign with Him, including those who were martyred during the tribulation because of the Word of God and the testimony of Jesus.

During the millennial reign of Christ, the nations will go up to Jerusalem every year for the Feast of Tabernacles to honor and worship Him.[34] "Every knee will bow and every tongue will confess that Jesus is Lord, to the glory of God the Father."[35] Jesus' rule will be the fulfillment of the Creator's intended desire for the earth before the fall of man. Paul described how creation "waits eagerly for the revealing of the sons of God....For the creation was subjected to futility, not willingly, but because of Him who subjected it, in hope that the creation itself also will be set free from its slavery to corruption into the freedom of the glory of the children of God."[36]

Many teachers in the early church reasoned that Christ would come at the end of six thousand years of recorded history and reign during the seventh millennium. They further believed the millennial reign of Christ would be followed by His eternal reign in heaven with the saints. There are numerous scholars in the premillennial school who presently hold to this view.

Satan will be bound during Christ's millennial reign, unable "to deceive the nations." When the thousand years are concluded, he will be loosed for a brief period of time. The great deceiver of nations will assemble a host of rebels in one final effort to overthrow the rule of Christ, but fire will fall from the heavens and destroy them all. Satan will be cast into the lake of fire where the antichrist and the false prophet are already being tormented day and night forever.[37]

Other than Daniel and John, no prophet was given such an extensive vision of Christ's millennial reign as was given to Ezekiel. After describing various events leading up to Christ's coming, the battles to be fought, descriptions of the Temple and the millennial city of Jerusalem, Ezekiel penned the very last verse of his writings: "The city shall be 18,000 cubits round about; and the name of the city from that day shall be, *Adonai Shammah* 'The Lord is there.'"[38]

THE JUDGMENT

After unbelievers are raised from the dead at the end of the millennial reign of Christ, they will stand before the Great White Throne to be judged for what they have done.[39] "And if anyone's name was not found written in the book of life, he was thrown into the lake of fire."[40]

The judgment that will take place after the millennial reign of Christ will not be a judgment for believers, but for unbelievers. The ultimate judgment of all believers was rendered when Christ took our sins upon Himself at Calvary. Paul said, "Therefore there is now no condemnation for those who are in Christ Jesus."[41] Before the resurrection of unbelievers, all of the redeemed will already have been gathered with Christ. They will have already celebrated the great Marriage Feast of the Lamb, returned with Him in glory, and reigned with Christ during His millennial reign.

REPLACEMENT THEOLOGY

The proponents of "replacement theology" (mostly those who hold to the amillennial view) are those who claim God's promises and covenants made to Israel have either been abrogated or have been taken over by the church because of Israel's rejection of Christ when He was on earth. Countless verses in both the Old and New Testaments contradict such claims.

In his book *The Apocalypse Code*, Hank Hanegraaff launched a vitriolic attack on premillennialism in general and on Tim LaHaye in particular, mostly for his *Left Behind* series. Hanegraaff could not disguise his anti-Israel bias when he made this preposterous statement:

> While one might well defend the right of the secular state of Israel to exist, the contention that the modern state of Israel is a fulfillment of biblical prophecy is indefensible. In truth, since coming under the exclusive control of modern Israel, Jerusalem has demonstrated a far greater resemblance to the harlot city spoken of by the prophets than to the holy city spoken of by the psalmists.[42]

Martin Luther maintained that God was finished with the nation of Israel. While his views on this matter were largely based on his amillennial position, it needs to be understood the whole culture of Luther's day was decidedly anti-Semitic. Jews had been expelled from Austria in 1421, from Spain in 1492, from Lithuania in 1495, and from Portugal in 1497. As many displaced Jews sought refuge in Germany, the hostility of the general population toward the Jews greatly intensified. Still, there is no justification whatsoever for Luther's vitriol and writings against Jews. Sadly the influence of Luther's writings and an anti-Semitic attitude continued in Europe for centuries, culminating during the dictatorship of Adolph Hitler.

The Case Against Replacement Theology

God affirmed His covenant with Abraham when he was ninety-nine years old: "I will give to you and to your descendants after you, the land of your sojournings, all the land of Canaan, for an everlasting possession; and I will be their God."[43] The key word in this promise to Abraham is *everlasting*. God repeated His everlasting covenant regarding the land to Isaac and again to Jacob.[44]

God, who is never inclined to exaggeration, defined His covenant with Israel even as the nation was about to be carried off to captivity for their many acts of disobedience.

> Thus says the Lord, Who gives the sun for light by day and the fixed order of the moon and the stars for light by night, Who stirs up the sea so that its waves roar; The Lord of hosts is His name: "If this fixed order departs from before Me," declares the Lord, "then the offspring of Israel also will cease from being a nation before Me forever." Thus says the Lord, "If the heavens above can be measured and the foundations of the earth searched out below, then I will also cast off all the offspring of Israel for all that they have done," declares the Lord.[45]

The promises of God are immutable! The rising of the sun every morning, the appearance of the moon and stars every evening, and the tides of the sea twice each day are all affirmations that God's covenant with Israel is still intact.

Proponents of replacement theology maintain the establishment of the modern nation of Israel has nothing whatsoever to do with the Jews of the Bible. But in order to take this position, its adherents have to both deny the clear teaching of Scripture and the reality that the nation of Israel exists today! After nearly two thousand years, God has brought back the people of Israel from their exile, just as He promised in His Word. The Jews have returned with their language, culture and religious heritage still intact. God preserved the land from which the Jews were exiled in AD 70, and He preserved the city of Jerusalem and the Temple Mount, both of which are the centerpiece in biblical prophecy regarding end-times. These are undeniable facts!

It is hard to fathom how anyone can read the Bible's prophecies concerning the Jews returning to their own land at the close of the age and not be able to see the fulfillment of these prophecies. The focus of the whole world today is on the Middle East in general and on Israel in particular, just as the prophets foretold.

Paul took up this issue in his letter to the Romans when he asked, "I say then, God has not rejected His people, has He?" Answering his own question, Paul wrote: "May it never be! ...God has not rejected His people whom He foreknew."[46]

Paul described Israel as an olive tree, from which some of the branches had been broken off so that the Gentiles could be grafted in. Speaking of the Jews, he said: "And they also, if they do not continue in their unbelief, will be grafted in, for God is able to graft them in again....and so all Israel will be saved....for the gifts and the calling of God are irrevocable."[47]

Old and New Testament prophecies make it clear God intends not only to bring the Jews back to their land in the last days, but He also intends to bring them to faith in Jesus Christ. The Lord spoke through the prophet Zechariah concerning Israel at the time of His return: "I will pour out on the house of David and on the inhabitants of Jerusalem, the Spirit of grace and of supplication, so that they will look on Me whom they have pierced; and they will mourn for Him, as one mourns for an only son...."[48] Then the prophecy of Paul will come to pass: "And so all Israel will be saved...."[49]

UNTIL THEN

God's grace will continue to flow abundantly through the church until the rapture. Then, with His church safely gathered in heaven, the Lord will again deal with Israel during the seven years of tribulation. Why is it so difficult for anyone to believe God still loves the Jews, or that He will never break His covenant with them? It is unfathomable to believe anyone could embrace the teachings of Paul in Romans and yet deny the reality of his words: "For I am not ashamed of the gospel, for it is the power of God for salvation to everyone who believes, *to the Jew first and also to the Greek."* [50]

In 1850 a German scholar, J. H. Kurtz wrote these remarkable words: "As the body is adapted and destined for the soul, and the soul for the body; so is Israel for that country and that country for Israel. Without Israel, the land is like a body from which the soul has fled; banished from its country, Israel is like a ghost which cannot find its rest."[51]

As the Zionist movement got underway in the late nineteenth century, many Christians saw the connection of the Jews returning to their land and numerous biblical prophecies. In his book *Jesus is Coming,* William E. Blackstone stated: "If Israel is beginning to show signs of national life and is actually returning to Palestine, then surely the end of this dispensation is nigh, even at the doors."[52]

Of course not everyone saw it that way. R. C. H. Lenski, the much acclaimed Lutheran theologian, saw the return of the Jews to Palestine from his amillennialist perspective. In Lenski's commentary on Luke's Gospel, written in 1934, he said: "The Zionist movement today is the latest attempt of the Jews to repossess their land, and it has failed." He went on to say "Jerusalem shall continue to be trampled by the Gentiles until the Second Advent of Christ."[53] Exactly fourteen years after Lenski made this statement, the nation of Israel was reborn. The reunification of Jerusalem came about over forty years ago in 1967.

In 1891 a group of clergy, professional men, mayors and members of the U.S. congress presented President Benjamin Harrison with a petition to back the reestablishment of the State of Israel. The first paragraph stated:

Why not give Palestine back to them again? According to God's distribution of nations, it is their home—an inalienable possession from which they were expelled by force. Under their cultivation it was a remarkably fruitful land, sustaining millions of Israelites, who industriously tilled its hillsides and valleys. They were agriculturists and producers, as well as a nation of great commercial importance—the center of civilization and religion.[54]

Ultimately God has the last word concerning the return of the Jews to their land. It is not up for discussion or debate. God will not go back on His covenants with Abraham, Isaac, Jacob or David.

> For Zion's sake I will not keep silent, and for Jerusalem's sake I will not keep quiet, until her righteousness goes forth like brightness, and her salvation like a torch that is burning. The nations will see your righteousness, and all the kings your glory; and you will be called by a new name which the mouth of the Lord will designate. You will also be a crown of beauty in the hand of the Lord, and a royal diadem in the hand of your God. It will no longer be said to you, "Forsaken," nor to your land will it any longer be said, "Desolate"; but you will be called, "My delight is in her," and your land, "Married;" for the Lord delights in you, and to Him your land will be married."[55]

For the first time in centuries, there is a Jewish church in Israel today with several thousand Jewish believers worshiping in about seventy congregations. Hundreds more Israelis who have embraced Jesus Christ as Savior still live within their communities. Across the globe literally thousands of Jews have given their hearts to Jesus Christ and acknowledged Him as their Messiah. This too is a sign of the Lord's soon return!

ISRAEL OR PALESTINE?

It is amazing how many Christian scholars, books and maps still identify the land of Israel as "Palestine in the time of Jesus." There was no Palestine in the time of Jesus! There never has been a sovereign country called Palestine. From 1948 until the 1960s, the Arabs living there rarely referred to themselves as Palestinians. Most Arabs living in the West Bank and Jerusalem carried Jordanian passports and called themselves Jordanians. Those living in Gaza identified themselves with Egypt. Though the term *Palestine* was widely used, even by the Jews from AD 135 to 1948, the land was, is and forever shall remain Israel.

God Himself first gave the name Israel to Jacob and then to the nation! The word Israel is used in the Bible to describe the land or the nation several hundred times. It is used in almost every book of the Bible, both in the Old and New Testaments. There is scarcely a word in the Bible used more often than the word *Israel*. God repeatedly identifies Himself as "the God of Israel."

Jesus was not born in Bethlehem of the West Bank; He was born in Bethlehem of Judea, Israel. Jesus did not ascend to heaven from a hilltop in Palestine but from the Mount of Olives in Israel. At His coming Jesus' feet shall stand on the lofty summit of Israel's Mount of Olives. The Lord will not suddenly appear in a Muslim mosque but, according to Malachi, He shall suddenly come to His Temple.[56] Jesus Christ shall reign as King of kings and Lord of lords not from some Palestinian capital but from Jerusalem, Israel — God's own city! God Himself referred to Israel as "My land."[57] "But who can endure the day of His coming? And who can stand when He appears?"[58] In that day let the man or woman arise who will find the courage to tell the Lord that His land should be called by any other than the name He has chosen — ISRAEL!

Chapter 2

RATTLING OF THE BONES

When Ezekiel had his vision in a valley filled with dry bones, God asked him this question: "Son of man, can these bones live?" After informing the prophet of His plan to resurrect the bones, God said to him:

> "Son of man, these bones are the whole house of Israel; behold, they say, 'Our bones are dried up, and our hope has perished. We are completely cut off.' Therefore prophesy and say to them, 'Thus says the Lord God, Behold, I will open your graves and cause you to come up out of your graves, My people; and I will bring you into the land of Israel.'"[1]

There have been numerous times in history when the Jewish people surely must have felt as though their bones were dried up, their hope had perished, and they were completely cut off. Such an occurrence took place in AD 70 when Rome destroyed Jerusalem and the Temple. At that time most of the surviving Jews were scattered or exiled throughout the Roman Empire.

The Jews unquestionably felt their bones were dried up as they endured centuries of persecution and disgrace while living in Europe and the Middle East. They must have felt as though their hope had perished during the Spanish Inquisition when Jews by the thousands were tortured and murdered in the name of Christ. Approximately 200,000 Spanish Jews were cut off on August 3, 1492, as King Ferdinand and Queen Isabella ordered all Jews to leave Spain. The day Columbus set sail to find the new world, his ships passed Spanish vessels in the harbor that were filled with condemned Jews who were about to be taken out to the high seas and thrown overboard.

It is doubtful, however, Jews ever felt as bereft of hope or so completely cut off as when six million of their race perished in the death camps of Nazi Germany. Regrettably, the wounds inflicted on the Jewish people during the Nazi era are being reopened in the twenty-first century by a new wave of Holocaust deniers. Leading this assault on human intelligence and common decency is Mahmoud Ahmadinejad, Iran's current president. Ahmadinejad believes Israel's existence as a nation is directly connected with the Holocaust. Discredit the Holocaust, he reasons, and you discredit any justification for the existence of the Jewish nation. He also has another Holocaust in mind — the destruction of Israel.

YAD VASHEM

Yad Vashem is a beautiful but somber memorial to the six million Jews who were murdered in the Holocaust (Shoah). It stands on a wooded hillside in Jerusalem as a constant reminder of the best and worst that is in the heart of man. The worst is seen in the heart-breaking displays and images of suffering Holocaust victims; the best is symbolized through numerous trees planted on the grounds of Yad Vashem and dedicated to the "righteous Gentiles" who risked or gave their lives to save Jews from Hitler's "Final Solution of the Jewish Problem." Several hundred Gentiles, including Corrie ten Boom from Holland, Oscar Shindler from Germany and Raoul

Wallenberg from Sweden, are honored at Yad Vashem by the State of Israel for their selfless acts of love and courage.

Yad Vashem, means "a memorial and a name." It comes from Isaiah 56:5: "To them I will give in My house and within My walls a memorial and a name ... which will not be cut off." Yad Vashem typifies the Jewish spirit as it rises from the depths of despair and seizes the hope of a new day. This inspiring memorial stands not only as a tribute to millions who died, but also as a testimony to the living that God's promise spoken through Ezekiel will be fulfilled—"Behold, I will open your graves and cause you to come up out of your graves, My people; and I will bring you into the land of Israel."[2]

THE FIRST PALM SUNDAY

Five days prior to His crucifixion, Jesus astounded His disciples as He stood with them on the Mount of Olives and prophesied the destruction of Jerusalem and the Temple.

When He approached Jerusalem, He saw the city and wept over it, saying, "If you had known in this day, even you, the things which make for peace! But now they have been hidden from your eyes. For the days will come upon you when your enemies will throw up a barricade against you, and surround you and hem you in on every side, and they will level you to the ground and your children within you, and they will not leave in you one stone upon another, because you did not recognize the time of your visitation."[3]

Though Jesus was about to suffer unimaginable agony, the tears that flowed that day were not for Himself but for the Jewish nation that had rejected their Messiah. Through His tears Jesus saw the gleaming white stones of Herod's Temple that had taken forty-six years to complete. From His vantage point, Jesus could see the priests offering sacrifices on the high altar and the money changers swindling the people.

As Jesus looked down from Olivet's lofty heights, He saw the city's inhabitants moving about the streets, unaware the King of Glory was about to enter through the Eastern Gate. He gazed upon Herod's hundred-room palace and the elaborate homes of the wealthy in the upper city. He saw the humble dwellings of the common people nestled in Jerusalem's lowest valleys. On that first Palm Sunday, Jesus beheld the city of Jerusalem and the Temple not in the splendor of their present form but rather in the utter desolation that was to come.

Jerusalem was teeming with people who had come for the Passover celebration. Little did they know this Passover would fulfill all the other Passovers—past, present and future. No longer would God require little lambs be slain and offered upon the Temple altar. Within the shadow of the Holy Place, God was about to offer Himself as the sacrificial Lamb who would forever take away the sins of the world.

THE DESTRUCTION OF JERUSALEM

In the year AD 70, Titus, son of Emperor Vespasian, marched on Jerusalem in order to put down a revolt that had begun four years earlier. Jews by the thousands poured into Jerusalem as they fled Rome's advancing legions. The city quickly became overwhelmed by the vast number of refugees pressed together within its walls. Ordinarily the population of Jerusalem was less than fifty thousand, but as people gathered for the Passover, and as still more came to escape death at the hands of the Romans, the city's population swelled to over a million, according to an account by the first-century historian Flavius Josephus.

Among those who had sought the protection of Jerusalem's massive walls were Jewish zealots. Josephus referred to them as terrorists. They had been fighting the Romans in the northern part of the country, but behind the walls of the cramped city, they fought one another for turf and domination. Two militant groups, the Zealots and the Sicarii, even took over the Temple and used it for their base of operations. Death and mayhem ruled Jerusalem's streets long before the Romans ever approached.

Four Roman legions, each with six thousand men, arrived at the outskirts of the city. Two legions set up camp on Mount Scopes, while Titus' own Tenth Roman Legion encamped on the Mount of Olives opposite the Temple. General Titus stood on the Mount of Olives at or near the place where Jesus had wept over the city and made His amazing prophecy concerning the city's destruction. There, Titus devised his strategy for capturing the highly fortified city.

Titus' carefully crafted plan turned out to be exactly what Jesus had prophesied nearly forty years earlier. He called for the construction of an earthen embankment and a wooden wall to hem in the city's residents. Virtually every tree around Jerusalem was cut down in order to complete this project. Few trees would grow on the Judean hills until the Jews returned to plant them nearly two thousand years later.

The siege of Jerusalem lasted over five months. Food became so scarce that hundreds died daily of starvation. Some of the city's residents resorted to cannibalism in order to survive. Josephus described how Jews ventured outside Jerusalem's walls at night to forage for food, only to be captured and killed by the Romans. Literally hundreds of crosses with crucified Jews lined the perimeter of the city. Because wood was so scarce, the Romans crucified as many as three Jews on a single cross. According to Josephus instead of killing their starving captives, sometimes the Romans cut off their hands and sent them back into the city. Without hands they could not fight, but alive they could still crave food.

Titus constructed an earthen ramp against the northern side of Jerusalem's walls, the only side of the city that did not have a deep valley beneath it. When the ramp was finished, he set up siege towers and battering rams. Eventually the walls were breached and Roman soldiers forced their way into the city. Although the Roman legions met stiff resistance, they prevailed. The Jewish fighters retreated to the Fortress of Antonio and then into the Temple compound where they held out for another few days.

Titus and his men broke through to the Temple area on the ninth of Av, AD 70. Amazingly, it was on the ninth of Av in 586 BC that Nebuchadnezzar had razed Solomon's Temple. The half-starved defenders of Jerusalem were no match for the vicious attack they faced from the trained and disciplined Roman army. Josephus described the carnage on the Temple Mount as horrific. Bodies of both Romans and Jews were strewn on the altar and even inside the Temple sanctuary.

Titus made every effort to save as many of the precious contents of the Temple as possible—the seven-branch candelabra, the altar of incense and other priceless furnishings. These Temple treasures were eventually taken to Rome and put on display. According to Josephus, Titus did not want the Temple destroyed, but the anger of his troops and their greed for the Temple's gold proved too much for the Roman officers. Without warning the Temple became a burning inferno.

The Roman soldiers dismantled the Temple stone by stone in order to get at the gold that had melted into the cracks. The huge stones of the sanctuary were sent crashing onto the streets below. Jesus' prophecy was fulfilled to the last detail—"not one stone will be left on top of another." Some of the stones thrown down from the Temple in AD 70 may be seen today in Jerusalem's new Archaeological Park. The Temple was so thoroughly destroyed that its exact location atop the Temple Mount remains a matter of debate to this day.

Josephus described yet another amazing fact—Christians were not present in Jerusalem when it was destroyed. Remembering Jesus' words of warning, they had fled the area. Jesus had told them: "But when you see Jerusalem surrounded by armies, then recognize that her desolation is near. Then those who are in Judea must flee to the mountains, and those who are in the midst of the city must leave, and those who are in the country must not enter the city." [4]

In biblical times the natural instinct when threatened by an advancing army was to run to the walled cities for protection. It must have taken a tremendous amount of faith on the part of Christians living in and around Jerusalem to go against this prevailing wisdom and run away from the protective walls of the city. Christians today should likewise heed the words of Jesus and diligently prepare for His appearing.

GOD'S CARETAKERS

During the Jews' long exile, the land of Israel became the occupied territory of one nation and then another—the Romans, Persians, Arabs, Seljuks, Crusaders, Mamelukes, Ottoman Turks and finally the British. From AD 70 until 1948, no nation ever rose up to govern itself on that little piece of real estate called Israel. Instead the land was always occupied territory. From the time of the Romans to the British occupation of Palestine, each occupying force was nothing more than a caretaker of God's own land.

Israel was renamed *Syria Palestina* in AD 135, after Emperor Hadrian put down the last Jewish revolt. The anglicized word *Palestine* came to be used much later. He rebuilt Jerusalem and called it Aelia Capitolina. During the time of Hadrian, Jews were forbidden to enter Jerusalem, as the Romans sought to rid the country of all Jewish influence. Hadrian constructed pagan temples over Christian holy places, and he erected a Temple to Jupiter on the Temple Mount.

Throughout the centuries there has always been a Jewish presence in Israel. Sometimes the Jewish population was extremely sparse, but so also was the population of the Arabs. It is estimated that during the four hundred years when the Ottoman Turks ruled (1517-1917), there were never more than 400,000 people living in the whole country at any one time. The total population of Jerusalem at the turn of the twentieth century was less than 12,000, including both Jews and Arabs.

Between 1900 and 1947, the population of Palestine began to swell. As the Jews developed the land and as jobs became plentiful, Arabs from the surrounding countries began to pour into the country. Today the per capita income of Arabs living within Israel is greater by far than the per capita income of Arabs who live in surrounding Muslim countries. Many Arabs in the West Bank would rather live under the control of the Israelis than under the control of Hamas or Fatah.

THE LAND DURING THE EXILE

Israel lay in ruins for centuries. Most of the trees, olive groves and vineyards had been cut down. Without trees and cultivation the land turned into desert and malaria-infested swamps. This too was in keeping with biblical prophecies. "I will make the land desolate so that your enemies who settle in it will be appalled over it."[5] Isaiah prophesied regarding the land: "I will lay it waste; it will not be pruned or hoed, but briars and thorns will come up. I will also charge the clouds to rain no rain on it."[6]

Samuel Clemens, the American author who was better known by his pen name Mark Twain, visited the Holy Land in 1863. After riding through the countryside, he wrote in his dairy:

> There is not a solitary village throughout its whole extent—not for thirty miles in either direction. There are two or three small clusters of Bedouin tents, but not a single permanent habitation. One may ride ten miles thereabouts and not see ten human beings. To this region one of the prophecies is applied, "I will bring the land into desolation; and your people which dwell there shall be astonished at it. I will scatter you among the heathen, and I will draw out a sword after you; and your land shall be desolate and your cities waste." No man can stand here by deserted Ain Millahah and say the prophecy has not been fulfilled.[7]
>
> ...A desolate country whose soil is rich enough, but is given over wholly to weeds—a silent mournful expanse.... A desolation is here that not even imagination can grace with the pomp of life and action....We never saw a human being on the whole route....There was hardly a tree or a shrub anywhere. Even the olive and the cactus, fast friends of a worthless soil, had almost deserted the country.[8]

These are amazing statements from an avowed agnostic, who was impressed not with the land's restoration but with its utter devastation.

THE JEWISH NATION IS REBORN

The rattling of the bones began in earnest in 1897 as Theodor Herzl organized the first Zionist Congress in Basel, Switzerland and presented his vision for a Jewish state in Palestine. Herzl, who is called "the father of modern Israel," traveled throughout Europe trying to convince Jews that they should embrace the Zionist vision. He died at age forty-four from a series of heart attacks; nevertheless, his vision lived on, and Zionism became the driving force behind the establishment of the Jewish nation. Shortly after Israel was founded, Herzl's remains were laid to rest on a hillside overlooking Jerusalem. His grave is the centerpiece of Israel's National Cemetery located on a wooded hill in Jerusalem that bears his name—Mt. Herzl.

In the late 1800s and early 1900s, Jews began making their way to Palestine in order to turn Herzl's vision into reality. With the assistance of wealthy Jews, including Baron Edmond de Rothschild and Moses Montefiore, the Jewish National Fund was established for the purpose of purchasing large tracts of land for Jewish development from the Turkish government and Arab landowners. Most of the land was little more than desert and swamps. Collective farm communities, called kibbutzim, were established to clear the fields, drain the swamps, and bring life back to the devastated land. Over the next fifty years, the "rattling of the bones" continued as Jewish settlements dotted the landscape from the border with Lebanon in the north to Beersheba in the south.

A major turning point in the establishment of a Jewish state came in 1917 when Great Britain defeated the Ottoman Turks and gained control over Palestine as well as other portions of the region. A British document known as the Balfour Declaration set forth the concept of a Jewish homeland.[9] The original plan provided for the establishment of a Jewish homeland in all of present-day Jordan, including what is now called the West Bank, the Gaza Strip, as well as the present boundaries of Israel. The British, desiring to appease the Arabs, lopped off the eastern-most portion of the proposed Jewish homeland in 1922 and created the Hashemite Kingdom of Jordan. At that point Jordan should have become the Palestinian state, and the entire region west of the Jordan River should have become the Jewish state, but that was not to be.

In 1947 a commission of the United Nations recommended the narrow strip of land west of the Jordan River be divided into two states, one for the Jews and the other for the Arabs. According to the plan, Jerusalem was to become an international city under the authority of the United Nations. Thus out of the whole area that should have been the Jewish homeland, only a small sliver of land would be allotted to the Jews. Jewish leaders accepted the plan, even though they were concerned over the division of the land. On November 29, 1947 the United Nations voted to partition Palestine into two states—one for the Jews and the other for the Arabs.

Two world wars and a Holocaust later, Herzl's vision and God's plan turned into reality. On May 14, 1948 David Ben-Gurion, the first Prime Minister of Israel, announced the birth of the State of Israel. The first government to recognize the new Jewish nation was the United States of America.

Exactly eleven minutes after Ben-Gurion's announcement, President Harry S. Truman officially announced America's support for the new Jewish nation. The Chief Rabbi of Israel visited President Truman in 1949 and told him, "God put you in your mother's womb so that you could be the instrument to bring about the rebirth of Israel after two thousand years." Hearing that comment, tears started rolling down Harry Truman's cheeks.[10]

The Arabs would have no part of the plan to carve up Palestine into two states. For them it was all or nothing. The State of Israel was born struggling to survive. That night bombs fell on Tel Aviv, as five Arab nations declared war on Israel and began their offensive to drive the Jews into the sea. Israel's War of Independence ended in victory on July 9, 1948. The Jewish state lost 6,074 lives during the war, one percent of their population. It was a heavy price, but the tiny nation endured.

Prior to 1948 an estimated 850,000 Jews were living in the Persian Gulf countries. That number was cut in half shortly after Israel was established, as one Arab state after another expelled its Jewish residents. Large numbers of Jews continued living in Yemen until the 1970s, when they were transported by the plane loads to

Israel. Today Jews are forbidden from entering Saudi Arabia; while Jordan has laws forbidding Jews from owning property or becoming citizens.

Other wars between Israel and her neighbors followed in 1956, 1967 and 1973. Two wars were fought in Lebanon. The first was fought in 1982 against the Palestine Liberation Organization and their allies; the second war was fought in the summer of 2006 against Hezbollah. Presently Hezbollah has all but taken control of Lebanon. This terrorist organization, armed and financed by Iran, is little more than a surrogate for Syria and Iran. Hezbollah has at least 20,000 short and long-range missiles aimed at Israeli towns and cities. Though the United Nations has 3500 peace-keeping troops in the area, war could break out at any time.

THE DEAD SEA SCROLLS

In AD 70, the year Israel went into exile, scrolls from the Temple were taken to the region of the Dead Sea, where they were placed in clay jars and hidden away in caves. Included among the irreplaceable treasures was a copper scroll which described Temple rituals and the location of precious Temple treasures hidden within the Dead Sea caves.

Those same scrolls, known today as the Dead Sea Scrolls, were discovered in 1947 when Muhammad edh-Dhib, a Bedouin shepherd, went searching for a lost goat. After throwing a stone into a small cave and hearing something break, he went in and discovered forty-five clay jars filled with ancient documents. The scrolls were hidden in the year Israel went into exile and discovered the year that the United Nations partitioned Palestine and authorized the establishment of the Jewish state. Was this a coincidence? Hardly! Unless, of course, you spell coincidence—G-O-D!

PRESENT-DAY REALITIES

The War of 1967 came about as five Arab nations prepared to destroy Israel, but before they could launch their attack, Israel took preemptive action. In just six hours, Israel gained complete air superiority by taking out the air forces of Egypt, Jordan and Syria. In just six days Israel destroyed the military capability of five enemy nations. This war brought significant changes to the region. The Israeli Defense Forces captured the Sinai and the Gaza Strip from Egypt; the Golan Heights from Syria; the West Bank, East Jerusalem, the Old City and the Temple Mount from Jordan.

After the 1967 War, Israel offered to return the conquered lands for a formal peace settlement, but the Arabs refused. From 1967 to the present day, efforts to draw permanent boundaries have been thwarted by Arab leadership. Thankfully, a peace treaty between Israel and Egypt was signed in 1979, and a similar treaty between Jordan and Israel was signed in 1994.

Many believe the Palestinian issue could have been settled in 2000, when President Bill Clinton led negotiations at Camp David between Yasser Arafat and Prime Minister Ehud Barak. A peace agreement that would have given the Palestinians ninety-five percent of the West Bank, all of the Gaza Strip and a portion of Jerusalem was turned down by Arafat. Within a few days, Arafat orchestrated an intifada (uprising) that cost the lives of thousands of Palestinians and Israelis. Arafat's decision to reject statehood for the Palestinians set back their cause by many years, perhaps permanently. His decision also gave several terrorist organizations, including Hamas and Fatah, a greater incentive to pursue the path of violence instead of the path of peace.

In August 2005 Israel unilaterally withdrew from the Gaza Strip. Their withdrawal included the abandonment of several large settlements and the removal of 8500 Jewish settlers. Shortly after the Israelis withdrew from the Gaza Strip, their abandoned settlements were either destroyed or turned into Hamas strongholds. The Palestinians used these same settlements to fire missiles into Israeli towns and settlements in the Negev.

Ehud Olmert became acting Prime Minister on January 4, 2006, after then Prime Minister Ariel Sharon suffered a massive brain hemorrhage. Olmert became Israel's twelfth Prime Minister officially on April 15 of the same year. In August the new Prime Minister faced a war with Hezbollah in Lebanon. The thirty-three-day war did not go well for Israel; at best it ended in a stalemate. Hezbollah and their supporters soon claimed victory. Since the war, Hezbollah has been rearmed by Iran and Syria; the terrorist organization now boasts of its readiness to resume hostilities against Israel.

Early in 2006 elections were held in the Gaza Strip. The terrorist organization Hamas won control of the Palestinian legislature, but the presidency remained in the hands of Mahmoud Abbas, leader of the Fatah organization. Because Hamas leaders were adamant about not recognizing Israel's right to exist, the European Union and the United States withheld funds from the Palestinian Authority, and Israel refused to hand over tax money it had collected on behalf of the Palestinians.

Not long after the 2006 elections, Hamas and Fatah began to attack one another in the Gaza Strip and the West Bank, until an all-out civil war seemed inevitable. Through the intervention and influence of several Arab states, Hamas and Fatah were able to form a unity government, but it was doomed from the start. Hamas and Fatah battled each other in the streets of Gaza throughout the first half of 2007. They assassinated each other's leaders and committed numerous acts of terror on one another. Finally in June 2007, Hamas gained the upper hand, forcing Fatah to yield control of the Gaza Strip to them. Since then, a new paradigm has developed in Gaza and the West Bank, causing Europe, the United States, Israel and several Arab states to reassess their roles in the region. With Hamas in control of the Gaza Strip and Fatah the dominant force in the West Bank, prospects for peace are dim; war with Israel may be inevitable.

Hamas set out at once to turn the Gaza Strip into what some have termed "Hamasstan," by mandating sharia law on everyone, including Christians. Within hours of their takeover of Gaza, Hamas terrorists broke into the Roman Catholic Church and destroyed every cross and Bible they could find, before setting the buildings on fire. Christians in Gaza are now facing greater restrictions and persecution than they have ever known.

During the first half of 2007, the United States and Israel sent millions of dollars worth of military supplies into Gaza in order to prop up President Mahmoud Abbas and his Fatah forces. Unfortunately many of the guns and supplies ended up in the hands of Hamas.

Israeli intelligence reports stated Hamas had seized 800,000 rounds of ammunition, 7400 American M-16 assault rifles, eighteen armored personnel carriers, seven armored jeeps, eight trucks equipped with water cannons and fourteen military bulldozers.

Immediately following Hamas' takeover of the Gaza Strip, the United States sent an estimated $86 million in cash and military supplies to Palestinian Authority President Abbas in the West Bank, in an effort to strengthen his hand. At the same time, Israel released 256 Fatah prisoners as a gesture of good will and handed over $700 million in tax money to the Palestinian Authority. There is little doubt much of the aid will end up in the hands of Hamas. The present situation causes one to consider what could have happened had the West succeeded with its peace plans. If the proposed Palestinian state had become a reality, in all likelihood it would now be under the control of the terrorist organization Hamas.

On several occasions in biblical times, confederations of enemy nations joined forces against Israel. But before the attacks took place, they turned on one another instead. Biblical history has a way of repeating itself. Surely the hand of God has protected Israel from a peace settlement that would have left them at the mercy of their enemies. You can be certain, however, the European Union and the United States will continue to promote another peace plan that will ask the Israelis to give away more land and make additional concessions to the Palestinians.

THE DESERTS ARE IN BLOOM

One of the most significant signs relating to Christ's return is being fulfilled in Israel right now. It is written in Isaiah:

The wilderness and the desert will be glad, and the Arabah will rejoice and blossom; like the crocus it will blossom profusely and rejoice with rejoicing and shout of joy....For waters will break forth in the wilderness and streams in the Arabah.[11]

God is not given to exaggeration. What He says, He will do, and what He declares will happen! While this prophecy will have its ultimate fulfillment during the millennium, there is no doubt the desert regions of Israel are in blossom today.

The Arabah region of Israel, located just below the Dead Sea, receives on average about three inches of rain per year. Because the ground is so barren and the weather is so hot, it is beyond comprehension how anything or anyone could survive living there, yet the desert landscape is being transformed into a highly productive region.

The road that leads from the Dead Sea to Eilat is filled with surprises for the traveler. Unexpected patches of green break the monotony of the barren landscape. Along the way one sees groves of date palms rising from the desert floor. There are greenhouses filled with flowers, while row upon row of plastic tents protect a variety of vegetables from the blistering sun. From time to time, one sees herds of dairy cattle. The drive from the Dead Sea to Eilat leaves no room for doubt concerning the fulfillment of Bible prophecy—the deserts are blooming.

The Negev

The Negev Desert, located in the south-central interior of Israel, was home to Abraham, Isaac and Jacob. Today it is home to nearly 500,000 people. The Negev comprises about sixty percent of Israel's territory but only eight percent of its population; this includes Israel's fourth-largest city, Beersheba, with its 200,000 residents.

Beersheba is home to many industries and technology companies. The city's impressive medical complex trains doctors, nurses and medical technicians; it also offers some of the finest medical care and research in the world. Many Russian Jews settled in Beersheba in the 1990s, some of whom are highly skilled scientists, doctors and engineers.

David Ben-Gurion encouraged Israelis to move into this region and make the desert bloom. Ben-Gurion and his wife Paula took his own advice and settled in a Negev kibbutz called Sde Boker. Ben-Gurion University of the Negev, located in Beersheba, leads the way in the development of desert farming, agriculture and medical research. A branch of the university is located at Sde Boker. David Ben-Gurion and his wife are buried there at a site overlooking a desert valley where the children of Israel once camped as they made their journey to the Promised Land.

Water is in short supply in the Negev. The northern portion of the Negev receives about twelve inches of rain a year, while the southern half receives between three and six inches. In fields near Beersheba, winter wheat and other assorted crops extend as far as the eye can see. These crops depend on both the winter rains and irrigation.

Flowers are among the most extensively raised crops in the Negev. Every day fresh flowers from Israel are flown by the plane loads to the flower market in Amsterdam, the flower capital of the world. God declared the deserts of Israel would blossom profusely, and that is exactly what is happening today.

There is plenty of water 2000 feet beneath the Negev, however, it is very brackish. The salty water was a disappointment when it was first discovered, yet it has turned into a blessing because of the numerous and unusual crops it produces.

Fish in the Desert

One of the strangest agricultural components in Israel's Negev is fish farming. Who would expect to see fish being raised in the desert? But scores of fishponds in the Negev are swarming with carp, mullet and tilapia, sometimes called St. Peter's fish. The brackish water beneath the Negev, which naturally remains about 100 degrees Fahrenheit, has proven to be an excellent resource for breeding fish. Fed by computerized machines the fish are harvested and shipped to stores and restaurants all over the country.

One kibbutz in the Negev is now raising shrimp. This non-kosher creature would likely stir the ire of Israel's Orthodox Jews, if the kibbutz was located closer to civilization. The kibbutz is presently producing several hundred tons of shrimp a year and selling them to restaurants and fish markets in Tel Aviv where kosher food is not always demanded. A report published in *Israel Today* stated only one-third of Israel's 4,399 restaurants and coffee shops are kosher.[12]

Periodically water from the fish ponds is drained onto the desert floor where it causes grasses to spring up. The fields are also nourished by the brackish irrigation water pumped from beneath the Negev. Herds of dairy cattle that graze on these grasses produce very sweet milk. Several dairy farms have been developed in the area as a result. One dairy farm produces ice cream which they sell in their grocery store and to nearby restaurants.

Food in Abundance

Tomatoes are being raised in the Negev. The Israelis discovered regular and cherry-sized tomatoes go into stress and retain more of their sugar when produced in the Negev's saline water. These tomatoes are marketed as "Desert Sweets" in Israel, and large quantities are exported to Europe.

The kibbutz at Sde Boker is presently experimenting with shrimp, lobster and eel. They are also raising a special type of algae which sells for several hundred dollars a pound. It is used in nutritional supplements and some cosmetics.

In the Galilee region of northern Israel, rainfall is sufficient to cultivate fields that produce some of the highest yields per acre in the world. Crops raised in Galilee include wheat, corn, cotton, as well as a variety of fruits and vegetables.

The Carmel mountain range along Israel's northern coast produces some of the most excellent wines found anywhere in the world, while the Jordan Valley and the coastal areas of Israel produce abundant citrus crops and vegetables. A bountiful banana crop is harvested each year from fields close to the Sea of Galilee. Israel's farms produce beef, chicken, turkey, vegetables and fruit in supply ample enough to feed the nation and export a twenty percent surplus. Israel is now sufficient in producing its total food requirements, although numerous food products are imported.

The only thing that seems to be lacking in Israel is oil. Former Prime Minister Golda Meir liked to tell how Moses and the children of Israel wandered about the region for forty years before settling on the only piece of real estate in the Middle East without oil. While a few oil and gas reserves have been discovered in Israel, research and drilling continue in hopes of finding more.

THE LAND OF MILK, HONEY
AND TECHNOLOGY

As one considers Israel's many accomplishments in the development of their land and resources since its founding in 1948, two aspects of Israel's economy that tend to be overlooked are research and technology. Daniel's prophecy that knowledge would increase at the close of the age is certainly being fulfilled in Israel, and it is having a positive influence on the nation's economy.

Approximately 105,000 students are presently enrolled in Israel's colleges and universities. Twenty-one percent of all students and fifty percent of all Ph.D. candidates specialize in the sciences and medicine. Thirteen percent specialize in engineering. Many highly skilled scientists from Europe and Russia have immigrated to Israel, a brain-drain for those countries but a scientific boon to the Jewish state.

Israel has more college graduates per capita than any other nation in the world; consequently the Jewish nation has become an economic and technological powerhouse. By population Israel is ranked one-hundred in size among the nations of the world, yet it is ranked twenty-first in per capita GDP and twenty-third in per capita income, life expectancy and educational standards.[13] The World Economic Forum in its 2006-2007 Global Competitiveness Report ranked Israel number three in the field of technology. It had been listed twenty-third in the previous year's report.[14]

Israel's technological achievements spring from both their economic goals and their need to excel in order to survive. Even before the nation was founded, Jews living in the Holy Land placed a high priority on education and scientific research, especially in the areas of agriculture and military capability. Israel produces sophisticated guns, tanks and guidance systems, not to mention their nuclear capability. Israel has shared its knowledge about irrigation techniques and raising crops in desert regions with the Palestinians and with several drought-prone nations in Africa. This humanitarian effort on the part of the Israelis has received little or no coverage in the press.

The oldest educational institution in the country is the Israel Institute of Technology (Technion), founded in 1924. The Hebrew University in Jerusalem was founded in 1925, and the Weizmann Institute of Science came into being in 1946. Since then many other educational institutions and research centers have been created throughout the country.

Israel ranks near the top of nations that are on the leading edge of technological development in computers, software, electronics, wireless communications, digital networks, drugs and a variety of medical devices. Electronic components have emerged as the country's leading industrial sector. There are over 1800 high-tech companies operating in Israel. International corporations, including Intel, IBM, Motorola, Hewlett Packard, Johnson and Johnson, Bristol Myers-Squibb, General Electric and Siemens, conduct extensive business in Israel. In 2006 billionaire Warren Buffett invested over $4 billion in an Israeli technology company.

The list of Israel's achievements extends into all areas of scientific research and development. Agricultural achievements include:

- Drip irrigation and computer-generated drip irrigation with nutrients.
- Plant genetics that produce higher yielding and more disease-resistant crops.
- Scientific cattle-breeding has led to one of the highest yields in milk production in the world.
- Disease-resistant seeds and biological pest controls.
- Development of crops that grow under the most arid conditions.

In the field of medicine, Israel has contributed the following:

- Pioneered laser surgery. Israel produces and uses state-of-the-art surgical lasers.
- The Histocan, a tiny air-driven camera that detects early cancerous lesions.
- The IRE (Irreversible electroporation) targets cancer cells without harming adjacent healthy tissues.

- Vaccine against human papilloma virus that causes cervical cancer in women.
- Pioneered cardiac stents.
- Pioneered organ transplants.
- First-care bandages for self-application to wounds.
- Sure-Closure Skin system to replace costly skin grafts and close large wounds.
- Ultrasound imaging systems and faster MRI systems.
- A glove device that can stimulate movements in a paralyzed hand or arm.
- Bar-Ilan University has developed an advanced electro-optical blood cell sorting device to diagnose and detect early stages of cancer.
- The Jerusalem College of Technology developed a new thermal sensor that makes thermal-imaging readings more precise during an angiogram.[15]

What God has done for Israel and the Jewish people in the past sixty years is truly remarkable. Those who take the time to sit down and read the prophecies concerning the reestablishment of the nation of Israel along with prophecies dealing with the restoration of the land will come away with an overwhelming sense of being a witness to the fulfillment of all these things. Each of these fulfilled prophecies brings us closer to the return of the Lord Jesus Christ. Yes, God is truly blessing Israel, but the best is yet to come for this nascent Jewish nation; His Name is *Yeshua HaMoshiach*, Jesus the Messiah.

Chapter 3

PROPHECY ACCORDING TO DANIEL

Daniel was one of the greatest men who ever lived. He was among the first captives to be carried off to Babylon by King Nebuchadnezzar (605 BC). Throughout the entire captivity period, God used Daniel as a stabilizing influence for his people. The stories of Daniel in the book that bears his name are not fanciful tales, as some claim, but true accounts of a faithful servant of God.

In the darkest hours of human history, God has always raised up men and women of faith and integrity. Daniel was such a man for his time. Known for his piety and strength of character, he continues to serve as an example of righteous living. In this age when so many are advocating compromise and accommodation with the forces of evil, we desperately need men and women who will faithfully stand for the truth of God. A little poem many of us learned as children is a worthy challenge for Christians today:

Dare to be a Daniel,
Dare to stand alone!
Dare to have a purpose firm,
Dare are make it known.

Some of the most detailed prophecies in Scripture are found in the book of Daniel. They are so precise, in fact, liberal scholars have labeled Daniel a mythological figure and dated his book to the time of Antiochus IV (175-164 BC), rather than the time of the Babylonian captivity. These scholars concluded no one could possibly have had such precise insights into the flow of human history; therefore Daniel had to have been written long after these events took place, but in a style in which the writer only appeared to be looking toward the future. However, Ezekiel identified Daniel as a person of great wisdom and righteousness, and Jesus Christ affirmed Daniel as both a prophet and author.[1]

Alva J. McClain, one of the most astute Bible scholars of the twentieth century, disarmed the liberal critics when he stated:

> But no critic has ever dared to suggest a date for the Book of Daniel as late as the birth of our Lord. Yet Daniel's prophecy of the Seventy Weeks predicts to the very day Christ's appearance as the Prince of Israel. Therefore the critics have done their worst, no matter where they place the date of the book, the greatest time-prophecy of the Bible is left untouched. And on this prophecy, the whole case of the critics goes to pieces.[2]

Liberal theologians who claimed the Book of Daniel was written in the second century BC were dealt another blow when a copy of Daniel dating to 100 BC was found among the biblical manuscripts now known as the Dead Sea Scrolls. It would have been impossible in so brief a period of time for the Book of Daniel to have been accepted as part of the Jewish Scriptures had it been written during the time of Antiochus IV.

The Book of Daniel was written in Hebrew and Aramaic. The detailed prophecies of Daniel are critical to understanding end-time events in general and the Book of Revelation in particular. Nebuchadnezzar's dream, as interpreted by Daniel, described various world empires from the time of Nebuchadnezzar to the coming of Christ. Daniel was given a vision of the reign of the Ancient of Days, as well as a detailed account of the antichrist and the seven years of tribulation. Perhaps the most important prophecy of all is contained in Daniel's vision of the seventy weeks of years and the coming Messiah.

NEBUCHADNEZZAR'S DREAM

In the second year of his reign, King Nebuchadnezzar had an unusual dream. He summoned his wise men to tell him the dream and its interpretation. After his wise men assured him not a man on earth could reveal what the king had asked, Nebuchadnezzar commanded all the wise men of Babylon be killed. Daniel and his three close friends, Hananiah, Mishael and Azariah, took the matter to the Lord in prayer; then He revealed to Daniel both the contents of the dream and its revelation.

As Daniel stood before King Nebuchadnezzar, he assured him his wise men had correctly stated that no man could render such a revelation, but the God in heaven had made known to Daniel both the dream and its interpretation. Then Daniel described a great statue; its head was made of gold, its breast and arms of silver, its belly and thighs of bronze, its legs of iron and its feet partly of iron and partly of clay. In Nebuchadnezzar's dream "a stone, cut out without hands struck the statue on its feet of iron and clay and crushed them." Upon impact the stone pulverized the statue so that not a trace of it could be found. "The stone that struck the statue became a great mountain and filled the whole earth," said Daniel.[3] This stone is a description of Jesus Christ when He returns in glory to establish His kingdom and rule the nations of the earth.

The concept of Christ as "the Rock" is found in various portions of Scripture. The Song of Moses describes the Lord as "the Rock of salvation."[4] Moses brought water from the Rock in the desert, not once but twice. On the first occasion, Moses was instructed to "strike the Rock" and water would come forth;[5] the second time he was told to "speak to the Rock" and it would yield water.[6] But on the second occasion, Moses did not obey God; instead he struck the Rock in anger, consequently God would not allow him to lead the people into the Promised Land. At first glance this punishment may seem harsh until you realize the Rock that Moses struck was Christ. Because the Rock is a type of Christ, it could only be struck once. The Bible states: "Christ was offered once to bear the sins of many."[7] Paul wrote:

> For I do not want you to be unaware, brethren, that our fathers were all under the cloud and all passed through the sea; and all were baptized into Moses in the cloud and in the sea; and all ate the same spiritual food; and all drank the same spiritual drink, for they were drinking from a spiritual rock which followed them; and the rock was Christ.[8]

The meaning of Nebuchadnezzar's dream could not be made clearer.

> "You, O King," said Daniel, "are the head of gold. After you there will arise another kingdom inferior to you, then another third kingdom of bronze, which will rule over the earth. Then there will be a fourth kingdom as strong as iron....In that you saw the feet and toes, partly of potter's clay and partly of iron, it will be a divided kingdom; but it will have in it the toughness of iron, inasmuch as you saw the iron mixed with common clay. As the toes of the feet were partly of iron and partly of pottery, so some of the kingdom will be strong and part of it will be brittle. And in that you saw the iron mixed with common clay, they will combine with one another in the seed of men; but they will not adhere to one another, even as iron does not combine with pottery."[9]

Daniel went on to describe the establishment of the Messianic kingdom which will forever replace all earthly kingdoms and can never be destroyed. There is not a hint in Daniel that the kingdom to be set up at the end of the age is an allegory or merely spiritual in nature. To the contrary, a literal Messianic kingdom will be established on earth by the direct hand of God.

In chapters seven and eight of Daniel, portions of the same vision are expanded and further explained. The first world empire to arise was Babylon (the head of gold); it was followed by the Medes and Persians (breast and arms of silver). The third empire, Greece (belly and thighs of bronze), came to power through Alexander the Great when he swept the world and lamented there were no more worlds to conquer. After his death at age thirty-three, Alexander's empire was divided into four parts.

The fourth empire, represented in the statue's legs, depicted the Roman Empire when it was divided into two parts, with the Eastern portion of the empire being ruled from Constantinople, while the Western portion remained centered in Rome. Daniel's vision extended into the future, as it described a revived Roman Empire (its feet partly of iron and partly of clay) that will come into existence under the leadership of ten kings (the ten toes). Daniel identified a leader, called "the little horn," (the antichrist), who will arise and dominate the other kings in the confederation. The antichrist will then wage war with the saints for three and a half years.

The eighth chapter of Daniel records how the angel Gabriel was sent to Daniel in order to give him "an understanding of the vision." Daniel was shown both the future of the Jewish nation and the Gentile world. The prophet was also shown the rise of the antichrist and the coming reign of the Messiah. According to Daniel's prophecy, the Messiah will come "with the clouds of heaven, and with dominion, glory and a kingdom...which will not be destroyed."[10]

Most scholars agree that portions of Daniel's prophecies in chapter eight were fulfilled through Antiochus IV who ruled Syria in the second century BC. As Antiochus returned from an attack on Egypt, he swept through Jerusalem and slaughtered approximately 40,000 Jews. Antiochus, who called himself "Theos Epiphanies" (the god who reveals himself), desecrated the Temple by offering a pig on the altar and setting up an image of the Greek god Zeus in the Temple sanctuary.

These and other despicable acts caused a priest named Mattahias and his five sons to lead a revolt against Antiochus. The revolt was

77

successful, and the sons of Mattahias ruled the country until Rome conquered the region in 63 BC. The most famous of Mattahias' five sons was Judas, known also as Maccabaeus (the hammer).

Shortly after Antiochus was defeated, the Temple was cleansed. A one-day supply of oil for the menorah lasted eight days. This miraculous event became an important festival in Judaism which is known today as Hanukkah. This celebration, mentioned in the tenth chapter of John, is also called the Feast of Dedication or the Festival of Lights.

Without a doubt Antiochus Epiphanies foreshadows the antichrist; yet one cannot claim he fulfilled all the prophetic events described by Daniel. Christ spoke of Daniel's prophecy regarding the desecration of the Temple as a future event.[11]

The skepticism of the Bible's critics concerning the prophecies of Daniel continues to focus on the fact the prophet so accurately described the rise of four consecutive world empires from the time of Nebuchadnezzar to the time of Christ—Babylon, the Medes and Persians, Greece and Rome. However, if Daniel was written in the second century BC (which it was not), it would still leave the prophecy concerning the rise of the Roman Empire in place. Rome would not control the region for another hundred years (63 BC).

Furthermore, the liberal critics are unable to explain the detailed prophecy of Daniel's seventy weeks. If Daniel was written in the second century BC (which it was not), the critics are left to explain Daniel's prophecies concerning the appearance of the Messiah on Palm Sunday and the destruction of Jerusalem in AD 70.

DANIEL'S SEVENTY WEEKS

Seventy weeks have been decreed for your people and your holy city, to finish the transgression, to make an end of sin, to make atonement for iniquity, to bring in everlasting righteousness, to seal up vision and prophecy and to anoint the most holy place. So you are to know and discern that from the issuing of a decree to restore and rebuild Jerusalem until Messiah the Prince there will be seven weeks and sixty-two weeks; it will be built again, with plaza and moat, even in times of distress. Then after the sixty-two weeks the Messiah will be cut off and have nothing, and the people of the prince who is to come will destroy the city and the sanctuary. And its end will come with a flood; even to the end there will be war; desolations are determined. And he will make a firm covenant with the many for one week, but in the middle of the week he will put a stop to sacrifice and grain offering; and on the wing of abominations will come one who makes desolate, even until a complete destruction, one that is decreed, is poured out on the one who makes desolate.[12]

While reading the words of the prophet Jeremiah, Daniel understood the seventy years of captivity in Babylon were about to end for Israel. With that knowledge Daniel entered into a prolonged period of prayer. Wearing sackcloth and ashes, the aged prophet began to intercede for Israel by confessing the many sins that had brought them into captivity.

There is a great parallel between the spiritual condition of Israel at the time of Daniel and the spiritual condition that presently exists in America. Our country is moving further away from God with every passing day. There are not enough people on their knees pleading for this nation, and even fewer who are weeping over our manifold sins. Our nation is in great danger of God's judgment. If Christians do not arise soon to intercede on behalf of America and call for national repentance, judgment is sure to come.

In direct answer to his prayers, Daniel received a visitation from the angel Gabriel in the ninth hour of the day, giving him "insight with understanding." Before the Temple was destroyed in 586 BC, the Jews gathered for prayer each day at the time of the evening sacrifice (the ninth hour). Daniel faithfully observed the same hour of prayer even though the Temple no longer existed and he was languishing in exile.

The general consensus among premillennialists is that Daniel's seventy weeks are weeks of years, not weeks of days. As a rule amillennialists do not allow for any kind of literal interpretation of Daniel's prophecies, nor do they offer a satisfactory explanation as to their meaning. "Seventy weeks have been decreed for your people and your holy city." The literal rendering of this passage would be *seventy sevens or seventy weeks of years are determined for your people and your holy city.* There is no doubt the timeline referenced here specifically refers to the Jewish people and Jerusalem.

The concept of weeks of years was well understood by Daniel and every Jew, because God had instructed the people of Israel to plant and harvest their lands for six consecutive years and leave them fallow throughout each seventh year (the Sh'mita Year).[13] The fact Israel had violated God's law for 490 years, the Lord determined their captivity in Babylon would last for seventy years in order that the land could enjoy its Sabbath rests. After each forty-nine years (7x7), God instructed the nation of Israel to observe a year of Jubilee, during which time ownership of lands that may have been sold or lost would revert back to the original or rightful owners.[14]

The number seven appears in the Book of Revelation more than fifty times; this includes the seven spirits of God, the seven seals, the seven trumpets and the seven vials. The number seven (shalem) is used throughout the Bible to denote perfection and completeness. It has the same root as the Hebrew word for peace (shalom).

Gabriel told Daniel the seventy weeks of years would begin with the decree to rebuild Jerusalem, and Israel would continue as a nation until sixty-nine weeks of years were completed.[15] According to Nehemiah, the decree to rebuild Jerusalem was issued by King Artaxerxes on March 14, 445 BC. Alva McClain uses calculations developed by Sir Robert Anderson in his book *The Coming Prince,* in order to show the sixty-nine weeks of years ended precisely on the day Jesus rode into Jerusalem on a donkey to present Himself as the Messiah. Sir Robert Anderson multiplied 69 years x 7 x the 360 days in the Jewish calendar and came up with a total of 173,880 days. Beginning with March 14, 445 BC when the order to rebuild Jerusalem was given, this number of days concluded on April 6, AD 32, as calculated according to the Gregorian calendar with its 365 days per year. God revealed to Daniel the exact day (Palm Sunday) when Jesus would enter Jerusalem and present Himself as Israel's Messiah.

Four days prior to each Passover (the tenth day of Nissan), the people of Israel were instructed to choose from their flocks the lambs to be offered on Passover. It was on that precise day God announced His selection of Christ as "the lamb of God who takes away the sins of the world." As Jesus sat on the Mount of Olives weeping over Israel's rejection of their Messiah, He spoke about the significance of that very day: "When He approached Jerusalem, He saw the city and wept over it, saying, 'If you had known in *this day,* even you, the things which make for peace! But now they are hidden from your eyes.'"

As shouts of Hosanna and praises rang out, the Pharisees asked Jesus to rebuke His disciples. Jesus answered, "I tell you if these become silent, the stones will cry out."[16] Jesus spoke the words *"If you had known this day,"* because the *day* He rode into Jerusalem on a donkey (Palm Sunday) had been marked out on God's calendar as the day when Christ would present Himself as Israel's Messiah.

The Bible speaks of Jesus coming to earth "in the fullness of time." Jesus Himself told His disciples on several occasions, "My *time* has not yet come." God had marked out a day for Jesus' birth, for His crucifixion, for His resurrection and for His ascension. All the events in the life of Christ took place at the exact time and place of God's choosing. This same principle will be applied when Christ returns for the church and when He comes again in glory.

THE PARENTHESIS

The period of time (gap or a parenthesis) between the sixty-ninth week and the seventieth week of Daniel's prophecy is referred to as the "church age." This gap in which we are now living represents the season of harvest when the church is commissioned to go into the world with the gospel, "to the Jew first and also to the Greek."[17]

During most of the long gap between the sixty-ninth and the seventieth weeks, the Jews were exiled from the land of Israel. (However, there never was a time since their exile in AD 70 that some Jews were not living in Israel.) Now with the Jews returning to their land, one may assume the start of the seventieth week is not far off. The seventieth week described by Daniel will begin after the rapture of the church takes place and at the start of the seven years of tribulation.

Several prophecies in Scripture help us to better understand the gap between the sixty-ninth and the seventieth weeks. Isaiah prophesied Christ's first coming when he wrote, "For a child will be born to us, a son will be given to us...." The same prophecy continues without interruption to describe His second coming: "And the government will rest on His shoulders; and His name will be called Wonderful Counselor, Mighty God, Eternal Father, Prince of Peace."[18] At the beginning of His ministry, Jesus stood in the synagogue in Nazareth and read from Isaiah 61 concerning His first coming, but He stopped reading abruptly in the middle of the second verse because that which followed related to His second coming.[19]

Daniel prophesied the following events would occur after the sixty-ninth week:

- The Messiah will be cut off and have nothing (the crucifixion).
- The people of the prince (Rome) will destroy the city and the Temple (AD 70).

According to Daniel, at the close of the seventieth week, which is the seven years of tribulation, Jesus Christ shall return in clouds of glory and perform the following as they relate to Israel:

- finish the transgression,
- make an end of sin,
- make atonement for iniquity,
- bring in everlasting righteousness,
- seal up vision and prophecy,
- and anoint the most holy place.

Each event described by Daniel will be fulfilled as Israel acknowledges Jesus Christ as their Messiah and mourns over the One whom they have pierced.[20] The regathered nation of Israel will at last embrace Christ's atoning death on the cross.

The Lord spoke with great tenderness regarding His plan for Israel at the end of the seven years of tribulation and at His coming:

"Comfort, O comfort My people, says your God. Speak kindly to Jerusalem; and call out to her, that her warfare has ended, that her iniquity has been removed, that she has received of the Lord's hand double for all her sins."[21]

One should not surmise because God extends His grace to the church during a certain period of time and then deals with Israel during another period of time, there are two differing covenants of redemption. Both Jews and Christians are brought to faith in exactly the same way—by grace through faith in the once-for-all sacrifice of Jesus Christ on the cross.

There are, however, a growing number of liberals and even some evangelicals who teach what is called the "two covenant" theory of the atonement. They claim God has one way of redeeming the Gentiles and another way of redeeming the Jews. Therefore they conclude evangelism to Jews is unnecessary, since God has already made provision for them through special "revelation." The theory of two covenants is not in accord with the Scriptures.

In each of his missionary journeys, Paul always went first to the Jewish synagogue to preach the gospel; only then did he take the gospel to the Gentiles. Some of the Jews responded to Paul's witness and received Jesus as their Savior. Paul wrote: "For there is no distinction between Jew and Greek; for the same Lord is Lord of all, abounding in riches for all who call on Him; for 'Whoever will call on the name of the Lord will be saved.'"[22]

Liberals today actually promote a multi-covenant theology of salvation, in which they teach there are separate plans of salvation for Jews, Christians, Muslims, Buddhists, etc. This doctrine, commonly called "universalism," is deceiving millions and placing them on a fast-track to hell. Paul reminded us of the true path to salvation when he said: "There is one body and one Spirit, just as you were called in one hope of your calling; one Lord, one faith, one baptism, one God and Father of all who is over all and through all and in all."[23]

When you walk down the streets of heaven, it will not matter who you meet, be it Jew or Gentile, from Adam to the last person to be redeemed, everyone in heaven will have the same testimony—I am here because Jesus Christ died for me! None, including Moses, will boast they were saved by keeping the law; all who have been redeemed will have been saved under one covenant—the Covenant of Jesus' blood and righteousness.

THE SEVENTIETH WEEK

The seventieth week (seven years) of Daniel was the subject of much of Jesus' Olivet Discourse (Matthew 24) as well as most of the prophecies in the Book of Revelation. The seventieth week, which focuses on Israel, will begin at the time of the rapture of the church and conclude with Christ's glorious appearing with His saints.

The seven-year period will see the rise of the antichrist (the little horn) and the false prophet. It is foolish to speculate about the identity of the antichrist; Paul informs us prior to the coming of Christ, the man of lawlessness will be revealed.[24]

The antichrist will arise and assume power over the confederation of ten kings from the revived Roman Empire. Do not forget that a large portion of the ancient Roman Empire included present-day Turkey, Syria, Jordan, Lebanon, Iraq and portions of Iran. John Walvoord, among others, expressed the belief the antichrist will likely come from this region of the world. Chuck Missler cites several biblical passages that describe such a person as an "Assyrian."[25]

At the start of the tribulation, the antichrist will make a covenant with Israel that will enable the Jews to have access to the Temple Mount and restore the Temple services. But half way through the seven years, he will break the covenant and attack them. "He will speak out against the Most High and wear down the saints of the Highest One by altering laws."[26]

If the antichrist should arise from the Islamic world, the words *altering laws* could refer to the imposition of Islamic (sharia) law. This may be what is meant when Daniel stated the antichrist will "fling truth to the ground and perform its will and prosper."[27] While one may not be able to understand the full scope of the antichrist's rule, it is clear he will control the entire Middle East region and eventually the rest of the world. Without entering into speculation, the Scriptures (Ezekiel 38 and 39) clearly state the Islamic world will be at the very center of end-time events.

THE MARK OF THE BEAST

The Book of Revelation describes another aspect of the rule of the antichrist, when he requires everyone, rich and poor, to accept a mark on their right hand or on their forehead. No one will be able to buy or to sell except the one who has the mark, either the name of the beast or the number of his name. The number of the beast is 666 (Revelation 13:18).

Only a few years ago, such a system of identification could not have been imagined. Today modern technology makes this prophecy fully plausible. Even now some social engineers have called for microchips to be embedded under the skin of individuals for the purpose of obtaining an immediate readout of their personal and economic history. They claim such an information retrieval system would be useful for airport security, immigration, passports, banking and general commerce. One can only wonder how long it will be until existing technology will make the implantation of microchips mandatory.

WE ARE ON THE WINNING SIDE!

At the end of the tribulation (Daniel's seventieth week), the antichrist will gather his armies and invade "the Beautiful Land." The battle to end all battles will take place in the Valley of Armageddon. While the devastation to Israel and the world will be great in that hour, the Lord and His hosts will descend from heaven with His saints! The antichrist and all his forces will be utterly destroyed by Christ.

Jesus said that immediately following the tribulation of those days, "then the sign of the Son of Man will appear in the sky, and then all the tribes of the earth will mourn, and they will see the Son of Man coming on the clouds of the sky with power and great glory."[28]

Then the fullness of the Lord's promises to Israel will come to pass as spoken through the prophet Jeremiah:

> "For I know the plans that I have for you," declares the Lord, "plans for welfare and not for calamity to give you a future and a hope. Then you will call upon Me and come and pray to Me, and I will listen to you. You will seek me and find Me when you search for Me with all your heart. I will be found by you," declares the Lord, "and I will restore your fortunes and will gather you from all the nations and from all the places where I have driven you," declares the Lord, "and I will bring you back to the place from where I sent you into exile."[29]

Whatever happens, we may be confident of this—God is in control! From the moment our hearts receive God's free gift of salvation in Jesus Christ, the Holy Spirit empowers us to live in the reality of Christ's VICTORY! Paul reminds us we are more than conquerors through Him who loved us. There is no need for fear or alarm as we witness the signs of the times. Jesus said, "...when you see these things happening, recognize that the kingdom of God is near."[30]

The heavenly benediction of God's love and grace are ours forever. As we consider God's plan of redemption, may we bow in humility and praise to receive His gracious benediction:

> Now to Him who is able to keep you from stumbling, and to make you stand in the presence of His glory blameless with great joy, to the only God our Savior, through Jesus Christ our Lord, be glory, majesty, dominion and authority, before all time and now and forever. Amen.[31]

Chapter 4

THE RISE OF A WORLD GOVERNMENT

> *It was also given to him to make war with the saints and to overcome them, and authority over every tribe and people and tongue and nation was given to him (Revelation 13:7).*
>
> *He will speak out against the Most High and wear down the saints of the Highest One, and he will intend to make alterations in times and in law; and they will be given into his hand for a time, times and half a time (Daniel 7:25).*

The Scriptures are very clear—at the time of the tribulation a world ruler (the antichrist) will rise to dominate the earth. Although the antichrist will gain power on a platform of peace, he will be ruthless in his dealings. The fact the antichrist will "make war with the saints" means his government will be anti-Christian and anti-Israel, especially during the last half of the tribulation.

According to the Book of Revelation, every person on earth will be required to accept "a mark on their right hand or forehead" in order to buy or sell.[1] People throughout the world will be required to worship the antichrist, much as the Caesars demanded worship from everyone living in the Roman Empire. However, the Bible gives a stern warning to those who accept the mark of the antichrist or worship him: "If anyone worships the beast and his image, and receives a mark on his forehead or on his hand, he will drink of the wine of the wrath of God."[2]

While we do not know precisely what form the antichrist's government will take, the Bible warns us a global government is coming. A hundred years ago, prophecies describing such a government were little understood, but today we are better able to comprehend both its development and the motivation behind it because these concepts are actually being established.

Norman Cousins, honorary chairman of Planetary Citizens and president of the World Federalist Association, stated: "World government is coming, in fact, it is inevitable. No arguments for or against it can change that fact."[3] The concepts of a world government, a world justice system, world trade initiatives and a global currency have been promoted for many years.

Strobe Talbott, an official in the State Department during the Clinton administration, was quoted in a *Time* magazine article:

> Here is one optimist's reason for believing unity will prevail over disunity, integration over disintegration. In fact, I'll bet that within the next hundred years, nationhood as we know it will be obsolete; all states will recognize a single, global authority. A phrase briefly fashionable in the mid-20th century—"citizen of the world"—will have assumed real meaning by the end of the 21st.
>
> The best mechanism for democracy, whether at the level of the multinational state or that of the planet as a whole, is not an all-powerful Leviathan or centralized super state, but a federation, a union of separate states that allocate certain powers to a central government while retaining many others for themselves.[4]

The universal government at the end of the age will be ushered in on the wings of political expediency. Its formation and support will come about as some type of global crisis occurs, such as an economic collapse, a perceived environmental disaster, a major terrorist attack or a nuclear confrontation. Any of these occurrences could cause the inhabitants of the earth to gravitate towards anyone who promises a solution. Eventually opposition to global government will be tantamount to treason.

THE COUNCIL ON FOREIGN RELATIONS

One of the most influential organizations promoting global government today is the Council on Foreign Relations (CFR). Founded in 1921 the CFR was largely responsible for the formation of the United Nations. Just about every U.S. president and secretary of state since Franklin D. Roosevelt has been a member of the CFR. Membership in the CFR is by invitation only. Politicians, corporate leaders, celebrities and representatives from the academic world make up this quasi-government organization. The organization has both a broad membership and an inner circle which controls its agenda. The CFR is funded by some of the world's richest families and members of the international banking community.

The CFR has proposed the establishment of governmental regions throughout the world, such as the European Union. Presently they are endeavoring to develop a regional form of government in North America through the cooperation of government leaders in Mexico, the United States and Canada.

One of the most influential publications in the world is *Foreign Affairs,* a journal of the Council on Foreign Relations that regularly promotes world federalism. Richard Cooper, a former undersecretary of state during the Carter administration, wrote an article in *Foreign Affairs* in which he offered a plan for a world currency and a one-world bank: "I suggest a radical alternative scheme...the creation of a common currency for all industrial democracies, with a common monetary policy and a joint Bank of Issue to determine that monetary policy."[5]

In 2007 Benn Steil, director of international economics at the Council of Foreign Relations, wrote an article for *Foreign Affairs* in which he stated: "the world needs to abandon unwanted currencies, replacing them with dollars, euros, and multinational currencies as yet unborn." He went on to assert the dollar and the euro are temporary currencies, perhaps necessary today, but eventually they should be replaced by a new multinational currency. "Monetary nationalism is simply incompatible with globalism," he said.[6]

Other "radical alternative schemes" of the CFR have been turned into law and made official policy of our government in the past fifty years; more are sure to follow as CFR members at the highest levels of government are empowered to implement CFR plans. Knowledgeable critics of the CFR often refer to it as "a shadow government."

Rear Admiral Chester Ward, who was part of the Council on Foreign Relations for sixteen years, resigned because of the organization's desire "to bring about the surrender of the national sovereignty and the national independence of the United States." He wrote:

Once the ruling members of the CFR have decided that the U.S. government should adopt a particular policy, the very substantial research facilities of the CFR are put to work to develop arguments, intellectual and emotional, to support the new policy, and to confound and discredit, intellectually and politically, any opposition.[7]

THE TRILATERAL COMMISSION

The Trilateral Commission was formulated in 1972 by David Rockefeller, chairman of the Council on Foreign Relations and chairman of Chase Manhattan Bank. It was formally established in 1983 through the leadership of Zbigniew Brezinski, national security adviser to President Jimmy Carter. The Trilateral Commission has three major goals—a one-world economy, a one-world government and a one-world religion. Membership in the organization is comprised of elitists from North America, Europe and Japan—

regions which control the vast riches of the world. Most of America's trade agreements were engineered by the Trilateralists. James W. Wardner described the agenda of the Trilateral Commission:

> They seek an age of post-nationalism when, devoid of ethnic culture and history, the social, economic and political values esteemed by the Trilateral "volunteers" will be transformed into universal values. That is, a universal economy, a universal government (appointed, not elected), and a universal faith. Likeminded government officials and business leaders are to carry out national and international policy formation. There must be "more technical focus and lesser public awareness." This lessens the chance for people to grasp the overall scheme of the world managers and organize serious resistance.[8]

GLOBAL PROBLEMS
REQUIRE GLOBAL SOLUTIONS

For years we have witnessed the globalization of the economy and religion, much of it influenced by the United Nations. There is a growing mindset that global problems require global solutions. Military units under the auspices of the United Nations or international coalitions are becoming more acceptable to most countries than military units from individual nations, especially the United States.

In April 2007 at a White House ceremony, President George W. Bush, German Chancellor Angela Merkel and Jose Manuel Barroso, current president of the European Council, signed "The Transatlantic Economic Integration," an agreement creating a permanent body that commits the U.S. to a "deeper transatlantic economic integration." According to *WorldNetDaily*, the agreement established a new Transatlantic Economic Council to be chaired on the U.S. side by a cabinet-level officer in the White House and on the EU side by a member of the European Commission. After the signing President Bush stated: "It is a recognition that the closer that the United States and the EU become, the better off our people will be."[9]

The International Monetary Fund and the World Bank are largely responsible for shaping today's one-world economy. Nearly all financial markets throughout the world are now interconnected. A decline in any major country's financial market has an immediate ripple effect on other markets throughout the world.

Trade alliances, such as the Common Market in Europe, the Organizations of American States and the North American Trade Agreement (NAFTA), have opened world markets to most nations. As a result the United States continues to rack up staggering trade deficits. On any given month, the U.S. trade deficit exceeds $55 billion, yet our national leaders claim these deficits are good for our economy. One can only wonder how the United States or any other nation can continue to operate with an economy based on deficits and debt.

At the present time, foreign governments hold approximately twenty-five percent of our nation's $8.5 trillion debt and fifty percent of our U.S. treasury notes. China and Japan hold over $1 trillion in U.S. treasury notes.[10] If and when foreign governments no longer have faith in the American dollar or wish to do us harm economically, our nation could be faced with dramatically higher interest rates. This, in turn, would produce a major depression that would impact the entire global economy. For several years now, the American dollar has been sliding against several major currencies. OPEC has indicated it may have to base the sale of its oil on the euro, rather than on the American dollar.

In recent years we have witnessed the creation and development of the European Union (EU) with its centralized government and monetary system. The EU, presently composed of twenty-seven states, has a combined population of 490 million. The European Union's gross domestic product now stands at $14 trillion, "making it the world's largest economic bloc and a magnet for job-seekers."[11]

The euro has become one of the strongest currencies in the world. While major European nations continue to operate their own system of government, there has been a decided shift of power, especially in matters of economic issues from individual countries to Europe's centralized government. It is now considered politically incorrect for EU nations to promote any kind of nationalism.

In the meantime the world finds itself in a nuclear arms race, as smaller nations seek to acquire nuclear capability. If Iran is successful in building nuclear weapons, they will become the tenth nation to possess nuclear arms. Nuclear-armed North Korea, India, Pakistan and Russia already pose a threat to world peace. If terrorist organizations or unscrupulous dictators are able to get their hands on these weapons or nuclear components, we could experience the most horrible disaster the world has ever known. Such a nuclear event would not only cause death and mayhem of indescribable proportions, it would bring down the entire global economy.

One can easily see how a world dictator could come to power under such circumstances, offering a wounded world a new start at peace and prosperity. To say that the masses of humanity would quickly gravitate to such a person is a gross understatement. Yet with each passing day, the likelihood of such an eventuality comes more clearly into focus.

The coming world government will be a godless structure. Its utopian promises are an illusion. The lion will not lie down with the lamb when the antichrist is in power. Though he masquerades as "the Prince of Peace" and though most people will fall for his promises, the antichrist will ultimately bring about a world peace based on brute force and tyrannical power. The world may experience a measure of peace under the antichrist for a brief period of time, but according to Scripture, that peace will be shattered.

THE NORTH AMERICAN COMMUNITY

There are events unfolding today in the United States so incredible, it is difficult to imagine how any patriotic American could ever consider endorsing them. An example is the proposed North America Community, an ongoing effort to merge the United States with Canada and Mexico, much like the European Union. This proposal, drafted by the Council on Foreign Relations, has the support of some of the most powerful and elite members of our government. The CFR has called for a common security border with Canada and Mexico to be established by 2010.

In 2006 Dr. Robert Pastor, vice-chairman of the Council on Foreign Relations Task Force on North America, appeared before a panel of the Senate Committee on Foreign Relations and called for erasing the borders between the United States, Mexico and Canada. Among other things Pastor stated: "What we need to do is forge a new North American Community. Instead of stopping North Americans on the borders, we ought to provide them with a secure, biometric Border Pass that would ease transit across the border like an E-Z pass permits our cars to speed through tolls."[12]

The CFR's proposed North American Community, to be implemented by 2010, supposedly will retain "respect for the sovereignty" of all three nations. Nevertheless it calls for:

- A common currency to be called the "amero."
- A common border around all three countries.
- Military and law enforcement cooperation among all three countries.
- A common border-pass so that residents and goods can freely move among the three countries. This pass will eliminate the need for passports.
- Expand the temporary migrant program to include the full mobility of labor among the three countries.
- Bring people from Canada and Mexico into the U.S. Department of Homeland Security.
- Harmonize all visa and asylum regulations, as well as "entry screening."
- Construct a superhighway from Mexico through the center of the United States and into Canada.
- The United States is to establish a fund to finance the education of 60,000 Mexicans in U.S. colleges and universities.
- Establish a North American inter-parliamentary group and executive commission to govern its rules and regulations without interference from any country's government.

The North American Community proposal is moving through all three governments one piece at a time. Elements of the plan were endorsed at a meeting held at Baylor University, Waco, Texas, March

23, 2005 by former Canadian Prime Minister Paul Martin, former Mexican President Vicente Fox and President George W. Bush. The three leaders committed their respective governments and signed an agreement called "The Security and Prosperity Partnership of North America (SPP)." A joint-statement following the signing said: "In a rapidly changing world, we must develop new avenues of coopera-tion that will make our open societies safer and more secure, our businesses more competitive, and our economies more resilient." Since the meeting in Waco, twenty or more trilateral groups have been formed by the three governments to move the plan forward. The White House has established offices for the SPP in the U.S. Department of Commerce.

In the controversial "Secure Borders, Economic Opportunity and Immigration Reform Act of 2007, a bill that was defeated in the U.S. Senate in June of that same year, a provision for the acceleration of the Security and Prosperity Partnership was put forward. It read: "It is the sense of Congress that the United States and Mexico should accelerate the implementation of the Partnership for Prosperity to help generate economic growth and improve the standard of living in Mexico, which will lead to reduced migration."[13]

The momentum for promoting the North American union plan was reported by *WorldNetDaily* as follows:

A powerful think tank chaired by former Senator Sam Nunn and guided by trustees, including Richard Armitage, Zbigniew Brezinski, Harold Brown, William Cohen and Henry Kissinger, is in the final states of preparing a report to the White House and U.S. Congress on the benefits of integrating the U.S., Mexico and Canada into one political, economic and security bloc. The final report, published in English, Spanish and French, is scheduled for submission to all three governments by September 30, 2007, according to the Center for Strategic and International Studies.[14]

The Council on Foreign Relations has called for the implemen-tation of "the Social Security Totalization Agreement, negotiated between the United States and Mexico." This plan would place all

Mexicans who work in the United States in our Social Security system.[15] One cannot imagine the tax increase that would be required to finance this scheme, especially since the existing Social Security program is presently in danger of bankruptcy.

A follow-up conference to the Waco agreement, sponsored by the Canadian Council of Chief Executives, took place in Banff, September 2006. Some of the participants included Defense Secretary Donald Rumsfeld, George Shultz, James Woolsey, Doris Meissner, Robert Pastor, William Perry, James Schlesinger and top officials of both Mexico and Canada.[16]

Lou Dobbs of CNN remarked on his news program:

> President Bush signed a formal agreement that will end the United States as we know it, and he took the step without approval from either the U.S. Congress or the people of the United States....[17] Americans must think that our political and academic elites have gone utterly mad, at a time when three and a half years, going on four, after September 11, we still don't have border security, and this group of elites is talking about not defending our borders, finally, but rather creating new ones.[18]

Early in 2007 the Department of Transportation granted permission for one hundred Mexican trucking companies to have "unlimited access to U.S. roads to haul international cargo from Mexico to locations throughout the country." On returning the Mexican trucks will be allowed to carry cargo from the U.S. into Mexico. "The intent is for the Mexican trucking operations in the U.S. to be indistinguishable from U.S. trucking operations," said a DOT spokesperson.[19]

BUILDING A MEGA-HIGHWAY
FROM MEXICO TO CANADA

The construction of a colossal 4000-mile NAFTA highway system from Mexico to Canada, at an estimated cost of $183 billion dollars, is now on the drawing boards. The highway, which will follow existing I-35, will be 1200 feet wide and extend from the Mexican border through Texas and the Midwest and eventually into Canada. Construction could take up to fifty years. Preliminary plans call for the highway to have ten lanes, a high-speed rail system and gas, oil and water pipelines. The project is to be financed by Cintra Concesiones de Infraestructureas de Transporte, S.A., a foreign investment consortium based in Spain. Cintra will own the leasing rights to the highway for fifty years. According to *WorldNetDaily*, Cintra is represented in the U.S. by Bracewell and Giuliani, Rudy Giuliani's Houston-based law firm.[20]

Commenting on this proposed superhighway, Patrick J. Buchannan stated:

The American people never supported NAFTA, and they are angry over Bush's failure to secure the border—but a shotgun marriage between our neighboring nations appears prearranged. Central feature: a ten-lane, 400-yard-wide NAFTA superhighway from the Mexican port of Lazaro Cardenas, up to and across the U.S. border, all the way to Canada. Within the median strip dividing the north and south car and truck lanes would be rail lines for both passengers and freight traffic, and oil and gas pipelines.

As author Jerome Corsi describes this Fox-Bush auto-bahn, container ships from China would unload at Lazaro Cardenas, a port named for the Mexican president who nationalized all U.S. oil companies in 1938. From there, trucks with Mexican drivers would run fast lines into the United States, hauling their cargo to a U.S. customs inspec-tion terminal—in Kansas City, Mo. From there, the trucks would fan out across America or roll on into Canada. Similar superhighways from Mexico through the United States into Canada are planned.

According to Corsi, construction of the Trans-Texas Corridor, the first leg of the NAFTA superhighway, is to begin next year (2007).

The beneficiaries of this NAFTA superhighway project would be contractors who build it and the importers and outlet stores for the Chinese-manufactured goods that would come flooding in. The losers would be U.S. longshoremen, truckers, manufacturers and taxpayers.

The latter would pay the cost of building the highway in Mexico and the United States, both in dollars and in lost sovereignty of our once-independent American republic.[21]

The construction of this mega-highway system is set to begin in Texas in the very near future. The Texas legislature tried to halt the project in its tracks through legislation passed in June 2007, but Texas Governor Rick Perry vetoed the measure. Many people in Texas are alarmed to see this project going forward, because it will consume tens of thousands of acres of valuable farmland, and because the proposed mega-highway will have limited access, bypassing many cities and towns from one end of Texas to the other.

Every American should keep a watchful eye on these CFR proposals that are being implemented without the sanction of Congress and without the support of the American people. The unwillingness of political leaders to protect our border with Mexico, their efforts to sanction illegal immigration and pay for the healthcare, education and Social Security of some twelve to twenty million illegal immigrants are all connected to the plan to create the North American Community by 2010. Other than Lou Dobbs on his nightly CNN news program, the media is largely ignoring this assault on American sovereignty.

It is likely the North American Community will come into existence, if not by 2010 certainly by 2020. If those who control the monetary system force a collapse of the American dollar, the amero will come into existence very quickly. Under the right set of circumstances, the American people could accept the institution of the amero as a means to save not only the economy but their own finances as well. In any event it will be a giant leap toward a global government.

GLOBAL GOVERNMENT AND TECHNOLOGY

One of the signs of the last days as described by Daniel is an increase in knowledge. It is incomprehensible how swiftly our civilization is changing in the twenty-first century. Laser and computer-assisted surgeries have transformed what were once fatal diseases into routine maintenance. Computer chips now control our thermostats, refrigerators, automobiles and about any major or small appliance you can name. Guidance systems that once were used to control missiles are now used to help us drive our automobiles. A tiny computer chip is now being inserted under the skin of animals and pets with an amazing amount of information about their ownership and medical records. Such a chip could be used to control every aspect of individual lives, if and when the government is so inclined.

Writing in the *Toronto Star,* Kevin Haggerty discussed the use of implanted microchips in the not too distant future.

> By the time my four-year-old son is swathed in the soft flesh of old age, he will likely find it unremarkable that he and almost everyone he knows will be permanently implanted with a microchip. Automatically tracking his location in real time, it will connect him with databases monitoring and recording his smallest behavioral traits.
>
> Most people anticipate such a prospect with a sense of horrified disbelief, dismissing it as a science-fiction fantasy. The technology, however, already exists. From this point forward, microchips will become progressively smaller, less invasive, and easier to deploy. Thus, any realistic barrier to the wholesale "chipping" of Western citizens is not technological but cultural. It relies upon the visceral reaction against the prospect of being personally marked as one component in a massive human inventory.[22]

Consider how much information about you is already stored on government, medical and business computers—credit history, medical history, employment records, driving records, insurance records, etc. Go into most any automobile dealership to buy a new car, and within a few minutes they know your entire credit history. Like it or not, our lives are already an open book for most anyone to read. A prophecy teacher once remarked, "If you're not paranoid, it's because you're not paying close enough attention."

KNOWING THE REAL THING
FROM THE COUNTERFEIT

It is no small matter that before Christ comes again to establish His Kingdom, the antichrist will come first to organize his own counterfeit kingdom. He will promote himself as the world's savior and messiah. He will claim for himself what truly and rightly belongs only to God. Then, as now, many will be captivated by his deceptions and drawn to his counterfeit program, rather than to the real thing.

The Gospel of John begins with these words: "In the beginning was the Word, and the Word was with God, and the Word was God." A literal translation of *the Word* in Hebrew would be: "In the beginning was the *dabar,* (meaning the real thing) and the *dabar* (the real thing) was with God, and the dabar (the real thing) was God." It is the Holy Spirit who enables us to embrace not the counterfeit but "the real thing." Believing in "the real thing" makes all the difference in this life and in the life to come.

Many people today are falling for the counterfeit in religion and in various aspects of their daily lives. Everything counterfeit is worthless, whether it's money, faith or a savior. There is only One who is real, and His name is Jesus. A counterfeit messiah is coming, but those who know the *Dabar* (the real thing) will not be fooled. The apostle John declared, "But as many as received Him, to them He gave the right to become the children of God, even to those who believe in His name, who were born, not of blood nor of the will of the flesh nor of the will of man, but of God."[23]

Chapter 5

THE RISE OF A WORLD RELIGION

The concept of a world religion at the end of the age comes largely from a description in Revelation of a religious leader (beast) who rises to prominence and exercises great spiritual influence throughout the earth. John stated this individual will cause people who dwell on the earth to worship the "first beast," (the antichrist). Foremost among his exploits will be an agenda of deception. Here is the key to understanding the nature of religion at the end of the age.

In times past numerous scholars of prophecy were inclined to believe a one-world church would emerge during the last days, largely through the influence of the Roman Catholic Church, or an ecumenical organization such as the World Council of Churches. What seems to be emerging, however, is not a world church but rather a world religion.

The Bible does not specifically teach all churches or religions at the end of the age will be organized under one unified structure or even under one leader; rather it seems more likely people on earth will develop a common religious and political understanding based on humanistic values. The influence of the false prophet who will arise at the time of the tribulation will enable him to deceive the masses, in order that the whole world will follow the political agenda of the antichrist. The antichrist will use organized religions to implement his programs, but in the end they will be but a means for him to achieve his ultimate objectives.

THE WORLD RELIGION IS HERE NOW!

The foundation of the coming world religion is being established on secular humanistic values that now dominate mainline churches and secular institutions. The same values are also being promoted by the media and the entertainment industry. In the religion of end-times, it is man, not God, who will be the supreme authority in matters of faith, doctrine and practice. These values are presently motivating liberal denominations to pass resolutions and position statements on moral and social issues that are based on popular opinion rather than on the Scriptures.

Throughout much of the world, there is a growing belief all religions are valid expressions of truth, and each religion has something unique to contribute to man's understanding about a supreme being. Whether it's Islam, Christianity, Buddhism, Hinduism or even witchcraft, the central elements of the one-world religion are tolerance, understanding, diversity and pluralism. Each religion and religious concept has a place at the table, except Bible-based Christianity and long-established biblical absolutes.

Is Brahma Our Heavenly Father?

On July 12, 2007, a Hindu cleric gave the opening prayer in the United States Senate. Rajan Zed, director of interfaith relations at a Hindu temple in Reno, Nevada, was invited to offer the prayer by Senate Majority Leader Harry Reid. Zed is the first Hindu to offer a prayer in the Senate.

Hindus certainly have the right to freely worship and pray in this country, but to ask a Hindu cleric to say a prayer in the United States Senate is a sad commentary on our nation's deteriorating spiritual condition. We are not one nation under Brahma. Our motto is not "In Brahma We Trust." America owes it existence to the God of the Old and New Testaments. Whatever hope our nation may have for the future is not going to come from Allah, Brahma or any other god; our hope will come from the God and Father of our Lord Jesus Christ.

While Hindus pray to a supreme god called "Brahma," they also pray and worship literally thousands and thousands of lesser gods. Zed's prayer was as follows:

We meditate on the transcendental glory of the deity supreme [Brahma], who is inside the heart of the Earth, inside the life of the sky and inside the soul of the heaven. May he stimulate and illuminate our minds."

In many ways Senator Harry Reid's comments after Zed's prayer were more disconcerting than the prayer itself. Reid said, "I think it speaks well that someone representing the faith of about a billion people comes here and can speak in communication with our heavenly Father regarding peace."[1] Equating Brahma with "our heavenly Father" is just another installment in the indoctrination of the American people to worship at the altar of the politically correct, nonsectarian, government god. The irony of the Hindu cleric's prayer in the chamber of the United States Senate is that Christian chaplains who are invited to pray at the opening of Senate sessions are encouraged not to pray in the name of Jesus Christ.

The Cost of Discipleship
Christians who dare to affirm biblical absolutes will not be tolerated in the new world religion. Even now those who uphold the rights of the unborn, the elderly and the seriously handicapped through their opposition to abortion, euthanasia and assisted suicide are labeled *as rightwing extremists*. Those who uphold traditional family values by standing against homosexual perversions, same-

sex marriages and same-sex adoptions are branded as *homophobes* and *bigots*. Those who challenge any aspect of Islam are called *Islamophobes*. Those who believe Jesus Christ alone is the world's only Savior are accused of being *exclusionary* or *intolerant*. Fifty years ago those who affirmed these same foundational Christian beliefs were called orthodox Christians; today they are branded as religious fanatics.

In March 2007 the former chairman of the Joint Chiefs of Staff, General Peter Pace, outraged the cultural elitists and the homosexual community when he stated his belief homosexuality and adultery are immoral. In an interview with a reporter from the *Chicago Tribune*, General Pace stated:

> I believe homosexual acts between two individuals are immoral and that we should not condone immoral acts. I do not believe the United States is well served by a policy that says it is OK to be immoral in that way. As an individual, I would not want acceptance of gay behavior to be our policy, just like I would not want it to be our policy that if we were to find out that so-and-so was sleeping with somebody else's wife, that we would just look the other way, which we do not. We prosecute that kind of immoral behavior.[2]

As it turned out, these forthright statements may have cost General Pace his job. It was extremely disappointing when President George W. Bush did not reappoint this highly decorated and exceptionally capable Marine to another term as chairman of the Joint Chiefs of Staff.

Rosie O'Donnell created media frenzy over her comment that Christian fundamentalists and Islamic fundamentalists are equally dangerous. A few years ago, Ted Turner blathered "religion is for losers," meaning Christianity, of course. Ted and Rosie are not alone in their negative assessments about Christianity. Bible-believing Christianity is the enemy of those who are espousing the new global religion and conformity to our politically correct culture. The social engineers have decreed Bible-believing Christianity must be marginalized; the authority of Scripture must be challenged; and the law of God (the Ten Commandments) must disappear from the public consciousness. Of course all of these things are taking place right now in one degree or another!

Christians must be silenced!
In several Western nations, anti-hate legislation has been or is being passed to restrict Christians from voicing their opposition to a global agenda. The secularists know as long as Christians are allowed to influence society, their liberal agenda may never be realized. Christians must be silenced. The cultural elitists are determined to turn biblical values into crimes by labeling them "hate-speech." Anti-hate legislation is already being used against Christians in Canada, Australia, Sweden, the Netherlands and Germany. Bob Unruh has cautioned anti-hate legislation may be coming to America:

> Two Christians in Australia have been indicted for criticizing Islam, and another for criticizing Zionism. A filmmaker has been threatened with arrest for using the word "homosexual" rather than "gay." Now a German priest faces jail time for publicly criticizing abortionists, and in Holland, "fornicators" and "adulterers" are protected classes and cannot be criticized. All of these are courtesy of the concept of federal "hate crimes" legislation, which unless defeated soon could be mandatory in the United States.[3]

State and federal legislators are working to pass anti-hate bills that will severely limit the free speech of all Americans. Their legislation is primarily directed at Bible-believing Christians. Unless Christians rise up now to stop this madness, it is only a matter of time until they are successful.

THE ONE-WORLD RELIGION IS CHRIST-LESS

The principal enemy of the one-world religion is Jesus Christ; nearly everything about Him is hated by our modern culture. Those who embrace the concepts of a unified religion have a mandatory rule: DON'T INVOKE THE NAME JESUS! Whether it is a pastor offering an opening prayer at a city council meeting, a chaplain offering a prayer in the halls of Congress or a military chaplain in uniform offering a prayer at a public gathering, all are instructed, explicitly or implicitly, not to invoke the name of Jesus. The American people are being conditioned to bow only at the altar of the politically correct, non-sectarian, government god who has no connection with Jesus Christ. When people speak of a "non-sectarian prayer," they really mean: "Don't mention the name of Jesus." But if you take *Christ* out of the word Christian, what do you have left? I-A-N, which means—"I Am Nothing."

Thirty-two students and faculty members of Virginia Tech in Blacksburg, Virginia were senselessly gunned down by a crazed killer on April 16, 2007. After a memorial convocation the following day, the Evangelical Lutheran Church in America (ELCA) issued a press release announcing—"ELCA Pastor Delivers Christian Message at Virginia Tech Convocation." What they did not mention, however, was the fact the man who delivered the so-called "Christian message" failed to mention the name of Jesus Christ, even though the vast majority of those assembled were Christians.

ELCA chaplain William H. King was the last of four members of the religious community at Virginia Tech to speak at the convocation. The first speaker, a Muslim, mentioned Allah; the second speaker, a Buddhist, mentioned the Dalai Lama; the third speaker, a woman Rabbi, quoted from Ecclesiastes; but when the time came for the Christian representative to speak, he never mentioned the only One who could have brought hope and comfort to those assembled—Jesus Christ.

Each Christmas season the courts are deluged with lawsuits seeking to prevent the display of nativity scenes on public property or keeping public school choirs from singing songs that mention Christ. For the past several years, Christmas trees placed on the White House lawn and in front of the nation's Capitol have been referred to as "Holiday Trees." The word *Christmas* is being abandoned by stores, banks and assorted corporations who prefer to decorate their places of business with benign wishes for a "Happy Holiday Season."

Each Christmas season protests and legal challenges are put forward by Christian organizations in the hope of turning back the clock to better times. The fact is, however, even if the witness of the gospel was put on display in Macy's Department Store window, the assaults on Christianity would not cease. These anti-Christian efforts are like a runaway freight train bearing down on our nation.

In 2006 the College of William and Mary in Williamsburg, Virginia removed a brass cross from the altar in their historic chapel, in order to make it "less of a faith-specific place."[4] On February 12, 2007 the same college was the scene of a Sex Workers Art Show which featured topless dancers, a striptease artist, demonstrations of sex toys and a question and answer session with male and female prostitutes.[5] Apparently, the cross of Christ is offensive at this former Christian institution, but pornography and debauchery are not. The college found out removing the cross and sponsoring the sex show were extremely costly after a longtime supporter informed school officials he would not be making a planned $12 million donation. Although the cross was finally brought back to the chapel, it was not returned to the altar; instead it was placed in a glass case.

Christian honor students who earn the right to deliver the valedictorian address at their commencement exercises are free to say just about anything they like except, of course, the name of Jesus. A few years ago, one school in the Midwest turned off the microphone when a young woman mentioned her gratitude to Jesus Christ as she was giving her valedictorian address.

Incredibly, the most alarming aspect in the rise of a world religion is the participation and cooperation of vast portions of the Christian church. Mainline churches and liberal clergy are in the vanguard of efforts to foist a *Christ-less,* politically-correct form of religion upon society. These efforts represent a mindset that has been taking shape for the past several decades in the Christian church and in our society. It is this mindset of the antichrist that is laying the groundwork for the new global religion.

A POLITICALLY-CORRECT SOCIETY
AND THE ONE-WORLD RELIGION

Liberals in our society are constantly calling for the "separation of church and state." Some claim it is in the Constitution, but just ask them to find it! Most Americans do not realize the words "a wall of separation between church and state" are not in the Constitution; they were drafted by Thomas Jefferson in a letter to the Danbury Baptist Association in 1802. Comments regarding Jefferson's statement were described in the *Citizen* magazine:

Jefferson's initial draft reveals his understanding that the federal government simply lacked jurisdiction over religion. So who gave us the wall of separation that renders prayers at graduations and in public parks unconstitutional? The author of that wall was not Jefferson, but U.S. Supreme Court Justice Hugo Black, appointed by Franklin Roosevelt in 1937 and who served until his death in 1971. In a number of rulings he helped write, Black used Jefferson's language, but not Jefferson's meaning. Black's separationist leanings became more aggressive over time, resulting in rulings that ordered the removal of religious instruction, prayer and Bible reading from public schools and bans on graduation prayers and the posting of the Ten Commandments.[6]

Those who are so quick to invoke the name of Thomas Jefferson in their efforts to remove God from every vestige of this nation's life should quote his words affixed to the Jefferson Memorial in Washington DC:

God who gave us life gave us liberty. Can the liberties of a nation be secure when we have removed a conviction that these liberties are the gift of God? Indeed I tremble for my country when I reflect that God is just, that his justice cannot sleep forever.

It is ironic religious liberals who are clamoring the loudest about "the separation of church and state" are actually the ones who have joined with leftwing politicians and judges around the country to fashion exactly the opposite result. Religious and secular liberals have become allies in removing the God of our founding fathers from public life and replacing Him with a politically-correct, government god! Organizations, such as the American Civil Liberties Union (ACLU), Americans United for Separation of Church and State, and People for the American Way have joined forces with liberal politicians and mainline denominations to remove God from public life and discourse.

Here is the motivation for using only nonsectarian prayers at public functions. Here is the motivation for having the words "under God" removed from the Pledge of Allegiance. Here is the motivation of those who would have the words "In God We Trust" removed from our coins. And here is the motivation for removing the Ten Commandments from our schools and public buildings.

"Way too much Jesus..."

An evangelical pastor who was invited to give the opening prayer at a session of the Ohio State Legislature in Columbus, Ohio set off a firestorm in May 2007 when he made multiple references to Jesus in his prayer. An article on the front page of the *Columbus Dispatch* stated: "House wants preachers to tone it down." The article began: "Excessive evangelizing. Too many controversial topics. And way too much Jesus....Too many guest ministers are invoking the name of Jesus during their prayers, a no-no under House guidelines which, based on a 1983 U.S. Supreme Court ruling, requires such prayers to be nondenominational, nonsectarian and non-proselytizing."[7] The Jesus-has-got-to-go movement is running at full speed in today's society, and most Christians are allowing it to happen.

There is essentially no difference between being required to offer a prayer to the politically correct, non-sectarian state god being promoted in America today and participating in the Caesar worship that existed in the days of the Roman Empire. Christians in the early church were ordered to stop saying "Jesus is Lord," and declare their loyalty to the state by saying "Caesar is Lord." All any Christian had to do in Roman times to keep in the good graces of government officials was to refrain from saying "Jesus is Lord," and instead quote the non-sectarian prayer of the state—"Caesar is Lord." Essentially all one has to do today to stay in the good graces of those promoting the new state religion is refrain from praying in the name of Jesus Christ.

One cannot help but contrast today's compromising clerics with those early Christians who chose death rather than deny the name of Jesus! Those stalwart men and women of God died with the name of Jesus on their lips. It is alarming to see how many Christian clergy in the twenty-first century are willing to accommodate the worship of the secular god by refusing to pray in Jesus' name at any public function. Little wonder liberal denominations have jettisoned from their hymnals such glorious songs as "Faith of Our Fathers" and "Onward Christian Soldiers."

Belief in the politically correct, nonsectarian, government god also requires our history books be revised in order to remove any hint our founding fathers ever acknowledged the role of God in establishing our nation, or ever intended to include Him in the nation's founding documents. This flies in the face of the facts, of course, but facts are not nearly as important to the revisionists as is their agenda to rid the nation of any mention of God.

It is the belief in a politically correct, non-sectarian, government god that has enabled both church and society to embrace homosexuality, abortion, pornography and just about every other evil one can name. Obviously if there is no God, neither can there be moral absolutes. This is the mindset that has prompted the ACLU's lawsuits against the Boy Scouts of America because of that organization's refusal to allow homosexuals in positions of leadership. This is the mindset that has prompted United Way organizations across the country to stop funding the Boy Scouts. It is the mindset that has caused government agencies to forbid the Boy Scouts from using public parks or public buildings. Apparently an organization that seeks to mold young men "for God and country" is a little more than our godless culture can bear.

THE FIRST SIGN OF CHRIST'S COMING —
DECEPTIONS

Jesus' question— "When the Son of Man comes, will He find faith on the earth?"— is also a prophetic statement regarding the spiritual condition that will exist on earth at the close of the age.[8] When Jesus sat with His disciples on the Mount of Olives, they asked Him, "What will be the sign of Your coming and of the end of the age?" Jesus answered them, "See to it that no one misleads you....*Many* false prophets will arise and mislead *many.*"[9]

The magnitude of deceptions being perpetrated within the church today is mind-boggling. Deceivers are everywhere. You would have to lock yourself away in a cave on a deserted island to avoid contact with them. Even then the devil would not leave you alone.

Only a few years ago, you could have walked into most any mainline church in the country and found at least some semblance of orthodoxy coming from the pulpit. Today, however, the very essence of the Christian faith is being challenged in ways not seen before. Amazingly most church members have not a clue anything is amiss. They walk in and out of their churches Sunday after Sunday unaware they are being served generous portions of poisons that threaten the salvation of their very souls. The typical church member today has little or no concept of what constitutes the true and living gospel of Christ. That is the tragedy of our times! They are no longer able to distinguish the truth from a lie.

Some deceptions today are so subtle they challenge even the most discerning believer. The new vocabulary of the global religion sounds just like the old vocabulary, but the words have been given new meanings. For example the word *inclusive* was once used to indicate all sinners are welcome to partake of God's forgiveness and grace; now the word is used to promote the acceptance of sinful life-styles and immoral sexual practices. The meanings of other words that have been changed include *atonement, justice, family, marriage* and even the name *Jesus.*

We are living in an age of apostasy in which men and women cloaked in clerical garments dare to mount their pulpits and preach lies and apostasy to the people. One of the raging debates posed in the modern church is over the authenticity and reliability of the Scriptures. Is the Bible truly God's Word or does it merely contain the Word of God?

Vast portions of the church teach the Bible is a book written by man, and it is filled with myths, inaccurate statements and untruths. Some church leaders question the authenticity of Christ's miracles, while others are rewriting the Bible to make it conform to their own perverted theologies. Every false doctrine and every evil practice being perpetrated on the church today is due to the fact the Bible is no longer viewed as the inspired, infallible and inerrant Word of God.

There are millions who attend church every Sunday and never hear the pure Word of God. Jesus' letters to the seven churches of Revelation help us to understand the consequences of apostasy, compromise, tolerance of evil and disobedience to His Word. Within mainline denominations are those who question or deny the most fundamental doctrines of Christianity, including the virgin birth and the bodily resurrection of Jesus Christ. The damage being caused by these false teachers is beyond comprehension.

Though today's church is riddled with false teachers and practitioners of evil, God will preserve His true church, the pure and spotless bride, for the coming of the Bridegroom! As Christians it is our responsibility to keep our portion of the church pure in doctrine and life. When false teachings and unbiblical practices enter, it is our duty to resist and expunge them, if possible, but we never have the choice of accepting them. God calls us to stand for the truth and remain faithful to the end.

SAVING JESUS

A full-page ad on the back cover of a national periodical stated: "Ever feel Jesus has been kidnapped by the Christian Right?" Then in letters an inch and a half high is the title of a course called "SAVING JESUS." The ad claims the course is taught by "leading religious voices of our day."[10] The extent to which this course and others like it are being offered in congregations throughout the United States and Canada is most troubling. After reviewing the contents of the course, one can only conclude if these leading voices from several mainline denominations are leading people anywhere, it is straight into hell.

THE SPIRIT OF THE ANTICHRIST!

It is imperative Christians become aware of the spiritual poisons being dispensed in the name of Jesus Christ, not only in liberal mainline denominations but also in evangelical churches. "SAVING JESUS" is not an anomaly; courses like it are being taught to unsuspecting church members all over the country. True Christian doctrine is being eroded throughout the church in order to make ready for the new doctrines of the one-world religion!

These false doctrines are nothing more than the old heresies the devil has used to deceive the church throughout the centuries. Those who are espousing these teachings, however, are looked upon as distinguished clergy and highly respected theologians within the mainline churches.

In addition to promulgating their poisonous teachings, these so-called scholars are endeavoring to brand all who uphold the Bible's teachings as extremists and religious fanatics. Thus you will find courses like "SAVING JESUS" or books such as *Rescuing the Bible from Fundamentalism* are part of a deliberate attack on orthodox Christians! These masters of deceit have declared Bible-believing Christians are the real enemy of both church and society.

If you are looking for a sign of the times, look no further! This is the spirit of the antichrist and it is among us today! Paul wrote: "But the Spirit explicitly says that in later times some will fall away from the faith, paying attention to deceitful spirits and doctrines of demons."[11]

THE DOCTRINES
OF THE ONE-WORLD RELIGION

The world religion being foisted upon humanity today despises moral absolutes and the certitude of God's Word. The mission of those who promote this global faith is to convince church members the Bible is antiquated and must change with the times. At the very least, church members must be taught to look upon the Bible as just another book, no more or no less holy than the scriptures of other religions. Furthermore the global religionists believe the concept of sin must be eradicated and people must be convinced truth is ever changing.

The proponents of the one-world religion are out to rid the church of any concept Christ is the world's only Savior, and they are endeavoring to destroy all belief in Christ's atoning death for the sins of the world. This is one of the chief reasons Islam has become the darling of the ecumenical movement.

In the theology of the one-world religion, the concept of salvation does not focus on the world to come but rather on justice and equality here and now. Social justice and equality have become the mantra in most mainline churches today. The new theology demands Christians adopt the feminist agenda and buy into the right of women to do with their bodies whatever they please. They further claim the Bible, hymns, sermons and church literature must be cleansed of all masculine images. When referring to God, terms such as *God* and *goddess* are often used interchangeably.

As evidence that the radical new theology is being accepted in much of the church, the Baltimore-Washington Conference of the United Methodist Church announced the reappointment of a woman pastor to her present congregation. That would hardly be news, except the woman pastor underwent a sex-change operation and is now a male pastor. Before her re-appointment at St. John's United Methodist Church in Baltimore, she was called Ann Gordon. Now as a man who is serving the same parish, she is called Drew Phoenix. Goodbye Pastor Gordon, and hello Pastor Phoenix! What once would have been a scandal in the church is not even a blip on the radar screen.

A radical new theology is being embraced by nearly all the mainline churches via their pulpits, curricula, tapes and seminars, and it is being taught in nearly all mainline seminaries. The venerable gurus of the one-world religion have taken the stage to impart their revelations and to lead the world to adopt what they claim is a new and better way. In addition to the pulpits of America, these venerable apostles of apostasy are being granted a platform to enlighten and indoctrinate the general public on a host of media outlets.

Those who have been self-commissioned for the task of "SAVING JESUS" from Bible-believing Christians are renowned within the mainline churches and academia for their denials of foundational doctrines of Christianity, yet most Bible-believing Christians remain uninformed about the extent of their influence.

RITA NAKASHIMA BROCK

Rita Nakashima Brock, one of the "SAVING JESUS" instructors, frequently speaks at events in mainline denominations. Brock says her number one goal is convincing people the doctrine of the atonement is a betrayal of Christianity.

During a breakfast meeting at the General Assembly of the Presbyterian Church (USA) in Birmingham, Alabama, June 19, 2006, Brock stated: "One of the great controversies to emerge from Re-Imagining [Conference, 1993] was our rejection of the atonement, the idea that the torture and execution of Jesus Christ saved the world." Brock further stated:

My theological career has been spent dismantling that doctrine. I want to tell you today that I am convinced that atonement theology is the deepest betrayal of Christianity ever perpetrated. It is not just one way to understand salvation, but a betrayal of salvation, a doctrine that abandoned the life and ministry of Jesus Christ for loyalty to Caesar and his legions.

In an article entitled "The Mask of Violence," Rita Brock and Rebecca Parker made the following statement:

The actual historical event of Jesus' crucifixion was neither sweet nor saving. In Jesus' time, the Romans occupied all of Palestine. The Romans suppressed resistance by terrorizing the local population. Crucifixion was their most brutal form of capital punishment. It took place in full public view to teach a lesson through terror. To say that Jesus' executioners did what was historically necessary for salvation is to say that state terrorism is a good thing, that torture and murder are the will of God.[12]

Another statement in the same article declared: "You couldn't look at Jesus on the cross and see there, as the old liturgy said, 'one perfect sacrifice for the sins of the whole world'...You couldn't look on the man of sorrows and give thanks to God without ending up a partner in a thousand crimes."[13]

The realization these false teachers are being given a platform in mainline churches and via the media to discredit the atonement of Christ should outrage every true believer.

JOHN SHELBY SPONG

John S. Spong, a retired Episcopal bishop, not only wants to save Jesus from orthodox Christians, he wants to *Rescue the Bible from Fundamentalism*, the title of one of his books. Within this book he sets forth concepts that question foundational doctrines of Christianity—the virgin birth, the bodily resurrection of Christ, His miracles and many historical accounts as set forth in the Scriptures.

In the same book Spong wrote: "Jesus could not have imagined such an idea as Albert Einstein's theory of relativity."[14] What an astounding statement! If only Jesus had lived in the present century instead of the first century, He might have known as much about science as Albert Einstein or even Bishop Spong. According to Spong, it is likely the apostle Paul was a homosexual.[15] Here again is another one of Spong's astounding statements! If only Paul could have lived in our enlightened age, he would not have had to hide his homosexuality; moreover Spong could have ordained Paul and given his ministry some real stature.

In yet another chapter entitled "Christmas and Easter: Ultimate Truth and Literal Nonsense," Bishop Spong comments on Luke's account of the nativity:

Am I suggesting these stories about the virgin birth are not literally true? The answer is a simple and direct 'Yes.' Of course these narratives are not literally true. Stars do not wander, angels do not sing, virgins do not give birth, magi do not travel to a distant land to present gifts to a baby, and shepherds do not go in search of a newborn savior. I know of no reputable biblical scholar in the world today who takes these birth narratives literally. Does that mean that the virgin birth story is not literally true? Let me answer this categorically. The virgin birth tradition of the New Testament is not literally true. It should not be literally believed.[16]

In the appendix of his book *Here I Stand,* Bishop Spong makes the following dogmatic statements which he would like to see debated in the church:

- The miracle stories of the New Testament can no longer be interpreted in a post-Newtonian world as supernatural events performed by an incarnate deity.
- The view of the cross as the sacrifice for the sins of the world is a barbarian idea based on primitive concepts of God that must be dismissed.
- Resurrection is an action of God, who raised Jesus into the meaning of God. It therefore cannot be a physical resuscitation occurring inside human history.
- There is no external, objective, revealed standard written in Scripture or on tablets of stone that will govern our ethical behavior for all time.
- Prayer cannot be a request made to a theistic deity to act in human history in a particular way.[17]

Bishop Spong denies the bodily resurrection of Christ, preaches salvation without the atonement and heaven without hell. Spong also sanctions the ordination of homosexuals and endorses same-sex marriage.

The reason people are leaving the Episcopal Church and other liberal mainline churches by the tens of thousands is not simply because of their acceptance of homosexuality; they are also leaving because these churches have abandoned true biblical doctrine. Thank God for clergy in the mainline churches who are finding the courage to lead their people out of such apostasy; and thank God for the laity who are leaving their apostate denominations with or without their leaders.

JOHN DOMINIC CROSSAN

Just about anybody with a television has seen John Dominic Crossan at one time or another. He regularly appears on the news programs and the religious specials of most major networks. In the 2006 Christmas season, Crossan appeared on several television programs and assured his audience just about everything in the Christmas narrative did not happen as the Bible says it did. Crossan assured viewers Jesus was not born in Bethlehem; there were no wise men, no star, no shepherds and no escape into Egypt.

John Crossan, who now resides in Florida, was born in Ireland. A former Roman Catholic priest, he is now Emeritus Professor of Religious Studies at De Paul University in Chicago. Crossan is co-chairman of the Jesus Seminar, a group of scholars who determined a few years ago Jesus actually said only about eighteen percent of what is attributed to Him in the Gospels.[18] According to Crossan and other Jesus Seminar participants, the Christ of the Apostles' Creed is purely "mythical, except that he was from Nazareth and suffered under Pontius Pilate."[19]

Crossan believes the Bible is filled with metaphors and myths, none of which are to be taken seriously. He specifically refuses to acknowledge any literalness to Christ's birth, miracles, parables, resurrection or ascension. He believes biblical passages that describe Jesus' divinity are not to be taken literally.

One of the most ludicrous propositions set forth by John Crossan was given on a televised Easter special and in one of his books *The Historical Jesus*, as he expressed his belief that Jesus was never buried after his crucifixion. Crossan said, Jesus' body was eaten by dogs or left to rot on a garbage heap.[20]

In a speech at Unity Church of Dallas, September 24, 2006, Crossan commented in his introduction that Bible-based Christian extremists have hijacked Christianity and American foreign policy. Like Spong and Brock, Crossan is determined to marginalize Bible-believing Christians in order to give his heretical teachings credibility.

Crossan's book *The Historical Jesus* portrays Jesus as a "peasant Jewish cynic," whose teachings got him into trouble with both Jewish and Roman authorities.[21] According to Crossan, Mark's gospel actually ended at Mark 15:39 with the words of the centurion, "Truly, this man was the Son of God." The remaining portion of Mark, according to Crossan, is not credible. He believes the entire resurrection narrative was developed by the early Christians after Christ's death, with or without the knowledge that Jesus' body was consumed by dogs or left to rot on a garbage heap.

One can almost hear the melodious hymns Crossan's followers might sing at their Easter morning services: "Because He Doesn't Live," "My Hope is Built on Less and Less," "Tell Me the Story of Jesus, It Won't Take Very Long." And, of course, they might end with a rousing verse or two of "Who Let the Dogs Out?!"

MARCUS BORG

Marcus Borg was born into a Lutheran family in northeastern North Dakota. As a youth he attended church and professed a firm belief in Jesus Christ. Borg stated that as the years went by, he came to believe less and less in the traditional teachings about God or Christ.

Marcus Borg graduated from Concordia College in Moorhead, Minnesota (ELCA) and from Union Seminary in New York. He received a doctorate from Oxford University. A member of the infamous Jesus Seminar, Borg has written several books in which he explained his unorthodox theological positions, including *Meeting Jesus Again for the First Time* (1994) and *The God We Never Knew* (1997).

Borg states in his autobiography:

I realize God does not refer to a supernatural being 'out there,' rather I began to see the word 'God' refers to the 'sacred' at the center of existence, the 'holy mystery' which is all around us and within us. I now see that the Christian tradition — including its claims about Jesus — is not something to be believed but something to be lived in.[22]

In one of the "SAVING JESUS" sessions, Borg asks: "If Christianity is not primarily about an afterlife, what is it all about? If the Bible is not historically correct, how are we to read it?" Like previously mentioned scholars, Borg believes any concept of Christ's atonement for the sins of the world is absurd. He says the atonement gives God a very poor image. It is clear all of these scholars are offering unsuspecting people water from the same poisoned well.

Writing on the significance of the cross, Borg stated:

Then there's the cross as the once and for all sacrifice for sin. If we literalize that language, as much of conventional Christianity has done, the only way God can forgive sins is if adequate sacrifice is offered: Somebody has got to be punished, and that person is Jesus. Also, only those people who know and believe in that story can be saved. Thus, literalizing that language is a slur on the character of God. If you see Jesus' death as part of the divine plan, as part of the will of God, that suggests that God required the suffering of this immeasurable great man. It is never the will of God that an innocent person be crucified, and to suggest that is to suggest something horrible about God.[23]

Borg goes off into the mystic fog of the twilight zone when he states: "To be a Christian, I would say, is to live within the Christian tradition as a metaphor of the sacred, and also as a sacrament of the sacred....It's about entering into a relationship with *suchness,* with *is-ness.* I think of God, to use very abstract language, as is-ness without limits."[24] Borg's books and teaching are being widely promoted not only in the "SAVING JESUS" series but also in churches and seminaries across the nation.

WHEN ENOUGH IS ENOUGH

In recent years church members by the tens of thousands have been leaving mainline denominations, as it becomes increasingly clear they have been taken over by those who have perverted or, in some cases, abandoned the Christian faith altogether. Membership in several mainline church bodies has been cut nearly in half over the past twenty years.

We have been taught to believe schisms are a bad thing, but that is not always the case. While it is sad to see divisions take place in any church, it is biblically mandated Christians take their stand on the Word of God. Men and women of faith have left or are leaving their Bible-denying churches because their denominations have been hijacked by those who have abandoned orthodox Christianity. They have left or are leaving because of their unwillingness to be part of such deceptions and apostasy. They have left or are leaving not to destroy the church but to save it. There comes a time when people of faith must rise up and say to their compromising denominations and clergy—"Enough is enough."

EVANGELICALS FACE DECEPTIONS

Deceptions and false teachings are not exclusive to liberal mainline churches; they are also present in evangelical and nonaligned churches. In recent years especially, evangelical Christianity has been inclined to go after the latest trends in worship and theology. While some congregations and pastors may be rightly motivated, so many are driven by the latest gimmicks and fads.

Instead of relying on the power of God's Word, there are evangelical pastors who are turning their worship services into an hour of entertainment. Some have gone so far as to remove the cross from their sanctuaries in order to attract those who might be offended by such Christian symbols. Others have introduced rock music into their services in order to attract a more youthful crowd. Church-growth leaders advise pastors to avoid preaching on controversial topics such as homosexuality and abortion. Whatever works seems to be the standard.

Pastor Jay Erickson, who served as a parish pastor in the Association of Free Lutheran Congregations and as a field representative for the Hauge Lutheran Inner Mission from 1988 until his death in 1992, had a great burden to see the churches return to the life-changing proclamation of the Word of God. He wrote:

> I well remember as a youth hearing the late Pastor Joseph Stump, then a new Christian. Preaching in his dynamic manner with piercing conviction he would say, "Without a Blood-bought, Holy Ghost-wrought experience of salvation, you are still lost." He spoke such words with deep conviction because he himself had been in the Lutheran ministry for some ten years before he was awakened and converted.
>
> His messages struck home as piercing arrows to the unsaved hearers. One evening while Pastor Stump was preaching at a Gospel tent service in Westby, Wisconsin, a young man in his thirties rose during the sermon, unable to wait until its finish. He asked in urgent desperation, "Will someone please pray for me, I'm lost!"
>
> That service quickly became a glorious prayer meeting, as others in the audience became acutely aware of their lost condition and began to seek help and prayer.
>
> Those were the days of fearless preaching, reminiscent of the apostles after Pentecost. Deep conviction marked their message, penetrating conscience and bringing forth a cry for mercy.
>
> There can be little doubt that the lack of similar response to the Gospel in our day is largely due to a weak and ineffective proclamation of God's holy Law. If preached at all, the message is couched in language designed to soften the blow, thus it fails to pierce the conscience and to awaken the sinner.

The kind of preaching Pastor Jay Erickson described has all but disappeared, even in conservative, Bible-believing churches. Today so many churches market Christ instead of preach Christ.

Some Christians like to study the great revival preachers of years past and yearn for such an experience in our time. While we marvel at the dynamic power of the Holy Spirit that attended their services, it is doubtful evangelists such as Charles Finney, Dwight L. Moody and Billy Sunday would get invited to very many mainline or evangelical churches today, not unless, of course, they toned it down a bit.

Leonard Ravenhill got it right when he said:

Brethren, when we get humble enough, and low enough, and desperate enough, and hungry enough, and concerned enough, and passionate enough, and broken enough, and clean enough, and prayerful enough, then God will send us a revival that equals and surpasses the awakening this country experienced in the days of Charles Finney.[25]

PROSPERITY THEOLOGY

One of the greatest deceptions taking place in the evangelical scene today is prosperity theology. *Time* magazine published a story concerning several well-known clergy whose entire ministries are centered on this teaching.[26] However, prosperity theology is not only being preached by the religious stars of television, it now extends to even small rural churches. The purveyors of prosperity theology are legion.

Many prosperity preachers live lavish lifestyles in multi-million-dollar homes. They rake in money hand over fist. They wear expensive clothes and adorn themselves with expensive jewelry as supposed "proof" God's primary objective is to prosper His saints. A number of famous television evangelists fly around the country in their own multi-million dollar jet planes, paid for by their respective ministries. Sadly, prosperity preachers have to rely on the poor and downtrodden to send them money so they can continue to live in luxury.

The focus of prosperity theology is SELF! What is in it for ME? Its central message is "How to get God to give you everything you want." Here in America prosperity theology sells! On any given day, television evangelists carry on like carnival barkers: "Write to me today for your prayer cloth which I have prayed over, and don't forget to send your generous love offering." Another pitches, "Write to me today for your holy water and be anointed with healing, and don't forget, when you write, send me money." Still another invites the fleeced sheep of his television flock to "plant a seed of faith today by sending me a thousand dollars. If you do this, God will turn you from rags to riches."

While it is true God's blessings flow mightily on His children, the blessings do not always take the form of material wealth. In whatever ways God chooses to bless our lives, we should be thankful, but God help those who make personal prosperity the focus of their faith.

When Peter encountered the crippled man at the Temple gate, he told him: "I do not possess silver and gold, but what I do have I give to you: In the name of Jesus Christ the Nazarene—walk" (Acts 3:6). There was a day when the church was poor in the things of this world but rich in the supply of God's grace. Today much of the church is rich in the things of this world but poverty-stricken when it comes to a demonstration of God's power. Few are the churches in America that can say, "Silver or gold, we have none," and fewer still are those who can say, "Rise up and walk."

It is dangerous to construct a theology around personal prosperity. Such a theology diminishes the gospel's call to follow Christ, regardless of benefits or costs. Prosperity theology, with its false promises of wealth, health and success, is a false gospel. Its teachings not only contradict the Bible, they mock the Lord who had no home of His own or even a tomb in which to be buried. Prosperity theology flies in the face of Jesus' words, "If anyone wishes to come after Me, he must deny himself, and take up his cross daily and follow Me."[27]

Prosperity theology is an affront to millions of Christians who must rely on the Lord daily for the basic necessities of life. It flies in the face of saints who denied everything for the sake of Christ. It flies in the face of countless missionaries who left home, family and possessions to witness the gospel in some impoverished land. And it flies in the face of Christian martyrs who counted their lives as nothing when compared to their faithfulness to Christ.

God help us, especially here in the United States of America, to realize power, fame, wealth, and even good health are not measured in the kingdom of God as they are on earth. When the roll is called up yonder, the Lord will commend believers whose good deeds were totally unknown even to their closest friends—men and women of faith who served the Lord not for what they could get out of it, but in praise and gratitude for all they had received from His hands.

Possessions in this life are temporal, while treasures laid up in heaven are eternal. As God chooses to bless us here on earth, everything we have should be used to His glory. If He calls us to a life of self-denial and sacrifice, we should praise Him all the more. We have nothing that we have not received from His hands. When this life is over, saint and sinner will leave all their worldly goods behind. Jesus instructed us: "Do not store up for yourselves treasures on earth...but store up for yourselves treasures in heaven...for where your treasure is, there your heart will be also."[28]

THE EMERGENT CHURCH

A movement within the evangelical camp that bears watching is "the Emergent Church." The title of this movement reveals its primary objective—to transform the traditional and evangelical church into a form more acceptable to the modern culture. The Emergent Church movement is not an organization or a physical entity; rather it is a method or an approach to ministry. This highly questionable movement has many adherents from varied backgrounds. They mostly operate in newly formed and independent congregations, although an increasing number of clergy in established evangelical and mainline churches are buying into the methods of the Emergent Church as well.

While a few goals of the Emergent Church may have some validity, their tactics and practices leave much to be desired. It is true our culture is not at all inclined to listen to what the church has to say, but it is unconscionable for any pastor or church body to water-down the absolutes of Scripture or compromise Christian doctrine in order to witness to the gospel in the twenty-first century. There is no difference witnessing Christ in the twenty-first century than there was witnessing Christ in the first century. The heart of man remains as it was—desperately wicked and LOST! People do not need psychology, sociology, or entertainment; people need the Lord. They need to know they are sinners, and they need to know there is a Savior.

Those connected with the Emergent Church have a tendency to soft-peddle moral absolutes. Some of their leaders claim if you do not find ways to do an endrun around controversial issues, you will turn off the very people you want to reach. Churches and pastors who buy into this approach make it a point not to speak often, if at all, about social and moral issues that threaten to destroy our nation. Emergent Church leaders tell pastors, "Don't say anything that might be construed as being offensive or political."

But it does not stop there. Emergent Church leaders use the same approach with the gospel by going easy on traditional messages about sin, the atonement, the blood of Christ, etc. Preaching is out in the Emergent Church; while dialogue is in. A considerable number of those associated with this movement seem to have a leftwing political bias and are very critical of conservative churches and pastors.

On a PBS program that examined the Emergent Church, it was stated:

> People are encouraged to tangibly express their spirituality. Many are weaving together elements from different religious traditions, especially Catholicism and Eastern Orthodoxy. Some are discovering medieval mystical practices, such as walking the labyrinth, but adding decidedly modern twists. It's a pick your own approach that also stresses community and social justice. One Emergent Church set up a prayer corner in which they burn incense.

Note the similarity between the Emergent Church and the approach used by John Dominic Crossan and Bishop John Shelby

Spong. While the Emergent Church tends to be more orthodox, it too believes that orthodoxy is no longer able to connect with the modern culture. In both the liberal church and the Emergent Church, there seems to be a sense the end justifies the means. Do whatever it takes to reach the masses. Success is found not so much in the work of the Holy Spirit as it is in new and creative ways to "do" church.

The Emergent Church has captured the attention of liberals in Holland, Michigan where a church called "The Journey" was organized in 2007, through the cooperation of area United Church of Christ congregations. The pastor of the new congregation stated: "We're going to be trying to get people in touch with their spirit, to have a deep relationship with the divine. The sermons are going to be based on the Bible, but they will also use other sacred sources, such as the Qur'an or something Gandhi or the Dalai Lama said. So it's the Bible-plus." He indicated the new church will be "a progressive Christian church with some of the evangelical emergent movement mixed in."[29]

The whole approach to ministry in the Emergent Church flies in the face of the unchanging truth of God's Word. The Bible tells us, "The word of the cross is foolishness to those who are perishing, but to us who are being saved it is the power of God." (1 Corinthians 1:18).

BACK TO THE BIBLE

While it may be appropriate for churches to use a variety of methods to reach the lost with the gospel, it is never right to proclaim less than the whole counsel of God, nor is it appropriate to do anything that contradicts the clear teachings of Scripture. Paul told Timothy, "Preach the word; be ready in season and out of season; reprove, rebuke, exhort, with great patience and instruction."[30] He also warned him the day would come when "they will not endure sound doctrine; but wanting to have their ears tickled, they will accumulate for themselves teachers in accordance to their own desires, and will turn away their ears from the truth and will turn aside to myths."[31]

Today most people are not looking for a church where the Word is preached in its truth and purity, but one that agrees with their already preconceived belief systems. And there are plenty of clergy who are ready to accommodate them.

Any church where the true preaching of the Word is not central in all it does is doomed to fail in its mission, no matter what approach it uses. Today many churches are highly successful in drawing crowds and entertaining them, but total failures when it comes to seeing lives transformed through the life-changing power of the gospel.

Neither the efforts of man nor his methods can ever reach the hearts of the lost; they can only be brought to Christ through the witness of the true gospel and the energizing power of the Holy Spirit. "Jesus Christ is the same yesterday and today and forever."[32] God's Word is unchanging. The church needs to reclaim the passion of Paul who said, "For I determined to know nothing among you except Jesus Christ, and Him crucified."[33]

Many pastors seem willing to try almost anything, if it means their congregation will grow and prosper, anything, that is, but the pure proclamation of the Word of God. Proclaiming the Word worked for Paul and the apostles; it worked for our grandparents, and it still works today! Music, programs and strategies will never succeed unless they are Christ-centered and scripturally sound. Surely it is time for the churches to get back to the Bible. God, give us a heart like Paul's, so that we may declare: "Woe is me if I do not preach the gospel."[34]

BE FAITHFUL UNTO DEATH

The one-world religion is being formed at this moment with the full cooperation of mainline churches, evangelicals and individuals who profess Christ. Masses of humanity are being deceived into believing all religions are essentially the same, whether it's Buddhism, Hinduism, Islam or Christianity.

Like Caesar worship of old, many professing Christians see nothing wrong with bowing their knees to a politically correct, nonsectarian, government god or to a god who is the figment of someone's imagination. But the Bible has commanded us: You shall have no other gods before Me!

There are no Hindu gods; there is no Buddhist god; there is no Islamic god; and there certainly is no politically correct, non-sectarian, government god! "Hear, O Israel! The Lord is our God, the Lord is one! You shall love the Lord your God with all your heart and with all your soul and with all your might."[35]

What makes the difference if people embrace the one-world religion during the time of the tribulation or if they embrace it today? Those who claim to love the Lord and yet affiliate with a church or denomination they know deep in their hearts has gone over to the enemy are on a dangerous path. With eternity in view, what could possibly be more important than being faithful to the Lord throughout the days of our lives?

The battle for the church and the nation is being fought today whether we like it or not, or whether we want to be part of it or not. We are either part of the problem or part of the solution. We are either standing for Christ or we are not! In times like these, our Lord commands we hold the blood-bought ground. His Word instructs us to put on the whole armor of God and having done all to stand, STAND![36]

SECTION TWO

MILITANT ISLAM, A CLEAR AND PRESENT DANGER

Despite the media's extensive coverage of the subject of terrorism, the public still lacks a substantive understanding of Islamic radicalism, the danger it poses, and the extent to which it operates in the United States — in our cities and even in our halls of government.

Steven Emerson

There are still Americans who are unable or unwilling to recognize the nature or the extent of the threat presented by radical Islam. Whether motivated by naïve wishful thinking or rigid political correctness, they assert that Islam is a "moderate," "tolerant," and "peaceful" religion that has been hijacked by "extremists." They ignore the repeated calls to jihad, Islamic holy war, emanating from the government-controlled mosques of so-called moderate Islamic countries such as Egypt, Pakistan, and Indonesia. They refuse to accept that in the Muslim world, extreme is mainstream.

Brigitte Gabriel

MILITANT ISLAM,
A CLEAR AND PRESENT DANGER

INTRODUCTION

We all remember where we were and what we were doing that fateful morning of September 11, 2001. For most of us the day began like any other. Shortly after 8:45 a.m. news bulletins flashed, announcing fire and smoke were coming from the north tower of the World Trade Center. First reports suggested a light plane might have accidentally hit the building, but within a few minutes, fire and smoke were seen billowing from the second tower. Television cameras already on the scene captured images of the second plane flying into the south tower of the World Trade Center. At that moment we knew America was under attack.

Around 9:45 a.m. a news bulletin announced the Pentagon had been attacked and the White House had been evacuated. Before we could catch our breath, the two tallest buildings in the nation crashed to the ground. Horrendous scenes of devastation and panic filled our television screens, as people fled for their lives through thick clouds of smoke and debris. But it was not over; still another news report informed us a fourth hijacked plane had crashed in Western Pennsylvania.

The FAA stopped all flights from entering or leaving the country. Flights already in the air were diverted and ordered to land at the closest airport. The military scrambled fighter planes, but for a time they were uncertain about where to fly, or if they should shoot down passenger planes deemed to be controlled by terrorists. Trading on the New York Stock Exchange was halted; the stock market would not reopen for seven days. All day and into the night, Americans watched in stunned disbelief as the surreal tele-vised images continued to emanate from New York, Washington and Pennsylvania. It seemed every emotion known to man ebbed and flowed within us that day.

As the hours wore on, it became clear Islamic terrorists were behind the attacks. For the first time in modern history, Americans collectively felt a wave of insecurity sweep over us. We knew after 9/11 the United States would never be the same again. We also knew our country was just as vulnerable to major terrorist attacks as any other nation on the planet.

The nation's pain was intensified as television reports from Gaza and numerous cities in the Middle East showed Muslims dancing in the streets, celebrating the despicable attacks on America and their so-called victory over the "Great Satan." In Egypt and Jordan, two of America's allies in the region and recipients of billions of our tax dollars, Muslims openly demonstrated their joy over the attacks on the United States. Even in England Muslims took to the streets to praise Allah for the terrorist attacks on America.[1]

Initially it was thought as many as 10,000 people might have been killed in the several attacks. Thankfully the finalized number was closer to 3000. Family members waited by their phones for calls from missing loved ones that never came. Stories about daring rescues and selfless acts of heroism boosted our morale. That day we saw the worst of the enemy and the best of the American spirit. Flags were hoisted throughout the nation, as churches and synagogues filled with people who needed to know God was still in control.

Since that September day, we have learned a great deal about Islamic terrorism, but most Americans still have little understanding about the Islamic teachings from which it springs. As Christians we have been naïve enough to believe everyone who is *religious* must be motivated to practice love and tolerance. Nothing could be further from the truth when it comes to Islam. Islam may be the only religion in the world, other than forms of Satanism, whose official doctrines instruct its adherents to hate and kill.

There is no comparison between the commands of love taught by Jesus Christ and the commands of hate taught by Muhammad. With all their faults and failures, Christians have been the driving force in opposing tyranny and oppression throughout the world. Christianity has given rise to democracy and freedom wherever its influence has been felt. The West is head and shoulders above all Islamic countries in medical advances, industry, economics and technology. Were it not for the oil beneath their soil, most Islamic states in the Middle East would be just as backward today as they were in the days of Muhammad.

As one reads the Scriptures and discerns the times in which we live, the prophetic texts point more and more to Islam as the spirit of the antichrist that will rise in the last days. Islam fits the description of the antichrist in so many ways, especially through its wanton acts of violence and hatred of Israel.

Islam is a false religion. Allah is not the God of the Bible. The Jesus of the New Testament is not the Jesus of the Qur'an. The foundations of Islam are built on its repeated denials of Jesus Christ as the incarnate Son of God. Their religion looks upon Him as a mere man, a prophet who cannot rise higher than the second heaven.

The satanic influences of Islam are seen in its efforts to mock the cross of Christ, mimic His ascension and distort His glorious return. Islam fulfills Bible prophecy through its hatred for Israel and its fraudulent claims to its land, Jerusalem and the Temple Mount. Islam has perverted the Bible's teachings concerning many matters and individuals, including Abraham, Isaac and Ishmael. The satanic influences of Islam are also visible in suicide bombings and wanton acts of violence committed in the name of Allah.

The apostle John identifies the antichrist for us:

Who is the liar but the one who denies that Jesus is the Christ? This is the antichrist, the one who denies the Father and the Son. Whoever denies the Son does not have the Father; the one who confesses the Son has the Father also.[2]

Beloved, do not believe every spirit, but test the spirits to see whether they are from God, because many false prophets have gone out into the world. By this you know the Spirit of God: every spirit that confesses that Jesus Christ has come in the flesh is from God; and every spirit that does not confess Jesus is not from God; this is the spirit of the antichrist, of which you have heard that it is coming, and now it is already in the world.[3]

It is imperative Christians study the Bible, become informed about Islam and read the daily news in order to better understand the prophetic signs unfolding around us. The stage is set; the leading characters are assuming their roles as the earth moves ever closer to the shout and the trumpet call that will announce the return of Jesus Christ.

Chapter 6

MUHAMMAD,
THE MAN AND THE MYTH

Muhammad, the founder of Islam, was born near Mecca in AD 570. Orphaned when he was six years of age, Muhammad was raised by his grandfather for two years, and then by an uncle. His family was part of the Koreish clan, the official guardians of the Ka'aba.

A merchant by trade, Muhammad traveled on business throughout the Middle East where he learned about other religions and cultures, including Judaism and Christianity. Muhammad became disgusted with the idolatry and crude religious practices of the pagan Arabs, especially their wonton killing of unwanted baby girls.

Muhammad was twenty-five when he married Khadija, a wealthy widow fifteen years his senior. They had two sons and four daughters; both sons died in infancy. His daughter Fatima married Ali bin Abi Talib who eventually succeeded Muhammad. Khadija was Muhammad's only wife for twenty-five years.

Freed from financial concerns after his marriage, Muhammad often went off in seclusion to a mountain called Hira, near Mecca, where he meditated and prayed in a cave. Muhammad claimed the angel Gabriel came to him in a series of visions and revealed portions of the Qur'an. He first thought his visions had come from evil spirits (jinn), but Khadija encouraged him to accept the revelations as a gift from Allah. The visions and encounters with Gabriel continued for 23 years, during which time the entire Qur'an was disclosed to Muhammad. There are numerous accounts of Muhammad having seizures, during which he experienced some of his visions and revelations. At one period when the visions ceased, he became so depressed he seriously contemplated suicide.

Muhammad adapted some of his teachings from Judaism and Christianity. The Qur'an states, "God has established for you the same religion enjoined on Noah, on Abraham, on Moses and on Jesus" (Sura 42:13). Muhammad taught Adam, Abraham, Moses and Jesus were all Muslim prophets, but He considered himself to be the last and greatest of all the prophets sent by Allah.

It is written in the Qur'an Jesus foretold Muhammad's coming: "And remember, Jesus, the son of Mary, said: 'O Children of Israel! I am the messenger of Allah sent to you, confirming the Law which came before me, and giving Glad Tidings of a Messenger to come after me, whose name shall be Ahmad'" (Sura 61:6). Muslims identify "the Comforter," whom Jesus promised to send, as the Prophet Muhammad.[1] While Muhammad believed earlier revelations from Allah included the Old and New Testaments, he claimed both had been perverted by Jews and Christians, and the Qur'an was Allah's final and only true revelation.

MUHAMMAD'S ASCENSION TO HEAVEN

A major event in the life of Muhammad was his night journey or ascension into heaven. Likely Muhammad reasoned if the New Testament Jesus ascended to heaven, he would do likewise. Muhammad's fantasized journey carried him on a winged-horse, Boraq, from Mecca to the "farthest mosque," according to the Qur'an. Islamic tradition later claimed the "farthest mosque" was the site of the Dome of the Rock in Jerusalem; however, references to Jerusalem are not in the Qur'an. According to Muhammad the angel Gabriel escorted Muhammad from the "fartherest mosque" into the seven levels of heaven, but he returned to earth the same night.

Muhammad met John the Baptist and Jesus in the second heaven. Jesus greeted him: "You are welcome, O pious brother and pious Prophet." He met Joseph in the third heaven, and in the sixth heaven he encountered Moses. Finally when Muhammad arrived in the seventh heaven, he saw Abraham. He learned from Allah that Muslims should pray fifty times daily; but after some negotiations, the number was reduced to five.[2]

MUHAMMAD TURNED ON THE JEWS

Muhammad began to proclaim his teachings in Mecca. His messages contained three basic themes — there is only one sovereign God; there is a resurrection and judgment for all men; and believers should practice acts of charity to the poor. The idol-loving population of Mecca was not impressed with Muhammad, his visions or his messages. When he began telling them about being transported into the seven heavens, the protests grew more intense and threatening. Because of their rejection and hostility, Muhammad and his followers were forced to flee to the city of Yathrib (Medina) in 622, where he became rich and powerful by robbing caravans and taxing those he conquered.

There were Jews living in the Arabian Peninsula from the time of the Babylonian captivity; others had come after the Temple's destruction in AD 70. At first Muhammad called Jews and Christians "People of the Book" and spoke about them with considerable respect, but after they rejected his teachings, he referred to Jews as "pigs" and "monkeys," and to Christians as "infidels." When Muhammad turned on Jews, they were treated with great severity.[3]

Initially Muhammad and his followers faced Jerusalem to pray; but after growing hostile to the Jews, he taught all prayers should be offered while facing Mecca. When the Jews of Medina refused to accept Muhammad's teachings, he had about 800 Jewish men beheaded in one day and sold their wives and children into slavery.[4] Historic accounts say the killing went on all day and into the night.

MUHAMMAD TAKES UP THE SWORD

From the beginning Muhammad planned for Islam to dominate the world. He initially taught: "Let there be no compulsion in religion" (Sura 2:256); later he abrogated (revised or substituted) this teaching: "Kill those who join other gods" (Sura 9:5). Muhammad established three alternatives for his enemies—convert, submit or die. Those who chose to submit were treated as second-class citizens and made to pay taxes. This teaching continues to be the primary motivation and the driving force behind the expansion of Islam.

In 630 Muhammad and 10,000 followers marched on Mecca. Its inhabitants accepted him and his religion without opposition. One of his first acts was to circle the Ka'aba seven times, cleanse it of its 360 idols and proclaim it as Islam's most holy place. The pre-existing pagan ritual of circling the Ka'aba and kissing the stone inside it were made part of Islam's rituals, as were other pagan observances including the month of Ramadan.

Christians lived in various parts of the Middle East from the earliest days of the church. But in the time of Muhammad, the Christian community was largely composed of Egyptians, Greeks and Nestorians. The latter were condemned by the Council of Ephesus in 431. The Nestorians questioned certain aspects of Christ's divine and human natures. It appears they had considerable influence on Muhammad's beliefs; this may explain why some of his understandings of Christianity were distorted and unorthodox.

MUHAMMAD'S MANY WIVES

Muhammad claimed while he was on his night journey to heaven, Allah had married him to three women—Mary the mother of Jesus, Miriam the sister of Moses, and the wife of Pharaoh. Even more marriages awaited him upon his return to earth.

Muhammad was married to his first wife Khadija for twenty-five years, but after her death he remarried. In fact he was married to at least eleven wives at the same time, even though the Qur'an permitted Muslim men to marry but four. "Marry women of your choice, two or three, or four" (Sura 4:3). The Qur'an gave a special exception for Muhammad to marry many wives; however, this exception was for him only (Sura 33:50). Muhammad added several verses to the Qur'an to accommodate his numerous marriages and other circumstances in his life.

Islamic tradition tells of Muhammad's great sexual prowess, but most Westerners in the twenty-first century would consider his actions to be criminal. Muhammad married Aisha, the daughter of Abu Bakr, when she was just six; he consummated the marriage with her when she was only nine. He gave his own daughter Fatima in marriage to his cousin Ali bin Abi Talib when she was twelve.[5] Another of Muhammad's wives, Zainab, had been the wife of his adopted son, but after Muhammad admired her, his son divorced Zainab so that she might be free to marry the Prophet.

THE PRIMARY DIVISIONS IN ISLAM

Following Muhammad's death in 632, a schism developed within Islam that continues to this day. The largest group, the Sunnis, wanted the entire Muslim community to choose Muhammad's successors, but another group, the Shiites, wanted the leader of Islam to be directly descended from Muhammad. Those in the second group regarded Ali, Muhammad's cousin and son-in-law, to be the rightful heir of Muhammad and leader of Islam.

Muhammad's father-in-law Abu Bakr was chosen as the successor to Muhammad. Under his leadership (632-634), Abu Bakr was able to unite all the tribes in the Arabian Peninsula; however, an estimated 70,000 Muslims who had opposed him were put to death in the process.[6] Abu Bakr was succeeded by Umar Abu Hafsa who ruled from 634 to 644. Umar extended Islam's influence in the Middle East through conquests. After Umar was murdered, he was succeeded by Uthman bin Affan, and the wave of bloodshed continued.

Caliph Uthman was responsible for the development of an authorized version of the Qur'an. He too was murdered and succeeded by

Ali bin Abi Talib, Muhammad's cousin and son-in-law. Ali's rule was also one of significant violence, in which tens of thousands were put to death. Ali eventually met the same fate as his predecessors when he was murdered in Kufa, Iraq.[7] The first four successors of Muhammad are called "the rightly guided caliphs," because they tried to enforce Islamic law and protect Islamic society from outside influences.

Sunnis now comprise about eighty-five percent of all Muslims. Iran is predominately Shiite, as are about sixty percent of the residents of Iraq. The Sunnis and Shiites have ruthlessly killed and terrorized one another in Iraq and elsewhere for centuries over a feud that began in the seventh century. In many parts of the Islamic world, Sunnis fight Sunnis and Shiites fight Shiites, because the violence produced by their religion is truly indiscriminate in manifesting its venomous hatred. Even so, Sunnis and Shiites always seem to find common ground in their hatred for Israel and the United States.

THE ANTICHRIST DIMENSIONS OF ISLAM

When considering the spirit of the antichrist, one must begin with Muhammad. A Muslim commentary claims the coming of Muhammad was prophesied in the Bible. Two passages are cited; the first is from Deuteronomy:

> "I will raise up a prophet from among their countrymen like you, and I will put my words in his mouth, and he shall speak to them all that I command him. It shall come about that whoever will not listen to My words which he shall speak in My name, I Myself will require it of him."[8]

An Islamic commentary concluded that this passage describes Muhammad, who is "like Moses," because he too gave a comprehensive law and code of life. It further states Muhammad came "from among their brothers" through Ishmael, and Allah put his words in Muhammad's mouth through the revelation of the Qur'an. The fact Muhammad took on himself prophecies relating to Jesus Christ is in keeping with the Bible's description of the antichrist.

Muslims use a passage from the Gospel of John to prove Muhammad, not Jesus, was the prophet mentioned in Deuteronomy 18:

Now this was John's testimony, when the Jews of Jerusalem sent priests and Levites to ask him who he was. He did not fail to confess, but confessed freely, "I am not the Christ." They asked him, "Then who are you? Are you Elijah?" He said, "I am not." *"Are you the Prophet?"* He answered, "No."[9]

An Islamic commentary draws attention to margin notes published in the *NIV Study Bible*, referencing this verse in the Gospel of John with the passage in Deuteronomy 18. Though this verse clearly relates to Jesus Christ, the Muslim commentary uses it as proof Muhammad, not Jesus, is the prophet mentioned in Deuteronomy.[10] Many of Muhammad's teachings were nothing less than a perversion of Christianity and Judaism.

Martin Luther (1483-1546) believed Muhammad possessed the spirit of the antichrist. He penned his famous hymn "Lord Keep Us Steadfast in Thy Word" even as Muslim hordes were threatening the gates of Vienna.

Lord, keep us steadfast in Thy word:
Curb those who fain by craft or sword
Would wrest the kingdom from Thy Son,
And set at naught all He hath done.

Lord Jesus Christ, Thy power make known;
For Thou art Lord of lords alone;
Defend Thy Christendom, that we
May evermore sing praise to Thee.

O Comforter of priceless worth,
Send peace and unity on earth;
Support us in our final strife,
And lead us out of death to life.

Chapter 7

THE TEACHINGS OF ISLAM

The word *Islam* means "submission to God" or "it is peace." The word *Muslim* means "those who submit" or "those who have peace." Islam is not just a religion; it is both a spiritual and a legal system that controls the lives of those who practice the teachings of Muhammad. It is their religion and government. Therefore Muslims find it extremely difficult to make any distinction between what they do in their daily lives and how they conduct themselves religiously.

THE FIVE PILLARS OF ISLAM

Five Pillars reflect the essence of the Islamic religion. No Muslim may expect mercy from Allah unless these five pillars are faithfully observed.

1. The Creed (Shahada). The Muslim creed states: "There is no God but Allah, and Muhammad is his prophet." These words are spoken into the ear of a new born baby. Muslims want these words to be the last words they hear or utter prior to death. The Shahada is presumably the first thing a Muslim says each day upon waking and the last thing spoken before going to sleep. A person may convert to Islam by reciting the Shahada three times from the heart.

2. **Prayers** (Salah). Muslims pray five times each day—sunrise, noon, mid-afternoon, sunset and late evening. Each day Muslims are expected to recite seventeen prayers. Prayers are said while standing, bowing, kneeling and in prostration. All prayers must be offered while facing Mecca; the direction of Mecca is clearly marked in mosques, shrines and other places of prayer.

While Muslims have no official Sabbath day, they gather at the mosque to pray each Friday. Muhammad chose Friday for assembly because the Jews worshipped on Saturday, and Christians already had taken Sunday. When women are present at the mosque, they must remain separated from the men. No one is permitted to wear shoes inside the mosque. At Friday services a spiritual leader, called an imam, gives a sermon. It is not unusual for sermons to be little more than tirades against Jews, Christians and the United States. Sermons are also used to incite acts of violence and to promote jihad against the perceived enemies of Islam.

The call to prayer is sounded five times each day from a minaret located next to a mosque. In times past the call to prayer was given by a man called a *muessin*; today the call to prayer is often recorded and electronically amplified. The English translation of the call to prayer is as follows:

God is Great. (repeated four times)
I testify that there is none worthy of worship except God. (repeated twice)
I testify that Muhammad is the messenger of God. (repeated twice)
Come to prayer! (repeated twice)
Come to success! (repeated twice)
God is Great! (repeated twice)
There is none worthy of worship except God.

Before praying Muslims purify themselves by washing their faces, hands, elbows, feet and ankles, and they rinse out their mouths three times. A man is considered unclean if he even touches a woman before prayer.

As an aid to prayer, Muslims use a string of ninety-nine beads, one for each of the ninety-nine names of Allah. The Crusaders adopted the use of these beads when they occupied the Holy Land; later they introduced them into the Roman Catholic Church as the Rosary.

3. **Almsgiving** (Zakat). Almsgiving is an important aspect in the celebration of Ramadan. Muslims are required to give 2.5 percent of their possessions to the poor. While there are legitimate charitable works in Muslim communities, some Islamic charities, especially in the United States and Europe, are nothing more than fronts to collect money for terrorist organizations. A U.S. government report stated: "Of the eight obligatory categories of disbursement of Muslim charitable donations, two are for funding jihad or holy war."[1] Over the past few years, several Muslim charities in the United States have been closed by agencies of the government.

4. **Fasting** (Swam). During Ramadan Muslims are expected to abstain from food, drink and sexual relations from sunrise until sunset (self-purification). Each day the fast is broken with the evening meal. Muslims are not permitted to drink alcohol or eat pork any time.

5. **Pilgrimage** (Hajj). Muslims who are physically and financially able are required to make a pilgrimage to Mecca at least once during their lifetime. Only Muslims may enter Mecca. The Hajj includes a visit to Muhammad's tomb in Medina. A type of the Hajj was practiced by pagan Arabs long before the beginning of Islam; it involved visiting the Ka'aba.

An official Saudi web site describes the Hajj as it is practiced today:

The rites of the Hajj, dating to the time of Abraham, include circling the Ka'aba seven times and running seven times between the mountains of Safa and Marwa to commemorate Hagar's search for water and for her son Ishmael. Those making the Hajj also stand together in the plain of Arafat and pray for God's forgiveness. After sunset, the pilgrims process towards Mecca, stopping at Muzdalifah until the brightness of day appears on the eastern horizon. Here, the pilgrims collect seven pebbles and carry them to Mina. As they arrive in the valley, they trek along a two-level pedestrian walkway some 100 yards wide toward the three stone pillars called the Jamarat, which are meant to represent Satan. The pilgrims are required to cast pebbles they have collected at the Stone Pillar of Aqabah while praising God, in a symbolic rejection of Satan. As the pilgrims approach along the walkway, they join those already at the pillar and, after hurling their pebbles, circle toward the exit ramp in the direction of Mecca.

About two million people make the Hajj to Mecca every year. Pilgrims who enter Saudi Arabia through Jeddah are transferred to Mecca via a modern superhighway in a fleet of 15,000 buses. They are taken to the Mina Valley, about four miles northwest of Mecca where they are housed in thousands of air-conditioned tents. Kitchens are scattered throughout the encampment, as are medical stations and banks of telephones.

All pilgrims must put on a special garment called the "ihram," in order to enter into a "state of spirituality and purity." According to the official Saudi web site, all who make the Hajj say this prayer: "Here I am at your service, oh Lord, here I am—here I am. No partner do you have. Here I am. Truly, the praise and favor are yours, and the dominion. No partner do you have." The words "no partner do you have" refer to their belief Allah has no son, meaning, of course, Jesus Christ. Numerous verses in the Qur'an repeatedly deny the divinity of Christ.

The Shiites add two additional pillars to their belief system. The sixth pillar is jihad, to preserve and protect the Islamic religion and all Islamic lands. The seventh pillar is to perform good works and avoid all evil thoughts and deeds.

JIHAD

Islam teaches jihad has two dimensions—first, a personal inner struggle to follow all the teachings of Muhammad; secondly, participation in a war proclaimed through a fatwa (official declaration) against the enemies of Islam and Allah. While moderate Muslims stress the first definition, radical Islamic groups stress the latter.

The jihad taught in the Qur'an and by Islamic leaders all over the world is not peaceful; rather it promotes the establishment of Islamic law (sharia) in every country on earth. A primary reason the United States has become the enemy of the jihadists is because of our efforts to expand democracy in the Middle East. Democracy and Islam are incompatible. Sharia law does not come from democratic governments but from Allah. Any attempt to diminish or modify sharia law by individuals or human governments is not only foreign to Islam, it is considered anathema and the ultimate reason jihad exists in the first place.

Dr. David Bukay, a teacher in the Political Science Department at the University of Haifa, offers insights into the second definition of jihad:

The Islamists start their politics of hatred and jihadi ideology from infancy. The children learn to hate before everything, even without knowing why: at home, in mosques, in madrasses, and in summer camps. They hate Jews and Americans, because they are what they are, and not because they know anything about American or Israeli foreign policy. The hatred is in their drink and the air they breathe, and this is the fuel that directs and motivates the massacres, lynches, and murders. Above all, they are fully convinced that these are the demands of their religion.[2]

Moshe Sharon, a teacher of Islamic history at the Hebrew University in Jerusalem, clarifies how the peaceful definition of jihad has been translated into the more violent version.

What happens if Jews and Christians don't want to live under the rules of Islam? Then Islam has to fight them and this fighting is called jihad. Jihad means war against those people who don't want to accept the Islamic superior rule. That's jihad.[3]

MUHAMMAD

Muslims do not worship Muhammad, though they believe he is the last and greatest of all the prophets sent to earth by Allah. According to Islamic teaching, when Jesus spoke about sending "the Comforter," He was not referring to the Holy Spirit but to Muhammad.[4] "And remember, Jesus, the son of Mary, said: 'O children of Israel! I am the messenger of Allah to you, confirming the Torah before me, and giving Glad Tidings of a messenger to come after me, whose name shall be Ahmad'" (Sura 61:6).

The Caner brothers, in their book *More Than a Prophet*, point out the Greek word for "comforter" is *parakletos,* meaning "famed" or "praised." The Arabic term translated "praised" is *Ahmad*. It is similar to Ahamad, a variant spelling of Muhammad.[5]

THE QUR'AN

Islam's scriptures are contained in the Qur'an (Koran in English), which they refer to as "the Mother of Books." The word *Qur'an* literally means "recital" or "reading." According to Islam it contains the words of Allah. Muhammad claimed the Qur'an's 114 chapters (sura) and 6200 verses were given to him directly by the angel Gabriel over a period of twenty-three years. Each sura begins "In the name of God, the Lord of Mercy, the Giver of Mercy."

As he could neither read nor write, Muhammad never wrote down any of its contents. The Qur'an was first given to Muhammad in oral form. Bits and pieces of the Qur'an were written by others on stones, palm leaves and parchment. Eventually Muhammad's sayings were gathered and recorded in a haphazard fashion, rather than in any chronological order. The Qur'an, for example, begins with the longest chapters and concludes with the shortest chapters.

According to Islam the original Qur'an was written on stone tablets which are kept in heaven. The Qur'an is the final revelation of God to man and supersedes all other previous revelations, specifically the Old and New Testaments. Muslims claim the Bible is incomplete without the Qur'an. They teach both the Old and New Testaments were corrupted by errors which the Qur'an amended and corrected. They also recognize the Apocrypha as well as several other extra-biblical works.

At first there were at least four versions of the Qur'an, but Caliph Uthman established an authorized version still in use today. Devout Muslims endeavor to memorize the entire Qur'an in Arabic. Even young Muslim children around the world are trained to memorize the Qur'an in Arabic. They consider the original Arabic language of the Qur'an to be the only authentic version. Often when Christians quote from the Qur'an in a language other than Arabic, Muslims cry "foul" and claim it is not an accurate translation, but this is not true.

The Doctrine of Abrogation

Verses in the Qur'an are often contradictory. Since Muslims claim the Qur'an is a perfect revelation, one would assume these contradictions would pose a problem, but the Islamic doctrine of *abrogation* explains and corrects all such matters. This doctrine was examined by Alvin Schmidt and reported in *The Lutheran Witness*.

> When two or more passages in the Koran are in conflict or contradict each other, the more recent passage(s) Muhammad reportedly received from Allah via the angel Gabriel usually abrogates (repeals) the earlier passage in question.
>
> The Koran states: "Whatever communications We abrogate or cause to be forgotten, We bring one better than it or like it. Do you not know that Allah has the power over all things?" (Sura 2:106)
>
> When passages were abrogated, they continued to be part of the Koran. Because abrogated verses are never deleted and because the public does not know about the doctrine of abrogation, or which verses have been abrogated, Muslims

propagandists can (and do) easily deceive the non-Muslim public by citing certain abrogated verses as though they were still valid, thus falsely presenting Islam in a positive light.

It illustrates with Sura 2:256, "There is no compulsion in religion." Later passages state: "Fight those who do not believe in Allah, nor in the latter day, nor do they prohibit what Allah and His apostles have prohibited, nor follow the religion of truth." (Sura 9:29). "I will cast terror into the hearts of those who disbelieve, therefore strike off their heads and strike off every fingertip of them." (Sura 8:12).

These verses and others like them, called the "Sword verses," abrogate those that speak of peace' or tolerance." Thus when the promoters of Islam cite passages from the Koran to show Islam as a religion of peace, we must not let ourselves be deceived by verses that have been abrogated.[6]

Schmidt points out the doctrine of abrogation is an orthodox teaching of the Qur'an and is not an anti-Islamic concept.[7]

Even though the Bible predates the Qur'an by hundreds of years, many so-called historical facts contained in the Qur'an are either incorrect or in direct conflict with biblical accounts. Some of these distortions may be due to the fact Muhammad acquired information from people whose knowledge about Christianity and Judaism was either limited or in error, but most of the distortions were obviously contrived.

Islam's crude and thinly veiled attempts to hijack elements of Judaism and Christianity and incorporate them into its religion should be obvious to anyone with a basic knowledge of the Bible. At a White House dinner celebrating the end of Ramadan in 2005, President George W. Bush referred to the Qur'an as "the Word of God." Such references by professing Christians, while deemed politically correct in today's society, are false and misleading. The Qur'an is not inspired by God; it is not Scripture, and it certainly is not God's Word.

OTHER SOURCES OF AUTHORITY

The Muslims' second most holy book is the Hadith. Its ninety-three chapters are divided into two parts, the sacred and the prophetic. The sacred portion reveals the words of Allah as spoken through Muhammad, in addition to those found in the Qur'an. The prophetic portion contains the gathered sayings of the Prophet Muhammad. While the Hadith does not have quite the same status as the Qur'an, its contents are fully authoritative in Islam. Many of the sayings in the Hadith concerning killing and violence are even more objectionable than those contained in the Qur'an. Muslims look to the Hadith to better understand what is expected from them in various areas of life. The Sunna, which is especially important to the Sunni Muslims, is comprised of the social and legal mandates. The Sira, biographies of Muhammad, and the Tfsir, an Islamic commentary, are also highly regarded by Muslims.[8]

THE KA'ABA

At the time of Muhammad, the Ka'aba (Beit-Allah), located in Mecca, was already an ancient center of pagan worship dedicated to 360 gods, including the pagan god Allah. *Ka'aba* is an Arabic word meaning "cube," and refers to a black rock located in the structure. Ancient Muslim lore claims Gabriel gave the stone to Adam. The stone was venerated by pagan Arabs long before Muhammad made it part of Islam. Muslims claim the Ka'aba was originally built by Adam; after its destruction in the flood, it was rebuilt by Abraham and his son Ishmael.

THE JESUS OF ISLAM

The Jesus of the Qur'an and the Jesus of the New Testament are two entirely different persons. The Jesus of the Qur'an is not divine, nor is He the Son of God. The Jesus of the Qur'an was created, as was Adam. Though viewed as a Muslim prophet, their Jesus is not considered superior to other prophets, especially Muhammad.

While Muslims teach Jesus was born of a virgin, they deny He actually died on a cross or was raised from the dead. The Qur'an claims Allah substituted someone else to die on the cross (Judas), and Allah took Jesus directly to heaven. "They said, 'We killed the Messiah Jesus, son of Mary, the messenger of God.' They did not kill him, nor did they crucify him, but the likeness of him was put on another man (and they killed that man)" (Sura 4:157).

Islam does not believe Jesus gave his life to atone for the sins of mankind. They view the Christian doctrine of Jesus being equal with God as an unforgivable sin. Since nothing is more central to Christianity than the death, burial, resurrection and divinity of Jesus Christ, how could there possibly be any confusion over the relationship between the Jesus of Christianity and the Jesus of Islam?

SALVATION ACCORDING TO ISLAM

Salvation may be obtained by believing in the oneness of Allah, believing in the revelations of Muhammad and believing in life after death. The essence of Islam is not to know Allah but to obey him. Islam has no concept of an approachable, loving and knowable God. This is in stark contrast to Jesus' words about obtaining eternal life: "This is eternal life, that they may know You, the only true God, and Jesus Christ whom You have sent."[9]

There is no concept of redemption in Islam; salvation is based entirely on one's good deeds outweighing the bad deeds on the scales of judgment. "Then those whose balance is heavy, they will be successful. But those whose balance is light will be those who have lost their souls; in Hell will they abide" (Sura 23:102-103).

Even Muhammad was fearful about his own salvation: "By Allah, though I am the Apostle of Allah, yet I do not know what Allah will do to me" (Hadith 5:266). It is hard to imagine how anyone could follow a religion whose leader was unsure of his own salvation!

According to the Qur'an, the only way to be absolutely sure of going to Paradise is to die as a martyr (shahid) for Allah and Islam (jihad). This is the primary teaching that motivates suicide bombers. A martyr of Islam is assured of heaven, where he will be given seventy-two virgins and a beautiful mansion. Otherwise on

154

judgment day, Muslims must appear before Allah and hope their good works will be considered sufficient enough for them to enter Paradise.

Muslims are assured of entering the fires of hell if they abandon the true faith (Islam). "Whosoever turns back from his religion and dies as a disbeliever...they will be dwellers of the Fire" (Sura 2:217). In many Muslim countries, conversion to Christianity or another religion means a death sentence. These killings, called "honor killings," are usually performed by family members or individuals who kill for Allah.

RAMADAN

Ramadan is a month-long celebration of the Qur'an's revelation to Muhammad, although it was practiced as part of a pagan ritual long before Muhammad made it part of Islam. During Ramadan Muslims are expected to fast, donate money to the poor, seek forgiveness and recite special prayers. The last ten days of Ramadan include the "Night of Destiny," when Gabriel first revealed the Qur'an to Muhammad. Muslims who worship Allah on this night are promised great reward.

Ramadan begins with the new moon of the ninth month in the Islamic calendar. During this celebratory month, Muslims are forbidden to eat or drink during the daylight hours, and they must refrain from sexual intercourse. The fast-breaking meal each day in Ramadan is called *iftar*. Ramadan concludes with a three-day feast called Eid al-Fitr, a time of celebration and exchanging of gifts.

THE STATUS OF WOMEN IN ISLAM

Most Western women would think it hell on earth to live under the teachings and traditions of Islam. Women are considered property and subservient to men in every way. In strict Islamic societies, women are not permitted to acquire an education. From childhood they live under the domination of their fathers and brothers. After marriage they live under the authority of their husbands and sons. A married woman may not leave the house without the permission of her husband or her sons; she must walk behind her husband and kneel behind him for prayer.[10]

For radical Muslims, Islamic law and tradition requires women when outside their homes to be covered from head to toe so that men will not look at them with lust. The outer covering, called an abaya, must be loose-fitting. Muhammad did not require a woman to cover her face; the veil was developed by more radical sects over the years. Strict Muslims require women to wear a veil over their faces (niqab), with only a small slit for their eyes. The headscarf worn to cover just the hair is called a hajib. The word comes from the Arabic word *hajiba,* meaning to hide or conceal. The longer partial cloak that covers the head and upper body is called a khemar. In most Islamic countries, women typically wear long dresses and veils over their faces.

To what extent are Islamic laws that require women to be veiled being enforced today? An incident in Saudi Arabia in March 2000 best describes how strict some Muslims are in this regard. Fifteen girls who were trapped in a fire at their school removed their outer clothing, including their veils, in order to escape the fire. When they reached a point of exit, the religious police of Saudi Arabia would not let them out of the burning building without being fully covered. All fifteen girls perished.[11]

Since Mamoud Ahmadinejad came to power in Iran, the Iranian vice-police have been stopping women on the streets if they are not appropriately dressed. Even men have been detained for "not observing the proper dress code" by wearing tight pants or short-sleeve shirts.[12] The same condition now exists in the Gaza Strip, since it was taken over by Hamas. Even Christian women in Gaza are now required to observe the Islamic dress code.

Middle East Media Research Institute, which monitors Muslim television, released a video of an exchange on Saudi television between a Muslim cleric and Buthayna Nasser, a female newscaster. Nasser was reacting to the demand all women who appear on Saudi television should have their faces covered. She told the cleric, "Sir, when I appear on TV, and when I claim my right to play a role in this professional field, I demand that my face, which constitutes my identity, be seen. Under no circumstances am I prepared to have my identity to be obliterated."

Television audiences in Saudi Arabia who are not accustomed to such dissent, especially from women, were shocked as Nasser went on to charge that Saudi youth were being brainwashed by Islamic clerics. She said beginning in elementary school and continuing through university, students are subject to rote memorization, and "whoever dares to argue or to question anything is called upon to ask for Allah's forgiveness. He is told that this will get him into hell."

The Qur'an permits husbands to beat their wives for acts of disobedience (Sura 4:34). According to the Qur'an, women taken captive in battle may be sold as slaves or, if desired, used for sexual pleasures. Muhammad actually married one of his "desirable captives."

In most Muslim countries, children may be given in marriage, but according to sharia law, they may not be married until they are nine. *Time* magazine reported in 2001:

> In Iran the legal age for marriage is nine for girls, four-teen for boys. The law has occasionally been exploited by pedophiles who marry poor young girls from the provinces, use and then abandon them. In 2000 the Iranian Parliament voted to raise the minimum age to fourteen, but this year, a legislative oversight body dominated by traditional clerics vetoed the move. An attempt by conservatives to abolish Yemen's legal minimum age of fifteen for girls failed, but local experts say it is rarely enforced anyway. (The onset of puberty is considered an appropriate time for a marriage to be consummated.)[13]

Women who are part of moderate Muslim communities are not subjected to the same rigid dress codes as are their fundamentalist counterparts. Muslim women in moderate Islamic countries and in the West are often seen in modern attire as they work in offices and attend educational institutions. However, as the influence of radical Islam increases in moderate Arab countries and in the West, radical

Muslims are demanding that all women wear traditional head coverings and veils.

HONOR KILLINGS—
ISLAM'S DIRTY LITTLE SECRET

Honor killings are common in many Islamic communities. The most likely victims of honor killings are those who convert to another religion and women whose conduct is not in keeping with Islamic standards or codes of morality. Even women who are raped can be targeted for death by members of their own family. Most honor killings are committed by family members.

A report from a German publication stated six Muslim women living in Berlin in 2005 were victims of honor killings within a space of four months. In each case the women were trying to break out of the servitude imposed by their Islamic culture. The six women were killed by their husbands or family members for "besmirching the family's Muslim honor." Two were stabbed to death in front of their young children, two were shot, one was strangled, and another was drowned. Many honor killings are never reported, but according to the report, over forty killings have been documented in Germany since 1996.[14] Honor killings are commonly practiced in nearly all Islamic countries.

In July 2007, a Muslim in Jordan was sentenced to six months in jail for killing his pregnant sister in order to "uphold his family's honor." The woman was pregnant with her former husband's child. The Jordanian court said the woman's "shameful behavior deviated from tradition and harmed her family's honor." The court further justified its lenient sentence, saying it was warranted because of the "state of fury" that had led to the woman's slaying. About twenty women are victims of "honor killings" in Jordan every year. Likely those are only the reported cases.[15]

The New York-based Human Rights Watch, in a report entitled "A Question of Security: Violence Against Palestinian Women and Girls," stated nearly one-quarter of Palestinian women are victims of domestic violence, abuse or rape, but governmental agencies do nothing to protect them. The report, conducted between November

2005 and early 2006, further stated, "Palestinian women and girls who report abuse to the authorities find themselves confronting a system that prioritizes the reputations of their families in the community over their own well-being and lives." The report observed that Palestinian laws reduce penalties for men accused of honor killings or attacks against female relatives who commit adultery, and they absolve rapists who agree to marry their victims. In addition there has been an increase in incest cases, and fathers do not deny it. They say, "I have a right to her body over others" or "I want her to go to her husband experienced."[16]

ALLAH OF ISLAM IS NOT THE GOD OF THE BIBLE!

Muhammad taught Allah is the God of Jesus and Moses. But saying it does not make it so. It is a known fact the name Allah was used prior to the establishment of the Islamic religion. Muhammad's father's name was Abd-Allah, meaning "slave of god." Allah was the chief god among the many gods worshiped in the Ka'aba. Scholars claim pre-Islamic Arabs connected the god Allah with the moon. To this day the moon plays a significant role in the Islamic religion. The crescent moon is their chief symbol, and the entire Islamic calendar is based on the cycles of the moon.

Today many Jews and Christians, including a growing number of evangelicals, seem eager to recognize Allah as being the same God who is worshiped by Christians and Jews. Those who equate Allah with the God of the Scriptures really have not a clue as to authentic Islamic beliefs; most have never read the Qur'an. Others base their opinion on the fact Muslims are monotheistic and some of their teachings were taken directly from Judaism and Christianity. Yet when examined in the light of the Bible, their arguments cannot hold up.

The ELCA claims
Muslims and Christians worship the same God!

The Evangelical Lutheran Church in America (ELCA) has produced several studies and articles in which they emphatically claim Muslims "worship the same God, revere the same prophets, and obey the same spiritual commandments that we do."[17] This statement is patently absurd. Muslims and Christians do not worship the same God, nor do they even come close to obeying "the same spiritual commandments," because Islam's commandments come from an entirely different source.

Another ELCA statement declared, "All three of these traditions [Christianity, Judaism, and Islam] are religions of 'the book,' stressing the importance of using scripture to discern God and God's will for mankind."[18] This ELCA study equates the Qur'an and the Old and New Testaments; it also refers to the Qur'an and the Bible as being "the book," as if both are one book and carry the same authority. If, as the ELCA study claims, God's will and truth are expressed in the Qur'an, then His will and His truth cannot be expressed in the Bible. One of them is a lie!

Still another ELCA study declares, "Islam is a close cousin of Judaism and Christianity, and the spiritual practices of many Muslims merit study and appreciation by other monotheists."[19] One can only wonder if the author of this ELCA study means Christians should practice jihad, honor killings or if Christian women should start wearing veils, accept beatings from their husbands or start memorizing the Qur'an.

CHRISTIANS MUST LEARN TO DISCERN

Even the most cursory examination of the Qur'an should cause anyone to conclude the god of Islam is not the God of the Bible. Allah can not be the God and Father of our Lord Jesus Christ, since Islam denies Christ's divinity, His death on the cross and His resurrection. According to the Islamic religion, the words of the Qur'an were inspired by Allah. If Allah is indeed the one who inspired the Old and New Testaments, how could the Qur'an and the Bible possibly contradict each other?

The Qur'an is filled with one contradiction after another, even though it claims to have been written by one man over a period of twenty-three years. The various books of the Bible were written hundreds of years apart by many different authors, yet the books of the Bible support, confirm and compliment one another. There is not a single fulfilled prophecy in the Qur'an, while the Bible is filled with literally hundreds of fulfilled prophecies. It is an affront to God for any Christian to equate the Qur'an with the Bible. When Jesus prayed, "Sanctify them in the truth; Your word is truth,"[20] He was not referring to the Qur'an.

Chapter 8

IS ISLAM A RELIGION OF PEACE?

The politically correct mantra continues to declare "Islam is a religion of peace." If you believe a host of liberal preachers, politicians and celebrities, you will likely agree with this statement. However, if you engage in a serious study of Islam or listen to the morning news, you may be inclined towards an opinion based more on reality.

Every Friday imams around the world preach violence to those gathered at the mosques. Over 100 verses in the Qur'an and dozens more in the Hadith advocate the expansion of Islam through violence. A verse in the Qur'an, called "the verse of the sword," states: "But when the forbidden months are past, then fight and kill the pagans wherever you find them, and seize them, beleaguer them, and lie in wait for them at every outlook post." (Sura 9:5).

Not long before he died, Muhammad said to his followers on Mount Arafat, "After today there will no longer be two religions existing in Arabia. I descended by Allah with the sword in my hand, and my wealth will come from the shadow of my sword. And the one who will disagree with me will be humiliated and persecuted."[1] This message of Muhammad represents the primary reason why Islamic states in the Arabian Peninsula are so strongly opposed to any presence of Christianity, and why they prohibit non-Muslims from practicing their faith. It also explains why Osama bin Laden and other radical Islamic leaders have been determined to get all foreign troops to leave the region.

Muhammad was personally responsible for the deaths of thousands. He was present for the execution of 800 Jews in Medina. He had a woman poet put to death in Mecca for criticizing him. Muhammad believed in holy wars, calling them jihad. He commanded his followers to "fight in the cause of God" (Sura 2:244). "And when you meet the Unbelievers, smite at their necks" (Sura 47:4). Muhammad was involved in no fewer than twenty-six battles. Several times he ordered the execution of hundreds of his perceived enemies. The first four leaders (caliphs) of Islam focused on the expansion of Islam through war. This violent expansion lasted for over 650 years and cost over a million lives. Calling Islam a religion of peace defies history and reality.

Moderate Muslims claim jihad refers mostly to a spiritual battle or a personal struggle to follow the teachings of Allah. However, all radical Muslims use the Qur'an's teaching about jihad as license to attack and kill their perceived enemies. Moderate Muslims are wrong when they try to pass off their peaceful interpretation of jihad without taking into account what the term has meant in the past, and what it means today to millions of Islamic extremists. Moderate Muslims and their allies like to quote the few verses in the Qur'an that speak of peace, while failing to mention the scores of verses that promote hatred and violence. Muslims who speak of Islam as a religion of peace are referring to an enforced silence of all opposition that will come when the whole world is living under Islamic law. Until then, radical Muslims continue to advocate the use of violence and coercion against their enemies.

In the book *Inside Islam*, Bernard Lewis states if Muslims are fighting in the war for Islam and for God, they reason their opponents are fighting against God.[2] He further states, "In the classical Islamic view, to which many Muslims are beginning to return, the world and all mankind are divided into two: the House of Islam and the House of Unbelief, or the House of War, which is the duty of Muslims ultimately to bring to Islam."[3]

An Islamic biographer describes the manner in which Muhammad took care of his enemies in Medina: "The apostle of Allah, may Allah bless him, sat with his companions and they were brought in small groups. Their heads were struck off. They were between six hundred and seven hundred in number."[4]

Emir and Ergun Caner, two former Muslims who converted to Christianity, describe the difference between Jesus Christ and Muhammad: "Jesus Christ shed His own blood on the cross so that people could come to God. Muhammad shed other people's blood so that his constituents could have political power throughout the Arabian Peninsula."[5]

TERRORISM AND ISLAM

One should not consider Islam as being a peaceful religion without taking into consideration the manifold terrorist organizations that carry out their nefarious activities in the name of Islam and Allah. The list of terrorist groups is staggering; at least thirty known organizations are operating globally with millions of members. Furthermore, these terrorists groups are supported by sovereign Muslim governments, charitable-front organizations and by individual Muslims around the world.

The Muslim Brotherhood

The Muslim Brotherhood is a worldwide jihadist movement that gave birth to Hamas, the Palestinian Islamic Jihad and al-Qaeda. Osama bin Laden and his deputy Ayman al-Zawahiri are members of the Muslim Brotherhood. Their motto is "The Quran is our constitution, the prophet is our guide; Death for the glory of Allah is our greatest ambition." The stated goals of Brotherhood members in the United States are to propagate Islam in America, fund jihad and back Israel's destruction. Related Muslim groups in the United

States include the Saudi-backed Muslim Student Association, the Islamic Society of North America and the North American Islamic Trust which owns and controls eighty percent of all mosques in America and Canada.

The Council on American-Islamic Relations (CAIR)

The Council on American-Islamic Relations (CAIR), one of the most respected Islamic organizations in America, is considered by some authorities to be a supporter of terrorist organizations. Sources for a PBS documentary stated the Washington-based Council on American-Islamic Relations is connected through its forerunner to the Islamic Association for Palestine, a front group for Hamas.[6]

According to Judicial Watch, several CAIR staffers were convicted on terrorism-related charges. CAIR's founder, Omar Ahmad, allegedly told a group of Muslims they are in America not to assimilate but to help assert Islam's rule over the country.[7]

In the meantime, various agencies of the United States government treat CAIR as though it is part of our home security. The Department of Homeland Security took CAIR officials on a tour of our Customs screening operations at O'Hare International Airport in 2006, after the organization complained about the treatment Muslims were receiving at various airports. CAIR has been asked by several government agencies and even by the military to conduct sensitivity training sessions.

One law enforcement source stated that CAIR representatives sit on the FBI's community advisory board and "routinely lodge complaints about case agents who question mosque leaders and followers." The same source also stated the FBI "seldom makes a raid in the Muslim community without first contacting CAIR officials."[8]

In 2007 the Department of Homeland Security made $24 million available to nonprofit organizations "deemed high-risk for a potential international terrorist attack." CAIR immediately issued an alert to American mosques and other Islamic institutions, saying they should immediately apply for the funds.[9]

Judicial Watch president Tom Fitton said while CAIR has done a good job of portraying itself as a "champion for all Muslims and has been very effective in making themselves out to be the ACLU of Arab-Americans, they are a narrow interest group funded by terrorist-associated organizations, and they've knowingly assisted violent Muslim Arab groups." CAIR should be considered "a foreign-based, subversive organization," according to Fitton.[10]

If there is one piece of good news regarding CAIR, it is their membership has been in a steady decline since 2001. A report in the *Washington Times* revealed that membership in CAIR dropped from 29,000 in 2000 to less than 1,700 in 2006. But several wealthy donors are supplying the necessary funds to keep them in business. In 2000 they had eight offices in the United States; today they have thirty-three offices. While the size of their membership has declined, the same can not be said for their influence with U.S. government officials, in spite of the fact the Justice Department named CAIR as "an unindicted co-conspirator" in a federal case against another foundation charged with providing funds to terrorists.[11]

Al-Qaeda

Al-Qaeda, a Sunni terrorist organization, was founded by Osama bin Laden in 1988. In 1993 al-Qaeda bombed the World Trade Center in New York. Their failure to bring the buildings down and thereby create an economic disaster prompted them to try again on September 11, 2001. In 1998 bin Laden issued a fatwa against Jews and Crusaders, the latter being the United States. His fatwa called for the killing "of Americans and their allies—civilian and military." He called on Muslims everywhere "to plunder their money wherever they find it."

Osama bin Laden made good on his threats. A partial list of al-Qaeda's terrorist attacks includes:

- The bombing of the United States embassies in Tanzania and Kenya on August 7, 2000; 257 people were killed and over 4,000 were injured.
- The bombing of the USS Cole in Yemen harbor on October 12, 2000; 17 were killed, 39 were injured. There was no retaliation by the United States.

- The bombing of the World Trade Center and the Pentagon, September 11, 2001; 3000 were killed, thousands were injured.
- Four trains were bombed in Madrid on March 11, 2004; 157 were killed, hundreds were injured.
- Three underground trains and a bus were bombed in London, July 7, 2005; 52 were killed, over 700 were injured.[12]

In 2002 bin Laden sent a 4,000-word message to the United States, explaining al-Qaeda's rationale for their attacks. He called on the people of the United States to convert to Islam: "The first thing we call you to is Islam. It is to this religion that we call you, the seal of all previous religions."

Much of the violence in Iraq and Afghanistan during the past five years has been caused by members of al-Qaeda. The fire bombings in London and Glasgow in June 2007, in which several medical doctors were implicated, were traced to connections with al-Qaeda. This terrorist organization remains the most serious threat to European and American security. According to a National Intelligence Agency report released in July 2007, the strength of al-Qaeda has increased in recent years to levels not seen since September 2001.

Americans have a short memory, but you may be certain the list of attacks by al-Qaeda will continue to grow if liberal and naïve politicians do not secure our borders and stop hamstringing law enforcement agencies with politically correct policies and regulations.

Hezbollah

Hezbollah (Party of God) had its beginnings in 1982 in Lebanon. It is comprised of Shiite Muslims and funded largely by Iran, although Syria is complicit in many of their activities. Hezbollah was the first terrorist organization to employ suicide bombings. Today there is a close working relationship between al-Qaeda and Hezbollah, including sharing of training bases.

By any standard Hezbollah is a terrorist organization. The people of the United States discovered that fact when they bombed our embassy on April 18, 1983, killing sixty-three people, including seventeen Americans. On October 24 of the same year, Hezbollah bombed our Marine barracks in Beirut, killing 241 US military personnel. These actions were followed by numerous kidnappings and hijackings of American citizens over a period of several years. Hezbollah in Saudi Arabia was responsible for bombing the Khobar Towers in which nineteen American servicemen were killed and hundreds were wounded.

Over the years, Hezbollah has been armed with modern and sophisticated weaponry, as was evidenced in their war with Israel in the summer of 2006. Reports from Israeli intelligence reveal since their war with Israel in 2006, Hezbollah has been rearmed by Iran and Syria. It is estimated they now have 20,000 short and long-range rockets ready to fire into Israel. Israeli intelligence also reported Iran continues to smuggle sophisticated weapons and long range missiles into Lebanon under the not-so-watchful eyes of the United Nations' peace-keeping forces. The Hezbollah flag is now flying over southern Lebanon in violation of peace arrangements with the United Nations. In June of 2007, Hezbollah detonated a road-side bomb, killing five members of the UN peace-keeping forces.

Hezbollah, with the support of Iran and Syria, wants to seize control of the government of Lebanon. Though they have been included in the Lebanese cabinet and legislature, Hezbollah wants total dominance over Lebanon's Christian and Sunni populations. Should they succeed in taking over Lebanon, their regime will ultimately be controlled from Tehran and Damascus.

Hamas

Hamas (The Islamic Resistance Movement), founded by the Muslim Brotherhood in 1987, is a Sunni-Palestinian terrorist organization that functions mostly in the West Bank and the Gaza Strip; however, its influence reaches into Europe and the United States. The primary goal of Hamas is the complete destruction of Israel and the establishment of a Palestinian state in its place.[13]

The military wing of Hamas has been able to obtain thousands of rockets and small arms to strike Israel. In addition, they have acquired a number of anti-aircraft missiles which could be used against civilian airliners flying in or out of Ben Gurion Airport in Tel Aviv. Israeli intelligence confirmed hundreds of anti-tank missiles,

Qussams and Katyusha rockets are now in the hands of Hamas-led forces. These weapons make it possible for Hamas to strike deeper into Israel with more accuracy and ferocity. Hamas fields its own military wing called the Mujahadin. A high-ranking Israeli military official stated that Hamas now has "a full-fledged army of 13,000 troops, consisting of four brigades stationed in various areas of the Gaza Strip.

The extent to which Hamas and other Palestinian terror groups have been able to smuggle weapons into the Gaza Strip is staggering, according to reports from the Israeli Defense Forces. Palestinian terror groups have learned Hezbollah-like tactics, such as the use of anti-tank weapons and the construction of a network of underground bunkers and tunnels. Hezbollah and Hamas have been training Palestinian militants in the Sinai desert, just south of the Gaza Strip. According to Israeli intelligence, a substantial number of Hamas' military leadership has been trained in Iran.

The most notable achievement thus far for Hamas was its military victory over Fatah and the Palestinian Authority in the Gaza Strip in June 2007. Over the past twenty years, Hamas has been responsible for scores of suicide bombings against Israeli civilians. The charter of Hamas calls for the destruction of Israel and the establishment of a Palestinian state. Their charter further states, "There is no solution for the Palestinian question except through jihad."[14]

Hamas is financed by Iran, Saudi Arabia and indirectly by funds given to the Palestinian Authority by the United States and the European Union. In 2006 Iran gave $120 million to Hamas and pledged to send them $240 million in 2007. Furthermore, Israeli intelligence claims Iran was a partner in Hamas' takeover of the Gaza Strip.

Like Hezbollah, Hamas enjoys a great deal of popular support because of its social welfare programs that include hospitals, clinics, orphanages, etc. Syria permits senior operatives of Hamas to live in and direct operations from its territory, and it continues to assist Hamas in smuggling weapons into the West Bank and Gaza. Hamas has taken the leadership in educating and indoctrinating Palestinian children, using textbooks and materials supplied by Saudi Arabia.

Secretary of State Condoleezza Rice brokered a deal in November 2006, in which Israeli control over the Egypt-Gaza border was replaced by Egyptian and Palestinian security officials who are supposed to be observed by European monitors. However, Israeli intelligence claims the European monitors have looked the other way as wholesale smuggling operations have taken place. The Israelis also claim smuggling tunnels that snake between Egypt and the Gaza border are "thriving."[15] One Israeli military official called the network of tunnels "an underground city." Abu Ahmed, northern Gaza leader for al-Aqsa Martyrs Brigade, told a reporter:

> We are turning Gaza into south Lebanon. We learned from Hezbollah's victory that Israel can be defeated if we know how to hit them, and if we are well prepared. We are importing rockets and the knowledge to launch them, and we are also making plans for battle. The Sinai is an excellent ground for training, the exchange of information and weapons and for meetings on how to turn every piece of land into usable territory for a confrontation with Israel. The Katyusha rockets we fired (into the Israeli Negev) show we can have every weapon we need. It is only a matter of a small period before Gaza is ready for war.[16]

Other Terrorist Organizations and Their Tactics

Islamic radicals believe they are obligated to overthrow any government if it refuses to apply Islamic laws. Governments of moderate Islamic countries, such as Jordan and Egypt, must constantly protect themselves from extremists.

Other terrorist groups operating in Gaza and the West Bank include Fatah, the military arm of the Palestine Liberation Organization; the al-Aqsa Martyrs Brigade, a Fatah affiliated movement; the Palestinian Islamic Jihad; and Izzadin Kassam, an armed branch of Hamas. The Popular Front for the Liberation of Palestine (PFLP) operates mostly out of the Bethlehem area.

Hamas now controls the Gaza Strip, while Fatah remains in control of the West Bank. This division of the Palestinians' territory makes it extremely difficult for further peace efforts with Israel to proceed. It may be Fatah and the Palestinian Authority will be able to negotiate with Israel over the future of the West Bank, but even that is highly unlikely, since they are likewise determined to destroy Israel. As for Gaza, it remains a powder keg ready to blow at any moment.

David Bukay offers a profile of terrorists who have attacked Israel in recent years. His description does not meet the profile most people have about suicide bombers.

From September 2000 until May 2003, 197 suicide bombers were sent on suicide actions, among them 35 women. Of all the 115 successful murderers, 65 percent had university education, and 50 percent came from al-Najah University. They were not hungry or miserable. They were in total repulsion of Jews and Zionism, and motivated by dehumanization of Israeli existence.

The leaders of Islamic fundamentalist terrorist groups are members of the middle and upper class. They have university education and many, with doctoral degrees, are physicians and engineers. They never declared that the reasons for their activity were poverty or ignorance. They speak of Western crusaderism, which they want to expel, and of Israeli aggression which they aspire to destroy. They have no program for social progress, economic well being, improving health, or broadening education to the masses....The leadership of al-Qaeda prove this reality clearly. Bin Laden is a multi-millionaire with an MA degree in public administration from the University of Jeddah. His deputy, Ayman al-Zawahiri, is a surgical physician from the upper class in Egypt.[17]

PEACE IRANIAN STYLE

The government of Iran was taken over through a revolution led by the Ayatollah Khomeini in 1979. Since then Iran has been dominated by Islamic radicals. The eyes of the world are on Iran because of their nuclear ambitions and their announced intentions to destroy Israel. Iran poses a great danger not only to Israel but also to the whole world. The government of Iran is directly responsible for the deaths of hundreds of our brave U.S. service men and women in Iraq.

Mahmoud Ahmadinejad, Iran's current president, has set his nation on a collision course with the West that may end in a nuclear confrontation. However, it was the Ayatollah Khomeini who first issued the call for a jihad with the West. Immediately prior to his death, Khomeini stated:

> Islam makes it incumbent on all adult males, provided they are not disabled and incapacitated, to prepare themselves for the conquest of countries so that the writ of Islam is obeyed in every country of the world. But those who study Islamic Holy War will understand why Islam wants to conquer the world....Those who know nothing of Islam pretend that Islam counsels against war. Those (who say this) are witless. Islam says: Kill all the unbelievers just as they would kill you all! Does this mean that Muslims should sit back until they are devoured by (the unbelievers)! Islam says: Kill them (non-Muslims), put them to the sword and scatter (their armies). Does this mean sitting back until (non-Muslims) overcome us? Islam says: Kill in the service of Allah those who may want to kill you! Does this mean that we should surrender to the enemy? Islam says: Whatever good there is exists thanks to the sword and in the shadow of the sword! People cannot be made obedient except with the sword! The sword is the key to Paradise, which can be opened only for Holy warriors! ... Does this mean that Islam is a religion that prevents men from waging war? I spit upon those foolish souls who make such a claim.[18]

Iran continues to develop nuclear arms, even though the United Nations has ordered them to stop and has imposed numerous sanctions. Thus far the sanctions have had little success in slowing down their nuclear program. Brian Ross and Christopher Isham reported on an ABC news report:

Iran has more than tripled its ability to produce enriched uranium in the last three months, adding some 1,000 centrifuges which are used to separate radioactive particles from the raw material. The development means Iran could have enough material for a nuclear bomb by 2009, sources familiar with the dramatic upgrade tell ABC news.

The sources say the unexpected expansion is taking place at Iran's nuclear enrichment plant outside the city of Natanz, in a hardened facility 70 feet underground. The addition of 1,000 new centrifuges, which are not yet operational, means Iran is expanding its enrichment program at a pace much faster than U.S. intelligence experts had predicted.[19]

In June 2007, the US House of Representatives passed a nonbinding resolution that called on the UN Security Council to charge Mahmoud Ahmadinejad under the genocide conventions. The UN charter requires all UN members to "refrain in their international relations from the threat or use of force against the territorial integrity or political independence of any state." Only two congressmen voted against the resolution — representatives Dennis Kucinich from Ohio and Ron Paul of Texas.

PEACE SAUDI STYLE

Saudi Arabia's population is predominately Sunni Muslim. Wahhabism, a most extreme and militant form of Islam, is observed as the state religion of Saudi Arabia. Adherents of Wahhabism consider all Shiites to be apostates, and they want to see Islam made the dominating religion throughout the whole world.

Saudis live under the strict enforcement of Islamic law (sharia). Beheadings, stoning, public beating and cutting off hands and feet are all part of the legal structure of the country. Christians are arrested and prosecuted if they publicly display a Bible or any Christian symbol. The religious police, visible throughout the country, regularly arrest people for failing to live up to Islamic standards of conduct and for not wearing appropriate attire as prescribed by sharia law.

Western corporations doing business in Saudi Arabia must be certain their representatives comply not only with the letter of the law but also with cultural standards. U.S. military personnel who are there to defend and protect the Saudis may not witness or display any form of Christianity while in public. Male and female airline employees who fly to Saudi Arabia from Western nations must wear clothing and conduct themselves according to Islamic standards.

The Saudis, supposedly one of our staunchest Arab allies in the Middle East, spend billions of dollars from oil profits to promote their radical brand of Islam throughout the world. They especially delight in funding the spread of Islam in American colleges and universities. In 2006 Georgetown University received $20 million from Saudi Prince Alwaleed bin Talal. The university renamed its Center for Muslim-Christian Understanding to the Alwaleed bin Talal Center for Muslim-Christian Understanding. However, those who have examined the Center's agenda say "the Christian part of their projects is conspicuous by its absence."[20] In the last few years, the Saudis have donated $20 million to set up Islamic studies at the University of Arkansas; $5 million went to University of California in Berkeley and $22.5 million was given to Harvard.[21]

The Saudis fund religious schools across the globe, including Great Britain and the United States. They publish textbooks that promote Wahhabism and advocate violence and hatred against Jews and Christians. While Saudi officials claim to have cleaned up their textbooks, recent studies indicate that is not the case. NBC News reported the following teachings are included in textbooks currently being produced in Saudi Arabia:

- Jews and Christians are enemies of Muslims.
- Every religion other than Islam is false.
- The hour of judgment will not come until the Muslims fight the Jews and kill them.
- An eighth-grade textbook equates Jews with "apes" and Christians with "swine."
- A tenth-grade textbook claims a Muslim's life is worth twice that of a non-Muslim.[22]

The New York Times quoted from a textbook for tenth graders produced by Saudi Arabia:

"After examining a number of scriptures which warn of the dangers of having Christian and Jewish friends…it is compulsory for the Muslims to be loyal to each other and to consider infidels their enemy." This statement comes straight from the Qur'an, "O believers, do not hold Jews and Christians as your allies. They are the allies of one another; and anyone who makes them his friends is surely one of them" (Sura 5:50).[23]

The Saudi government has paid for the construction of hundreds of mosques in the United States, Canada and Europe, and yet there is not a single church in Saudi Arabia. They operate the Islamic Saudi Academy in Alexandria, Virginia where Wahhabism is both taught and practiced. In addition the academy uses Saudi textbooks that condemn Jews and Christians as infidels and enemies of Islam.

Ali al-Amed, executive director of the Washington-based Saudi Institute, a leading Saudi opposition group, gave this assessment of another Saudi-sponsored school in Fairfax, Virginia: "It is a school that is under the auspices of the Saudi Embassy. So the minister of education appoints the principal of the school, and the teachers are paid by the Saudi government." Ali al-Amed also said he examined the academy's textbooks and saw passages promoting the hatred of non-Muslims. For example, the eleventh-grade text says one sign of the Day of Judgment will be when Muslims fight and kill Jews, who will hide behind trees and say: "Oh Muslim, oh servant of God, here is a Jew hiding behind me. Come here and kill him."[24]

The Saudis are among the world's top financiers of terrorism. U.S. authorities have "traced millions of dollars received by major jihadi terror groups like Hamas and al-Qaeda back to Saudi and other foreign Islamic charities. They also have traced illegal contributions by U.S. Muslim charities, such as the Holy Land Foundation."[25]

The Saudis must laugh all the way to the bank as they deposit billions of American oil dollars into their accounts, then use the money to promote Islam and support terrorist organizations devoted to the destruction of America and Israel. Literally thousands of extremists that are now destabilizing Muslim and Western nations were trained in Saudi Arabia. And lest we forget, fifteen out of the nineteen hijackers who attacked the United States on September 11, 2001 were from Saudi Arabia. With friends like the Saudis, who needs....Well, you know the rest.

TOLERANCE IS A ONE-WAY STREET

While Muslims demand tolerance from everyone else, they seldom offer it to others. Criticisms of Muhammad or Islam are met with a most vicious response. The cartoons of Muhammad published in Denmark, books critical of Islam and comments by Pope Benedict XVI in 2006 all served as catalysts to set off waves of violence throughout the Muslim world. At the same time, Muslims regularly insult Jews and Christians and question the authenticity of the Holocaust without a word of protest being uttered by their so-called spiritual leaders.

When the dictator of Pakistan, Pervez Musharraf, spoke at the United Nations in 2006, he asked the international body to ban "the defamation of Islam." Less than a year later, the United Nations Human Rights Council adopted a resolution urging nations to pass laws prohibiting the dissemination of ideas that "defame religion." From the overall content of the resolution, it is clear they were not referring to the defamation of Judaism or Christianity but only of Islam.

In 2007 the European Union issued a classified handbook advising government officials and spokesmen not to link Islam and terrorism in their statements. The handbook banned words such as "jihad," "Islamic" or "fundamentalist." Previously the European Union had stated the term "Islamic terrorism" was to be replaced by "terrorists who abusively invoke Islam."[26]

Muslim leaders, the media and liberal politicians in Washington criticized President George W. Bush for referring to terrorists as "Islamic Fascists." Though Bush's definition was accurate, White House speech writers quickly jettisoned that description from presidential speeches and press releases. Daniel Pipes described the Muslims' motives this way:

> The Muslim uproar has a goal — to prohibit criticism of Islam by Christians and thereby impose Shariah norms in the West. Should Westerners accept this central tenet of Islamic law, others will surely follow. Retaining free speech about Islam, therefore, represents a critical defense against the imposition of Islamic order.[27]

Then there is Dr. Akbar S. Ahmed who wants everyone to believe the whole Islamic community stands ready to dialogue with the religions of the world. In the book *Inside Islam,* he stated:

> In spite of the similarities, [between Islam and Christianity] many in the West think of Islam as the civilization most likely to clash with the West. September 11, 2001, confirmed this idea for many. However, it is also worth noting that there are many who believe in an idea opposite to that of the clash of civilizations, and that is the idea of the dialogue of civilizations. And it is worth pointing out that this idea was presented to the United Nations in 1998 by President Mohammed Khattami of Iran. Because his country is known as a land of extremism and fanaticism in the West, people were taken aback, but the idea of dialogue is central to Islam.

However, Pope Benedict XVI did not find the Muslims quite so ready to enter into dialogue.

KILL THE POPE!

While visiting in Regensburg, Germany during the summer of 2006, Pope Benedict XVI delivered a lecture in which he called for a dialogue with the Muslims. Benedict, a brilliant scholar, quoted a fourteenth century Byzantine emperor who said, "Show me just what Muhammad brought that was new, and there you will find things only evil and inhuman, such as his command to spread by the sword the faith he preached." Instead of dialogue, much of the Muslim world went ballistic. Pakistan's legislature unanimously condemned Pope Benedict. An extremist group in Pakistan issued a fatwa calling on Muslims to rise up and kill the Pontiff. Officials in Turkey compared the Pope to Hitler and Mussolini.

Sheik Abu Saqer of Gaza stated in an interview, "The only Christian-Muslim dialogue that is acceptable is one in which all religions convert to Islam." He called for a "holy war" against the Pope, and declared the green flag of Muhammad would soon fly over the Vatican.[28] A sermon on the state-run station in Gaza declared Pope Benedict is "arrogant, stupid, and criminal," and he will be judged by Allah on the day "when eyes will stare in terror." In direct response to the Pope's remarks, Palestinians set fire to five Christian churches in the West Bank and the Gaza Strip.

In Somalia, where over a million Christians have been slaughtered in the past few years, Sheik Abubukar Hassan Malin urged Muslims to find the Pontiff and punish him for insulting the Prophet Muhammad and Allah. "Whoever offends our Prophet Mohammad should be killed on the spot by the nearest Muslim," he said. Apparently unable to get their hands on the Pope, they murdered a Roman Catholic nun instead.

Adjem Choudary, an Islamic radical in London, told a group of demonstrators at Westminster Abbey the Pope is now condemned to death.[29] In Mosul, Iraq, Paulos Iskander, a Syriac priest, was kidnapped and held for ransom. His kidnapers demanded the Pope apologize for his remarks against Islam before any negotiations could begin. A few days later, the priest was beheaded and a fourteen-year-old boy was crucified in al-Basra.

Al-Qaeda representatives in Iraq threatened to "destroy the cross and to slash the throats of those who believe in the cross." The Mujahedeen Sura Council, an umbrella organization of Sunni Arab extremists, issued a statement that threatened to take over Rome: "You infidels and despotic, we will continue our jihad (holy war) and never stop until God avails us to chop your necks and raise the fluttering banner of monotheism when God's rule is established governing all people and nations." They also warned an ultimatum will be given—"conversion to Islam or death by the sword."[30]

So much for Christian-Muslim dialogue!

ALLAH WANTS ME FOR A SUICIDE BOMBER

Today Muslim children are being trained from their earliest years to become suicide bombers (shahid). A video entitled "Ask for Death" that featured two 11-year-old girls was shown on government-run television in Gaza; it depicted the glory of martyrdom (shahada). Some of the dialogue went as follows:

Host: You described shahada as something beautiful.
Walla: Shahada is very, very beautiful. Everyone yearns for shahada. What could be better than going to Paradise?
Host: What is better, peace and full rights for the Palestinian people, or shahada?
Walla: Shahada. I will achieve my rights after becoming a shahada.
Yussra: Of course shahada is a good thing. We don't want this world, we want the afterlife. We benefit not from this life, but from the afterlife. The children of Palestine have accepted the concept that death by shahada is very good. Every Palestinian child aged, say twelve, says, 'Oh Allah, I would like to become a shahid.'[31]

Another telecast that aired March 8, 2007 on Palestinian television further demonstrated the murderous ways of Islamic extremists and their willingness to exploit their own children. The telecast centered on two children of Rim Al-Riyashi who blew herself up at a border crossing on January 14, 2004. Three years later Hamas representatives interviewed her two young children. The script of the interview is as follows:

Interviewer: "Let's talk with the two children of the jihad-fighting martyrdom-seeker Rim Al-Riyashi, Dhoha and Muhammad. Dhoha, you love Mama, right? Where did Mama go?"
Dhoha: "To Paradise."

Interviewer: What did Mama do?"
Dhoha: "She committed martyrdom."
Interviewer: "She killed Jews, right?"
Interviewer: How many did she kill, Muhammad?"
Muhammad: "Huh?"
Interviewer: "How many Jews did Mama kill?"
Muhammad: "This many..."
Interviewer: "How many is that?"
Muhammad: "Five."
Interviewer: "Do you love Mama? Do you miss Mama? Where is Mama, Muhammad?"
Muhammad: "In Paradise."
Interviewer: "Dhoha, what would you like to recite for us?"
Dhoha: "In the name of Allah the Merciful the Compassionate: When comes the help of Allah, and victory, and you see people entering the religion of Allah in troops, then celebrate the praise of your Lord, and ask His forgiveness, for He is ever ready to show mercy." (Sura 110:1-3).[32]

Early in 2007 Hamas broadcast a television program for children, featuring a costumed character dressed like Mickey Mouse. The Hamas Mickey Mouse ranted on about how Jews and Americans should be killed. This type of satanic-inspired education reminds one of the words of Jesus: "It is inevitable that stumbling blocks come, but woe to him through whom they come! It would be better for him if a millstone were hung around his neck and he were thrown into the sea, than that he would cause one of these little ones to stumble."[33]

RECRUITING SUICIDE BOMBERS

How can radical Islamic leaders get people to strap bombs to their bodies and kill themselves and others? First, they teach them the virtues of dying for Allah. Secondly, they make them outlandish promises, some from the Qur'an and others from Islamic traditions.

As soon as the first drop of your blood is shed in jihad, you will feel no pain, all your sins will be forgiven, and you will be transported instantly to paradise where you will recline comfortably for eternity on plush green cushions, to be lavished with the choicest meats, the finest wines and endless sex with seventy virgins. In addition, all of your family members will be admitted into heaven as part of your reward.[34]

Believing they are about to enter Paradise, terrorists usually recite verses from the Qur'an and shout "Allahu Akbar" (God is the greatest) as they carry out their suicide missions.

It is increasingly common for young women to carry out suicide bombing missions. In some cases, they may have committed an infraction of Islamic law, such as an illicit sexual act that brought disgrace to themselves and their families. Rather than face death through an honor killing, they are given the option of making amends by becoming a suicide bomber. These suicide-bombing cases have been documented by Israel.[35]

An internal Pentagon report has linked terrorist violence with the commands of the Qur'an. While the White House tried to avoid linking the two, the report, entitled "National Strategy for Combating Terrorism," stated: "Most Muslim suicide bombers are in fact students of the Qur'an who are motived by its violent commands — making them, as strange as it sounds to the West, 'rational actors' on the Islamic stage."[36]

An article published by *WorldNetDaily* regarding this Pentagon report clearly shows the relationship between the teachings of Islam and the acts of suicide bombers. It stated:

The Pentagon report was produced by an intelligence unit called Counterintelligence Field Activity, or CIFA. It cites a number of passages from the Qur'an dealing with jihad, or "holy" warfare, martyrdom and Paradise, where "beautiful mansions" and "maidens" await martyr heroes. In preparation for attacks, suicide terrorists typically recite passages from six surahs of the Qur'an.

The Pentagon report further states: "His actions [suicide bomber] provide a win-win scenario for himself, his family, his faith and his God. The bomber secures salvation and the pleasures of Paradise. He earns a degree of financial security and a place for his family in Paradise. He defends his faith and takes his place in a long line of martyrs to be memorialized as a valorous fighter. And finally, because of the manner of his death, he is assured that he will find favor with Allah. Against these considerations, the selfless sacrifice by the individual Muslim to destroy Islam's enemies becomes a suitable, feasible and acceptable course of action."

Pierre Rehov, a French documentarian, interviewed the families of suicide bombers and would-be-bombers in an attempt to find out why they do it, says it's not a myth or fantasy of heretics. He says there's no doubt the Qur'an "promises virgins" to Muslim men who die while fighting infidels in jihad, and it's a key motivating factor behind suicide terrorism. "It's obviously connected to religion," said Rehov, who features his interviews with Muslims in a recently released film, "Suicide Killers." They really believe they are going to get virgins. He further states that Muslim clerics do not disavow the virgins-for- martyrs reward as a perverted interpretation of the Qur'an.[37]

Dave Hunt was right when he observed, "Islam does not bring peace. It never has and it never will. This is the result of its very nature. No Muslim can point to even one example in history where Islam ever brought peace. There is no peace even among Muslims themselves anywhere in the world today."[38]

Gregory M. Davis, an authority on Islam, has produced a feature documentary "Islam: What the West Needs to Know," and he has written a book *Religion of Peace? Islam's War Against the World*. Davis, who received his Ph.D. in political science from Stanford University, maintains "Islam is a violent, expansionary ideology that seeks the subjugation and destruction of other faiths, cultures and systems of government." He remarked:

The mistake Westerners make when they think about Islam is that they impose their own views of religion onto something decidedly outside Western tradition. Because violence done in the name of God is "extreme" from a Western/Christian point of view, they imagine that it must be so from an Islamic one. But unlike Christianity, which recognizes a separate sphere for secular politics ("Render unto Caesar what is Caesar's and unto God what is God's"), Islam has never distinguished between faith and power. While Christianity is doctrinally concerned primarily with the salvation of souls, Islam seeks to remake the world in its image.

According to orthodox Islam, Sharia law — the codified commandments of the Quran and precedents of the Prophet Muhammad — is the only legitimate basis of government. Islam is in fact an expansionary social and political system, more akin to National Socialism and Communism than any "religion" familiar to Westerners. Islamic politics is inevitably an all-or-nothing affair in which the stakes are salvation or damnation and the aim is not to beat one's opponent at the polls but to destroy him — literally as well as politically.

Our Leaders Don't Get It!

Prospects for peace between radical Islam and the non-Muslim world could not be bleaker. There is no way to negotiate peace with those who have announced their intention to kill you. The focus of the world is on the Middle East, just as the Bible said it would be at the close of the age. A host of Muslim countries are determined to destroy Israel and implement sharia law from one end of the globe to the other. America and Western nations are being deceived today by the mantra "Islam is a religion of peace."

One of those leading this mantra in Washington DC is Michael Chertoff, head of the Department of Homeland Security. Immediately after the British authorities foiled a plot by Muslim terrorists to blow up ten airliners over the Atlantic in August 2006, Chertoff sent out a one-page memo to Homeland Security staff stating there were "a significant number of extremists engaged in a substantial plot to destroy multiple aircraft flying from the United Kingdom to the United States." One DHS official remarked: "It's ridiculous. 'Extremists' could mean anyone. Who are we talking about here? Neo-Nazi extremists? Environmental extremists? It is so politically correct. If the head of Homeland Security cannot say it, who can?"[39] When the immigration bill was being considered in the Senate in 2007, Chertoff went on one news program after another in support of the bill and challenged anyone who suggested our porous borders were in any way a threat to homeland security.

In January 2007 Secretary of State Condoleezza Rice referred to Hamas as a "resistance movement," a term frequently used by European Union leaders. Hamas is one of the leading terrorist organizations in the Middle East with extensive cells in the United States. They have been on the State Department's terrorist list over twelve years.[40] By assigning this group the nomenclature "a resistance movement" instead of the Islamic terrorist organization they are, the danger posed to Israel and to the free world is greatly enhanced.

One leader who seems to understand the dangers America now faces is Robert S. Mueller, Director of the FBI. In June 2007 Mueller stated it is only a matter of time and economics before terrorists will be able to purchase nuclear weapons, and the world's law-enforcement community must unite to prevent it.[41] While the FBI has done an outstanding job of infiltrating terrorist operations and organizations, preventing them from carrying out their planned attacks, it is unlikely that they will be able to stop them all in time.

American politicians can join hands with moderate Muslims around the camp fire and sing a rousing chorus of Kum Ba Yah, but that will not make the terrorist threat go away. Devastating terrorist attacks and increased global warfare are inevitable if the American people and our leaders do not recognize the imminent danger we are facing from radical Muslims. We must stand up to them while there is still time.

Chapter 9

CONFLICTING FAITHS AND VALUES

News commentators and analysts have referred to the conflict between Islam and the West as a clash of civilizations, but it is really a clash of conflicting faiths and values. While there are substantive theological differences involving the whole spectrum of the Islamic religion, especially issues relating to Jesus Christ, the major difference between Christianity and Islam that prevents meaningful dialogue is Islam's culture of hatred. It is hard to dialogue with people who are determined to kill you.

The Qur'an teaches Islam must supplant all other religions. Islam views all other cultures and religions as enemies that must be opposed or subdued. Islamic values run counter to the values of most other religions. Lies and deceptions are viewed as moral, if they are done for the greater good of Islam. Treaties mean nothing; Islamic leaders speak one thing to the West in public and another thing to their people in Arabic. Yasser Arafat was a master of such deceit.

It is not that other cultures and religions are unwilling to coexist with Islam; Islam is unable or unwilling to coexist with them. Their religion is their government; and their government is their religion. Islam, by its own admission, desires to supplant every other religion and form of government on the globe. Therefore any treaty or peace agreement made with Islamic nations is tenuous at best.

LESSONS FROM HISTORY

Conflicts between Islam and the Jews have existed since the seventh century. Conflicts between Islam and Europe go back nearly as far. After conquering most of the Middle East and North Africa, the Muslims set their sites on the conquest of Europe. Their advance into Europe was halted by Charles Martel at the Battle of Tours in 732.

Few people realize conflicts between Muslim terrorists and the United States preceded the Revolutionary War, when Muslim pirates from Tunis, Morocco, Algiers and Tripoli raised havoc on the high seas by attacking ships that sailed under the flags of European nations and the Colonies.

After the United States was formed, Islamic pirates, who came to be called "the Barbary pirates," continued to attack American ships and kidnap their crews. Because the newly formed nation had no navy, President George Washington authorized extortion demands be paid to the Muslims in order to secure the release of American citizens. The American government continued making extortion payments to the Islamic terrorists for many years. According to historian David Barton, by the end of the John Adams' administration, extortion payments amounted to twenty percent of the federal budget.[1]

As attacks on American ships continued, President John Adams influenced Congress to organize the U.S. Navy. President Thomas Jefferson used the newly formed Navy to transport U.S. Marines to Tripoli and attack the Islamic terrorists who were operating from there. According to Barton it was from the Marine Corps' role in that first conflict with Islamic terrorists the opening line of the Marine Hymn is derived: "From the halls of Montezuma to the shores of Tripoli...."[2]

President Washington authorized John Adams, Benjamin Franklin and Thomas Jefferson to negotiate with the Muslim terrorists. David Barton wrote:

> When they inquired as to why the attacks on American ships were taking place, the Ambassador from Tripoli answered that it was written in their Koran that all nations who should not have acknowledged their authority were sinners; that it was their right and duty to make war upon them wherever they could be found and to make slaves of all they could take as prisoners; and that every Muslim who should be slain in battle was sure to go to Paradise.[3]

History demonstrates the motivation for Muslim terrorists to kill and destroy whomever they deem to be an enemy of their religion has not changed over the centuries. It also shows giving in to terrorist threats or attempting to appease them with financial payoffs does not work either. As the United States finally stood up to the Islamic terrorists and soundly defeated them in the late eighteenth and early nineteenth centuries, so also America and the world must stand up to them today!

A NEW KIND OF ISLAMIC INVASION

The immigration policies of many European countries and their demand for a cheap labor force have given rise to a major influx of Muslims from various parts of the world. The official Muslim population in Europe is listed at twenty million; some believe it may be closer to thirty million.

Bernard Lewis, an expert on Islam and Middle Eastern studies, believes Europe may become predominately Islamic by the end of the twenty-first century.[4] This is due in large measure to Europe's liberal immigration policies, the Europeans' low birth rate, as well as the Muslims' high birth rate. A case in point—the most popular baby boy's name in Great Britain and Belgium is Muhammad. The same is true in Amsterdam and in Malmo, Sweden where Muslims make up one-fourth of the population.[5] Islam is rapidly changing the culture and political landscape of most European and Scandinavian countries.

In an interview with the *Jerusalem Post*, Dr. Lewis said, "Muslims seem to be about to take over Europe." When asked what that might mean for European Jews, he responded: "The outlook for the Jewish communities of Europe is dim. Soon the only pertinent question regarding Europe's future would be, 'Will it be an Islamized Europe or Europeanized Islam?'"[6]

Muslims are not storming the gates of Western nations in order to take them by force; instead they are coming by the millions as immigrants. Once here, their desire to make Islam the supreme religion is just as great as that which prompted their warrior ancestors to invade Europe in past centuries. While Muslims are welcome in the nations of the West, the teachings of Islam make it difficult for them to assimilate into their host countries. Reports show the vast majority of Muslim immigrants still cling to the language and traditions of their home countries and of Islam.[7]

The political climate in the West is changing rapidly. Muslims control huge voting blocks that are influencing governmental policies in several European countries. The reluctance on the part of politicians in France, Germany and other European nations to stand with the United States in the War on Terror has been due in large measure to their perceived need to placate their Muslim constituents. As Islamic influence continues to grow in these countries, they will become even more inclined to side with Muslim interests. This does not bode well for what is about to descend upon the free world.

Prophecies regarding a revived Roman Empire in the last days are seen in a whole new light as the European Union becomes more Islamic in its make-up and geopolitical outlook. Surely the stage is being set for end-time events in ways we could not have imagined even a few decades ago.

MUSLIMS IN GREAT BRITAIN

Three million Muslims reside in Great Britain. More Muslims attend religious services each week in England than Christians.[8] Even though London has more mosques than any other Western city, efforts are underway to build a mosque in East London that will hold 70,000 worshippers, making it the largest mosque outside the Middle East.

The mega-mosque is being proposed by a Muslim group called Tablighi Jamaat. According to the FBI, this group has ties to al-Qaeda. Funding for the project will come from the Middle East said Abdul Khalique, spokesman for Tablighi Jamaat. "The mega-mosque is a mosque for the future, as part of the British landscape," Khalique added.

Dr. Irfan al-Alawi is among several Muslims in London who oppose the construction of the mega-mosque. He sees it as a threat to British national security and a way to increase the influence of Tablighi Jamaat. "Once youth have been brainwashed and been captured by the satanic ideology of the Tablighis, yes, it will come as a very hard-hitting movement," said al-Alawi. He asked, "Is the British government going to turn a blind eye on that and say, 'Let's go ahead and give these people a chance?' I don't think so. If they want a 9/11 in England, then by all means."[9]

There are one million Muslims living in London, half of them are under age twenty-five.[10] Some British now refer to London as "Londonstan." Mark Steyn, a Middle East expert, reported that over sixty percent of British Muslims say they want to live under Islamic law (sharia) in the United Kingdom.[11] A good case can be made sharia law is already being practiced by a significant number of Muslims living there, though in an unofficial way.

The BBC produced a radio program in 2006 entitled "Law in Action," in which they stated sharia law is voluntarily being used by some Muslims as an alternative to English criminal law. They cited cases where certain issues in the Islamic community, such as divorce and assault, were being handled by Muslim officials. They quoted Dr. Prakash Shah, a senior lecturer in law at Queen Mary University of London, who said "such tribunals could be more effective than the formal legal system."

Britain's growing Muslim population is having considerable influence on the nation's educational system. A report by Britain's Department of Education, released in 2007, stated that several public schools have stopped teaching history lessons that include mention of the Holocaust or the Crusades, "because its balanced handling of the topics would directly contradict what was taught in local mosques."[12]

Studies show although many Muslims have lived in Britain for years, today's youth are more inclined to view themselves as Muslims first rather than as British citizens. London has experienced numerous terrorist attacks perpetrated by their own Muslim citizens as well as highly educated immigrants. The firebomb attack in Glasgow, Scotland and the two failed-firebombs discovered in London in June of 2007 were the work of a terrorist cell that included several medical doctors.

Dame Eliza Manningham, head of the British MI5 a counter-terrorist agency, shocked her nation and much of the West when she stated: "Islamic militants linked to al-Qaeda are recruiting teenagers to carry out suicide attacks and plan to use chemical, biological or nuclear weapons if they get the chance." In a speech at Queen Mary College in London, Dame Manningham said the MI5 was presently monitoring about 200 networks engaged in some thirty plots, comprising more than 1600 individuals "who are actively engaged in plotting or facilitating terrorist acts here and overseas." She stated her agency had seen an eighty percent rise in its casework since the start of 2006. She added according to surveys among Muslims (living in Britain) as many as 100,000 people believed the July 7, 2005 atrocities were justified.[13]

A Sunni-Islamic group Hizb ut-Tahrir, with an estimated membership of 10,000 scattered throughout Europe, is causing great concern in Britain. Founded in Jerusalem as an offshoot of the Muslim Brotherhood, Hizb ut-Tahrir is openly anti-democratic and wants to establish a new world order based on uniting the world's 1.3 billion Muslims under a single caliph or successor to Muhammad. Hizb ut-Tahrir argues "Western-style democracy is incompatible with Islam because it allows people to be governed by laws other than those revealed by God."[14]

Great Britain is now paying dearly for its long-established liberal immigration policies. For years, they have allowed Muslims to travel to and from Britain without bothering to stamp their passports or keeping records concerning their whereabouts. British officials estimate 400,000 Muslims travel back and forth from Britain to Pakistan every year. They also know a considerable number of those traveling to Pakistan are connecting with al-Qaeda operatives and participating in their training camps. Many of these same British Muslims upon returning from Pakistan are then able to travel to the United States with a minimum amount of security because of travel agreements between Britain and the United States.

Just how much success Great Britain will have in its "war on terrorism" is unknown, because one of the first acts of Prime Minister Gordon Brown after he took office in June 2007 was to instruct the members of his government not to say "Muslims are terrorists," or use the term "war on terrorism." If the Islamic terrorists are not Muslims, what are they? They certainly are not Baptists, Anglicans or Presbyterians. Do they think that by not saying "war on terror," maybe the "—- on terror" will just go away?

MUSLIMS IN GERMANY

There are about three million Muslims living in Germany, with an estimated 200,000 new immigrants arriving each year. Approximately 1.9 million immigrants are Sunni Muslims who came from Turkey, mostly for economic reasons. While churches in Germany have been in decline for decades, Muslims have erected over 2500 mosques and places of worship. Islam is now the third largest religion in the nation.

There are about 500,000 Muslims living in Berlin where a large section of the city is called "Little Istanbul" by the locals. Many Germans refuse to enter the Islamic sections of the city out of fear of bodily harm. High unemployment among Muslims has caused tensions between Muslims and German citizens to increase.

A high percentage of Muslims do not even try to accommodate the German culture. Recent polls have shown most Muslims consider themselves Muslims first and Germans second. While Germany has been spared thus far from major terrorist attacks, their liberal policies have made it possible for Islamic radicals and terrorists to enter the country and hide inside their Muslim communities.

Several hijackers in the September 11 attacks on America, including Mohamed Atta, trained in Germany and belonged to an al-Qaeda cell in Hamburg. A German counterterrorism report stated about 900 members of the militant Lebanese Shiite organization Hezbollah are operating inside Germany today.[15] An American Defense Department report, published in 2007, revealed as many as 500 al-Qaeda operatives are working inside Germany and plotting attacks on American interests there.

Presently Germany has 700,000 Muslim voters, and that number is growing as more Muslims are recruited into the nation's more liberal political parties. Many believe Gerhard Schroeder's victory in 2002 was due in large measure to his Muslim supporters. German politicians on the left often pander to Muslim citizens by offering them roles in government and promising to promote policies that will conform to their culture and sharia law.

MUSLIMS IN FRANCE

Muslims number nearly five million in France, about ten percent of the country's total population. Some non-Islamic women who live in Muslim neighborhoods have been intimidated to wear head scarves when in public; others feel they must wear the abaya to placate their Islamic neighbors.[16]

High unemployment and radical Islamic teachings have brought riots and mayhem to the streets of France over the past several years, as Islamic young people have sought to voice their many grievances with the French government, mostly high unemployment and not large enough welfare payments.

Young Muslims in France seem to have a penchant for burning cars parked in the streets. In 2005 more than 4700 cars were set ablaze in France as older Muslims cheered them on. Political correctness and fear of retribution have caused French officials to refer to the rioters as "youths," rather than identifying them as Muslims.

About ten percent of all French voters are Muslims. Since the majority of Muslims living in France are under the age of twenty, their political significance will soon be felt at the highest levels of government and throughout the French culture, even more than it is today.

MUSLIMS IN THE NETHERLANDS

Approximately one million Muslims live in Europe's most crowded country, the Netherlands, where an estimated 30,000 new Muslims arrive every year. While most Muslims in the Netherlands immigrated from Turkey and Morocco, a sizeable number came from Iraq and Somalia. The largest mosque in Europe is located in Rotterdam. It is predicted within a decade Muslims could become the majority in Amsterdam, Rotterdam, Utrecht and The Hague. If you count only children under age fourteen presently living in these cities, Muslims already outnumber the native population. Muslim gangs frequently intimidate and harass the Dutch population on the streets, in shopping centers and at sporting events.

In 2004 filmmaker Theo Van Gogh made a critical documentary about Muslims living in the Netherlands. In November of the same year he was shot, his throat slit and a knife in his chest held a five-page manifesto that called on Muslims to rise up against the "infidel enemies" in the West.[17]

An example of Islamic influence is the planned construction of a Muslim hospital in Rotterdam. It will have separate sections for men and women. The men will be treated by a male medical staff, while female patients will be treated by an all-female staff. Non-Muslims will not be welcomed at the new hospital.[18]

A factor compounding tensions between the native residents and immigrant Muslim citizens is the nation's acceptance of homosexuals, prostitutes and a host of liberal policies, including the legalization of drugs. Calls by government officials for Muslims to accept the culture of The Netherlands mean they must also accept or tolerate what the Qur'an deems to be immoral.

MUSLIMS IN AUSTRALIA

Government officials in Australia are not making life easy for the Islamic radicals who are attempting to change Australian culture. Prime Minister John Howard asked Muslims to pledge their loyalty to Australia and her Queen. Australian Treasurer Peter Costello suggested some Muslim clerics might be asked to leave the country if they could not accept the fact Australia is a secular state. "If those are not your values, if you want a country which has sharia law or a theocratic state, then Australia is not for you," he said on national television.

Prime Minister Howard upset some Australian Muslims when he said:

Immigrants, not Australians, must adapt. Take it or leave it. I am tired of this nation worrying about whether we are offending some individual or their culture. Since the terrorist attacks on Bali, we have experienced a surge of patriotism by the majority of Australians.

However, the dust from the attacks had barely settled when the 'politically correct' crowd began complaining about the possibility that our patriotism was offending others. I am not against immigration, nor do I hold a grudge against anyone who is seeking a better life by coming to Australia. However, there are a few things that those who have recently come to our country, and apparently some born here, need to understand. This idea of Australia being a multicultural community has served only to dilute our sovereignty and our national identity. And as Australians, we have our own culture, our own society, our own language and our own lifestyle.

This culture has been developed over two centuries of struggles, trials and victories by millions of men and women who have sought freedom. We speak mainly English, not Spanish, Lebanese, Arabic, Chinese, Japanese, Russian, or any other language. Therefore, if you wish to become part of our society...Learn the language!

Most Australians believe in God. This is not some Christian right wing, political push, but a fact, because Christian men and women, on Christian principles, founded this nation, and this is clearly documented. It is certainly appropriate to display it on the walls of our schools. If God offends you, then I suggest you consider another part of the world as your new home, because God is part of our culture.

We accept your beliefs, and will not question why. All we ask is that you accept ours, and live in harmony and peaceful enjoyment with us. If the Southern Cross offends you, or you don't like "A Fair Go," then you should seriously consider a move to another part of this planet. We are happy with our culture and have no desire to change, and we really don't care how you did things where you came from. By all means, keep your culture, but do not force it on others.

This is our country, our land, and our lifestyle, and we will allow you every opportunity to enjoy all this. But once you are done complaining, whining and griping about our Flag, our Pledge, our Christian beliefs, or our way of life, I highly encourage you to take advantage of one other great Australian freedom, the right to leave. If you are not happy here then leave. We didn't force you to come here. You asked to be here. So accept the country you accepted.[19]

How refreshing it would be if American leaders had the courage to speak the truth as did Prime Minister John Howard.

Liberal politicians in Australia have joined Canada and some European countries in passing a law that makes it a crime to "vilify" people of other religions. This so-called anti-hate law has curtailed free speech, even in pulpits. In 2006 two Australian pastors were convicted of "vilifying" Muslims by quoting verses from the Qur'an at a seminar on jihad. Fortunately, their appeal was upheld and the verdict was overturned; the case must now be retried in the lower courts again. Thus far the pastors have incurred court expenses of approximately $500,000.

MUSLIMS IN THE UNITED STATES

The Muslim population in the United States is estimated to be between three and six million. No one knows the exact number because the Census Bureau does not ask about religious affiliation. There are an estimated 1200 mosques in the United States; most have been built with donations from the government of Saudi Arabia, while several are being served by radical imams.

The majority of Muslims living in America do not have a history of engaging in acts of violence, but their assimilation into our society continues to be a major issue. Consequently, serious problems exist within Islamic communities that threaten harm to the nation unless they are corrected. According to a poll conducted by the *New York Post* in 2007, one in four young Muslims in the United States believes suicide bombings against innocent civilians are sometimes justified. The FBI has documented, and in some cases shut down, several Muslim charities engaged in supporting known terrorist organizations. Most Islamic terrorists who were discovered and arrested in this country were operating under the cover and protection of their Islamic communities. Thanks to Saudi Arabia, the vast majority of the mosques in this country are under the leadership of imams who promote Wahhabism, one of the most extreme and radical forms of Islam.

Muslim Influence in Public Education

Islam is increasingly being taught in the public schools of America. Christian parents have challenged classes on Islam in the Byron Union School District in Contra Costa County, California. But the Ninth Circuit Court of Appeals in San Francisco ruled these classes do not violate any laws. (This is the same Court that ruled children were in violation of the Constitution by saying the words "under God," in the Pledge of Allegiance.) The U.S. Supreme Court rejected an appeal on this case, thus the Islamic indoctrination of our children will continue in America's school districts.

Daniel Pipes reported the New York City Department of Education opened an Arabic-language *public* secondary school in Brooklyn in 2007. The Khalil Gibran International Academy will serve students grades six through twelve and offer multicultural curriculum and intensive Arabic language instruction.[20]

In Ohio a seventh grade social studies textbook presents Islam as a peaceful religion and makes an emphatic but erroneous theological statement that the god of Islam is the same God who is worshipped by Jews and Christians. It is highly remarkable secular educators who normally call for "the separation of church and state" are able to take on the role of theologian in both defining and teaching what they deem to be true Christian doctrine when it suits their purposes. Jews, Christians and Muslims do not worship the same God, even though liberals claim it is so.

Junior Scholastic magazine, distributed in elementary schools across America, published an article in 2006 in which they promoted a school (madrassa) in Pakistan. The article quotes Mohammad Yusef as saying: "There is no terrorism in Islam. Anyone who commits violent attacks in the name of Islam is wrong. Most Muslims want a world that is peaceful, in which there is no terrorism and people live together without fighting. We want a world where the teachings of Allah are followed—a world in which people are modest in attitude and appearances."[21] This statement is very revealing because it begins with a lie—"There is no terrorism in Islam." The same statement ends with a veiled description of Islam's true agenda— to bring about a world "where the teachings of Allah are followed and everyone is modest in attitude and appearances." The only way there will be a world without terrorism or a world where people live together without fighting is when Islam controls the globe. The description about all people living in a modest attitude and appearance will happen when everyone in the world is living under sharia law.

In public schools across America, students are asked to participate in Muslim prayers, recite verses from the Qur'an and assume Muslim names. One Muslim prayer quoted in a public school textbook states: "In the name of Allah, the Compassionate, the Merciful. Praise be to Allah, Lord of Creation, The Compassionate, the Merciful, King of Judgment-day! You alone we worship, and to You alone we pray for help, Guide us to the straight path."[22] One need not wonder how the Ninth Circuit Court of Appeals would have ruled if the course had been about Christianity and had included Christian prayers. In the meantime, has anyone seen the ACLU protesting this ruling?

Colleges and universities across America are remodeling their facilities and revising their rules in order to accommodate members of the Islamic faith. Special rooms for ritual washings, separate living arrangements in dorms, Islamic chapels and paid Muslim chaplains are all becoming part of the annual budgets of American colleges and universities. Some colleges have decided to close their campuses in observance of certain Muslim holy days. At Syracuse University in New York, for example, they have designated "Eid al Fitr," the celebration of the end of Ramadan, as an official school holiday.

Muslim Influence in the Military

The United States Academy at West Point, New York had only two Muslim cadets in 2001; in 2006 there were thirty-two. The Academy opened a worship hall for the Muslim cadets, complete with a pulpit facing Mecca.[23] A similar mosque was dedicated in 2006 at the Marine headquarters in Quantico, Virginia, the first of its kind in the history of the Corps. An estimated 10,000 Muslims are now serving in the various branches of the U.S. military. The Pentagon is presently engaged in a program to recruit as many Arab-speaking Muslims as possible.

Muslim prisoners at Guantanamo Bay, Cuba are served meals in keeping with their religion. Inmates may choose from a menu of 113 Muslim-appropriate meal selections. In addition, every prisoner is given a Qur'an, skull cap and beads. The Muslim chaplain has set up a special program to train guards to be more sensitive to the religious customs of Muslim prisoners.[24]

Muslim Influence in Other Areas

In November 2006 six Muslim imams were ejected from a U.S. Air flight due to what airline staff felt was suspicious behavior. It turned out those ejected from the flight were Muslim clerics returning from a convention. After that incident Islamic leaders demanded a special place of prayer be provided inside the Minneapolis/St. Paul Airport. The imams filed a law suit against U.S. Airlines and the passengers who reported them. Another issue at the Minneapolis/St. Paul airport took place when Muslim taxi drivers refused to haul passengers who carried alcoholic beverages or blind passengers with guide dogs.

Approximately 170,000 Muslims presently reside in the Minneapolis/St. Paul area. A number of Muslims who work in Target stores and at grocery chains have objected to being required to handle pork or alcohol products. Other Muslims in the Twin Cities have protested not being given time off from their jobs to engage in Islamic prayer rituals. In each case, Muslims are demanding the American culture yield to their demands.

Prisons in the United States have become indoctrination centers for Islamic radicals. Muslim prison chaplains, at taxpayers' expense, are given free reign to teach and indoctrinate inmates. In his book *Islam in the Big House,* Steven Schwartz states: "Radical Muslim chaplains, trained in a foreign ideology, certified in foreign-financed schools, and acting in coordination to impose an extremist agenda, have gained a monopoly over Islamic religious activities in American state, federal, and city prisons and jails."[25]

Hidden among America's Islamic communities are terrorist sleeper cells and those who support them through charitable-front organizations. Few Muslims living in America have publicly disavowed acts of terror by Islamic radicals. Most have been silent about denouncing terrorist organizations such as al-Qaeda, Hezbollah, Hamas and Islamic Jihad. Hamas has developed the largest network of cells in the United States. These cells are operating within Boston; New York City; Laurel, Maryland; Potomac, Maryland; Washington, D.C; Herndon, Virginia; Springfield, Virginia; Raleigh, North Carolina; Boca Raton, Florida; Ft. Lauderdale, Florida; Philadelphia; Cleveland; Charlotte; Orlando; Tampa; Detroit; Houston; Columbia; Missouri; Plainfield, Illinois; Kansas City, Kansas; Chicago; Denver; Oklahoma City; Arlington, Texas; Dallas; Tucson; Seattle; San Francisco; Santa Clara; Los Angeles and San Diego.[26]

Steven Emerson in his book *Jihad Incorporated* states FBI agents have expressed concern over Hamas operatives who currently have the capacity to carry out terrorist attacks on American soil.[27] Emerson also cites Khalid Mishaal, political head of Hamas, as saying Hamas is in a battle with the United States and Israel, and he has called on Muslims worldwide to join with the al-Mahdi Army of Iraqi cleric Muqtada Al-Sadr to fight against American forces in Iraq.[28]

It is shocking to learn that Islamic terrorists and their co-conspirators in the West have managed to secure jobs in airports, security agencies and even inside the halls of governments. Four terrorists were arrested in 2007 in a plot to ignite fuel-storage tanks and pipelines at JFK Airport in New York. One of them had been employed by the airport for several years.

Consider the case of Abdurahman Alamoudi who was president of the American Muslim Council and a supporter of Hamas and Hezbollah. Alamoudi had a high-level security clearance and the trust of high officials in Washington. He worked with President Clinton and the American Civil Liberties Union (ACLU) to get approval for the guidelines now used to teach Islam in public schools. Alamoudi appeared with President George W. Bush at a prayer service following the September 11, 2001 attacks on the United States. He was arrested in 2003 for attempting to launder money and send it to Syria.

Mark Steyn describes some of Alamoudi's shocking points of infiltration and influence:

> Alamoudi is the guy who until 1998 certified Muslim chaplains for the United States military, under the aegis of his Saudi-funded American Muslim Armed Forces and Veterans Affairs Council. In 1993, at an American military base, at a ceremony to install the first imam in the nation's armed forces, it was Mr. Alamoudi who presented him with his new insignia of a silver crescent star. He's also the fellow who help devise the three-week Islamic awareness course in California public schools, in the course of which students adopt Muslim names, wear Islamic garb, give up candy and TV for Ramadan, memorize suras from the Koran, learn that "jihad" means "internal personal struggle," profess the Muslim faith, and recite prayers that begin "in the name of

Allah," etc....Mr. Alamoudi was also an adviser on Islamic matters to Hillary Rodham Clinton.[29]

Another revealing case is that of Fawaz Damra, a Palestinian who came to the U.S. in the mid-1980s and became an imam in the largest mosque in Ohio. In that capacity he participated in numerous interfaith gatherings, especially after September 11, 2001.

In 2004 Damra was convicted of concealing his ties to terrorist groups when he applied for U.S. citizenship. At his trial prosecutors presented proof of his involvement with other Islamic leaders in raising money for the Palestinian Islamic Jihad. They also showed a video of a speech he made in Chicago in 1991, in which he said Muslims should be "directing all the rifles at the first and last enemy of the Islamic nation and that is the sons of monkeys and pigs, the Jews."

Prior to serving as imam in Cleveland, Damra served as imam of a mosque in Brooklyn, New York. His successor at that mosque was Omar Abdel-Rahman who was convicted in 1995 of a failed plot to blow up New York City. Damra was deported to the West Bank in 2006.[30]

Unless Western leaders wake up and face the hard cold facts about the religious ideology at the root of terrorism, the United States and our Western allies are going to experience the most devastating terrorist attacks we have ever known. These attacks will surely set the stage for a wide range of prophetic events foretold in the Scriptures. Unless the truth about the Islamic religion is taken into consideration by the American people, and soon, we have little chance of achieving victory or stopping the next assault that will surely come.

WE ARE AT WAR
WITH MILITANT ISLAM!

Militant Islam is a clear and present danger to the entire world. It has three basic goals—the total destruction of Israel, the downfall of the United States and the establishment of Islam as the dominant religion of the world. The hatred of radical Muslims for the United

States is exceeded only by their hatred for Israel. They also have a burning hatred for non-Muslims and for all governments that have not yet committed to Islamic law (sharia).

TERRORISM IS NOT GOING AWAY

Robert Spencer, an authority on Islamic terrorism, reported Islamic jihadists have perpetrated over 5,000 terror attacks since September 11, 2001.[31] He explained all of the September 11 hijackers were Muslims, as were the July 7, 2005 London bombers, and the Madrid train bombers of March 2004. Spencer stated:

All the plotters in the 2006 international airplane hijacking attempts were Muslims. All were working on the basis of Islamic theology. Why must officials continue not to notice this? To ignore this is to give up voluntarily the one thing that may make it possible to spot the perpetrators of a terror attack before it happens, and head it off. In other words, it is suicidal.[32]

The Jerusalem Post reported the Israeli Defense Forces and Shin Bet, an Israel Security Agency, uncovered a Nablus-based terror cell which was manufacturing explosive suicide belts with a liquid explosive material unable to be identified by metal detectors. One person wearing such a belt was caught when he was stopped in Jerusalem for a routine ID check.[33] Nablus is a city in the West Bank presently controlled by Fatah and the Palestinian Authority.

While not all Muslims are terrorists, of course, the number of Muslims who want to forcefully establish Islamic law (sharia) and impose their Islamic way of life on everyone across the globe is astounding. It has been suggested only fifteen to twenty percent of all Muslims are truly radicals. If that is so, it means as many as 250 million Muslims throughout the world are intent upon killing us or subjecting us by force, if we do not conform to their way of life and beliefs.

Bridgitte Gabriel, a knowledgeable and highly articulate expert on Islamic terrorism, offers insight into this matter:

...There are still Americans who are unable or unwilling to recognize the nature and the extent of the threat presented by radical Islam. Whether motivated by naïve wishful thinking or rigid political correctness, they assert that Islam is a 'moderate,' 'tolerant,' and 'peaceful' religion that has been hijacked by 'extremists.' They ignore the repeated calls to jihad, Islamic holy war, emanating from the government-controlled mosques of so-called moderate Islamic countries such as Egypt, Pakistan, and Indonesia. They refuse to accept that in the Muslim world, extreme is mainstream.[34]

Islamic terrorists are among us!

The Islamic terrorists are among us right now in the United States, Canada, Great Britain, Europe and elsewhere. As you read this book, the terrorists are plotting to kill as many people as they can. It is not a question of *if* Islamic radicals will attack us, but only *when* they will attack us. Mahmoud Ahmadinejad of Iran, Kim Jong Il of North Korea and all their ilk are only too willing to supply the terrorists with weapons of mass destruction.

America and various Western nations have taken numerous precautions at airports, utility plants, schools, etc., but we know from watching the terrorists operate in Israel, Iraq and Great Britain, the finest security in the world cannot stop those who are intent on murder and mayhem, especially when they are willing to die for their diabolical cause. We also know as long as the security of this country is hamstrung by left-wing ideologies and politically correct policies, we do not stand a chance of even slowing down, much less thwarting, the diabolical schemes of the terrorists.

Israel has made great strides in stopping the terrorists and suicide-bombers since they erected a wall to separate their nation from the Gaza Strip and the West Bank. Unfortunately, America's borders are so porous, between twelve and twenty million illegal immigrants are presently living in this country. Politicians in both parties want to grant them immunity from prosecution and set them on the path to citizenship. In the meantime, legal and law-abiding immigrants are required to pass through mountains of red tape and wait for months, sometimes for years, before they are permitted to come here. Somehow the unfairness of our immigration policies eludes those in Washington.

The violent and powerful Mexican and Colombian drug cartels move millions of dollars worth of drugs and countless illegals across our southern border every single day. The more they can succeed in this endeavor, the more they will be inclined to smuggle in terrorists and weapons.

The dictator of Venezuela, Hugo Chavez, operates a program from his country in which Muslims are taught to speak Spanish and then smuggled into the United States through Mexico. Chavez, who has a million-man army, is developing alliances with China, Iran, North Korea and Russia. In 2006 Hugo Chavez and Vladimir Putin announced Russia would sell twenty-two Sukhoi Su-30 Russian jet fighters to replace Venezuela's aging F-16 fleet. The deal also includes 100,000 newly developed AK-103 rifles. We may soon face problems at our own doorstep greater than the threats emanating from the Middle East.

Today liberal politicians and members of the liberal media in this country are complaining about profiling, wiretaps and interrogation techniques being used by our government. The liberals have been accusing our military of mistreating terrorists and violating their human rights! All the while, Islamic Fascists are kidnapping civilian workers, news reporters and members of our military, cutting off heads, mutilating and torturing with impunity. It is about time the liberals in this country start talking about the right of the American people to be defended from Islamic terrorists who operate without conscience or moral boundaries. President George W. Bush and respected leaders of our military have repeatedly stated America does not engage in torture.

William Gawthrop, former head of a counterintelligence and counterterrorism program at the Pentagon, warned the Pentagon needs to study the prophet Muhammad and his military doctrine if it wants to beat the growing number of jihadists. He said:

> As late as 2006, the senior service colleges of the Department of Defense had not incorporated into their

curriculum a systematic study of Muhammad as a military or political leader.

The U.S. does not have an in-depth understanding of the war-fighting doctrine laid down by Muhammad, how it might be applied today by an increasing number of Islamic groups, or how it might be countered. The jihadists in Iraq and Afghanistan are simply following the example of Muhammad and using his military doctrine in the Qur'an as a manual of warfare. The Pentagon needs to develop a broad new strategy to deal with the threat from Islamic terrorists. But to do so, officials must first overcome the political taboo of linking Islamic violence to the religion of Islam, including the Qur'an and the Hadiths, or traditions of Muhammad, and exploiting critical vulnerabilities and controversies within the faith itself."[35]

BECAUSE THEY HATE

Brigitte Gabriel, a Maronite Christian, lived through years of Islamic violence and terror in Lebanon. In her book *Because They Hate,* she describes the atmosphere of hatred that existed throughout that war-torn country.

Sunni and Shiite Muslims were taught to hate each other because of a theological disagreement more than twelve centuries old. Muslims in general hated the Christians over a theological disagreement even older, and the Christians hated the Muslims in return. The Christian clans mistrusted and feuded with one another; and the Druze were the odd people out. But everybody had one thing in common: we were all taught to hate Israel and the Jews.

In the universal hatred that was preached against the Jews, virtually no distinction was made between the Jewish religion and the Israeli state. In my Christian private school, we studied only the New Testament. I never saw the Old Testament, because it was considered the enemy's book. All I heard was "Israel is the devil, the Jews are demons, they are the source of all the problems in the Middle East, and the only time we will have peace is when we drive all the Jews into the sea."[36]

BECAUSE WE ARE TAUGHT TO LOVE

Contrast the teachings of Jesus Christ with the teachings of Muhammad. Jesus taught: "Love your enemies and pray for those who persecute you." Muhammad taught: "And when you meet the unbelievers, smite at their necks" (Sura 47:4). Militant Muslims are wrong when they promote hatred, but so are we if we allow their deplorable acts to make us hate them. Because we are at war with militant Islam, we need to recognize there are millions of Muslims who do not share the anger and hatred being promoted by Islamic radicals.

It is extremely difficult to witness to Muslims since they are in bondage to a religion of darkness. Many could be won to Christ if only Christians were willing to share the gospel with them. While most Islamic countries forbid Christian missionary activity of any kind, there are an estimated six million Muslims living here in the United States, and millions more are living in Canada, Europe and other places in the West. The only hope for all people, including Muslims, is Jesus Christ.

It is imperative we use our Christian influence to counteract tendencies in our society towards anti-Muslim sentiments. A Gallup poll taken in the summer of 2006, with 1000 participants, discovered thirty-nine percent of Americans were in favor of requiring Muslims in the United States, including American citizens, to carry special identification. Twenty-five percent said they would not want to live next door to a Muslim.[37]

While we may question many of Islam's teachings and practices, Muslims have the right to live in America without fear, discrimination or prejudice. Christians may not agree with their religion, but our attitude towards them should reflect true Christian love, as well as the American ideals of equality, liberty and justice. Admittedly this may present a huge challenge in the months and years to come, but our faith and our commitment to our American ideals must be honored and preserved.

A Marine Corps colonel, commenting on the conflict being waged between various Palestinian factions in the summer of 2007, said: "I hope they kill each other off. After all, they only want to destroy Israel." Such comments fall far beneath the teachings of Christ. There are thousands of innocent, peace-loving Palestinians living in the Gaza Strip and the West Bank, including Christian Arabs, who do not embrace the hatred demonstrated by Hamas, Fatah and a host of other terrorist organizations. They are, in fact, victims of the Islamic Facists.

While the God of the Bible is not the Allah of the Qur'an, and while the Jesus of the New Testament is not the Jesus portrayed in the religion of Islam, the God of the Judeo-Christian Scriptures loves Muslims. Christ died for Muslims. As Christians we must be careful not to allow our concern over their false teachings, threats or even their vicious terror attacks to diminish our love for them as a people, or our responsibility to witness the gospel of Christ to them.

Two brothers Emir and Ergun Caner were raised in a strict Muslim household in Columbus, Ohio. Yet someone in their neighborhood took the time to invite them to church where they were introduced to Jesus Christ. Today Emir Caner, who has a Ph.D. from the University of Texas, is Assistant Professor of Church History at Southeastern Baptist Theological Seminary in Wake Forest, North Carolina. Ergun Caner, who holds a Th.D. from the University of South Africa, is currently Professor of Theology and Church History at Criswell College, Dallas, Texas.

Walid Shoebat was born in Bethlehem of Judea, Israel. He became a member of the Palestinian Liberation Organization and participated in acts of terror and violence against Israel, according to his book *Why I Left Jihad*. Through studying the Bible, Walid came to realize both he and his religion were wrong, and he yielded his life to Jesus Christ. Today Walid has a most powerful witness regarding the gospel of Jesus Christ, and he unashamedly declares his support for Israel.

Literally thousands of Black Americans are being pursued by Muslim activists and converted to Islam. Christians should witness to Muslims with an even greater tenacity of purpose—to win them to Christ. Why? Because we are taught to love! Jesus said, "But I say to you, love your enemies and pray for those who persecute you, so that you may be sons of your Father who is in heaven."[38]

Chapter 10

RUSSIA AND THE
ISLAMIC CONFEDERATION

Formerly known as Persia, Iran was once the dominant power of the ancient world. Today Iran's president Mahmoud Ahmadinejad seeks to reclaim the nation's former glory by becoming the first Islamic nation in the Middle East to acquire nuclear weapons.

Shiites make up ninety percent of Iran's seventy-one million people; the remaining population is comprised of Sunni Muslims and small Islamic sects. Approximately ten thousand Jews live in Iran, as they have for centuries. Most of the Iranian people are not Arabs but Persians. Their official language is Farsi.

Iran is a theocratic republic that embraces the Shiite form of Islam as its official religion. It has been labeled by the U.S. State Department as a terrorist state, and with good reason. For years Iran has exported terror and supported terrorist organizations throughout the Middle East. They presently support Hezbollah in Lebanon, Hamas in Palestine and the Shiite extremists in Iraq. Undersecretary of State Nicholas Burns stated on a CNN news program in June 2007 there is irrefutable evidence the Iranians have transferred weapons to the Taliban in Afghanistan with the knowledge of the Iranian government.

Ahmadinejad was elected president of Iran in 2005. Prior to that time, he had served as the mayor of Tehran, a city with some seven million residents. The supreme leader of Iran is not Ahmadinejad, however. The man with the most power is the Grand Ayatollah Seyed Ali Khamanei who succeeded the Grand Ayatollah Khomeini in June 1979. Ahmadinejad could not proceed with any of his plans without the sanction of the Ayatollah.

Ahmadinejad sees himself on a divine mission to prepare the way for the Islamic messiah, known as the *Mahdi*. The Shiites refer to the Mahdi as the Twelfth Imam. Ahmadinejad's role, as he sees it, is to launch a holy war against Israel and the United States in order to hasten the coming of the Mahdi. Iran is working feverishly to obtain nuclear weapons; they may be only two years away from meeting that goal. Ahmadinejad, who refers to America as "the great Satan" and to Israel as "the little Satan," (an expression first conjured up by the Ayatollah Khomeini) has repeatedly called for the destruction of Israel and America.

The Iranian leader is determined to involve himself in the Palestinians' struggle against Israel. In a speech given in 2006, Ahmadinejad said: "Palestine is the front line of the Islamic nations in their struggle against the aggressive superpowers."[1] On February 1, 2007, seven members of the Iranian military, including a general in the Iranian Revolutionary Guard, were captured in Gaza by members of Fatah security forces.

Iran has succeeded in smuggling sophisticated arms and improvised explosive devices (IEDs) into the hands of Iraq's al-Qaeda terrorists and Shiite insurgents. These weapons have been responsible for the deaths of literally hundreds of American military personnel. The only response to this aggression from the United States thus far has been a low-keyed discussion by government leaders on whether or not we ought to enter into some sort of dialogue with Iran. A few brave hearts, such as Senator Joseph Lieberman of Connecticut, have recommended we bomb Iranian strongholds in or near Iraq.

A conference for terrorist leaders, entitled "A World without Zionism," was held in Tehran, October 26, 2005, during which Ahmadinejad declared: "Is it possible for us to witness a world without America and Zionism? But you had best know that this slogan and this goal are altogether attainable, and surely can be achieved. This regime that is occupying Jerusalem must be wiped from the map." The Iranian president then urged Muslims to prepare for the day when "our holy hatred expands" and "strikes like a wave."[2]

IRAN IN BIBLE TIMES

Persia's history is ancient, and its role in end-time events is significant. Biblical accounts relating to Persia date to Elam, son of Shem and grandson of Noah. The King of Elam, Chedorlaomer, was among the coalition of kings who attacked Sodom and carried off Abraham's nephew Lot. Abraham rescued Lot after defeating Chedorlaomer and the kings who were with him.[3]

The entire Middle East region came under the control of King Nebuchadnezzar of Babylon (605-562 BC). Many years later the Medes and the Persians became the dominant force in the region. The Medes and Persians were united under Cyrus II who defeated Babylon and ruled the region, as was prophesied by Daniel at the feast of Belshazzar.[4] King Cyrus decreed the Temple in Jerusalem should be restored.[5]

The Persian King Darius played a significant role in Israel's history when he gave the order for the work on the Temple to continue.[6] Queen Esther was married to King Xerxes I, known also as Ahasuerus (486-465 BC), when she saved the Jewish people in Persia from extermination. And it was Persian King Artaxerxes Longimanus I (464-424 BC) who commissioned Nehemiah to rebuild the walls of Jerusalem.[7]

THE FOCUS OF END-TIME EVENTS

Today most nations of the world are aligned either for or against Israel. Islamic nations, each with deeply rooted hatred for the Jews, surround the Jewish state. Even so-called moderate Islamic nations cannot disguise their hatred for Jews in general and for Israel in particular. Calls for Israel's destruction by Iran and numerous Islamic terrorist organizations are more than just threats; they are backed by active plans and military preparations. Such animosity against Israel at the end of the age was prophesied in the Scriptures. According to the Bible, Israel will be the focal point for end-time events.

Peace without Israel

There is a general consensus among most Western leaders until the Israeli/Palestinian situation is resolved, peace in the Middle East cannot be achieved. Since 1948 European and U.S. diplomats have been trying to come up with a workable peace plan between the Israelis and the Palestinians. There is one problem with such plans—neither the Palestinians nor the Islamic states in the region want peace with Israel. While most Israelis desire peace and would enter into a peace agreement today if it was fair, just and sincere, the Muslim's ultimate objective is to drive the Jews into the sea.

Efforts to create peace between Israel and the Palestinians have been thwarted by the unwillingness of Islamic governments and Palestinian terrorist groups to recognize Israel's right to exist. Some would-be-peacemakers have suggested that should the Israelis return to the pre-1967 borders, peace might be possible. Such a proposal begs the question of what prompted the wars of 1948, 1956 and 1967 when Israel existed within those borders.

Neither the Palestinians nor the surrounding Muslim nations have any intention of creating a Palestinian state at peace with neighboring Israel; they want every square inch of the Jewish state and Jerusalem as their capital, peace agreements and promises notwithstanding. Until the last Jew is driven from the land and Israel no longer exists, their enemies will go on attacking them.

One can easily see how the whole world will go after a charismatic leader who will come onto the world stage with what seems like a workable plan to bring peace to this troubled region. The Bible identifies that person as the antichrist. Even now the world stage is being set for the antichrist and his phony peace agreements.[8] Armageddon and the wars that will precede it may not be far off. The Bible describes a major attack on Israel by a group of nations at the time of the tribulation.[9] At the end of the tribulation, an even larger attack against Israel will take place.[10]

These prophecies are brought to mind as Iran's president, Mahmoud Ahmadinejad, continues to threaten Israel with annihilation. No one knows for certain what this maniacal leader might do, but it would be a tragic mistake not to take his threats seriously. If Iran is permitted to develop nuclear weapons and the capacity to deliver the same, anything could happen! A nuclear Iran will have repercussions for the entire world.

Since Iran is already furnishing arms to terrorist organizations, the likelihood they would make nuclear devices available to terrorist groups is extremely high. North Korea, Pakistan, China and Russia are also likely candidates when it comes to furnishing nuclear components to terrorist organizations. Few people in the West, especially politicians in Washington, seem to understand just how serious these threats have become.

Stop Him!

Benjamin Netanyahu, former Prime Minister of Israel, stated: "It's 1938 and Iran is Germany; and Iran is racing to arm itself with atomic bombs. Believe him and stop him. This is what we must do. Everything else pales before this." He also said: "No one cared then (1938) and no one seems to care now." Netanyahu insists Iran's nuclear and missile program "goes way beyond the destruction of Israel—it is directed to achieve world-wide range. It's a global program in the service of a mad ideology."[11]

Former Secretary of State Henry Kissinger said, "If Iran is allowed to produce nuclear weapons, the genie will be out of the bottle, and the whole world will be in grave danger."[12]

Newt Gingrich, former US Speaker of the House of Representatives, remarked:

> Israel is in the greatest danger it has been in since 1967...People are greatly underestimating how dangerous the world is becoming. Our enemies are quite explicit in their desire to destroy us. They say it publicly. We are sleep-

walking through this process as though it's only a problem of communication.

Our enemies are fully as determined as Nazi Germany, and more determined than the Soviets. Our enemies will kill us the first chance they get...If we knew that tomorrow morning we would lose Haifa, Tel Aviv, and Jerusalem, what would we do to stop it? If we knew we would tomorrow lose Boston, San Francisco, or Atlanta, what would we do? Today, those threats are probably one, two, five years away. Although, you can't be certain when our enemies will break out.[13]

President George W. Bush, Israeli Prime Minister Ehud Olmert and the United Nations have vowed Iran will not be allowed to develop a nuclear bomb. However, after all the challenges the United States has had to endure in Iraq, it is highly unlikely our country will embark on another Middle East conflict without extreme provocation. At the same time, leaders in Washington continue to insist when it comes to Iran's nuclear program "all options remain on the table." It is highly improbable Israel will attack Iran, unless, of course, it becomes an issue of survival or unless they are attacked first. Iran's proximity to Israel and Iran's ability to retaliate against Israel's population centers make an attack similar to the one Israel conducted against Iraq's nuclear facilities in 1981 very dangerous.

The United Nations is incapable of stopping Iran with or without sanctions. It is highly unlikely Russia and China, permanent members of the Security Council, will ever agree to go against their oil-rich Iranian ally. The sinister nature of the present Iranian government appeals to the oppressive governments of both China and Russia.

In 2006 then British Prime Minister Tony Blair commented to Western leaders on the dangers posed by Mahmoud Ahmadinejad: "I have never come across a situation of the president of a country saying they want to wipe out—not that they've a problem with, or an issue with, but want to wipe out another country.... Can you imagine a state like that with an attitude like that having nuclear weapons?"[14]

In an appearance on *Meet the Press,* Senator John McCain commented on Iran's nuclear ambitions: "...there is only one thing worse than using the option of military action, and that is the Iranians acquiring nuclear weapons. If Iran gets the bomb, I think we could have Armageddon."[15]

Intelligence sources indicated Iran's confidence has been bolstered by the tepid response of the United Nations to North Korea's underground tests of a nuclear weapon, as well as Britain's response to the capture of fifteen members of their military in March 2007. Unless the West finds its courage to stop Iran, Ahmadinejad will continue with his nuclear development.

PEACE, PEACE, BUT THERE IS NO PEACE

For several years Fatah and Hamas have been vying with one another for the control of the Gaza Strip and the West Bank. Hamas won the majority of seats in the legislature in 2006; however, Fatah retained control of the presidency of the Palestinian Authority. The two factions managed to set up a unity government which lasted for three months; then a civil war broke out in 2007, allowing Hamas to gain control of both the government and the military in Gaza. Fatah retained control of the West Bank, however. It is all but certain Hamas will eventually challenge Fatah for control over the West Bank or Fatah will challenge Hamas for control of the Gaza Strip.

The United States, with the cooperation of Prime Minister Ehud Olmert, tried to prop up Mamoud Abass and his Fatah forces in the first half of 2007 by sending supplies of arms and financial aid, but most of the guns and money ended up in the hands of Hamas.

Since Hamas' successful takeover of the Gaza Strip, the United States has been pouring millions of dollars into the hands of Mamoud Abass in the West Bank, hoping he will be able to put the peace process on track again. Aiming for the same objective, Israel released $700 million of the tax money they had been withholding from the Palestinian Authority. This policy seems to be aimed at isolating Hamas, but even if successful, this ill-conceived idea could end up producing a "three-state" solution — Israel and two separate

Palestinian entities. This is a very risky strategy, since Fatah is also determined to destroy the Jewish state. In 2007 when Hamas and Fatah were shooting at each other in the Gaza Strip, Mamoud Abass, the supposed *moderate* president of the Palestinian Authority, told the two sides to "stop fighting one another and turn their guns on Israel."

Over the next few years, the pressure exerted on Israel by Western powers to sign a peace agreement with the Palestinians is bound to be overwhelming. The United States and the European Union will ask Israel to give up more territory and offer major concessions on Jerusalem in order to achieve peace with the Palestinians. It will take a very strong Prime Minister who has the full backing of the Knesset to resist such pressure.

ISRAEL'S FRIENDS AND DETRACTORS

While the United States has been a strong supporter of Israel since 1948, there are an amazing number of influential people from both major political parties whose support for Israel is less than stellar. Some do not even try to disguise their bias against the Jewish state.

In 2006 a bi-partisan panel, headed by former Secretary of State James Baker and former congressman Lee Hamilton, was asked to formulate recommendations to help resolve the conflict in Iraq. Some of the panel's recommendations were little more than a capitulation and surrender to the terrorists. One recommendation called for the United States to put pressure on Israel to give up all claims to the Golan Heights. Another recommendation from the panel called for talks with Syria and Iran in order to enlist their help in stabilizing Iraq.

James Baker personally called on President Bush to organize an Arab summit to solve the dispute between Israel and the Palestinians. Baker's anti-Israel bias became evident to all when he indicated Israel would not be invited to participate.

The Jimmy Carter Factor

Former President Jimmy Carter has long sided with the Palestinians over Israel. In his book *Peace, Not Apartheid*, Carter described Israel as an apartheid state. He claimed Israel is largely responsible for the failures of the peace process, and he further stated Israel was responsible for the Christian exodus from the Holy Land; none of these statements is true. In 2007 Carter cautioned Iowa primary voters not to vote for any candidate who supports Israel over the Palestinians.

Fourteen members of the Carter Center advisory board resigned in protest over the former president's book. In their letter of resignation, the members stated: "You have clearly abandoned your historic role of broker in favor of becoming an advocate for one side."

Carter raised the ire of many Jews and supporters of Israel for berating Israel in his new book. Rabbi Marvin Heir, dean of the Simon Wiesenthal Center in Los Angeles, said: "President Carter has only himself to blame because his book was blatantly one-sided and unbecoming of a former President."[16]

Monroe Freedman, former executive director of the government's Holocaust Memorial Council during the Carter administration, revealed he once received a hand-written memo from then President Carter, stating Freeman's recommendations for council board members contained "too many Jews." The purpose of the Council was to establish the Holocaust Memorial Museum in Washington. Freedman said after revising the list with more non-Jews, he was "stunned" when Carter's office objected to a Holocaust scholar who happened to be a Presbyterian because his name sounded Jewish. Freedman said he decided to speak up after reading Carter's book.[17]

While speaking in Ireland at their eighth annual Forum on Human Rights in June 2007, Jimmy Carter said the Bush administration's refusal to recognize and accept Hamas' 2006 election victory was "criminal." He also blamed the Bush administration for Hamas' takeover of the Gaza Strip, saying "the United States and Israel decided to punish all the people in Palestine and did everything they could to deter a compromise between Hamas and Fatah." The former president's bias against Israel is one thing; his inability to distinguish between Islamic terrorists and a responsible Palestinian government is quite another. His statements reveal a distorted view that can be traced back to his own administration's failure to obtain the release of fifty-two American hostages who were held by Iran for 444 days.

Broken Promises

Politics continue to play a role in the way various governments view Jerusalem, Israel's capital. Succumbing to political pressure in 2006, Costa Rica and El Salvador moved their embassies from Jerusalem to Tel Aviv, leaving not a single foreign embassy in Jerusalem. In 1995 Congress voted to move the United States Embassy from Tel Aviv to Jerusalem, but neither Presidents Bill Clinton nor George W. Bush ever took the necessary steps to make it happen.

Prior to his election to the presidency in 2000, George W. Bush declared his first act as president would be to move our embassy to Jerusalem. In December 2006 President Bush again delayed moving the U.S. embassy for another six months, citing national security concerns. The President said: "Moving our embassy from Tel Aviv to Jerusalem now would complicate our ability to help Israelis and Palestinians advance toward peace and the president's two-state vision."[18]

MORE TROUBLE IN THE REGION

The terrorist organization Hezbollah is doing everything possible to seize control of the government of Lebanon. Even some Christian groups in Lebanon have aligned themselves with Hezbollah in an attempt to overthrow the present government, but they are making a tragic mistake. If Hezbollah gains control of the Lebanese government, these Christian parties will be cast aside and an Islamic state under sharia law will be established. Israel will end up facing a highly armed and dangerous enemy at its northern border such as it has not known before.

Israel attacked Hezbollah in the summer of 2006, after the terrorist organization killed two Israeli soldiers and kidnapped two others and after they rained down rockets on Israel's northern cities. Since the war Hezbollah continues to hold the two kidnapped Israeli soldiers, and it has been rearmed by Iran and Syria. Today Hezbollah possesses 20,000 short and long-range rockets ready to be launched into Israel, in spite of agreements that ended their war with Israel in 2006, and in spite of the fact thousands of UN peacekeepers are presently stationed in Lebanon to prevent a re-supply of arms.

Bashar Assad of Syria, who has a close relationship with Iran, wants political control over Lebanon and the return of the Golan Heights seized by Israel in 1967. Iran is determined to help the Shiite faction in Iraq gain control of the Iraqi government. To that end they continue to support the Iraqi insurrection by funneling men and weapons through Iraq's porous borders. The idea Iran can become a peace partner in Iraq is absurd; they are, in fact, instigators of and participants in the war itself.

In many ways the present situation in Iraq and the Gaza Strip mirror what is waiting on the rest of the world should Iran and the Iraqi Shiites have their way. If Iraq falls to the Shiites, the country will become a pawn of Iran and a haven for terrorists. Sunnis and Kurds in Iraq will be forced into surrender or engage in a civil war which will only result in a bloodbath. If Iraq falls to the radicals, the likelihood of the entire Middle East plunging into chaos seems all but inevitable.

If Lebanon falls to Hezbollah, if Gaza and the West Bank end up under the control of Hamas, and if Iran continues to gain dominance in the region, the present situation in the Middle East will degenerate into chaos in moderate Islamic countries. Such a possible outcome has Egypt, Jordan and the Persian Gulf states greatly concerned.

THE UNITED NATIONS

The United Nations is a failed organization, corrupt to the core. Even their most respected humanitarian projects have been pilfered by greedy governments, politicians and UN officials at the highest level. An anti-U.S.A. bias in the UN is no longer disguised. The President of the United States and our nation have been repeatedly maligned from the podium of the UN General Assembly.

UN leaders have never tried to disguise their bias against Israel. For years they have operated with a "blame Israel first" policy, no matter what happens in the Middle East. Over the years numerous resolutions condemning Israel have been drafted in the United Nations Security Council; most failed to pass only because of the veto power of the United States.

Dave Hunt in his book *Judgment Day* writes:

Israel has been a member of the United Nations for more than fifty years. Yet she is not allowed to take her two-year turn as one of the ten rotating nations (joining the five permanent ones) on the UN Security Council. Of the 191 current UN members, 190, including the worst terrorist nations, are allowed to take their turns on the Security Council—but not Israel. Nor is Israel...allowed to take a rotating term on the fifty-three member UN Commission on Human Rights.[19]

TROUBLEMAKERS

The Russian government, under the leadership of Vladimir Putin, is not a true friend of the United States or Israel. In fact, Russia with its advanced weaponry and nuclear arms remains a significant danger to the cause of world peace. Over the past several years, Russia has armed Iran and Syria with sophisticated arms, planes and rockets. Iran and Syria, in turn, have armed Hezbollah, Hamas and other terrorist organizations with the same weapons.

Just about anywhere you find a menacing dictatorship or a government with animus toward America or Israel, you will find the Russians giving them aid and support in one form or another. Whether it's Hamas, Hezbollah, North Korea, Venezuela, Syria or Iran, Russia seems to find some way to form an alliance with America's enemies, either through trade or by selling armaments to them.

In 1995 the Russians made an $800 million deal with Iran to build a nuclear plant in Bushehr and train over a thousand nuclear scientists. Much of the blame for the present crisis over Iran's nuclear program can be laid at the feet of Russia. Between 1989 and 1993, Iran acquired $10 billion worth of arms from Russia. Iran also signed a deal with Russia in November 2005 for an additional $1 billion worth of missiles and defense systems, including up to thirty Tor-M1 missile systems. Since that agreement, the missiles have been delivered. American officials have indicated Russia is negotiating to sell even more powerful long-range S-300 air defense missiles to Iran.[20] According to Israeli sources, Russia is planning to sell advanced MIG-31 fighter planes to Syria. This plane is capable of carrying guided missiles and striking twenty-four different targets simultaneously.

Russian president Vladimir Putin, who has taken more and more power for himself in recent years, is moving away from the democratic strides the Russian people have gained since the breakup of the Soviet Union. Senator Lindsey Graham of South Carolina referred to Putin as a one-man dictator. "He's a problem, not a solution, to most of the world's problems," said Graham. "He could help us with Iran if he chose to. He is becoming basically a one-man dictatorship in Russia."[21]

Communist China also has close ties with Iran, since China imports about ten percent of its oil from Iran. Every year the Chinese sell millions of dollars worth of arms to Iran; many have ended up in Iraq and Afghanistan. In 2005 the Chinese government signed a $70 billion agreement to modernize Iran's oil and gas fields. It is mostly the Chinese and the Russians who are preventing the West from halting Iran's nuclear ambitions. It is difficult to understand why the United Nations and major world powers are willing to allow Iran to go nuclear, in spite of warnings, sanctions and threats. One day the world will pay a huge price for such a foolhardy policy.

North Korea, Venezuela and Iran, each led by a brutal dictator, have become fast friends since they share a common enemy, the United States. Early in 2007 North Korea agreed to shut down its nuclear facilities if the United States agreed to give them millions of dollars and release North Korean funds that had been frozen. Still, it is unlikely North Korea will change its ways.

North Korea and Iran have been exchanging nuclear and missile technology for several years. North Korea has agreed to share information with Iran on underground nuclear testing. A senior European defense official stated: "The Iranians are working closely with the North Koreans to study the results of their last nuclear test. All indications are that the Iranians are preparing their own underground test. According to Western intelligence agencies, there has been an increase in the number of North Korean and Iranian scientists traveling between the two countries."[22]

IS THE ISLAMIC MESSIAH
CONNECTED WITH THE ANTICHRIST?

Muslim Shiites believe in a coming messiah who is called by various names—the Mahdi, the Twelfth Imam or the Hidden Imam. He is not, of course, the promised Messiah of the Bible, but rather an ancient imam who disappeared as a child in 941. Islam teaches the Mahdi, a direct descendant of Muhammad, will return to establish peace, justice and brotherhood on earth. To that end he will place the whole world under Islamic law (shiria). The cross will be taken down from each church spire, and Islam's star and crescent will rise in its place.

While Sunni Muslims believe in a coming messiah (the Mahdi), they do not believe in the Twelfth Imam. There is actually no mention of the Mahdi in the Qur'an. The lore regarding this Islamic messiah comes from later traditions. According to Shiite eschatology, the Mahdi will return to the Ka'aba in Mecca, from where he will reign over the earth for *seven years* before the final judgment. At the time of his coming, there will be a global war with catastrophic destruction. The Mahdi himself will muster an army and fight the enemies of God. After all Islam's enemies are defeated, he will establish his global government in the city of Kufa, located about 110 miles south of Baghdad.

A broadcast over official Iranian radio in January 2007 focused on the coming of the Mahdi, not setting a certain date but saying it was very soon. They claim when the Mahdi comes, the prophet Jesus will be with him. A speaker on the broadcast stated:

Another beautiful moment of the Savior's appearance is the coming down of Prophet Jesus from heaven. Hazrat Mahdi receives him courteously and asks him to lead the prayers. But Jesus says you are more qualified for this than me. We read in the book Tazkarat ol-Olia, "the Madi will come with Jesus son of Mary accompanying him." This indicates that these two great men complement each other. Imam Mahdi will be the leader while Prophet Jesus will act as his lieutenant in the struggle against oppression and establishment of justice in the world. Jesus had himself given the tidings of the coming of God's last messenger and will see Mohammad's ideals materialize in the time of the Mahdi.

No one believes more strongly in the coming of the Mahdi than Mahmoud Ahmadinejad. As the mayor of Tehran, Ahmadinejad widened the city's boulevards in order to make way for the coming of the hidden imam.[23] He constantly speaks about the return of the Mahdi and sees himself as the one who will prepare the way for his coming. One of the chief reasons Iran wants to help the Shiites take control of Iraq is to facilitate the return of the Mahdi. Since Ahmadinejad's views about the Mahdi are central to his governmental policies, the world could be in for a very bumpy ride during the next few years, especially if Iran succeeds in getting control of Iraq.

In a speech before the United Nations General Assembly in September 2006, Ahmadinejad offered these comments and a prayer:

> I emphatically declare that today's world, more than ever before, longs for just and righteous people with love for all humanity; and above all longs for the perfect righteous human being and the real savior who has been promised to all peoples and who will establish justice, peace and brotherhood on the planet.
>
> Oh, Almighty God, all men and women are your creatures and you have ordained their guidance and salvation. Bestow upon humanity that thirsts for justice, the perfect human being promised to all by you, and make us among

his followers and among those who strive for his return and his cause.[24]

Comparing the Mahdi with the Antichrist

One should not fail to see the similarity between the Muslim's messiah and the antichrist as described in Daniel and Revelation. This is not to say the Mahdi is the antichrist, but the Mahdi and other aspects of Islamic teaching have the hallmarks of the antichrist. The spirit of the antichrist is anything that opposes Christ.

The Bible reveals at the end of the age the antichrist will arise from a group of ten leaders in the revived Roman Empire. In the beginning his leadership will be somewhat obscure, though eventually he will succeed in elevating himself as the world ruler.[25] The antichrist will make a peace treaty with Israel for seven years, but according to the Bible, he will break it in three and a half years. He will also persecute the saints of God.

In Revelation 20 a description of the method of execution imposed on the saints who are killed during the tribulation because of their faith in Jesus Christ turns out to be the favorite method of execution used by radical Muslims today—*beheading*. This is very significant as it relates to present world conditions and the prophecies of Christ's coming.

> "And I saw the souls of those who had been *beheaded* because of their testimony of Jesus and because of the word of God, and those who had not worshipped the beast or his image, and had not received the mark on their forehead and on their hand; and they came to life and reigned with Christ for a thousand years."[26]

Iran's quest to become a nuclear power is moving forward in spite of declarations and demands by the United Nations. Should Iran succeed in their nuclear ambitions, it will become the *tenth* nuclear power in the world. That number could well coincide with the ten kings described in Daniel and the Book of Revelation. This fact gives cause for pause, since Ahmadinejad has stated his mission is to "pave the path for the glorious reappearance of Imam Mahdi; may Allah hasten his reappearance."[27]

According to the Bible, the antichrist will rise to power on a platform of peace.[28] Mahmoud Ahmadinejad, the harbinger of hatred against Israel and the United States, recently stepped forward to offer himself as a peacemaker of the Middle East. Many politicians in America and Europe seem eager to embrace Ahmadinejad or anyone else who can bring peace and stability to that part of the world. This is not meant to imply Ahmadinejad is the antichrist, but merely to point out if the world is willing to turn to him as a broker of peace in Iraq or anywhere else, one can readily see how the antichrist will be able to deceive the masses.

IRAN AND RUSSIA IN PROPHECY

The Persian Empire, which lasted from 539 to 331 BC, was the second portion of the statue in Nebuchadnezzar's dream that detailed the rise of four world governments; it was shown as the chest and arms made of silver.[29] As Babylon was known for its gold, Persia was known for its silver. Alexander the Great acquired between twelve and eighteen million pounds of silver when he captured Persia.[30] The Bible reveals Persia (Iran) will survive and go to war against Israel in the end-times.

Ezekiel 38 and 39 disclose how Persia will become part of a confederation of nations led by Gog of the land of Magog and Rosh. *Magog* is identified by the historian Josephus as being in the area of existing Islamic states that once were part of the Soviet Union, while *Rosh* is linked by conservative scholars to modern-day Russia. Ezekiel described a prince named Gog leading a mighty army from "the remote parts of the north." Prophecy scholars have always pointed to the fact the northern-most country from Israel is Russia. But strange as it may seem, Russia is now trying to claim the entire North Pole region with its oil and gas reserves. If Russia's claims are successful, it will give a whole new meaning to the Bible's description of "Gog leading an army from "the *remote* parts of the north."

Other nations identified in Ezekiel 38 and 39 include Libya (Put), Sudan (Ethiopia) and portions of Turkey (Gomer and Togarmah).

Ezekiel detailed how this confederation of nations would attack the restored nation of Israel in the last days. While there are differences of opinion among Bible scholars as to the precise identity of some of the nations mentioned in these two chapters of Ezekiel, there is little doubt regarding the identity of either Russia or Iran. All of these countries listed in these two chapters of Ezekiel are Islamic, except Russia.

Ezekiel 39 described a great battle that will bring about the destruction of all the forces arrayed against Israel. It will take seven months to bury the dead and seven years for Israel to dispose of all the armaments. This prophetic battle will likely take place prior to the tribulation or in its earliest stages. Most likely this invasion of Israel and the events surrounding it will give rise to the antichrist.

The Giant Hook

Today Iran and Russia are allied economically and militarily, even though they had been enemies for years. Ezekiel prophesied about Russia:

> "I will turn you about and put hooks into your jaws, and I will bring you out, and all your army, horses and horseman, all of them splendidly attired, a great company with buckler and shield, all of them wielding swords; Persia, Ethiopia [Cush] and Put with them, all of them with shield and helmet; Gomer with all its troops, Beth-togarmah from the remote parts of the north with all its troops — many people with you" (Ezekiel 38:4).

Mortimer B. Zuckerman, in an article in *US News and World Report*, quoted an American diplomat who described Russia's business with Iran as a "giant hook in Russia's jaw." It is amazing a diplomat would use the exact words of Ezekiel when describing Russia's involvements with Iran.[31]

Zuckerman also said:

> Iran today is the mother of Islamic terrorism. Tehran openly provides funding, training, and weapons to the world's worst

terrorists, including Hezbollah, Hamas, the Palestinian Islamic Jihad, and the Popular Front for the Liberation of Palestine, and it has a cozy relationship with al Qaeda. It has given sanctuary to major al Qaeda terrorists, including senior military commander Saif al-Adel, three of Osama bin Laden's sons, and al Qaeda spokesman Suleiman Abu Ghaith. It supports many of the barbaric terrorists in Iraq who are murdering innocent civilians in order to destroy Iraq's fragile hold on democracy. Through its 900-mile border with Iraq, Iran is flooding its neighbor with money and fighters. It is infiltrating troublemakers into Afghanistan, supporting terrorism against Turkey, sustaining Syria, and had a hand in the Khobar Towers bombing in Saudi Arabia.[32]

Iran is the central player on the world-stage!

When Robert Gates was being considered by the U.S. Senate for the cabinet post of Secretary of Defense, a senator asked him if he thought Iranian President Ahmadinejad was "kidding" when he denied the Holocaust and called for "wiping Israel off the map." Gates responded,

No, I don't think he's kidding. But I think that there are, in fact, higher powers in Iran than he. And while they are certainly pressing, in my opinion, for a nuclear capability, I think that they would see it in the first instance as a deterrent. They are surrounded by powers with nuclear weapons — Pakistan to their east, the Russians to the north, the Israelis to the west, and us in the Persian Gulf.

The senator then asked Gates, "Can you assure the Israelis that they will not attack Israel with a nuclear weapon, if they acquire one?" He responded,

No, sir, I don't think anybody can provide that assurance.... While Iran cannot attack us directly militarily, I think that their capacity to potentially close off the Persian Gulf to all exports of oil, their potential to unleash a significant wave of terror both in the Middle East and in Europe and even here in this country is very real....They could provide certain kinds of weapons of mass destruction, particularly chemical and biological weapons to terrorist groups. ...They have the capacity to do all of these things, and perhaps more than I just described."[33]

Some Israeli officials interpreted Gates' comments to mean the United States would not try to stop Iran from obtaining nuclear capability. They also took his words to mean a nuclear attack on Israel by Iran could happen. Gates' comments were quite unsettling to many Israelis.

The International Atomic Energy Agency (IAEA) reported in 2006 Egypt, Morocco, Algeria and Saudi Arabia have expressed interest in developing nuclear power for desalination purposes. Supposedly if and when these nations are ready to proceed, the IAEA said it will assist them to build their nuclear power plants.[34] Since that report Jordan has also expressed interest in developing nuclear power, and the IAEA has recommended to the United Nations Iran be permitted to hold on to certain components of their nuclear arsenal.

What will it take to awaken Western democracies to the threat that hangs over us like a mushroom cloud? Are our leaders so naïve as to believe all of this will just go away? As world conditions continue to deteriorate and take on an air of urgency, one is inclined to join the prophet Isaiah in crying out in prayer:

Oh, that You would rend the heavens and come down,
That the mountains might quake at your presence —
As fire kindles the brushwood, as fire causes water to boil —
To make Your name known to Your adversaries,
That the nations may tremble at Your presence![35]

KEEP YOUR EYES ON JESUS

As we witness the unfolding of end-time events, the Bible reminds us *to "fix our eyes on Jesus*, the author and perfector of faith, who for the joy set before Him endured the cross, despising the shame, and has *sat down* at the right hand of the throne of God."[36] If your name is written in the Lamb's book of life, there is absolutely nothing to fear in these last days, no matter how ominous the signs may become.

Jesus went to the cross not with fear but with joy, because He saw beyond the cross to the glories of heaven with all His saints. It is imperative Christians look beyond all the challenges of these troubled days prophesied in Scripture and see the everlasting prize awaiting us. Christianity is the only religion where the bad news is the good news for those who love the Lord. As various signs begin to take place, Jesus instructed us: "…straighten up and lift up your heads, because your redemption is drawing near."[37]

Consider where Jesus is today and what He is doing. According to Paul, Jesus is *seated* at the right hand of the throne of God where He *lives* to make intercession for us. If our Savior is calmly seated on the throne of His Father in heaven as these tumultuous events are about to unfold, then we certainly need to fix our eyes on Him.

Martin Luther captured this truth in his hymn "A Mighty Fortress is Our God:"

And though this world with devils filled, should threaten to undo us;
We will not fear, for God hath willed His truth to triumph through us.
The prince of darkness grim—we tremble not for him;
His rage we can endure, for lo, his doom is sure,
One little word shall fell him.

The devil, the antichrist, the false prophet and all those who do Satan's bidding will be destroyed, but believers shall rise to everlasting life and victory! As Luther said in this illustrious hymn—"The body, they may kill; God's truth abideth still; His Kingdom is forever."

SECTION THREE

GOD'S UNIQUE REVELATION OF PROPHECY

Prophecy has this unique characteristic that it often gives a panoramic view. It seems very evident that many of the prophecies of Isaiah and Jeremiah, and most emphatically of Ezekiel, must have a larger fulfillment than that which has already come to pass. Many of them are dated also by their relation to the Messianic ministry of Jesus. This puts them into that wide span of time that is indicated by the term "in the latter days."

C.M. Hanson

True prophetic study is an inquiry into these unsearchable counsels, these deep riches of Divine wisdom and knowledge. Beneath the light it gives, the Scriptures are no longer a heterogeneous compilation of religious books, but one harmonious whole, from which no part could be omitted without destroying the completeness of the revelation.

Sir Robert Anderson

GOD'S UNIQUE REVELATION OF PROPHECY

INTRODUCTION

The Bible is truly the living Word of God. Its sacred pages are filled with more truth than any of us will ever be able to comprehend this side of heaven. Every time believers open the Word, the Word is opened to them through the power of the Holy Spirit. Within the pages of the Bible are multifaceted messages of God's plan of salvation.

The story of Jesus Christ does not begin with Matthew, nor is it restricted to the New Testament. Jesus Christ is revealed from Genesis through Revelation. God's plan to send His Son as the Redeemer of mankind was not an afterthought, when other divine efforts proved to be lacking. God had purposed to send Christ to redeem us even before the foundations of the world were laid.[1]

The very first prophetic utterance concerning Jesus Christ was spoken by God to the serpent after he had deceived Eve into sinning:

"And I will put enmity between you and the woman, between your seed and her seed; He shall bruise you on the head, and you shall bruise him on the heel."[2] In this verse the words *her seed* are a prophecy of the virgin birth. As any biologist can attest, the woman has no seed; the seed that produces offspring comes from the man. Francis Monseth, Dean of the Association Free Lutheran Seminary in Minneapolis, said of this passage in Genesis, "It was as though God could not wait after the fall of man to announce the good news of the coming Redeemer of mankind."

Satan's efforts to triumph over Christ were prophesied in the words "you shall bruise him on the heel." Satan tried to kill Jesus when he was an infant. He tried to tempt Jesus away from His mission in the Judean wilderness. He thought he had won when Jesus was put to death on the cross, but unbeknown to the Deceiver was the fact God has a "third day." Death could not hold Him. Through His death on the cross Jesus fulfilled the prophecy—"He shall bruise you on the head." The powers of Satan were destroyed on the day now known as Good Friday. And the time is fast approaching when Christ shall cast the enemy of men's souls and all his demons into the lake of fire.

Throughout the Old Testament, glimpses of redemption's story may be seen, for example, through *types* or representations of God's ongoing drama to free us from the curse of sin and bring us back into fellowship with Himself. The Old Testament is filled not only with historical accounts of specific men and women but also with accounts that prophetically point to the life, ministry and eternal reign of Jesus Christ.

Abraham, who is called "the father of all who believe," is depicted in Scripture as a *type* of God the Father, while his son Isaac is depicted as a *type* of God's Son Jesus Christ. The biblical account of God directing Abraham to go to the land of Moriah where he was to offer his son Isaac on an altar of sacrifice is nothing less than a prophetic image of God the Father offering His Son Jesus Christ on Calvary.[3]

The seven feasts of Israel are more than just special days God directed the Jewish people to observe; they prophetically display God's eternal plan to redeem mankind. The drama of redemption is unfolded from the Feast of the Passover to the Feast of Tabernacles. The Passover bears witness to the Lamb of God's supreme sacrifice on the cross. The Feast of Trumpets prompts us to look forward to the day when "the trumpet shall sound and the dead shall be raised." And the celebratory Feast of Tabernacles is a witness to the Lord's eternal reign with His saints. Each of the seven feasts of Israel unfolds the greatest story ever told from the cross to the throne.

The Temple, a copy of God's throne in heaven, was a living illustration of the triune God—Father, Son and Holy Spirit. The Holy of Holies housed the Ark of the Covenant which symbolized the presence of God the Father; the table of showbread in the Holy Place depicted Christ as "the bread of life;" and the seven-branch candelabra symbolized the Holy Spirit. The Temple's sacrificial system was both a type and a graphic demonstration of the ultimate sacrifice made for us by Jesus Christ. Every lamb ever offered to God on the sacrificial altar pointed to Jesus Christ, the Lamb of God whose death took away the sins of the world.

The Old Testament records several appearances (theophanies) of Jesus Christ. Such appearances are recorded in Genesis 18:22; Genesis 32:30; Joshua 5:14-15; Judges 6:12, 22-23; Daniel 3:25; Daniel 7:13-14; Daniel 10:5-6 and Isaiah 6:1-5. While these and a few other appearances of the Lord had an immediate purpose for those who experienced them, they also foretold eternal truths that will be fulfilled at the close of the present age.

During numerous appearances of Christ in the Old Testament, people sensed they were in the presence of the Lord. Yet when the incarnate Christ walked this earth and taught the Word of God, many who saw Him and heard His incomparable teachings never realized they were standing in the presence of the God of Heaven. Christ wept over Jerusalem because the nation of Israel did not recognize the time of their visitation.[4] As Jesus Christ comes to us today through the witness of the Word, do we sense His presence? Do we realize as He opens His Word to us, we are standing on holy ground?

Chapter 11

THE JEWISH WEDDING, A PORTRAIT OF PROPHECY

A most amazing image in Scripture that helps us to understand God's plan of redemption and the hope of His coming is evidenced in the concept of marriage and the ancient Jewish wedding ceremony. At the dawn of creation, God established and sanctified marriage between a man and a woman. The meaning of marriage here on earth is magnified and sanctified through the marriage of Christ to His bride, the church.

Paul explains God's plan for marriage and the family here on earth by comparing marriage between a man and a woman with the union of Christ and His church. Paul concludes, "This mystery is great; but I am speaking with reference to Christ and the church."[1] A right understanding of God's design for marriage helps us to realize the magnitude of the sin being committed today by those who seek to destroy and desecrate the sacred institution of marriage.

In ancient times Jewish weddings involved several elements, wherein each represented an important aspect of redemption's story.

By examining the ancient rituals of a Jewish wedding, we are able to better understand many of Jesus' teachings and parables, especially as they relate to His second coming.

The first marriage, of course, was the union of Adam and Eve. Paul tells us Adam is "a type of Him who was to come."[2] After Adam was put into a deep sleep, God made Eve from one of Adam's ribs; then God presented Eve to Adam as his wife. "And they became one flesh...For this reason a man shall leave His father and mother and shall be joined to his wife, and the two shall become one flesh."[3]

Centuries later Christ's side was pierced on the cross. Through Christ's sacrificial death (sleep), the church is made "one" with Him. Paul said, "For since by a man came death, by a man also came the resurrection of the dead. For as in Adam all die, so also in Christ all will be made alive."[4] The theme of our "oneness" in Christ is presented several times in the New Testament through the depiction of the church as the bride of Christ.

The apostle John helps us to put this concept into perspective as he describes the scene of Jesus' death: "But one of the soldiers pierced His side with a spear, and immediately blood and water came out."[5] John writes: "For there are three that testify: the Spirit and the water and the blood; and the three are in agreement."[6] We are saved by the power of the Holy Spirit through faith in Christ who purchased us with His precious blood, and we are baptized with water into His body, the church. Jesus spoke of this truth when He said: "Truly, truly, I say to you, unless one is born of water and the Spirit he cannot enter the kingdom of God."[7]

THE BRIDE IS CHOSEN
AND PAYMENT IS GIVEN

Marriages in biblical times were usually arranged. A payment was made to the intended bride and her family. Abraham arranged for the marriage of his son, Isaac. According to Scripture Isaac is a type of Christ, as is evidenced in Genesis 22 and interpreted in Hebrews 11.[8] In Genesis 22 and 24, Abraham is presented as a type of God the Father.

Abraham sent a servant to find a bride for Isaac. Rebecca was actually chosen by God to become the bride of Isaac; she consented to marry Isaac even before meeting him. Peter captured this truth about our relationship with Jesus Christ when he said, "though you have not seen Him, you love Him...."[9] With the marriage agreement in hand, Abraham's servant presented Rebecca and her family with silver, gold and garments, as well as other gifts.

In redemption's story Jesus Christ paid the ultimate price for His bride through His death on the cross. All true believers (the church) have been chosen by God to become the bride of Christ.[10] Paul instructed the elders at Ephesus, "...Shepherd the church of God which He purchased with His own blood."[11]

THE BRIDE GIVES HER CONSENT

Even though marriages were arranged, the woman could refuse. According to Jewish custom, the groom offered his intended bride a cup of wine after he first drank from the cup. If she received the cup and drank from it, the covenant between them was sealed.

God often compared His covenant with Israel as being "a husband to them."[12] Today a man usually offers his intended a ring; if she accepts it, they become "engaged" to be married. As believers we are enabled by faith and the power of the Holy Spirit to consent to the divine relationship that brings us into union with Christ. No one is forced to receive Christ. The Bible's invitation is always, "Whosoever will, may come." Christ stands at the door of every heart saying, "Behold, I stand at the door and knock; if anyone hears My voice and opens the door, I will come in to him and will dine with him, and he with Me."[13]

The night before Jesus died, He drank from the cup and then gave it to His disciples saying, "Drink from it, all of you; for this is My blood of the covenant, which is poured out for many for forgiveness of sins. But I say to you, I will not drink of this fruit of the vine from now on until that day when I drink it new with you in My Father's kingdom."[14] In the Lord's Supper, we consent to Christ's gracious gift of salvation as we drink from the cup. Furthermore, Paul reminds us, "For as often as we eat this bread and drink this cup, we proclaim the Lord's death until He comes." Participation in the Lord's Supper reminds us not only have we been bought with a price, but we are the bride of Christ. Thus it is our duty to prepare ourselves for the day of His appearing. The marriage supper of the Lamb awaits us. "Blessed are those who are invited to the marriage supper of the Lamb." And He said to me, "These are true words of God."[15]

THE BETROTHAL

Upon the groom's payment and the woman's consent, the couple was pledged or betrothed to one another. The betrothal period usually lasted a year. Their marriage covenant could only be ended by death or a decree of divorce. The couple did not live together, but each went about preparing for their marriage and life together. The actual consummation of the marriage happened after all the preparations had been made. We who are the bride of Christ here on earth should long with anticipation for the Bridegroom to return from heaven to take us to His Father's house where we shall live with Him forever.

Mary and Joseph were betrothed, and "before they came together, she was found to be with child by the Holy Spirit." At first Joseph planned to "send her away secretly," that is to divorce her. But the angel Gabriel told him, "Do not be afraid to take Mary as your wife; for the Child who has been conceived in her is of the Holy Spirit." In obedience Joseph took Mary as His wife, and the rest is history— yours and mine!

THE RITUAL CLEANSING

The next element in the Jewish wedding involved a ritual of purification in an immersion bath. The ritual cleansing symbolized the bride's entrance into a new life with her husband. Everything in her past was washed away. Following this ritual the bride, dressed in her finest, was presented to her intended. He would treasure the image of her in his heart until he returned to claim her as his wife.

Paul described this ritual as having been fulfilled for us by Christ: "...having cleansed her by the washing of water with the word, that

He might present to Himself the church in all her glory, having no spot or wrinkle or any such thing; but that she would be holy and blameless."[16] As the bride of Christ, we have been washed in the waters of baptism and, by God's grace, dressed in robes of righteousness. "Therefore if anyone is in Christ, he is a new creature; the old things passed away; behold, new things have come."[17]

An inspiring gospel song captures this truth and rightly asks:

When the Bridegroom cometh will your robes be white?
Are you washed in the blood of the Lamb?
Will your soul be ready for the mansions bright,
And be washed in the blood of the Lamb?
Are you washed in the blood,
In the soul-cleansing blood of the Lamb?
Are your garments spotless? Are they white as snow?
Are you washed in the blood of the Lamb?[18]

THE BRIDEGROOM PREPARES A HOME

During the betrothal period, the groom prepared a place of residence for himself and his bride, adjoining his father's house. Within that residence he prepared a bridal chamber where they would spend their first seven days and nights together. When the groom's father was satisfied the addition to his house was completed, he authorized his son to return for his bride. None but the father knew when that authorization would be given. Thus the bride waited and watched with eager anticipation for her betrothed to come for her and for their marriage to be fulfilled.

Jesus said, "In my Father's house are many dwelling places; if it were not so, I would have told you; for I go to prepare a place for you. If I go and prepare a place for you, I will come again and receive you to Myself, that where I am, there you may be also."[19] At this very moment, Jesus Christ is in heaven preparing a place in His Father's house for His bride. Paul describes the prepared place this way: "But it is written, Eye has not seen, nor ear heard, neither have entered into the heart of man, the things which God hath prepared for them that love him."[20]

"But of that day and hour no one knows, not even the angels of heaven, nor the Son, but the Father alone."[21] Herein is the reason why Jesus said only the Father knew the time of His appearing. One glorious day the Father in Heaven will say, "Son, it's time. Go claim Your bride and bring her home."

THE BRIDE WAITS FOR THE GROOM'S RETURN

Each message of Jesus to the seven churches of Revelation was focused on the church (the bride) being ready for His return. Christ is not coming back for a harlot church but for His holy and spotless bride. As the betrothed was to keep herself only for her husband and be ready at any moment for his return, so too we must keep ourselves unspotted from the world, especially in an age when so many are unfaithful to Christ.

We watch with great sorrow as congregations and even whole denominations turn away from Christ by embracing false teachings and outright evil. Paul warned such things would happen in the last days, when people "will turn away their ears from the truth and turn aside to myths."[22] Surely that day is here! Today millions who call themselves Christians are totally unprepared to meet the Lord when He comes; indeed, many are playing the harlot.

THE BRIDEGROOM COMES!

The next aspect of the Jewish wedding occurred when the groom went to claim his bride. Having prepared a place for his bride, and having made all the required preparations for their wedding celebration, the son, with the sanction of his father, would set off to claim his heart's desire. Most often the groom would go for his bride late at night. It was called "stealing away the bride." As he approached her parent's house late into the night, his coming would be heralded by a shout and the sound of a trumpet, giving the bride a signal of his imminent arrival. This part of the wedding ceremony is described by the apostle Paul when Christ the Bridegroom returns for His bride: "For the Lord Himself will descend from heaven *with a shout,* with the voice of the archangel and *with the trumpet of God,* and the dead in Christ will rise first. Then we who are alive and remain will be caught up together with them in the clouds to meet the Lord in the air, and so we shall always be with the Lord."[23]

Near the one-year anniversary of their betrothal and sensing her groom would come soon, the bride and her attendants made the final preparations. Among the items needed for the procession from the bride's home to the groom's home were lamps to light the way in the darkness of the night.

In the parable of the ten virgins, Jesus describes this aspect of the Jewish wedding. Five of the bride's attendants were called wise because they had taken enough oil for their lamps in case the groom should be delayed. However, the other five did not have the foresight to adequately prepare; Jesus called them foolish because they had to hurry off to buy more oil. While they were gone, the bridegroom came, and the door to the marriage celebration was shut. Jesus compared this parable with the hour of His return to claim His bride, the church. "Be on alert then, for you do not know the day or the hour."[24]

THE MARRIAGE

Following Jewish tradition the groom and his bride went into their wedding chamber where the marriage was consummated through their sexual union. Then the groom went to the door and shared the good news with his groomsman who waited outside the bridal chamber. The news of the marriage's consummation was passed on to the wedding guests, and the wedding celebration was begun. John the Baptist alluded to this part of the wedding ceremony when he said: "He who has the bride is the bridegroom; but the friend of the bridegroom, who stands and hears him, rejoices greatly because of the bridegroom's voice. So this joy of mine has been made full."[25]

Let us rejoice and be glad and give glory to Him, for the marriage of the Lamb has come and His bride has made herself ready. It was given to her to clothe herself in fine linen, bright and clean; for the fine linen is the righteous acts of the saints. Then he said to me, "Write, 'Blessed are those who are invited to the marriage supper of the Lamb.'" And he said to me, "These are true words of God."[26]

The bride and groom remained in seclusion for seven days. Today we would call this "the honeymoon." This part of the Jewish wedding ceremony is a portrait of the church being raptured to heaven, where for seven years we shall be together with Christ. While the church is safely gathered in heaven, the wrath of God will be poured out upon the earth. How foolish for people to go through the tribulation when, by being ready (spiritually), they could be with Christ in glory.

Amillennialists, such as Hank Hanegraaff, criticize premillennialists for their belief the church will be safely gathered in heaven with Christ while the wrath of God is being poured out upon the earth.[27] However, this plan, clearly set forth in the Scriptures, was not devised by the premillennialists but by God Himself. The rapture of the church bears witness to God's overwhelming desire that "none should perish but that all should come to repentance." Hell is real and so are the judgments of God. This is the essence of salvation wherein God preserves His saints from His great and terrible wrath that will be poured out upon the earth.

IN MY FATHER'S HOUSE

Following the marriage supper, the groom escorted his bride to the home he had prepared for her. John's vision of the New Jerusalem coming down out of heaven is an image of the eternal dwelling place prepared for the bride by the Lord Jesus Christ.

"And I saw the holy city, new Jerusalem, coming down out of heaven from God, made ready as a bride adorned for her husband....Then one of the seven angels...spoke with me, saying, 'Come here, I will show you the bride, the wife of the Lamb.' And he carried me away in the spirit to a great and high mountain, and showed me the holy city, Jerusalem, coming down out of heaven from God, having the glory of God."[28]

The New Jerusalem will be our home with Christ our Savior for all eternity.

Today the world scoffs at the divinely established institution of marriage, but the covenant of marriage between a man and a woman will endure to the end of time. God's design for marriage and family as set forth in His Word should prompt us to desire for our marriage and family life to be the best it can be. By living out God's principles for marriage and family here on earth, we can experience a foretaste of heaven. The sacredness of marriage and the joys it brings are gifts from God. Those who remain unmarried during this earthly life will yet rejoice when they feast at the marriage banquet prepared for all who know and love the Lord.

The supreme question every person needs to ponder is this—Are you ready? Are you ready if the Lord should come today?

Chapter 12

SIGNS IN THE HEAVENS

"But immediately after the tribulation of those days THE SUN WILL BE DARKENED, AND THE MOON WILL NOT GIVE ITS LIGHT, AND THE STARS WILL FALL from the sky, and the powers of the heavens will be shaken. And then the sign of the Son of Man will appear in the sky, and then all the tribes of the earth will mourn, and they will see the SON OF MAN COMING ON THE CLOUDS OF THE SKY with power and great glory. And He will send forth His angels with A GREAT TRUMPET and THEY WILL GATHER TOGETHER His elect from the four winds, from one end of the sky to the other" (Matthew 24:29-31).

A n air of mystery surrounds Jesus' description of His return to earth with power and great glory at the end of the tribulation! But He makes clear—*the sign of His coming in that hour will be His coming.* All the inhabitants of the earth will look up and see the spectacular event unfolding, and they will all mourn! If, as the amillennialists claim, there is no rapture of the church, and the return of Christ is a one-time event for both the saved and the lost, why isn't any one praising the Lord at His coming? Why is everyone mourning? Why are some even pleading for the mountains and rocks to fall on them? "Fall on us and hide us from the presence of Him who sits on the throne, and from the wrath of the Lamb...."[1]

You may be certain of one thing—believers will not join the lost in mourning over Christ's appearing. On that glorious day when Christ returns, the redeemed will not be looking up *to* the sky; they will be looking down *from* the sky. The saints who have been purchased by the blood of the Lamb will appear in the air with the Son of God when He comes in the clouds of glory! Paul emphatically states: "For if we believe that Jesus died and rose again, *even so God will bring with Him those who have fallen asleep in Jesus.*"[2] When Christ comes for His church at the rapture, and when He comes in glory with His saints, the saints will not be mourning; they will be rising, rejoicing and praising the Lord.

KING OF CREATION

It is difficult to comprehend the full meaning of the supernatural and cataclysmic events Jesus described in Matthew 24 and elsewhere. Either natural or man-caused events could prevent the sun and the moon from giving their light. But perhaps the words of the prophet Joel hold the key to these events when he described a fierce war against Israel at the end of the age.

Blow a trumpet in Zion, and sound an alarm on My holy mountain! Let all the inhabitants of the land tremble, for the day of the Lord is coming; surely it is near, a day of darkness and gloom, a day of clouds and thick darkness. As the dawn is spread over the mountains, so there is a great and mighty people; there has never been anything like it, nor will there be again after it to the years of many generations....Before them the earth quakes, the heavens tremble, the sun and the moon grow dark and the stars lose their brightness.[3]

The prophet Zephaniah drew a similar picture of a great war that will take place not only in Israel but throughout the whole earth as well. He called it "a day of darkness and gloom, a day of clouds and thick darkness."[4] Several passages in Daniel and Revelation speak of a day when the sun and moon will not shine upon the earth because of overwhelming darkness. Could these passages be a description of a nuclear holocaust that will take place at the end of the tribulation?

Various biblical passages depict signs in the heavens that will occur prior to the time of Christ's return. One thing is certain, whenever the events unfold or whatever may be their cause, they will unfold exactly as the Bible describes them. The Lord neither exaggerates nor embellishes anything.

One should not be surprised to learn certain prophetic events surrounding the coming again of Jesus Christ will involve various aspects of creation, including the heavenly bodies. There are biblical accounts that describe the sun standing still, fire and brimstone raining down, and a star that guided men to the Christ-child.[5]

Most of the plagues inflicted by God upon Egypt involved the forces of nature. During the exodus God parted the waters of the Red Sea; twice He brought water from a rock in the desert. Each morning, except for the Sabbath, He gave the Israelites fresh manna and caused flocks of quail to fly into their camp. When Israel entered the Promised Land, God parted the waters of the Jordan River and caused the walls of Jericho to fall.

All through Scripture there are accounts of both natural and supernatural events caused by the direct hand of God—earthquakes, pestilence, winds, fire, floods and droughts. An earthquake took place on Good Friday, another on Resurrection morning when the stone was miraculously rolled away from Jesus' tomb. Jesus Christ is, after all, King of Creation.

EARTHQUAKES

Jesus spoke about certain events that will occur prior to His return, including wars, famines and earthquakes, and He compared them to "birth pangs." Since birth pangs increase in intensity and frequency prior to childbirth, many theologians interpret this to mean there will be an increase in the frequency and magnitude of these events prior to the Lord's second coming. Although the Bible does not specifically say there will be an increase in the frequency of earthquakes prior to the Lord's coming, it does reveal the magnitude of earthquakes will exceed any previous occurrences in the annals of history. Known fault lines and fault zones across the globe portend calamity for various nations, especially those regions that are densely populated. Scientists have even described how an "earthquake storm" might set off a series of quakes that could bring about worldwide devastation.

In the United States, people typically think of earthquake zones such as the San Andreas Fault in California that extends about 650 miles from Mexico to San Francisco. While a severe earthquake in that area would certainly be devastating not only to that region but to the whole country as well, a similar sized earthquake at the New Madrid Fault could be equally damaging to the nation and its economy. The New Madrid Fault runs through parts of Illinois, Kentucky, Missouri, Tennessee and Arkansas. Seismologists maintain there is a ninety percent chance a significant earthquake will take place in the New Madrid Fault region by the year 2040 and in California's San Andreas region within the next forty years.

Israeli scientists have warned of an impending earthquake that could kill thousands and leave hundreds of thousands homeless. Earthquakes frequently occur in Israel's Jordan Valley, which is part of the Rift Valley that runs from Africa to Turkey. Small fissures from this fault branch off through the Judean hills and across Jerusalem.

According to the prophet Zechariah, an earthquake will split the Mount of Olives in half at the time of the Lord's coming.[6] A fault-line presently exists underneath the Mount of Olives; it is just waiting for the Lord to say "NOW" and the Mount of Olives will split from north to south to form a large valley, through which water will flow from the Temple to the Dead Sea in the east and to the Mediterranean Sea in the west.[7]

HE IS COMING IN THE CLOUDS

Many believe the Bible's description of Jesus' ascension and His coming again in the clouds is purely symbolic, while others maintain these passages refer to atmospheric clouds above the earth. However, a comprehensive study on the subject prompts us to understand the biblical references to clouds, in association with the divine, transcend this material world, and they are all meant to be taken literally.

One could write an entire book on the subject of "clouds" as they relate to appearances of the Lord. References to the clouds that will surround Jesus at His coming in glory are not mere clouds in the sky, but rather they are the shekinah glory of God!

The word *shekinah* is not found in Scripture; it was used in later Jewish writings to describe the appearances and presence of God in the clouds as well as His presence in the Temple. Shekinah literally means "dwelling place" or a "royal place of dwelling." A Hebrew word used for atmospheric clouds in the Bible is *shachaq*, while the words used for clouds relating to the divine are either *nephele* or *anan*. Anan is also used to describe atmospheric clouds. Throughout the Bible these words are repeatedly used to describe the Lord's appearance in the clouds. Though the clouds may have concealed the fullness of God's glory, nevertheless they manifested His presence.

Clouds in the Wilderness

The Lord led the people of Israel out of Egypt with a pillar of cloud by day and a pillar of fire by night, and "the glory of the Lord appeared in that cloud."[8] The pillar of cloud and the pillar of fire were one and the same, though the cloud obviously had a different appearance at night than during the day. When the cloud moved the people of Israel moved; when the cloud stopped they stopped.[9]

The Lord appeared to Moses in a thick cloud on Mount Sinai.[10] He also appeared in a pillar of fire with a "very loud trumpet sound, so that all the people who were in the camp trembled."[11]

After the Tabernacle was completed, Moses was unable to enter "because the cloud had settled over it, and the glory of the Lord filled the tabernacle."[12] The Lord also appeared in the cloud over the

Mercy Seat in the Tabernacle.[13] The Mercy Seat itself represented the presence of God in the midst of the people of Israel.

Paul made a connection between the cloud that led the people into the Promised Land and our own salvation in Jesus Christ. "For I do not want you to be unaware, brethren, that our fathers were all under the cloud and all passed through the sea; and all were baptized into Moses in the cloud and in the sea; and all ate the same spiritual food; and all drank the same spiritual drink, for they were drinking from a spiritual rock which followed them; and the rock was Christ."[14]

The God of the Old Testament is the God of the New Testament. The rock from which the children of Israel drank in the desert, the manna which they ate every morning, the Passover lamb which they offered — all have their fulfillment in the person of Jesus Christ. The Lord who descended in a cloud on Mount Sinai, the great I AM, is the same Lord who will descend in the cloud on the Mount of Olives at the end of the age.

Clouds in the Temple

After Solomon finished building the Temple, the Ark of the Covenant was carried by the priests into the Holy of Holies. Then the priests assembled outside the sanctuary and sang praises to God, when suddenly "the house of the Lord was filled with a cloud, so that the priests could not stand to minister because of the cloud, for the glory of the Lord filled the house of God."[15] The first words uttered by Solomon at the dedication of the Temple were these: "The Lord has said that He would dwell in the thick cloud."[16] When Solomon concluded the dedication of the Temple, the shekinah glory of the Lord became even more intense.[17] Jews still associate the shekinah glory of God with both the Temple Mount and the Western Wall.

The Shekinah Glory and the Prophets

Isaiah had a magnificent vision of the Lord "sitting on a throne, lofty and exalted, with the train of His robe filling the temple.... And the foundations of the thresholds trembled at the voice of him who called out, while the temple was filling with smoke."[18] Isaiah was commissioned that day to carry the Word of God to a stubborn and rebellious people.

God's revelation to Daniel included a vision of the Son of Man coming to earth in the clouds. "And to Him was given dominion, glory and a kingdom that all the peoples, nations and men of every language might serve Him."[19]

One of the sad duties the prophet Ezekiel was called upon to perform was telling the people of Israel the glory of God had departed from the Temple in Jerusalem because of their many detestable sins. "Then the glory of the Lord departed from the threshold of the temple and stood over the cherubim."[20] The shekinah glory actually departed by way of the Eastern Gate and the Mount of Olives. And that is exactly how the shekinah glory shall return to the Temple at the coming of Christ—first from the Mount of Olives and then through the Eastern Gate.[21]

Later God remembered His covenant with Israel, and gave Ezekiel a vision of the millennial Temple and the coming of the Messiah. No prophetic message expressed by Ezekiel could have brought him more joy than to describe the Lord's presence returning to the Temple at the end of days.

> "And the glory of the Lord came into the house by the way of the gate facing toward the east. And the Spirit lifted me up and brought me into the inner court; and behold the glory of the Lord filled the house. Then I heard one speaking to me from the house, while a man was standing beside me. He said to me, "Son of man, this is the place of My throne and the place of the soles of My feet, where I will dwell among the sons of Israel forever."[22]

The Cloud and Jesus

At the time of Jesus' baptism in the Jordan River, a voice spoke from the heavens, "This is My beloved Son, in whom I am well pleased."[23] On the Mount of Transfiguration "a bright cloud overshadowed them, and behold, a voice out of the cloud said, 'This is My beloved Son, with whom I am well pleased; listen to Him!'"[24]

John described the event this way: "And the Word became flesh, and dwelt among us, and we saw His glory, glory as of the only begotten from the Father, full of grace and truth."[25]

Perhaps the most awesome appearance of the cloud came during Christ's ascension from the Mount of Olives. "He was lifted up while they were looking on, and a cloud received Him out of their sight."[26] People are often prone to think of the earth as being down and heaven as being up, or the ascension as merely a means of locomotion to remove Christ from the planet at the close of His ministry. However, the words *"a cloud received Him"* tell it all. At His ascension Jesus Christ was received into the shekinah glory of God, and instantaneously transported into heaven. According to the Scriptures He is coming back again in the same cloud of God's shekinah glory.

One of the amazing references concerning our Lord's coming in the clouds was given by Jesus Himself when He stood before Caiaphas, the high priest. At first Jesus kept silent, even though the Jewish authorities questioned Him relentlessly, and demanded in the Name of the living God He tell them whether or not He was the Christ, the Son of God. Jesus responded: "You have said it yourself; nevertheless I tell you, hereafter you will see the SON OF MAN SITTING AT THE RIGHT HAND OF POWER, and COMING ON THE CLOUDS OF HEAVEN."[27] Caiaphas became so furious with Jesus' answer he tore his robes.

The Lord stated the only sign that will be given when He returns in glory will be His personal, literal coming on the clouds of heaven. Paul emphatically stated to the church in Thessalonica when the Lord returns, He will come "with all His saints."[28] Hebrews 12: 1 even describes the saints as "a cloud of witnesses." To deny the literal coming again of Jesus in the clouds is to cast doubt on the Word of God itself.

The Cloud and the Two Witnesses

The Book of Revelation describes two witnesses who will appear in Jerusalem during the tribulation. They will preach and witness, and afterwards be killed. The two witnesses will be allowed to lie in the street for three and a half days; then they will be resurrected and taken up into heaven *in the cloud*. "And they heard a loud voice from heaven saying to them, 'Come up here.' Then they went up into heaven in the cloud, and their enemies watched them."[29]

Caught up in the Clouds

The clouds become intensely personal during the rapture of the church when believers will be caught up "in the clouds to meet the Lord in the air" and instantaneously transported to heaven.[30] While students of prophecy seem to focus mostly on the words "to meet the Lord in the air," the real impact of 1 Thessalonians 4:17 concerns the clouds; this reference is not about the earth's atmosphere but rather it speaks of our being caught up into the shekinah glory of God.

Paul described another aspect of the first resurrection and the rapture of the church in 1 Corinthians 15: "Behold, I tell you a mystery; we will not all sleep, but we will all be changed, in a moment, in the twinkling of an eye, at the last trumpet; for the trumpet will sound, and the dead will be raised imperishable, and we will be changed."[31] There is surely a connection between this divinely produced change or translation of our earthly bodies to our heavenly bodies and our being transported from earth to heaven. Both will be "in a moment, in the twinkling of an eye."

The Creator God is not bound by time or space. We will be changed and transported to heaven not in any earthly dimension but in the dimension of the divine glory. Christ's ascension and return as well as our being caught up into the presence of God Almighty transcend time and space. Christians should not think of heaven and God as being beyond the galaxies somewhere. While heaven is a real and literal place, it is not approachable by any device known to man. We shall be transported instantaneously to our heavenly home in the shekinah glory of God. Christ Himself will come for us, that where He is, there we may be also.

Every time believers look into the clouds, it should be a reminder that one day the Lord is coming back again "in the cloud" to receive us unto Himself.

Chapter 13

THE PROPHETIC MEANING OF THE SEVEN FEASTS OF ISRAEL

It is amazing how many prophecies have been woven into the Scriptures through historical events and religious observances. Scripture's multifaceted revelations prompted Paul to exclaim: "Oh, the depth of the riches both of the wisdom and knowledge of God! How unsearchable are His judgments and unfathomable His ways!"[1]

Nearly everything in Scripture has a depth of meaning beyond the obvious. As we read the Bible through the power of the Holy Spirit, the ordinary is transformed into the extraordinary. Scripture passages that may seem complete in and of themselves expand into prophetic revelations that stagger the mind. The seven feasts of Israel are illustrative of such expanding revelations. Though the feasts all begin with a single event to be recalled or celebrated, each feast is enlarged to prophetically encompass a portion of the divine panorama of redemption that stretches from the cross to the eternal reign of Christ.

God not only gave these feasts to Israel and commanded they be observed, but He continued to unfold their meaning in both the Old and New Testaments. From the Feast of the Passover to the Feast of Tabernacles, God's plan of salvation is revealed step by step, making known what was, what is and what is to come. The Bible clearly reveals each of the seven feasts has its fulfillment in the person and work of Jesus Christ.

Once the interconnectedness of Scripture's revelation is realized, other portions of God's Word come into focus with fresh meaning and new understanding. The fact these truths were there all the time causes us to wonder why we had not seen them before. We certainly can relate with the disciples on the road to Emmaus, whose hearts burned within them as Christ opened the Scriptures to them.[2]

THE FEAST OF THE PASSOVER

In the first month, on the fourteenth day of the month at twilight is the Lord's Passover (Leviticus 23:5).

The first Passover (Pesach in Hebrew) took place while the children of Israel were in bondage in Egypt. The feast was observed in connection with the tenth plague that threatened the first-born of every household in Egypt with death, both man and cattle. In order that the children of Israel might be spared from this judgment, God instructed each Israelite family to kill a lamb and apply its blood on the door posts and the lintel of their house. The lamb was to be eaten that same night, along with unleavened bread and bitter herbs. God further instructed the Israelites to be fully dressed, with sandals on their feet and staffs in their hands, as they ate the Passover meal. Although the Israelites had lived in Egypt for 430 years to the day, when those days were completed, God moved with amazing speed to send them on their way to the Promised Land. Such will be the suddenness of Christ's return for His church! When the trumpet is sounded, believers will be transported to the skies in the twinkling of an eye.

God said of this meal:

"It is the Lord's Passover....The blood shall be a sign for you on the houses where you live; and when I see the blood I will pass over you, and no plague will befall you to destroy you when I strike the land of Egypt. Now this day will be a memorial to you, and you shall celebrate it as a feast to the Lord; throughout your generations you are to celebrate it as a permanent ordinance."[3]

When I See the Blood

The Feast of Passover is clearly a type of Christ's redemptive sacrifice. The words *"When I see the blood I will pass over you"* were fulfilled as Christ shed His blood on Calvary. The blood of the Passover lamb posited on the door posts and lintels of the Israelites' houses was merely a token of what was to come. It was not so much the blood of a yearling lamb that caused the Lord to pass over the houses of the Israelites and spare their first born from death, as it was the ultimate sacrifice of the Redeemer centuries later. The first Passover prophetically looked forward to the ultimate Passover and to Jesus Christ, the Lamb of God. Every animal ever sacrificed to God was a type of the Lamb of God who was to come. The Bible tells us plainly, "For it is impossible for the blood of bulls and goats to take away sins."[4]

Today we look back 2000 years to the Savior's sacrifice on the cross; those who lived in the time of Moses had to look forward fifteen hundred years to the same event, but the power of Christ's supreme sacrifice is effectual for sinners throughout all the ages! This truth is made clear in Scripture: "By faith Moses, when he had grown up, refused to be called the son of Pharaoh's daughter, choosing rather to endure ill-treatment with the people of God than to enjoy the passing pleasures of sin, considering the reproach of Christ greater riches than the treasures of Egypt; for he was looking to the reward."[5]

The parallels between the celebration of the Passover meal and the death of Jesus Christ are manifold. The prophet Isaiah described the coming Messiah as the Passover lamb.[6] John the Baptist introduced Jesus by declaring: "Behold the Lamb of God who takes away the sin of the world!"[7] The meaning of God's Passover Lamb, Jesus Christ, is explained in various portions of the Bible; while references to the Lamb of God are recorded twenty-seven times in the Book of Revelation alone.

God directed the Passover lamb chosen by each family had to be a year-old male without blemish.[8] Because Jesus Christ was without sin, He alone was worthy to make atonement for the sins of the world. In like manner, only the Lamb of God in heaven is worthy to open the book with its seven seals and begin the countdown to eternity.

> I saw in the right hand of Him who sat on the throne a book written inside and on the back, sealed up with seven seals. And I saw a strong angel proclaiming with a loud voice, "Who is worthy to open the book and to break its seals?" And no one in heaven or on the earth or under the earth was able to open the book or to look into it. Then I began to weep greatly because no one was found worthy to open the book or to look into it; and one of the elders said to me, "Stop weeping; behold the Lion that is from the tribe of Judah, the Root of David, has overcome so as to open the book and its seven seals."... Then I looked and I heard the voice of many angels...and the number of them was myriads of myriads, and thousands of thousands, saying with a loud voice, "Worthy is the Lamb that was slain to receive power and riches and wisdom and might and honor and glory and blessing."[9]

The Passover Meal Reveals Jesus' Death

God told the children of Israel not a single bone of the Passover lamb was to be broken. This prophecy type was literally fulfilled immediately after Christ had died upon the cross. It was common for the Romans to break the legs of persons being crucified in order to hasten death; however, when the soldiers came to Jesus and "saw that He was already dead, they did not break His legs."[10] John revealed this fulfillment of Scripture by quoting Exodus 12:46

which refers to the Passover lamb. The same prophecy is also found in Psalm 34:20.

The Passover celebration has been modified by the Jewish community over the centuries through additional symbolism and rituals. This spring feast, now called the *Seder*, is central in the worship life of Judaism, especially since the destruction of the Temple. The Seder meal is presided over by the head of the household. Many aspects of the Seder as it is practiced today parallel the divine mission of Jesus Christ as the Lamb of God, but three examples will be sufficient for our consideration here.

Originally the Passover meal included eating the sacrificed lamb, either in family groups or in social groups. After the Temple was destroyed, a shank bone of a lamb was substituted for the sacrificed lamb. The shank bone of the lamb is a reminder of the lamb whose blood was applied to the lintel and doorposts of the Israelites' houses in order that the destroyer would pass over them. The Passover Lamb is Jesus Christ.

A second ingredient of the present-day Seder meal includes three pieces of unleavened bread or *matzah,* which are placed inside a linen bag with three separate pockets. Some Jewish sources suggest the three pieces of matzah represent the Patriarchs — Abraham, Isaac and Jacob. The matzah used today in the Seder is baked in such a way it is pierced and striped, symbolic of the words of Isaiah that He was *pierced* through for our transgressions and with His *stripes* we are healed."[11]

During the Passover meal, the middle matzah, which represents Isaac who was a type of Christ, is broken in half. One of the halves is then wrapped in a linen napkin and hidden away somewhere in the house for the children to discover later. Jesus, the second person of the Trinity who is symbolized by the Passover bread, was wrapped in a linen burial cloth and placed in a borrowed grave. Jesus identified Himself with the bread of Passover when He said, "Take and eat, this is my body given for you." Only eyes that have been opened by the Holy Spirit may truly comprehend the symbolism contained in this part of the Passover ritual.

During the meal the children are sent in search of the hidden matzah, also called the *afikomen.* After finding it they bring it to the head of the household who breaks it and offers a piece to each person at the Passover table as a reminder of the Passover lamb. Kevin L. Howard, in a most inspiring article in *Zion's Fire,* described the Christian significance of the Seder meal. He said the word *afikomen* is of Greek origin, not Hebrew, and simply means—*He came*. He also said the rituals involving the afikomen were not used in the time of Christ but were developed much later.[12] It is amazing how much of the present-day Passover ceremony clearly points to Christ, the second person of the Godhead, as the Jewish Messiah.

Four cups of wine are served with the Seder meal—the Cup of Sanctification, the Cup of Praise, the Cup of Redemption and the Cup of Acceptance. The night before His death, Jesus celebrated the Passover meal with His disciples in an upper room in Jerusalem. It was while offering the bread and the third cup, the Cup of Redemption, Jesus instituted the Lord's Supper. As He broke the bread and gave it to His disciples, He said, "This is my body which is given for you." Then He took the cup and gave it to them saying, "This is my blood." Few Christians today understand the abiding connection between the Passover meal and the Lord's Supper, or between Christianity and Judaism, or between the Old and New Testaments.

Jesus Christ is the Passover Lamb. John declared, "...the blood of Jesus His Son cleanses us from all sins."[13] Paul wrote: "Much more then, having now been justified by His blood, we shall be saved from the wrath of God through Him."[14] Paul also wrote: "In Him we have redemption through His blood, the forgiveness of our trespasses, according to the riches of His grace."[15]

Perhaps one of the most profound prophecies regarding the blood of Jesus Christ is found in Leviticus: "For the life of the flesh is in the blood, and I have given it to you on the altar to make atonement for your souls; for it is the blood by reason of the life that makes atonement."[16] This verse, from one of the oldest books of Scripture, is a portrait of Christ's redeeming sacrifice on the cross. Hundreds of years before anyone understood the scientific truth that the "life of the flesh is in the blood," the Pentateuch prophetically looked forward to the cross on which God would literally offer His own blood as an atonement for the sins of mankind. The passage also clearly states why God was so adamant in forbidding the children of Israel to consume anything containing blood.

The modern church seems determined to avoid either preaching or teaching about the blood of Christ. But where the sermons and hymns are bloodless, the people are lost. This is tragedy compounded, since a bloodless gospel is incapable of bringing anybody to salvation. The Bible states: "without the shedding of blood there is no forgiveness."[17] We are saved "through the blood of the eternal covenant, even Jesus our Lord."[18] Those praying for revival in the churches today need to include the petition: "O Lord, bring back the blood."

> There is a fountain filled with blood drawn from Immanuel's veins,
> And sinners plunged beneath that flood lose all their guilty stains.
> The dying thief rejoiced to see that fountain in his day,
> And there may I though vile as he, wash all my sins away.
> Dear dying Lamb, Thy precious blood shall never lose its power
> Till all the ransomed Church of God be saved to sin no more.[19]

THE FEAST OF UNLEAVENED BREAD

Then on the fifteenth day of the same month there is the Feast of Unleavened Bread to the Lord; for seven days you shall eat unleavened bread (Leviticus 23:6).

The Feast of Unleavened Bread, which lasts for seven days, immediately follows the Feast of the Passover. The names of these two feasts are used interchangeably. Prior to the Feast of the Passover, all leaven must be removed from the house. In the Scriptures leaven is associated with sin, hypocrisy and false teaching.[20] As Christians we understand our bodies are the temple of the Holy Spirit; therefore it is essential to "lay aside every encumbrance and the sin which so easily entangles us...."[21] Paul reminds us: "For Christ our Passover also has been sacrificed. Therefore let us celebrate the feast, not with the old leaven, nor with the leaven of malice and wickedness, but with the unleavened bread of sincerity and truth."[22] Paul said of Christ: "He made Him who knew no sin to be sin on our behalf, so that we might become the righteousness of God in Him."[23]

After Jesus fed the 5000 with five barley loaves and two fish, the crowd followed Him to Capernaum. The Jews sought for another sign and reminded Jesus of how their fathers had eaten the manna sent from heaven. He responded with these words:

"Truly, truly, I say to you, it is not Moses who has given you the bread out of heaven, but it is My Father who gives you the true bread out of heaven. For the bread of God is that which comes down out of heaven, and gives life to the world....I am the bread of life; he who comes to Me will not hunger, and he who believes in Me will never thirst."[24]

Paul also made the connection between Christ and the manna given to the children of Israel in the wilderness.[25]

The table of showbread in the Temple was identified by the Jews with their longed-for Messiah. Bethlehem, the town where Jesus was born, literally means "house of bread." Someone observed: "Jesus Christ was born in the 'house of bread,' so there might be bread in the house."

Christ died on the Feast of the Passover and His body was in the tomb on the Feast of Unleavened Bread. During the Seder the children are sent off in search of the hidden afikomen; upon finding it they return to the table rejoicing. This aspect of the Jewish Passover celebration witnesses to the fact the Messiah did not remain in the grave, nor did the Lord allow His body to see corruption.[26]

Both the Feast of Passover and the Feast of Unleavened Bread were literally fulfilled by Christ on the exact day of their celebration. There is some debate among theologians regarding the precise day Jesus was crucified because of the description given in the first three Gospels, and the description given by John in the fourth Gospel. There are, however, ample explanations for the differences.

Some Bible scholars have suggested Jews living in the northern part of Israel celebrated the Passover meal on the fourteenth of the month, while Jews living in Jerusalem and the southern part of the country celebrated it on the fifteenth. Some have further suggested two days were required in order to accommodate the sacrifice of so many lambs at the Temple. In his book *Bible Difficulties and Seeming Contradictions,* William Arndt offers a good explanation concerning this matter as it relates to differences about the Passover within the Jewish community during the first century.[27] Sufficient for our consideration is the absolute certainty Christ fulfilled both the Feast of the Passover and the Feast of Unleavened Bread on the precise days they occurred on the Jewish calendar.

THE FEAST OF FIRST FRUITS

"Speak to the sons of Israel and say to them, 'When you enter the land which I am going to give to you and reap its harvest, then you shall bring in the sheaf of the first fruits of your harvest to the priest. He shall wave the sheaf before the Lord for you to be accepted; on the day after the Sabbath the priest shall wave it'" (Leviticus 23:10-11).

The Feast of First Fruits comes on the first day of the week (Sunday), the day after the Sabbath of the Feast of Unleavened Bread. This feast is a celebration of the early harvest. In Hebrew it is called *Sfirat Haomer,* which literally means "the counting of the sheaf." It is a promise of the greater harvest to come. This feast is appropriately applied to Christ's resurrection.

Barley was the first crop to be harvested. Each man brought a sheaf of barley to the priest who waved it before the Lord in six directions—north, south, east, west, then up and down. This signified the God of Israel was the sustainer and giver of every aspect of life.

Jesus fulfilled this feast through His resurrection. Paul stated: "For since by a man came death, by a man also came the resurrection of the dead. For as in Adam all die, so also in Christ all will be made alive. But each in his own order: Christ the *first fruits*, after that those who are Christ's at His coming...."[28]

The concept of "first fruits" is mentioned seven times in the New Testament. Paul said: "He is also head of the body, the church; and He is the beginning, the first-born from the dead, so that He Himself will come to have first place in everything."[29] James wrote: "In the exercise of His will He brought us forth by the word of truth, so that we would be a kind of first fruits among His creatures."[30]

Easter, First Fruits or Resurrection Sunday?

Christ rose from the dead precisely on the Feast of First Fruits, the first day of the week. Today the celebration of the Lord's resurrection is commonly called *Easter*. For Christians, every Sunday should be a celebration of the Lord's resurrection. This is the reason the forty days of Lent do not include Sundays.

In 325 the Council of Nicea established the formula for determining the date of Easter—"the Sunday following the first full moon of the vernal equinox. (March 21)." Neither Emperor Constantine nor church officials wanted Easter to be connected with the Jewish Passover. The established formula was based on a pagan observance of an annual rite of spring for the goddess of fertility, Ishtar. Emperor Constantine, who assembled the Council of Nicea, wanted the church to make the celebration of Easter coincide with the pagan celebration of Ishtar. This feast was originally observed by the Babylonians and later by the Romans in honor of their fertility goddess Astarte; it involved fertility rites and incorporated symbols such as rabbits, eggs, etc.

Today a growing number of people, including many who call themselves Christians, do not have the slightest clue as to why Easter is celebrated, but its pagan roots are showing more than ever in stores and in public institutions. Much like Christmas, Easter has become commercialized without any connection whatsoever to its true meaning. In order to remove its pagan connections, Christians should call this day "Resurrection Sunday" or the "Festival of First Fruits." Easter is not celebrated much differently today than it was in 325 when Rome was still mostly pagan. Like Christmas, Easter seems to have been taken over by our pagan society.

The Feast of First Fruits should remind Christians of the eternal resurrection awaiting all who believe in Jesus Christ. Paul assured us: "But if the Spirit of Him who raised Jesus from the dead dwells in you, He who raised Christ Jesus from the dead will also give life to your mortal bodies through His Spirit who dwells in you."[31] He also wrote: "And not only this, but also we ourselves, having the first fruits of the Spirit, even we ourselves groan within ourselves, waiting eagerly for our adoption as sons, the redemption of our body."[32] In 1 Corinthians 15 and 1 Thessalonians 4, Paul elaborated on the resurrection to eternal life for all the redeemed children of God.

Another fulfillment of "first fruits" is evidenced in the Book of Revelation as it relates to the 144,000 Jewish saints who will be redeemed during the tribulation. "These are the ones who follow the Lamb wherever He goes. These have been purchased from among men as first fruits to God and to the Lamb."[33] The 144,000 will be first among the Jews who will be saved during the tribulation and at the coming of the Lord Jesus Christ.

Christ was crucified on the Feast of the Passover; His body was buried in the tomb on the Feast of Unleavened Bread; and He was raised on the Feast of First Fruits. Can you see the emerging pattern in God's grand design to show us His plan of redemption in the seven feasts? But there is more, much more! With God there is always more!

THE FEAST OF PENTECOST

You shall also count for yourselves from the day after the Sabbath, from the day when you brought in the sheaf of the wave offering; there shall be seven complete Sabbaths. You shall count fifty days to the day after the seventh Sabbath; then you shall present a new grain offering to the Lord (Leviticus 23:15-16).

Fifty days after the Feast of First Fruits is the Feast of Pentecost when Jews dedicate the early harvest to God. This feast is also a remembrance of the day Moses received the law on Mount Sinai. For

Jews, Pentecost represents the birthday of Judaism. For the church, Pentecost marks the coming of the Holy Spirit and the birthday of the church.

John declared: "For the Law was given through Moses; grace and truth were realized through Jesus Christ."[34] The connection between the Feast of Pentecost and Moses receiving the law on Mount Sinai is described in the book of Hebrews.

> For you have not come to a mountain that can be touched and to a blazing fire, and to darkness and gloom and whirlwind, and to the blast of a trumpet and the sound of words which sound was such that those who heard begged that no further word be spoken to them. For they could not bear the command, "If even a beast touches the mountain, it will be stoned." And so terrible was the sight, that Moses said, "I am full of fear and trembling." But you have come to Mount Zion and to the city of the living God, the heavenly Jerusalem, and to myriads of angels to the general assembly and the church of the firstborn who are enrolled in heaven, and to God, the Judge of all, and to the spirits of the righteous made perfect, and to Jesus, the mediator of a new covenant, and to the sprinkled blood, which speaks better than the blood of Abel.[35]

Ten days after the ascension, one hundred and twenty followers of Jesus, including His eleven disciples, were gathered in Jerusalem on the Feast of Pentecost. Suddenly the Holy Spirit descended upon them with the sound of a mighty rushing wind. The joy of the previous forty days spent in the company of the resurrected Christ was multiplied a hundredfold as the Holy Spirit entered each believer.

Empowered by the Holy Spirit, the small band of Jesus' followers left the confines of the house where they had been staying and went out into the streets of Jerusalem. Neither Jerusalem nor the world would ever be the same again! Beneath the shadow of the Temple, these Spirit-empowered believers witnessed the life-changing message of Christ. Jews from all over the world who had gathered for the Feast of Pentecost were amazed to hear the first proclamation of the gospel in their own languages.

As Peter's first sermon hit its mark, Jewish hearts, moved by the Holy Spirit, cried out, "Brethren what shall be do?" Peter extended the first invitation to come to Christ: "Repent and each of you be baptized in the name of Jesus Christ for the forgiveness of your sins; and you will receive the gift of the Holy Spirit. For the promise is for you and your children and for all who are far off, as many as the Lord our God will call to Himself." That very day three thousand Jewish believers were ushered into the Kingdom of God. The Bible says, "And the Lord was adding to their number day by day those who were being saved."[36] God's harvest of the redeemed had begun.

Throughout the centuries the church has been engaged in the work of gathering in the harvest, but there always seems to be a shortage of workers. In this age when so many Christians are caught up in their own personal interests, we need to pray as Jesus taught us: "The harvest is plentiful, but the workers are few. Therefore beseech the Lord of the harvest to send out workers into His harvest."[37]

One day the Lord Himself will send His angels to gather in the final harvest from the four corners of the earth and the heavens. In the meantime the church is under the directive of the Lord Jesus Christ to "go," "make disciples," "baptize," and "teach." Any church that is not carrying out this directive can not justify its existence.

During the Feast of Pentecost at the time of the Temple, two loaves of bread containing leaven were presented as a "wave offering." Zola Levitt said of these loaves:

Since they are baked with leaven, they represent sinful man (certainly not, for example, Jesus and the Holy Spirit, who are unleavened); and since they are "first fruits," they are redeemed or resurrected men. Obviously God was predicting here that the Church would be comprised of two parts, Jew and Gentile. We seem to think of the Church today as entirely Gentile, but of course it has always been part Jewish, since the Lord inevitably retains a remnant of His People. The greater body of Jews will join the Church in the kingdom at the Second Coming (Zechariah 12:10; 13:1) when "All Israel will be saved" (Romans 11:26).[38]

The first four feasts were fulfilled on the precise day of their celebration. The three remaining feasts await their fulfillment in God's ongoing drama of redemption.

THE FEAST OF TRUMPETS

"Speak to the sons of Israel, saying, 'In the seventh month on the first of the month you shall have a rest, a reminder by blowing of trumpets, a holy convocation. You shall not do any laborious work, but you shall present an offering by fire to the Lord'" (Leviticus 23:23-24).

The Feast of Trumpets is celebrated on the first day of the seventh month of Teshri. This feast marks the beginning of a period called the *ten days of awe* which ends on the Day of Atonement. During this time Jews are instructed to examine their hearts and through repentance seek God's forgiveness. The Feast of Trumpets is also called *Rosh Hashanah*, meaning "the head of the year." Teshri is the beginning of the new year in the Jewish civil calendar. The Jewish religious year begins with Passover in the month of Nisan. This is similar to the religious year in the church that begins with Advent, four Sundays before Christmas, even though the church also observes the civil calendar starting with January.

As the first three feasts of Israel take place in the month of Nisan and are connected to each other, so the last three feasts occur in the month of Tishri and are also connected to one another. Consequently the first three feasts are called the spring feasts, while the last three feasts are called the fall feasts. The fourth feast (Pentecost) occurs in the third month of the Jewish year, known as Sivan.

Those who hold to the premillennial view of eschatology believe the gap of time between the Feast of Pentecost and the Feast of Trumpets is symbolic of the church age which will end with the rapture of the church. The Feast of Trumpets will be fulfilled when the Lord comes to gather His church.

The Feast of Trumpets always begins with the new moon; in fact it is the only Jewish feast that falls precisely on the day of the new moon. Many years ago Jewish leaders changed the beginning of this feast from one to two days, largely because of the difficulty in determining the precise start of the new moon. The new moon occurs 29.5 days from the last new moon, which means the Feast of Trumpets can begin over a span of two calendar days. Therefore those in charge of sounding the trumpet to announce the start of the feast had to be extremely watchful about not missing the precise day and hour. The Scripture's admonition for believers to be ready for the trumpet call that will announce the coming of Christ for His church is rightly applied to this feast.

The trumpet used in the celebration of the Feast of Trumpets was the ram's horn (shofar), not the silver trumpet associated with other rituals. Extended blasts of the trumpet were sounded at the end of this feast, which may be the meaning of the Bible's description of Christ's return at "the last trumpet." Paul twice associated the sound of trumpets with the rapture when the church will be caught up to meet the Lord in the air.

> For the Lord Himself will descend from heaven with a shout, with the voice of the archangel and with the trumpet of God, and the dead in Christ will rise first. Then we who are alive and remain will be caught up together with them in the clouds to meet the Lord in the air, and so we shall always be with the Lord.[39]
>
> Behold I tell you a mystery, we will not all sleep, but we will all be changed, in a moment, in the twinkling of an eye, at the last trumpet; for the trumpet will sound, and the dead will be raised imperishable, and we will be changed.[40]

Moses, under the direction of the Lord, instituted the use of trumpets. Trumpets were sounded to break camp, call the people for assembly and summon them for war. They were sounded to announce the feasts, the Sabbaths and various holy days.

The sound of trumpets in Scripture is associated with a variety of divine appearances. God appeared to Moses on Mount Sinai with the sound of a "very loud trumpet, so that the people in the camp trembled."[41] Christ stated that prior to His coming in glory, He would "send forth His angels *with a great trumpet,* and they will gather together His elect from the four winds, from one end of the sky to the other."[42] The Book of Revelation speaks of seven trumpets that will emanate from the seventh seal. These trumpets will be sounded for each of seven specific judgments of God that will be poured out upon the earth.

The first four feasts were fulfilled on the exact day they were celebrated; this gives us reason to believe there will be a literal fulfillment of the last three feasts on the precise day of their celebration. However even with this understanding, we still do not know the day or the hour of the Lord's return. It is enough to know He is coming. Our hearts should reflect the sentiments of the apostle John when he closed the Book of Revelation with these words — "Come, Lord Jesus."

THE DAY OF ATONEMENT

"On exactly the tenth day of this seventh month is the day of atonement; it shall be a holy convocation for you, and you shall humble your souls and present an offering by fire to the Lord" (Leviticus 23:27).

The Day of Atonement, called *Yom Kippur* in Hebrew, is the holiest day of the year for the Jewish people. *Yom* means day, and *Kippur* means to pardon or to reconcile. Yom Kippur and the ten days of awe preceding it are all about repentance, contrition and forgiveness. It is a time of preparation for divine judgment.

Throughout the entire Day of Atonement, Jews are instructed to examine their hearts and confess their sins to God. A modern salutation given on Yom Kippur states: *"May you be inscribed in the Book of Life!"* Revelation 20:15 declares: "And if anyone's name was not found written in the book of life, he was thrown into the lake of fire." In Philippians 4:3, Paul wrote about his "fellow workers, whose names are in the book of life." In Exodus 32:32 Moses interceded with God by asking Him to blot out his name from "Your book," if it would save the children of Israel from God's wrath.

Yom Kippur was especially holy during the time of the Temple. On this one day of the year, the high priest, arrayed in garments of white, entered into the Holy of Holies to sprinkle the blood for the sins of the whole nation of Israel. Of the fifteen separate sacrifices observed at the Temple on the Day of Atonement, the high priest was responsible for them all.

Seven days prior to the Day of Atonement, the high priest left his personal residence and moved into special quarters at the Temple. Throughout the week he prepared himself by reading the Scriptures and having the Scriptures read to him. He rehearsed his duties over and over to be certain each would be properly carried out according to the law. A substitute priest was available just in case the high priest was unable perform his duties.

The night before this feast, the high priest was kept awake. As dawn broke over the Mount of Olives, the high priest began the first of his manifold tasks. Before the high priest could enter into the Holy of Holies, however, he had to sacrifice a bull for himself and his family in order to be cleansed of his own sins.

Early on the Day of Atonement, two male goats were presented to the high priest. He drew lots to determine which goat would be slain (*Chatat,* "for the Lord"), and which goat would be marked for the wilderness (*Azazel,* the scapegoat). Azazel was the name of the place in the Judean desert where the scapegoat was ultimately taken. The high priest tied a scarlet cord on each goat. This was to fulfill the Scripture, "Come now, and let us reason together, says the Lord. Though your sins are as scarlet, they will be as white as snow; though they are red like crimson, they will be like wool."[43] It is prophetic that the Roman soldiers mocked Christ prior to His crucifixion by adorning Him in a purple robe.

The High Priest Entered the Holy of Holies
Three Times on the Day of Atonement

The high priest actually entered into the Holy of Holies three separate times on the Day of Atonement. He first entered with a golden shovel of hot coals and incense which he offered until the room was filled with smoke. He momentarily withdrew from the Holy of Holies to pour the blood of the bull he had sacrificed earlier into a dipper-like vessel called a *mizrak*. With the gold mizrak in hand, the high priest, once again, entered the Holy of Holies and sprinkled the blood of the bull upon the foundation stone. The third time the high priest entered the Holy of Holies, he carried the mizrak filled with the blood of the goat that had been marked "for the Lord," and sprinkled the blood over the foundation stone. Finally blood from both the bull and the goat were mixed together and sprinkled in the Holy of Holies and on the horns of the altar of incense. Any remaining blood was poured out at the base of the outer altar.

With his functions concluded in the Holy of Holies, the high priest stood before the Eastern Gate and placed both hands on the scapegoat, symbolically transferring onto the goat the sins of the people of Israel. The scapegoat was then led off through the Eastern Gate, up the Mount of Olives and into the wilderness where it was set free. During the second-Temple period, however, the scapegoat was taken into the wilderness and thrown from a cliff to its death. The scarlet cord was taken from the goat's neck and placed on a rock before being sent to its death. The cord was made in such a way its color would change to white when placed in the sun, signifying the nation's sins had been forgiven. After the cord turned white, the good news was sent back to the high priest and to those gathered at the Temple.

Christ is Our Atonement

The Feast of the Atonement has been fulfilled through Christ's sacrifice on the cross, although some aspects of this feast await a future fulfillment that will center on Israel when they repent and turn to Christ upon His return.

Following His resurrection Christ entered into the Tabernacle in heaven where He presented the "once for all" offering of His own blood for the sins of the whole world. By doing so Christ became both the Victim and the Priest.

But when Christ appeared as a high priest of the good things to come, He entered through the greater and more perfect tabernacle, not made with hands, that is to say, not of this creation; and not through the blood of goats and calves, but through His own blood, He entered the holy place once for all, having obtained eternal redemption.[44]

The whole ritual of selecting the two goats, one for sacrifice and the other as the scapegoat, was fulfilled in the judgment hall of Pontius Pilate where Barabbas was set free and Christ was sentenced to death. It was customary for the Romans to release one prisoner in connection with the celebration of the Passover. "But the chief priests and the elders persuaded the crowds to ask for Barabbas and to put Jesus to death."[45] This was prophesied by the high priest Caiaphas when the Jewish leaders conspired to kill Jesus.

But one of them, Caiaphas, who was high priest that year, said to them, "You know nothing at all, nor do you take into account that it is expedient for you that one man die for the people, and that the whole nation not perish." Now he did not say this on his own initiative, but being high priest that year, he prophesied that Jesus was going to die for the nation, and not for the nation only, but in order that He might also gather together into one the children of God who are scattered abroad.[46]

Since the church will already have been gathered in heaven, it is clear the fulfillment of the Feast of the Atonement at Christ's second coming will uniquely relate to Israel. According to Zechariah, only one-third of Israel will survive the tribulation, but they all will yield their hearts to the Lord. "I will say, 'They are my people,' and they will say, 'The Lord is my God.'"[47] God spoke through Isaiah: "Speak kindly to Jerusalem; and call out to her, that her warfare has ended, that her iniquity has been removed, that she has received of the Lord's hand double for all her sins."[48] This passage will be fulfilled when the Lord gathers the nation of Israel at the time of His millennial reign.

During the tribulation two witnesses sent by God will confound the world with their testimony, even at the peril of their lives.

Eventually they will be killed by the antichrist, but after three and a half days they will rise from the dead and be transported into heaven in "the cloud."[49]

At the time of the tribulation, Israel will be attacked and nearly destroyed; but Christ will intervene at His coming and defeat the armies arrayed against Israel in the Valley of Armageddon.

The Day of Atonement is a somber celebration that calls for a fearful introspection in preparation for the coming judgment. Those whose lives have been redeemed through the blood of the Lamb need not fear the final judgment because Jesus has already paid our debt and taken our punishment! He has made us righteous through His finished work on the cross. The words of God given through His servant Jude are a source of comfort and hope to those who long for His appearing:

> But you, beloved, building yourselves up in the love of God, waiting anxiously for the mercy of our Lord Jesus Christ to eternal life. And have mercy on some, who are doubting; save others, snatching them out of the fire; and on some have mercy with fear, hating even the garment polluted by the flesh.
>
> Now to Him who is able to keep you from stumbling, and to make you stand in the presence of His glory blameless with great joy, to the only God our Savior, through Jesus Christ our Lord be glory, majesty, dominion and authority, before all time and now and forever. Amen.[50]

THE FEAST OF TABERNACLES

"Speak to the sons of Israel, saying, 'On the fifteenth of this seventh month is the Feast of Booths for seven days to the Lord'" (Leviticus 23:33).

The Feast of Tabernacles (Booths), known also as *Sukkot* in Hebrew, begins on the fifteenth day of Tishri. It commemorates the days when Israel lived in booths during their exodus from Egypt. The word *Sukkot* means booths. The Lord dwelt (tabernacled) with the Israelites in the wilderness throughout their wanderings. For forty years His presence overshadowed the Tabernacle which was located in the center of the camp.

The Feast of Tabernacles will be fulfilled when Christ reigns with His saints and tabernacles with Israel, not just for 1000 years but for eternity. Sukkot is the fall feast of harvest, fulfilled by the ingathering of all true believers in Jesus Christ.

> And I saw the holy city, new Jerusalem, coming down out of heaven from God, made ready as a bride adorned for her husband. And I heard a loud voice from the throne, saying, "Behold the tabernacle of God is among men, and He will dwell among them, and they shall be His people, and God Himself will be among them."[51]

The Levites were camped closest to the Tabernacle on three sides, in order that they could tend to their priestly functions. The other eleven tribes of Israel camped around the Levites and on all four sides of the Tabernacle. This too is a prophetic picture of the Lord dwelling in the midst of His redeemed for all eternity. In that glorious day, there will be no need for a copy of God's presence through either a Tabernacle or a Temple. John described the New Jerusalem: "I saw no temple in it, for the Lord God the Almighty and the Lamb are its temple."[52]

During the days between the Day of Atonement and the start of Sukkot, observant Jews still construct makeshift shelters outside their homes. These decorated and festive booths are gathering places for families, friends and neighbors throughout the seven days of Sukkot.

The Four Species

During the seven days when the Feast of Tabernacles is celebrated, four species are gathered and waved in petition and praise to God. This biblical directive states: "Now on the first day you shall take for yourselves the foliage of beautiful trees, palm branches and boughs of leafy trees and willows of the brook, and you shall rejoice before the Lord your God for seven days."[53]

The four species include a date palm frond, a bough of a myrtle tree, a willow branch (collectively called *lulav*) and a citron branch, called *an etrog*. The lulav is held in the right hand, while the etrog is held in the left hand. As the hands are held apart, the following prayer is recited: "Blessed are You, God our Lord, King of the Universe, Who has sanctified us with His commandments and commanded us to take the lulav." Then the hands are brought together, and the lulav is waved in the four directions as well as up and down as a prayer offering for abundant rain in the coming year. Throughout the Feast of Tabernacles, the four species were carried about and waved during various ceremonies.

The Water Libation

During Sukkot at the time of the Temple, the high priest went down to the Pool of Siloam (*Shiloah* in Hebrew means "the water is sent") and gathered water in a gold pitcher. Then he and a large number of worshippers processed back up to the Temple singing songs of praise as they went. When they reached the Water Gate, they were met by musicians who sounded the shofar and the silver trumpets. Water from Siloam and ceremonial wine were poured out simultaneously on the horns of the altar as a praise offering to God.

According to the Gospels, Jesus was present in Jerusalem for the Feast of Tabernacles. On the last day of the feast, Jesus stood in the Temple and cried out, "He who believes in Me, as the Scripture said, 'From his innermost being will flow rivers of living water.'"[54] The following day as Jesus was leaving the Temple precincts, He saw a man blind from birth. After applying clay to his eyes, Jesus told him to go wash in the pool of Siloam. "So he went away and washed, and came back seeing."[55]

The Feast of Tabernacles was a time of unprecedented joy at the Temple. The sages of Israel declared: "Whoever has not seen the Festival of the Water Libation has never experienced true joy."[56] The Water Libation festival, which was also celebrated each evening throughout the Feast, lasted late into the night. This event took place in the Women's Court where the men sang and danced to the sounds of joyful music. Those who desired could bring their own musical instruments and join with the Levitical musicians. Sukkot was one of the few times when flutes were played in the Temple.

As part of the Water Libation festivities, the Women's Court was illumined at night by rows of huge lamps towering about fifty feet into the air. According to an ancient Jewish text, when burning these lamps cast a glow bright enough to read by anywhere in the city.

The Bible describes how Jesus stood in the Temple and declared: "I am the Light of the world; he who follows Me will not walk in the darkness, but will have the Light of life."[57] The prophet Isaiah described Jesus' earthly ministry by saying: "The people who walk in darkness will see a great light; those who live in a dark land, the light will shine on them."[58] John identified Jesus as the "true Light which, coming into the world enlightens every man."[59] This truth of Jesus as the Light is borne out in the Book of Revelation where it is written, "And the city has no need of sun or of the moon to shine on it, for the glory of God has illumined it, and its lamp is the Lamb."[60]

Sacrifices and Prayers for the Nations

Throughout the seven days of Sukkot, seventy bulls were sacrificed on the altar and prayers were offered asking the Lord to bless all the nations of the world. Sukkot is not just a festival for the Jews; it is and has always been a festival for the nations. The Feast of Tabernacles (Booths) will find its ultimate fulfillment during the millennial reign of Christ when, as Zechariah prophesied, the people from all nations who survive the tribulation "will go up from year to year to worship the King, the Lord of hosts and to celebrate the Feast of Booths."[61]

During the days of the kings of Israel, a large platform was erected in the center of the Women's Court. Atop the platform a special booth was constructed for this feast, under which the king would stand and read from the Torah. The prophet Micah gave a prophetic word concerning this aspect of the feast when the Messiah reigns over the nations of the earth from Jerusalem:

And it shall come about in the last days that the mountain of the house of the Lord will be established as the chief of the mountains. It will be raised above the hills, and the peoples will stream to it. Many nations will come and say, "Come and let us go up to the mountain of the Lord and to the house of the God of Jacob, that He may teach us about His ways and that we may walk in his paths." From Zion will go forth the law, even the word of the Lord from Jerusalem. And He will judge between many people and render decisions for mighty, distant nations. Then they will hammer their swords into plowshares and their spears into pruning hooks; nation will not lift up sword against nation, and never again will they train for war.[62]

Simchat Torah

The Feast of Tabernacles continues to be a time of great celebration for Jews around the world. One of the happiest times to be in Israel is during the Feast of Tabernacles. Booths are erected everywhere. Most hotels construct large booths to accommodate their many Jewish guests who use the Feast of Tabernacles as a time for family gatherings. Special prayer services are conducted at the Western Wall throughout the entire seven days.

The day after Sukkot, the twenty-second day of Tishri, is called *Simchat Torah,* which is a celebration of the Torah. When the Temple stood, the Torah scrolls were joyfully paraded about with singing, dancing and prayers of thanksgiving. Today Simchat Torah is celebrated at the Western Wall in similar fashion.

From Pentecost to the very present hour, the message of the church has always been the same—THE KING IS COMING! But there is coming a day when all the redeemed of God, Jews and Gentiles from around the world, will gather to celebrate the Feast of Tabernacles; and with unified voices they shall make the most joyful proclamation ever heard upon the earth—THE KING IS HERE!

Chapter 14

PROPHECY THROUGH TYPES

Normally when we hear the term *prophecy,* we think of passages found in the Prophets or in various New Testament writings, but woven into the Scriptures are prophetic revelations called *types.* While types in the Bible have immediate relevance, they also point to some future event or person in God's unfolding drama of redemption. A type may be a person, a symbol or an event; it may even be a combination of the three. Types in Scripture most often represent or prefigure an event associated with some aspect of Christ's life and ministry. The fulfillment or object of a type is called the antitype. In almost every case, types are identified and explained in the Bible.

Both the Old and New Testaments possess a unity that defies comprehension, and types play a major role in that unity. Whether you are reading Genesis or Isaiah, the Gospels or the writings of Paul, types are interposed within the passages of the Bible. If a type is not made clear in the original source, often it is revealed in another part of Scripture. This is a fulfillment of Jesus' words: "But when He, the Spirit of truth, comes, He will guide you into all the truth."[1]

It is not possible to consider every type presented in Scripture, but even the study of a few types will expand one's understanding of both prophecy and the overall revelation of prophecy in the Bible.

ADAM AS A TYPE

In Genesis Adam is depicted as a type. Beyond the fact liberals question the historicity of Genesis, especially its teachings about creation and the flood, even those holding to a high view of Scripture sometimes fail to recognize the deeper meaning and relationship between Adam and Christ. Paul, under the inspiration of the Holy Spirit, described this relationship:

> Therefore, just as through one man sin entered into the world, and death through sin, and so death spread to all men, because all sinned—for until the Law sin was in the world, but sin is not imputed when there is no law. Nevertheless, death reigned from Adam until Moses, even over those who had not sinned in the likeness of the offense of Adam, who is a type of him who was to come.[2]
>
> For since by a man came death, by a man also came the resurrection of the dead. For as in Adam all die, so also in Christ all will be made alive…So also it is written, "The first MAN, Adam, BECAME A LIVING SOUL." The last Adam became a life-giving spirit. However, the spiritual is not first, but the natural; then the spiritual. The first man is from the earth, earthy; the second man is from heaven.[3]

NOAH AND THE ARK

Noah is presented in Matthew 24 as a type of the church that will be spared from the wrath of God at the close of the age. In His Mount Olivet discourse Christ compared His coming to the "days of Noah." He spoke about the continued routine of human activity until "the day" Noah entered the ark. Immediately following this statement, Jesus described a scene that surely relates to the rapture of the church, wherein two men would be in the field, one would be taken and the other left; He also described two women grinding at the mill, one would be taken and the other left. It should be further noted Christ identified the Bible's account of Noah and the flood as a literal event. If Christ taught the flood truly happened, who among His followers should doubt?

The Book of Hebrews described how Noah was warned by God "about things not yet seen," and "in reverence prepared an ark for the salvation of his household."[4] Peter presented Noah as a type of the church being spared from the wrath of God, when he wrote "the days of Noah, during the construction of the ark, in which a few, that is, eight persons, were brought safely through the water."[5]

ABRAHAM AND ISAAC

Abraham is called "the father of all who believe."[6] There is so much about this man's life every Christian should desire to emulate. Although Abraham was not perfect by any means, he was a man of great faith and unwavering obedience. On a few occasions, he ran ahead of God and sometimes took matters into his own hands, as though to help God make good on His promises. Such was the case when Abraham had sexual relations with his wife's servant, Hagar, in order to produce offspring, even though God had promised Abraham his descendants would come through his wife, Sarah. Regardless of such failings, Abraham walked with God throughout his life.

One day God called Abraham to leave the security of his homeland and family and travel to a distant place. At the same time, God made an everlasting covenant with Abraham and gave him the land of Israel as "an everlasting inheritance."

> "I will establish My covenant between Me and you and your descendants after you throughout their generations, for an everlasting covenant, to be God to you and to your descendants after you. I will give you and to your descendants after you, the land of your sojournings, all the land of Canaan, for an everlasting possession; and I will be their God."[7]

Moreover, God promised to make Abraham the father of a multitude of nations, and through his offspring the world would be blest.

In obedience to the Lord's command, Abraham set out, not knowing where he was going or what awaited him when he got there. Over the course of many years, the Lord tested Abraham's faith and obedience several times. However, no test was as difficult as the occasion when God directed Abraham to offer his son Isaac as a burnt offering.

For many people the account of Abraham going off to sacrifice his son is just another Bible story they learned as children. Some theologians have suggested this event in Abraham's life is an allegory of every man's search for a true understanding about God and acceptable ways to worship Him. Other theologians believe this event was God's way of telling Abraham not to engage in human sacrifices, as was the custom of his pagan neighbors. Frankly, none of these interpretations comes even close to the truth.

Abraham's willingness to offer his son Isaac as a sacrifice to God is a true story. While one may draw many legitimate lessons from this event, such as Abraham's obedience to God or Isaac's submission to his father, the account is not as much about Abraham and Isaac, as it is about God's plan to sacrifice His own Son for the sins of the world. Once this truth is understood, the event takes on a greatly expanded dimension.

In Genesis 22 Abraham and Isaac are both presented as types. Abraham is a type of God the Father, while Isaac is a type of God's Son, Jesus Christ. Abraham's willingness to sacrifice Isaac was a living demonstration of the drama of redemption that would be carried out on Skull Hill centuries later. While this incident focuses on Abraham's obedience to God, it is also a prophetic image of God's eternal plan to bring salvation to mankind. Few types in the Scripture are as transparent as this one.

In order to understand the meaning of Abraham and Isaac as types, it is necessary to turn to Genesis 22 and see verse by verse just how every portion of this account parallels actual events in Christ's passion and death.

God's Call and Abraham's Response

One day God called out "Abraham, Abraham!" The Patriarch answered as he had so many times before, "Here I am." It was God who had chosen Abraham, rather than Abraham who had chosen God. The Lord knew Abraham by name, and Abraham knew the voice of the Lord, two essentials for a meaningful relationship with the heavenly Father.

We must never forget the Lord, our Shepherd, knows each of us by name. "...And he calls his own sheep by name and leads them out...My sheep hear My voice, and I know them, and they follow Me...."[8] Before any of us ever thought of searching after the Lord, He came searching for us.

Abraham responded to the voice of God without hesitation, "Here I am." Whatever God wanted and wherever God directed him to go were settled issues for this man of faith. Abraham is our model in matters of faith and obedience.

God has a Place for You!

God told Abraham, "Take now your son, your only son, whom you love, Isaac, and go to the land of Moriah and offer him there as a burnt offering on one of the mountains of which I will tell you." The antitype of this text was revealed centuries later by John: "For God so loved the world, that He gave His only begotten Son, that whosoever believes in Him shall not perish, but have eternal life."[9] There would come a day when the Father in heaven would make the same journey with His Son to the same place and offer Him up as a sacrifice for the sins of the world—a truth that causes this story to take on eternal significance.

Abraham rose early the next morning, saddled his donkey and began a long and arduous journey with his son and two servants. Abraham cut the wood needed for the sacrifice. It is most revealing Abraham himself would undertake the back-straining task of splitting firewood, even though he had two strapping young men in his employ. Yet that is precisely what Abraham did. There are certain experiences of life that can never be assigned to another; this is especially true of our personal duty to believe and obey the Word of God.

Every aspect of our salvation is a free gift of God's grace. Down to the smallest detail, God gives it all; we only receive. Not only did God give His only begotten Son to die for us, He furnished the wood on which His Son would be crucified. God even created the men who would drive the nails into Christ's hands and feet. There is no aspect of salvation that does not belong to God alone!

After splitting the firewood, Abraham, Isaac and the two young men set off together "to the place" God had chosen. The fact God had in mind a specific place where this event was to take place is highly significant. God never does anything without a reason or purpose, and His purposes for choosing the precise location for Abraham to sacrifice Isaac would be made clear in due season. Paul wrote: "And we know that God causes all things to work together for good to those who love God, to those who are called according to His purpose."[10]

Strength for the Journey

The journey was long and difficult, over high mountains and deep valleys; it was not until the third day Abraham reached the point where he could see the place where God was leading him. The remarkable words "the third day" are a vital part of redemption's story. God always has a third day for those who believe! The agonies of our lives will inevitably bring us to God's third day of hope and resurrection. God's Word assures us, "Those who sow in tears shall reap with joyful shouting."[11] The Psalmist declared, "Weeping may last for the night, but a shout of joy comes in the morning."[12]

At this point in the journey, Abraham instructed his two servants: "Stay here with the donkey, the lad and I will go yonder and worship, and we will come back to you." Abraham's extraordinary faith enabled him to proceed to the appointed mountain of God where the imponderable act would occur. Abraham and Sarah had waited many years for the birth of Isaac; furthermore, God had promised Abraham's posterity would come through Isaac. Just how God would fulfill His promise was unknown to Abraham; yet he believed and traveled on to the place God was directing him.

Abraham's statement to his servants, "...the lad and I will go yonder and worship and we will come back to you"...is one of the most remarkable affirmations of faith in all the Scriptures. This statement is explained in the book of Hebrews:

> By faith Abraham, when he was tested, offered up Isaac, and he who had received the promises was offering up his only begotten son; it was he to whom it was said, "IN ISAAC YOUR DESCENDANTS SHALL BE CALLED." He considered that God is able to raise people even from the dead, from which he also received him back as a type.[13]

Even before Abraham left on his painful journey, he believed God would keep His promises regarding Isaac. If God required the death of Isaac, surely it had to mean He would raise him from the dead. Here, more than any other place in Scripture, we can understand why Abraham is called "the father of all who believe."

Abraham placed the wood for the sacrifice on his son Isaac, and he himself carried the fire and the knife. The Bible says: "So the two of them walked on together." Isaac is a type of Christ who bore His own cross to Calvary. "They took Jesus, therefore, and He went out, bearing His own cross, to the place called the Place of a Skull, which is called in Hebrew, Golgotha."[14]

Two other images from Christ's passion and death are displayed in Genesis 22. First, there is the image of Abraham going forth with the fire and the knife. "For God so loved the world that He *gave* His only begotten Son." The death of Jesus Christ was not due to the scheming plans of the Jewish leaders or the Romans; from the beginning it was in the heart of God to offer His Son for the sins of the world. Jesus said, "I lay down My life so that I may take it again. No one has taken it away from me, but I lay it down on My own initiative."[15]

Secondly, the image of Abraham and Isaac walking on together to the place of sacrifice is seen in the intimate conversation Jesus and His heavenly Father shared in the Garden of Gethsemane. "Father, if You are willing, remove this cup from Me; yet not My will, but Yours be done."[16] Had Jesus not added those closing words to His prayer, His ascension could have happened that night in the Garden of Gethsemane. If ever anyone deserved to have a prayer answered, it was the sinless Son of God; yet the Bible says, "He humbled Himself by becoming obedient to the point of death, even death on a cross."[17]

Behold the Lamb!

As Abraham and Isaac walked on together, the lad inquired, "Behold, the fire and the wood, but where is the lamb for the burnt offering?" Abraham responded, "God will provide for Himself the lamb for the burnt offering, my son." Abraham's words were more than an answer to his son's inquiry; they were both an affirmation of his faith and a prophecy that would be fulfilled not only that very day but also on the day when the Lamb of God would be nailed to the cross. The exact Hebrew translation of Abraham's words is this: "God will **provide *Himself* the lamb** for the burnt offering, my son!" When John the Baptist saw Jesus, he declared, "Behold the Lamb of God, who takes away the sin of the world." These words too were a prophecy regarding Jesus' sacrificial death.

At last Abraham and Isaac came to *the place* where God had instructed him to go. Abraham built an altar, arranged the wood, bound Isaac and laid him on the altar. One cannot imagine the pain that must have pierced the heart of Abraham as he prepared to sacrifice the son he loved more than life itself; nor can one know the agonizing thoughts of Isaac when he finally understood his role in the ceremony.

As Abraham stretched out his hand to slay his son, the angel of the Lord called out to him, "Abraham, Abraham!" The Patriarch responded, "Here I am." Whether the angel of the Lord was Christ or whether the divine voice was that of a heaven-sent messenger, we do not know for certain. But we do know why God intervened to spare Isaac from death and deliver Abraham from his most distressing hour. "Do not stretch out your hand against the lad, and do nothing to him; for now I know that you fear God, since you have not withheld your son, your only son from Me."

God never asked Abraham to do something He Himself was unwilling to do. The blood of Isaac could not have atoned for anyone. However, the day would come when the blood of God's Son would make full atonement for the sins of the whole world.

Abraham looked up and saw a ram caught in the thicket by his horns, "and Abraham offered him up for a burnt offering in the place of his son." Abraham's prophetic words that God would "provide Himself the lamb" were fulfilled at that very moment, but the ultimate fulfillment would occur many centuries later on a hill called Golgotha. On the day of Christ's crucifixion outside the walls of Jerusalem, there was no ram caught in the thicket waiting to spare God's Son from the ordeal of the cross or to prevent His Father's heart from being broken. On that day the antitype of Genesis 22, Jesus Christ, "bore our sins in His body on the cross, so that we might die to sin and live to righteousness."[18]

Jesus once remarked to the Jews, "Your father Abraham rejoiced to see My day, and he saw it and was glad." Surely Genesis 22 describes the meaning of the words "My day" in the life of Abraham.

On Mount Moriah, the Lord will Provide!

After Abraham offered the divinely furnished ram on the altar, he called the name of that place "The Lord Will Provide, as it is said to this day, 'In the mount of the Lord it will be provided.'" The place God had chosen for Abraham to offer his son Isaac was Mount Moriah.

If you go to Israel today and inquire about the location of Mount Moriah, you will be directed to the most hallowed place on earth — the Temple Mount! That sacred mountain, chosen by God as the place of Abraham's sacrifice of Isaac, would become the place where Solomon would build the Temple and the place where the shekinah glory of God would come down and dwell. Ultimately, it would become the one location on earth where the Lord provided for man's greatest need — redemption!

Gordon's Calvary and the Garden Tomb

The story of Abraham's willingness to sacrifice his son is far from over at this point. There is much more! At the northernmost point of Mount Moriah is a skull-shaped hill called Calvary. The three-acre site is known today as "Gordon's Calvary and the Garden Tomb."

In 1885 General Charles G. Gordon, a British military hero, was staying in the home of Horatio and Anna Spafford; both were very devout Christians. The Spaffords had moved to Jerusalem after losing most of their material possessions in the Chicago fire and after their four daughters were subsequently lost in a ship wreck. It was following the second tragedy Horatio Spafford penned his immortal hymn, "It is Well with My Soul."

Looking directly across from the Spafford's home, General Gordon saw the form of a skull-shaped rock on the side of a hill. After some serious study and investigation, he concluded it had to be the site of Christ's crucifixion. General Gordon later wrote:

> The morning after my arrival at Jerusalem, I went to the Skull Hill, and felt convinced that it must be north of the Altar. Leviticus 1:11 says that the victims are to be slain on the side of the Altar northwards (literally to be slain slant wise or askew on the north of the Altar); if a particular direction was given by God about where the types were to be slain, it is a sure deduction that the prototype would be slain in some position as the Altar; this the Skull Hill fulfills. The Latin Holy Sepulchre is west of the Altar, and therefore, unless the types are wrong, it should never have been taken as the site.[19]

General Gordon helped to secure the funds required to purchase the land around the Skull Hill. After the three-acre site had been purchased, excavations were begun at the site. Archaeologists discovered a tomb cut from solid rock in which only one person had ever been buried. They also discovered evidence proving the tomb was located in a rich man's garden. Beneath the garden and not far from the tomb, they found a huge cistern that held 175,000 gallons of water.

There are two sites in Jerusalem that claim to be the place of Christ's crucifixion and resurrection. In addition to Gordon's Calvary and the Garden Tomb, there is the ancient Church of the Holy Sepulcher, located a short distance west of the Temple Mount. The Church of the Holy Sepulcher was erected in the year 325 by

Emperor Constantine, several years after he had sent his mother to the Holy Land to search out sites associated with the life and ministry of Jesus Christ.

According to legend, Queen Helena, Emperor Constantine's mother, was brought to the site where the Church of the Holy Sepulcher now stands. She was shown three crosses supposedly discovered at the site. In order to determine which one was the true cross of Jesus, each cross was carried separately into the room of a sick woman. The first two crosses failed to change the woman's condition, but when the third cross was brought into her room, she was instantly healed. Thus, it is claimed Helena was not only able to identify the true cross of Christ, but also she was able to verify the site where He had been crucified and buried. Both accounts, the discovery of the true cross of Christ and the identification of the site of His crucifixion and burial, are pure fantasy. Helena arrived in the Holy Land nearly 300 years after the crucifixion and burial of Christ had taken place. In the meantime, Jerusalem had been destroyed and rebuilt twice.

Even though the Church of the Holy Sepulcher has been accepted for over 1600 years by the Roman Catholic Church and others as the site of Christ's crucifixion, burial and resurrection, numerous scholars have raised questions regarding its authenticity. The Church of the Holy Sepulcher stands on the site of an ancient rock quarry. The tomb inside the church, if there ever was one, has been destroyed. Archaeologists have never found any trace of a garden. Furthermore, the site does not meet the biblical descriptions.

Gordon's Calvary and the Garden Tomb are supported by both credible archaeological evidence and by various biblical descriptions. The Garden Tomb, located near the skull-shaped hill (the place of the skull), is in an area where ancient burial sites have since been located. Archaeologists have discovered indisputable evidence the area near Gordon's Calvary was once a stone quarry, and it had been used as a place for executions. Gordon's Calvary and the Garden Tomb are located near the Damascus Gate and an ancient highway. The Romans nearly always carried out executions along a busy thoroughfare.

Ruins of an ancient church, dedicated to the first Christian martyr Stephen, were found nearby. A cave located on Skull Hill is known today as Jeremiah's Grotto. This traditional site is believed to be the place where Jeremiah penned the words: "Is it nothing to you who pass this way? Look and see if there is any pain like my pain which was severely dealt out to me, which the Lord inflicted on the day of His fierce anger."[20]

Gordon's Calvary and the Garden Tomb meet the Scripture's description to the letter, especially its location at the northern-most side of Mount Moriah and its northern proximity to the Temple. While the Bible does not specify the northern part of Mount Moriah as the site of the crucifixion, all four Gospels — Matthew 27:33, Mark 15:22, Luke 23:33 and John 19:17 — describe Jesus' crucifixion at "the *place* of the Skull." The words *the place* are used four times in Genesis 22, repeatedly showing that God had a purpose in guiding Abraham to this location.

God required animals to be sacrificed on *the north side* of the altar.[21] He also instructed that the table of showbread, which was a symbol of the Messiah, be placed on the north side of the Holy Place.[22]

While this author is persuaded of the authenticity of Gordon's Calvary and the Garden Tomb as the true site of the crucifixion and the resurrection because of the archaeological and biblical evidence, this or any location is nonessential to salvation. What is essential to salvation is belief in Christ's death and resurrection. Paul declared: "...if you confess with your mouth Jesus as Lord, and believe in your heart that God raised Him from the dead, you will be saved; for with the heart a person believes, resulting in righteousness, and with the mouth he confesses, resulting in salvation."[23]

Those who visit the fabricated tomb inside the Church of the Holy Sepulcher, or those who enter the Garden Tomb quickly discover that each site bears witness to one great truth — both are empty. Jesus lives!

CHRIST AND MELCHIZEDEK

One of the most important types in Scripture is Melchizedek. The Bible identifies him as a type of Jesus Christ, our Priest and King. The role of Christ as High Priest is a neglected teaching in the church today. Of course it is imperative we focus on the redeeming work of Christ as Savior, since that is our entrance into the Kingdom of God. Likewise, it is essential that we focus on the return of Christ as King, since His coming will bring about the fulfillment of our redemption. Yet it is mystifying to find so little emphasis being given to the priestly office of Christ, since it is through that office we are enabled to access the throne of God and claim the victory over sin and death. The priestly work of Christ offers all believers innumerable blessings and benefits in this life and in the life to come.

Who was Melchizedek?

A meeting between Melchizedek and Abraham is described in Genesis 14. The two men met as Abraham returned from a battle in the region of Damascus, where he and 318 of his men had defeated the armies of four kings and rescued his nephew Lot. Melchizedek is identified as the king of Salem and a priest of God Most High (El Elyon). The Most High God is not only the God of Israel, He is God over the whole earth. Nebuchadnezzar learned to know El Elyon through Daniel, and said of Him "...the Most High is ruler over the realm of mankind and bestows it on whomever He wishes."[24] Gabriel told Mary she would bear "the Son of the Most High."[25] Mary sang the praises of the Most High God, "who has brought down rulers from their thrones."[26]

Melchizedek offered Abraham bread and wine, and said: "Blessed be Abram of God Most High, Possessor of heaven and earth; and blessed be God Most High Who has delivered your enemies into your hand." Then Abraham gave Melchizedek a tenth of all he had.

Melchizedek is mentioned in Psalm 110, in which David prophetically described the reign of Jesus Christ at the close of the age. David declared about Christ: "The Lord has sworn and will not change His mind, 'You are a priest forever according to the order of

Melchizedek.'" It was God who declared Melchizedek to be a type of Christ's priesthood.

The third time Melchizedek is mentioned in Scripture occurs in the Book of Hebrews, where both previous accounts, Genesis 14 and Psalm 110, are explained as having been fulfilled by Christ who is a High Priest according to the order of Melchizedek. *Melek* means King, while *Zedek* means righteousness. Melchizedek was the king of righteousness. He was also king of Salem, meaning the king of peace. Salem is understood by most scholars as referring to Jerusalem. Paul declared of Christ, "He Himself is our peace,"…and he obtained our peace "through the blood of His cross."[27] Christ is both the King of Righteousness and the King of Peace.

The Bible does not explain the meaning of Melchizedek's gifts of bread and wine, but such gifts were commonly given in Old Testament times as a gesture of friendship. The bread and wine are also descriptive of Christ's role as Priest, when He offered the Passover bread and wine to His disciples during the Passover meal. The bread of the Passover is Christ's body given on the cross; the wine of Passover is His blood shed for the sins of the world. When Christ was nailed to the cross, He made atonement for the sins of the world as both Victim and Priest.

The Bible places great emphasis on the fact Abraham saw himself as subservient to Melchizedek when he received Melchizedek's blessing and gave him a tenth of all he had. According to the Book of Hebrews, the fact Abraham was the beginning of Aaron's priestly line demonstrates the Levitical priesthood was inferior to Christ's priesthood.

Scholars continue to debate the precise identity of Melchizedek from the descriptions given in these three biblical sources (Genesis 14, Psalm 110 and Hebrews 7.) Jewish scholars teach Melchizedek was Noah's son, Shem, who was still living at this time according to the biblical timeline. Abraham's father Terah was a descendant of Shem who would have been head of that tribe. Therefore it would have been proper for Abraham to recognized Melchizedek's authority over him. Martin Luther held to this interpretation.

Others have suggested the appearance of Melchizedek was an appearance of the pre-incarnated Christ (a theophany) to Abraham.

The chief argument for this interpretation is the description of Melchizedek given in Hebrews: "Without father, without mother, without genealogy, having neither beginning of days nor end of life, but made like the Son of God, he remains a priest perpetually."[28]

At first glance this interpretation would seem to be an open and shut case, since it describes certain aspects of Christ's divine nature. However, the rendering of the original text does not state Melchizedek had no father or mother, but rather he was *without recorded genealogy* or there was no record of Melchizedek's ancestry.

Before Levitical priests could serve in the Temple, they were required to prove by their genealogy they were descendants of Levi. In Nehemiah's time, certain priests were disqualified because their genealogy could not be authenticated.[29] Further the text in Hebrews does not say Melchizedek *was* the Son of God, but he was *like* the Son of God, making him a type. If Melchizedek's appearance was a theophany, he could hardly have been a type of himself.

A third interpretation presents Melchizedek as the literal king of Salem and a priest of the Most High God. Because Melchizedek was a believer in the Most High God (El Elyon), it is possible he and Abraham may have known one another. Melchizedek came on the scene as king and priest without any credentials, other than his divine appointment to that office. God had arranged for the meeting between Abraham and Melchizedek to take place as a witness that Christ was both King and Priest, in every way superior to any other priesthood. Of these three interpretations regarding Melchizedek's identity, the third interpretation which affirms Melchizedek as a real person and a type of Christ is the choice of most conservative Bible scholars.

There is a humorous story about a preacher who gave a series of twelve sermons on Melchizedek. At the conclusion of his twelfth and final sermon, he said to his congregation, "So you see, brethren, we really don't know much about Melchizedek after all." Although our knowledge about Melchizedek may be limited, and though it may be difficult to unveil the mystery of Melchizedek, the Bible clearly states Melchizedek, king/priest of Salem, is a type of Christ who was, is and shall ever be the King of Peace, King of Righteousness and High Priest forever.

The Meaning of Christ's Priesthood

The author of Hebrews contrasts the priesthood of Aaron with Christ's priesthood *after the order of Melchizedek.* The Levitical priesthood was "a copy and shadow of the heavenly things."[30] The Levitical priesthood was temporary, as all Levitical priests died, but Christ's priesthood, after the order of Melchizedek, continues forever. Christ's priesthood was borne of righteousness and perfection, while the Levitical priesthood was replete with imperfections.

Under the Levitical code, the high priest entered into the Holy of Holies once a year to offer an atoning sacrifice for the sins of the people. Before undertaking this task, he was required to make atonement for his own sins. But Christ as High Priest after the order of Melchizedek did not need to offer up sacrifices for his own sins, because he was altogether sinless and His priesthood is superior in that He will not die. Since Christ offered the sacrifice of Himself "once for all," His priesthood renders the Levitical priesthood obsolete.[31]

The Bible teaches after Christ offered Himself on the cross, He entered "through the greater and more perfect tabernacle, not made with hands...and entered the holy place...and offered Himself without blemish to God...for this reason He is the mediator of a new covenant."[32] The mediator of the old covenant was Moses and the law. The priests of the Levitical order could only offer up animal sacrifices for the people, which they had to do repeatedly, but Christ as High Priest offered up Himself once for all. The Levitical priesthood was based on the law; Christ's priesthood is based on grace. John declared: "For the Law was given through Moses; grace and truth were realized through Jesus Christ."[33]

Christ our Intercessor

In His role as High Priest, Christ is seated at the right hand of God the Father, where "He always lives to make intercession for them."[34] One of the most comforting verses in the Bible states: "For we do not have a high priest who cannot sympathize with our weaknesses, but One who has been tempted in all things as we are, yet without sin. Therefore let us draw near with confidence to the throne of grace, so that we may receive mercy and find grace to help in time of need."[35]

Christ exercised his priestly role on the cross by offering up Himself for our sins, and He exercises His priestly office today as our intercessor. He is on our side. Christ not only enables us to live a Christian life, He is our life, as Paul declared, "Christ in you, the hope of glory!" Jesus Christ is perpetually before the Father's throne making intercession for His redeemed and giving us direct access to the Father. The power and beauty of our prayer-life is wrapped up in this aspect of the divine atonement—"He always lives to make intercession for them."[36]

Christ, Our Priest and King

Finally, Melchizedek foreshadows Christ as both King and Priest. Under the law Christ could not have been a priest because He was of the tribe of Judah, not Levi. Under the law no priest of Levi could become king. However, Christ, after the order of Melchizedek, is both King and Priest.

Zechariah wrote: "Yes, it is He who will build the temple of the Lord, and He who will bear the honor and sit and rule on His throne. Thus, He will be a priest on His throne, and the counsel of peace will be between the two offices."[37] In His millennial reign, Christ will rule as Priest and King from the Temple. "And the Lord will be king over all the earth; in that day the Lord will be the only one, and His name the only one."[38]

TYPES OF CHRIST IN THE EXODUS

The Bronze Serpent

Types in the Old Testament bear witness to the unity of the Scriptures. It was not until the New Testament was written that types and prophecies in the Old Testament could be fully understood. The old adage says it best—Christ is in the Old [Testament] concealed; Christ is in the New [Testament] revealed. Jesus Himself unveiled the meaning of several types associated with Moses when he led the Children of Israel out of Egypt.

As the Israelites wandered in the desert, they spoke against Moses, "Why have you brought us up out of Egypt to die in the wilderness?" In His anger God sent fiery serpents among the people, and they began to die. After they pleaded with Moses to intercede for them, God instructed Moses to make a fiery serpent of bronze and set it on a pole. If anyone was bitten by a serpent, he only had to look on the bronze serpent in order to live.

In Jesus' encounter with Nicodemus, He told him, "You must be born again." He also stated: "As Moses lifted up the serpent in the wilderness, even so must the Son of Man be lifted up; so that whoever believes will in Him have eternal life."[39] The message from the cross is always the same—"Look and Live!" Nicodemus came to understand these words in a most literal and personal way at Calvary.

The burial of Jesus was superintended by none other than Nicodemus.[40] Between his late-night encounter with Jesus and the event of Christ's death on the cross, Nicodemus became a changed man. As Nicodemus prepared Christ's body for burial, he truly looked on the One whom he had pierced. Even though Nicodemus was a member of the Sanhedrin, it is clear he had no direct role in Christ's death, but like us, his sin required Christ's atoning sacrifice.

The theme "Look and Live" is also found in Zechariah's prophecy; it concerns the actions and response of the Jewish people at the coming of Christ: "so they will look on Me whom they have pierced…."[41] As the post-resurrection accounts of Christ demonstrate, the marks of the nails remained in the glorified and resurrected body of Jesus Christ. One day not only the Jews but we ourselves shall *look* upon the wounds of the Savior and *live* for all eternity.

Christ, the Rock

It is amazing how many aspects of Israel's exodus from Egypt to the Promised Land are later identified by Scripture as types of Christ's redeeming work. In fact, the entire exodus experience is presented by the Scriptures as a type, whereby all the saints of God are brought from the bondage of sin and death into the Kingdom of life and freedom through the atonement of Christ. And little wonder, say most Bible scholars, since the Book of Exodus describes an angel who was sent by God "to bring you into the place which I have prepared....Be on your guard before him and obey his voice; do not be rebellious toward him, for he will not pardon your transgression, since My name is in Him."[42] Beyond all question, this passage refers to Jesus Christ in whom the very name of God dwelt.

There are two accounts of Moses bringing water out of a rock in order to quench the thirst of the Israelites. The first account in Exodus 17 details God's command that Moses strike the rock with his staff. The second incident, recorded in Numbers 20, took place many years later when the Lord instructed Moses to "speak to the rock," and water in sufficient measure would be supplied. However in the second incident, Moses, in a fit of anger, struck the rock with his staff, not once but twice. Though the water came forth as before, God said to Moses: "Because you have not believed Me, to treat Me as holy in the sight of the sons of Israel, therefore you shall not bring this assembly into the land which I have given them."[43]

Initially one might think God was being overly harsh with Moses for such a small infraction, yet the seriousness of Moses' act of anger and the magnitude of his disobedience is explained by Paul:

> For I do not want you to be unaware, brethren, that our fathers were all under the cloud and all passed through the sea; and all were baptized into Moses in the cloud and in the sea; and all ate the same spiritual food; and all drank the same spiritual drink, for they were drinking from a spiritual rock which followed them; and the rock was Christ.[44]

The rock from which the people were given water to drink "was Christ." God's instructions to Moses on the first occasion that he strike the rock point to Christ's death on the cross. The reason behind God's instruction to Moses on the second occasion that he should "speak to the rock," was to demonstrate Christ's atoning death was made "once for all" and never needed to be repeated.[45] Today we need only speak words of repentance, and the "blood of Christ will cleanse us from all unrighteousness."

Another lesson that may be learned from these two accounts of water being brought out of a rock is the abundance of water involved.

The total number of people whose thirst was assuaged by this miracle was at least one and a half million. According to the Bible the adult men alone numbered 600,000. The water must have flowed like a mighty river in order to supply so many people with water for an unspecified period of time. Today Christ offers the water of life to as many as will receive Him.

Several times during His ministry, Jesus identified Himself as the source of the water of life. He said to the woman at Jacob's well in Samaria: "Everyone who drinks of this water will thirst again; but whoever drinks of the water that I will give him shall never thirst; but the water that I will give him will become in him a well of water springing up to eternal life."[46]

During the Feast of Tabernacles at the time of the water libations, Jesus stood in the Temple and cried out in a loud voice for all to hear: "If anyone is thirsty, let him come to Me and drink. He who believes in Me, as the Scripture said, 'From his innermost being will flow rivers of living water.'"[47] Jesus is not only the source of living water; He is the living water! These words spoken by Christ referred to the outpouring of the Holy Spirit into the hearts of all believers. How foolish we are to spend our lives, as did the Israelites, grumbling and complaining, when the Lord freely offers us all we will ever need through the power of the Holy Spirit. "The Lord's loving-kindnesses indeed never cease, for His compassions never fail. They are new every morning; Great is Your faithfulness."[48]

Long before Moses was appointed to lead the children of Israel from the bondage of slavery in Egypt into the glorious liberty of the Promised Land, God had made provision for their every need to be supplied. The children of Israel did not have to complain or grumble about the lack of food, water or anything else. They only needed to seek the help of God through prayer. Christ assures all believers every need will be supplied by our Father in heaven.

Throughout Scripture "The Rock" is portrayed as a type of Christ. Moses exalted *the Rock* in his song of praise to the Lord.[49] David referred to God as "the Rock" on several occasions, including Psalm 18:46: "The Lord lives, and blessed be my rock; and exalted be the God of my salvation." Jesus told Peter He would build His church on "this rock and the gates of Hades will not overpower it."[50]

It is very clear from the context of this passage and from various other passages of Scripture, Christ did not tell Peter (the rock) He would build his church on him, but rather upon Himself, the Rock. Those who espouse the first interpretation need to understand that Peter (the rock) is only the type; Christ (The Rock) is the antitype.

Christ, the Bread of Life

The manna that was given to the children of Israel in the wilderness was a type of Christ. Every morning, except the Sabbath, manna appeared upon the ground. There was no need to gather more than was necessary for each day, except on the sixth day when a two day's supply was to be gathered. God faithfully supplied the Israelites with manna for forty years, until they entered into the land of Canaan.

Not long after Jesus had fed the 5000 near the Sea of Galilee, He made the connection between Himself and the manna. Speaking to the assembled crowd, Jesus said:

"Truly, truly, I say to you, it is not Moses who has given you the bread out of heaven, but it is My father who gives you the true bread out of heaven. For the bread of God is that which comes down out of heaven, and gives life to the world....I am the bread of life; he who comes to Me will not hunger, and he who believes in Me will never thirst....Truly, truly, I say to you, he who believes has eternal life. I am the bread of life. Your fathers ate the manna in the wilderness, and they died. This is the bread which comes down out of heaven, so that one may eat of it and not die. I am the living bread that came down out of heaven; if anyone eats of this bread he will live forever; and the bread also which I will give for the life of the world is My flesh."[51]

The application of the manna as a type continues to be fulfilled by Christ who is the source and essence of life. Christ as the "bread of life" is evidenced through the bread of Passover and the bread of the Lord's Supper, when He gave it to them saying "This is My body which is given for you; do this in remembrance of Me."[52]

CONCLUSION

There are many other types used in the Scripture that point us to Christ or some aspect of God's redemptive work. The identification of types will always open your mind to a deeper understanding of God's Word. Upon discovery types usually elicit a great **AHA** response when the Bible stories you learned in Sunday school come to life with new and deeper relevance. As you read the Bible and discover the many types God has given to reveal Himself and His redemptive purposes, you will experience many **AHA moments.**

Chapter 15

PROPHECY AND THE TEMPLE

Muslims presently control the Temple Mount, due in large measure to policies set in place by the Israeli government in 1967. Moreover, Muslims eagerly plan for the day when the entire city of Jerusalem will be in their hands as well. A few years ago, the Muslims created an annual event called "Jerusalem Day," in order to remind themselves and the world of Islam's ultimate goal of gaining full sovereignty over Jerusalem. The Muslim celebration is intended to offset an Israeli observance by the same name that marks the reunification of Jerusalem following the War of 1967.

Considering the magnitude of global issues now threatening world peace, it is amazing so much of the world's attention is being directed at Jerusalem and the Temple Mount. Yet biblical prophecy assures us both Jerusalem and the Temple Mount will be center stage in the last days.

Except for a few brief intervals, the Temple Mount has been in the hands of the Muslims since 636, when Caliph Umar Abu Hafsa seized it as part of his conquest of the region. Immediately prior to Umar's capture of Jerusalem, he set up an encampment on the

Mount of Olives, opposite the Temple Mount and close to the site of Christ's ascension. It was near the same location Jesus had wept over the city and prophesied its destruction. Titus planned his siege of Jerusalem in AD 70 from the same location.

Shortly after Caliph Umar captured Jerusalem, he oversaw the construction of a wooden structure that came to be called "The Mosque of Umar." The present octagonal building called "The Dome of the Rock" was erected in 691 by Caliph Abd el-Malik. The al Aqsa Mosque at the southern end of the Temple Mount was constructed in 710. The entire Temple platform, known in Scripture as Mount Moriah, was renamed the Haram esh-Sharif (Noble Sanctuary) by the Muslims. Many Islamic leaders now claim the Jewish Temple never existed on the site.

A few years ago, the Muslims enlarged the area beneath the Temple Mount known as Solomon's Stables; this newest place of prayer will accommodate up to 5,000 worshipers. During the construction process, hundreds of tons of dirt, stones and precious artifacts were hauled out and dumped. As a direct result, huge bulges developed in both the southern and eastern retaining walls of the Temple Mount. A passage concerning bulging walls is found in Isaiah: "Therefore this iniquity will be to you like a breach about to fall, a bulge in a high wall, whose collapse comes suddenly in an instant...."[1] This passage may be prophetic because Israeli authorities claim the Temple Mount is so unstable that even a small earthquake could bring down the al Aqsa Mosque and the Dome of the Rock. If the Temple Mount should collapse for whatever reason, you may be certain the entire Muslim world will blame Israel.

Today Muslims are determined to secure all rights to the Temple Mount for themselves. They want to ban Christians and Jews from ever setting foot on the site or even at the Western Wall. Since 2000 the Israeli government has cooperated with the Islamic custodians (the Waqf) to limit the times when non-Muslims may visit the Temple Mount. Even now Christians and Jews are not permitted to take their Scriptures, display any religious symbols, or pray while visiting the Temple Mount. These outrageous restrictions contradict long-established Israeli policy that guarantees free and open access to all holy places. Both Jews and Christians have as much right to pray and worship on the Temple Mount as do Muslims. These developments are helping to set the stage for end-time events and ultimately the coming of the antichrist.

The Temple Mount in Jerusalem stands ready to receive the King of Glory at His coming. It is of no significance to God that the Dome of the Rock and the al Aqsa Mosque are located there or that Muslims presently control access to the Temple Mount. When God is ready to change the status quo on the Temple Mount, no power on earth will be able to stay His hand.

Islamic claims to the Temple Mount and the Western Wall are fraudulent and will not stand! At the coming of Christ, not a centimeter of the Temple Mount or any part of Jerusalem will be under the control of anyone but King Jesus. Throughout the past centuries, the Lord has used several Gentile powers to preserve the thirty-five-acre Temple Mount until the "times of the Gentiles" are completed and He is ready to take it back again. Whether the Temple Mount will be cleared by an earthquake, by war or by some other means is a matter that need not concern us. When the hour comes for another Temple to be rebuilt, it will happen.

In order to better understand what is occurring now, we need to move beyond the present policies and politics of both the Israelis and the Muslims to see God's larger plan for the Temple Mount as announced in Scripture. However, to fully comprehend the Temple's prophetic role in end-time events, we need to start at the beginning.

THE TEMPLE'S LOCATION

Immediately after Moses and the children of Israel crossed over the Red Sea on dry land and the Egyptian forces were drowned trying to overtake them, Moses and the sons of Israel sang a song of praise and victory in which a most amazing prophecy concerning the Temple was given:

> You will bring them and plant them in the mountain of Your inheritance, the place, O Lord, which You have made for Your dwelling, the sanctuary, O Lord, which Your hands have established. The Lord shall reign forever and ever.[2]

Not only did Moses prophesy about the Temple and its location hundreds of years before it was built, it was revealed to him one day the Lord Himself would reign from that holy mountain. God revealed the location of the Temple to Abraham when He sent him to Mount Moriah to offer up his son Isaac. Specific reasons for this choice were covered in the previous chapter.

King David purchased the site of the Temple from the Jebusite, Araunah, who had used it as a threshing floor.[3] David paid Araunah fifty shekels of silver for his threshing floor, and later he paid six hundred shekels of gold for the whole mountain. Although God did not permit David to build the Temple because he had shed so much blood, his son Solomon was commissioned to construct the first and most elaborate of all the Temples that stood on the site.

After World War II, several proposals were put forward regarding the location of a homeland for the Jews. One proposal involved locating the Jewish state in Africa. This plan seemed viable to many people, including some Jewish leaders; however, there was just one problem — Africa was not the land God had given to Abraham, Isaac and Jacob as an "everlasting inheritance." Etched into Jewish hearts and ensconced in Jewish souls are the words of the psalmist: "If I forget you, O Jerusalem, may my right hand forget her skill. May my tongue cling to the roof of my mouth if I do not remember you, if I do not exalt Jerusalem above my chief joy."[4]

Israel's national anthem, "The Hatikvah," also captures a similar sentiment:

So long as still within our breasts the Jewish heart beats true,
So long as still towards the East, to Zion looks the Jew,
So long as still our hopes are not yet lost —
Two thousand years we cherished them —
To live in freedom in the land of Zion and Jerusalem.

On May 14, 1948, the nation of Israel was reborn on the same land God had promised to give to Abraham, Isaac and Jacob as an everlasting inheritance, and the same land from which they had been driven out by the Romans in AD 70. Nothing less than the direct hand of God could have brought about the rebirth of Israel after nearly 2000 years in exile.

Some have suggested Israel could relinquish the Temple Mount to the Muslims and construct their Temple on vacant land in or around Jerusalem. There is just one problem with such a plan—God Himself has chosen the site for the Temple, and there can be no other. Whenever the Temple will be rebuilt, it will be constructed on the site where all of the previous Temples have stood. God has chosen the same site for the Temple from which Christ will reign, namely on Mount Moriah!

While there may be some question as to the precise spot on the Temple Mount where the Temple once stood, there is no doubt at all about the location of the Temple Mount itself, all Islamic claims notwithstanding. This site is sacred because God chose it! It is sacred because God's shekinah glory once dwelt there, and it will dwell there again. When the next Temple is built, it will be established on Mount Moriah.

THE TABERNACLE

When Moses was on Mount Sinai, God gave him the blueprints for the Tabernacle: "According to all that I am going to show you, as the pattern of the tabernacle and the pattern of all its furniture, just so you shall construct it."[5] The Book of Hebrews makes clear Moses was required to carry out the design for the Tabernacle and its furnishings exactly as God had stated: "...just as Moses was warned by God when he was about to erect the tabernacle; for, 'See,' He says, 'that you make all things according to the pattern which was shown you on the mountain.'"[6]

In addition to the Tabernacle, God gave an exact description of how the furnishings were to be made, starting with the Ark of the Covenant. Why was God so concerned the Tabernacle and all its furnishings had to be constructed according to His exact specifications? The answer is plainly given in the Scriptures—the Tabernacle, its furnishing and various priestly functions were all copies of the Tabernacle (God's throne) in heaven!

Therefore it was necessary for the copies of the things in the heavens to be cleansed with these, but the heavenly things themselves with better sacrifices than these. For Christ did not enter a holy place made with hands, a mere copy of the true one, but into heaven itself, now to appear in the presence of God for us.[7]

Now the main point in what has been said is this: we have such a high priest, who has taken His seat at the right hand of the throne of the Majesty in the heavens, a minister in the sanctuary and in the true tabernacle, which the Lord pitched, not man.[8]

Glimpses of God's throne room in heaven were also given in the Book of Revelation. In many ways the descriptions of the heavenly sanctuary are like the earthly copy of the Temple given to King David.

Immediately I was in the Spirit; and behold, a throne was standing in heaven, and One sitting on the throne...And there were seven lamps of fire burning before the throne, which are the seven Spirits of God....[9]

And the temple of God which is in heaven was opened; and the ark of His covenant appeared in His temple....[10]

And the temple was filled with smoke from the glory of God and from His power; and no one was able to enter the temple until the seven plagues of the seven angels were finished.[11]

THE DESIGN OF THE TEMPLE

As Moses was given the instructions for the construction of the Tabernacle, David was given instructions for the building of the Temple, its contents as well as directives regarding the services of the priests.

Then David gave to his son Solomon the plan of the porch of the temple, its buildings, its storehouses, its upper rooms, its inner rooms and the room for the mercy seat…. "All this," said David, "the Lord made me understand in writing by His hand upon me, all the details of this pattern."[12]

Randall Price defines the word *pattern* as "original, proto-type, copy, duplicate, model, image, something like an architect's plan."[13]

THE TEMPLE SCENE

The Temple was the spiritual center for every Jew. The activities that took place in the Temple at the time of Christ were far too numerous to mention here, but they included many aspects of Jewish life. The Temple was the scene of daily sacrifices and incense offerings. Literally thousands of priests were engaged in various ceremonial duties and responsibilities.

The Temple served as the seat of the Sanhedrin, a ruling body composed of two parts. The high court rendered decisions and opinions concerning Jewish law, while the lower court issued decisions and opinions relating to lesser matters.

A Place of Prayer and Consolation

Both men and women went to the Temple courts in order to find comfort and consolation in times of sorrow and distress. Persons experiencing grief or distress were instructed to enter or leave the Temple by walking opposite of the established pattern, so those coming from the other direction might speak words of comfort and blessing to them. Since the practice of offering comfort was especially common with the women, it could have been the prophetess Anna had taken this ministry upon herself as she served in the Temple night and day for years.[14] As a widow she surely understood the meaning of grief and sorrow.

A Place of Purification

Jewish women came to the Nicanor Gate after childbirth, where they presented a lamb for a burnt offering and a young pigeon or turtledove for a sin-offering. If the parents could not afford the cost of a lamb, they were permitted by Jewish law to bring two young pigeons or two turtledoves, as did Mary and Joseph.[15] When Jesus drove out the money changers from the Temple precincts, He also drove out those who had been selling doves. Obviously, they had been observed cheating the poor. One cannot help but wonder if Jesus' parents were not among the poor people who had been swindled by the sellers of doves.

Lepers came to the Temple to be declared clean by the priests after eight days of purification. A special chamber was dedicated for this purpose. Another chamber located inside the Court of the Women was called the Chamber of the Nazirites. There, persons making vows to God for some special purpose would come to have their hair cut off. Paul went into this chamber with four men and participated in this ceremony.[16]

Large immersion pools (mikva'ot) were located outside several entrances to the Temple. These pools were used for the purification of those about to enter. Immersion pools for the priests were located within the Temple structure itself. In recent years archaeologists have discovered several immersion pools outside the southern part of the Temple Mount.

A Place of Joy and Praise

On any given day within the Temple precincts, the sounds of the trumpet and the shofar announced Sabbaths, festivals, prayer times and an assorted number of other religious ceremonies. The Levites served as the Temple musicians and singers. Musical instruments included trumpets, timbrels, cymbals, flutes, harps and lyres. Although a few non-Levites were permitted to play musical instruments, non-Levites could not be part of the choir. The flute was played only on a few occasions in the Temple because it was looked upon as a common instrument of the people, used mostly for weddings and funerals.[17] The only cymbals used in the Temple were played by the music director. The choir, which usually stood on the steps of the Nicanor Gate facing the Court of Israel and the sanctuary, offered praises to God with an array of Psalms and spiritual songs. On certain occasions, such as the Feast of Tabernacles, the choir stood on the opposite steps of the Nicanor Gate and faced the

congregation in the Court of the Women. The choir and the musicians enhanced the worship in the Temple and drew large crowds
when they performed.

A Place for Commerce and Giving

Jews came to the Temple to pay their vows, give alms and pay
the half-shekel Temple tax. A large trumpet-shaped container in the
Women's Court was used to collect offerings for the poor. Coins
dropped into the container rolled noisily around a brass bell-shaped
opening before descending through a funnel-shaped tube to the base.
The noisy offering was the basis of the Lord's admonition: "When
you give to the poor, do not sound the trumpet before you...."[18] At
this location Jesus witnessed the poor widow placing everything she
had into the container.

Because coins bearing the image of Caesar could not be used in
the Temple, money changers were on hand to exchange Roman coins
for Temple currency. People came to an area outside the northern
enclosure of the Temple in order to sell animals for sacrifice and
wood for the altar. Others brought oil for use in the Temple lamps
and wines for use in the libation offerings. The perfume makers,
seamstresses and weavers carried out their manifold tasks in special
rooms located in the Temple complex. One family in Jerusalem was
in charge of making the incense. A special chamber to store incense
was located near the outer altar.

A Place to Experience the Presence of God

Thousands entered the Temple precincts everyday, especially on
the major festivals such as Passover and the Feast of Tabernacles. The
Temple complex could accommodate as many as 100,000 worshippers; it was like a city within a city. One can imagine why it took
Mary and Joseph so long to find their young Son when He became
separated from them. They found Jesus in the Temple courts talking
with the teachers. Teaching and discussions were commonplace in
the Court of the Gentiles and on Solomon's portico.

The Temple was not only a feast for the senses, but a feast for the
soul as well. Thus David wrote: "I was glad when they said to me,
'Let us go to the house of the Lord.'"[19] He also declared with great

anticipation: "And I will dwell in the house of the Lord forever."[20] Numerous Psalms expressed the desire of the devout to enter the Temple and remain there forever.

> How lovely are Your dwelling places, O Lord of hosts! My soul longed and even yearned for the courts of the Lord; My heart and my flesh sing for joy to the living God. The bird also has found a house, and the swallow a nest for herself, where she may lay her young, Even Your altars, O Lord of hosts, my King and my God. How blessed are those who dwell in Your house! They are ever praising You...For a day in Your courts is better than a thousand outside. I would rather stand at the threshold of the house of my God than dwell in the tents of wickedness.[21]

It is little wonder the Lord made the following promises to His saints in Philadelphia:

> "He who overcomes, I will make him a pillar in the temple of My God, and he will not go out from it anymore; and I will write on him the name of My God, and the name of the city of My God, the new Jerusalem, which comes down out of heaven from my God, and My new Name."[22]

THE TEMPLE AT THE TIME OF CHRIST

King Herod, who ruled from 37 to 4 BC, rebuilt the Temple in order to please his Jewish subjects. What he constructed was truly remarkable in terms of architecture, engineering and beauty. The sages remarked: "He who has not seen the Temple has never seen a beautiful building in his life." Herod was a master builder. He also constructed elaborate palaces, arenas and fortresses throughout the country. Not since the days of Solomon had any king attempted to build on such a massive and grandiose scale.

Herodium, one of the fortress-palaces constructed by King Herod, was located a short distance from Bethlehem. It was there, according to Jewish historian Flavius Josephus, Herod was buried.

Many archaeological expeditions at Herodium failed to locate the ancient king's burial place, but in the spring of 2007 an archaeological team from the Hebrew University finally discovered his tomb. Herodium was destroyed by the Romans in AD 71; even so the rebel Bar Kokba occupied the site during his rebellion in AD 135.

King Herod began reconstructing the Temple by leveling the top of the mountain. His expansion included the construction of a huge retaining wall around the perimeter of the Temple Mount. By doing so Herod literally doubled the size of the Temple platform. The fact so much of the retaining wall is still standing today is a testament to ancient building skills. Several courses of immense stones from Herod's original retaining wall now comprise the Jews' most holy site — the Western Wall (*Kotel* in Hebrew).

The original retaining wall extends thirty to sixty feet below the present street level. A street and a shopping plaza near the Western Wall were discovered a few years ago as archaeologists dug some thirty to forty feet below ground at the southwest corner of the Temple Mount. Eventually they uncovered additional sections of the street and large portions of the original wall by digging a tunnel from the Kotel to the limits of the western enclosure.

As one walks through the Western Wall Tunnel, it is difficult to realize it was an open street during the time of Christ. The large stones used to construct Herod's retaining wall reveal the remarkable engineering skills known at that time. The largest stone visible inside the Western Wall Tunnel weighs nearly six hundred tons; it is twelve feet high, forty-five feet long and ten feet wide. Other stones in the wall are nearly as large, but most range in size from three to fifty tons. Not a bit of mortar was used to set any of the stones in place, yet each stone was fit so tightly a piece of paper could not be inserted between them. It took over forty-six years to complete the Temple complex.

Gentiles Welcome!

The Temple structure included a large area called the Court of the Gentiles. While Gentiles were permitted inside this court, they could not go beyond it. The fact Gentiles were welcomed at the Temple is in keeping with Isaiah's description: "For My house will be called a house of prayer for all the peoples."[23] In his prayer of dedication, Solomon prayed there would always be a place at the Temple for the Gentiles:

> Also concerning the foreigner who is not from Your people Israel, when he comes from a far country for Your great name's sake and Your mighty hand and Your outstretched arm, when they come and pray toward this house, then hear from heaven, from Your dwelling place, and do according to all for which the foreigner calls to You, in order that all the peoples of the earth may know Your name, and fear You as do Your people Israel, and that they may know that this house which I have built is called by Your name.[24]

God's provision for Gentiles to come to the Temple is descriptive of the present church age, as He sends His gospel to draw them into His Kingdom. It is also a prophetic description of Christ's millennial reign when people from all nations will gather in Jerusalem to worship the Lord in His Temple.

The Court of the Gentiles included the Royal Stoa located inside the southern wall of the Temple enclosure. The Stoa was built in the shape of a basilica with four rows of forty columns each.[25] Its central nave was forty-five feet wide and a hundred feet high. The historian Josephus said it took three men with outstretched arms to reach around one pillar. From the top of the Royal Stoa to the Kidron Valley below was a distance of four hundred and fifty feet. The southeast corner of the Stoa is believed to be the pinnacle of the Temple described in Matthew 4, as well as the general area from which Jesus drove out the money changers.

A wall with several gates separated the Court of the Gentiles from the Court of the Women. Both men and women were permitted to enter the Court of the Women, but Gentiles could not go there. Gentiles could be put to death for entering this part of the Temple. Paul was nearly killed by a mob when certain Jews accused him of bringing Greeks into this part of the Temple precincts.[26]

The Inner Courts

The Court of the Women, located directly in front of the sanctuary, was the scene of much activity. Fifteen steps led from the Court of the Women to the Nicanor Gate; women were not allowed to go beyond this gate, however. Inside the Nicanor Gate was the Court of Israel where only Jewish men were permitted to enter. Adjacent to the Court of Israel was the Court of the Priests where the outer altar stood and where the animals were slaughtered and prepared as sacrifices to be offered upon the altar.

The Sanctuary

Two massive doors led into the Temple sanctuary. When the doors were open, the entrance to the sanctuary was draped with a huge curtain. It took as many as ten priests to open and close these massive doors each morning and evening. Josephus said the sound of the doors closing could be heard in Jericho.

The Chamber of the Hearth served as living quarters for the priests on duty. Nearby, another chamber held their vestments. Each morning the priests cast lots to determine their respective duties for the day, including the priest who would burn the incense before the Holy of Holies.

The Temple sanctuary itself included a large front porch, the Holy Place and the Holy of Holies. Separating the Holy Place from the Holy of Holies was a magnificent veil made in two sections; its combined dimensions were sixty feet high by thirty feet wide. The veil was dyed in shades of blue, purple and scarlet, colors associated with Christ. The veil was embroidered with cherubim and other ornate symbols. This is the veil that was torn from top to bottom on the day Christ was crucified.

THE ARK OF THE COVENANT

The first piece of furniture the Lord instructed Moses to construct was the Ark of the Covenant. It was made of acacia wood and overlaid with pure gold. The acacia tree, which requires little water, is common in the desert regions of the Middle East. Four long poles, also made of acacia wood and overlaid with gold, were inserted through four gold rings attached to the Ark. The poles used to transport the Ark were kept in place even when it was resting in the Holy of Holies.

The top of the Ark was covered by a "mercy seat" made of pure gold. Two gold cherubim with their wings touching each other adorned the mercy seat where the presence of God rested. Two tablets of stone inscribed with the Ten Commandments were placed inside the Ark, along with Aaron's rod and a jar containing manna.

It is believed the Ark of the Covenant was captured and carried off to Babylon by King Nebuchadnezzar in 586 BC. The whereabouts of the Ark of the Covenant after the Babylonian captivity is a centuries-old mystery. The Holy of Holies remained empty until the Temple's destruction in AD 70. On the Day of Atonement when the high priest entered the Holy of Holies, he sprinkled blood on the foundation stone where the Ark would have been located.

Theories abound today regarding the whereabouts of the Ark of the Covenant. Some claim it is in an ancient church in Ethiopia; others say it is in Egypt or hidden away underneath the Temple Mount. Still others believe it was buried in a cave near the Dead Sea. Perhaps the theory with the most merit is found in the apocryphal Book of Second Maccabees. It states the prophet Jeremiah took the ancient Tabernacle and the Ark of the Covenant and hid them somewhere on Mount Pisgah, near the place where Moses had viewed the Promised Land. The account in Maccabees further states neither the Ark nor the Tabernacle will be found until the end of the age.

It was also in the writing that the prophet (Jeremiah), in obedience to a revelation, gave orders that the tent and the ark should accompany him, and that he went away to the mountain where Moses went up and beheld God's inheritance. And Jeremiah came and found a cave-dwelling, and he took the tent and the ark and the incense altar into it, and he blocked up the door. And some of those who followed him came up to mark the road, and they could not find it. But when Jeremiah found out, he blamed them and said, "The place shall be unknown until God gathers the congregation of his people together and shows them his mercy."[27]

Obviously if and when the Lord wants the Ark of the Covenant found, it shall appear. It is not necessary the Ark of the Covenant be found in order for the Temple to be rebuilt.

THE LAMP STAND

According to Scripture, the seven lamps of fire in the Temple represent the presence of the Holy Spirit.[28] The seven-branch lamp stand, also called *the menorah* or *the Golden Candlesticks*, was made of solid gold and fashioned from one piece. The Jews referred to the Temple as "the light of the world," and the symbol of that light was the menorah.

In Solomon's Temple ten seven-branch lamps were located on the southern wall of the Holy Place. Standing in two rows of five, each of the lamps was made of solid gold. In Herod's Temple only one menorah was used. The menorah was the only source of light in the Holy Place. Each day priests were chosen by lot to trim the lamps and replenish the oil. A three-step platform in front of the menorah enabled the attending priest to service the lamps without having to raise his arms above his head.

The Temple Institute in Jerusalem has crafted a menorah made of solid gold which they hope will be used in the next Temple. This menorah, costing about $5 million, is on display in Jerusalem.

THE TABLE OF SHOWBREAD

Ten tables of showbread were used in the Holy Place of Solomon's Temple. Only one showbread table was used during the second-Temple period, and it stood on the north side of the sanctuary. The table of showbread was constructed of wood and overlaid with gold. Twelve large loaves of bread in two rows of six were stacked on gold shelves, one on top of another. Two bowls of frankincense were placed on the table next to the showbread. Two priests brought fresh bread into the sanctuary each Sabbath, while two other priests took away the old bread. The bread was exchanged in such a way that twelve loaves were always on the table. The Jews looked upon the showbread as a symbol of the coming Messiah. During the Feast of Tabernacles, Jesus stood in the Temple and proclaimed in a loud voice: "I am the Bread of Life."

THE GOLDEN ALTAR OF INCENSE

The golden altar of incense stood in the middle of the sanctuary before the Holy of Holies. A priest, chosen by lot, burned incense on this altar each morning and evening. A priest could only perform this duty once in his lifetime, because offering the incense on the golden altar was deemed such an honor.

John the Baptist's father, Zacharias, was chosen by lot to offer the incense when the angel Gabriel appeared to him "standing on the right of the altar of incense." As was the custom, the priest was left alone while offering the incense. The Bible specifically states Gabriel's appearance to Zacharias was on the right (north) of the sanctuary. This may be a further sign pointing us to the location of Christ's crucifixion at the northern-most part of Mount Moriah.

Gabriel told Zacharias his wife Elizabeth would have a child, and they were to name him John.[29] Because Zacharias did not believe Gabriel at first, he was rendered mute until after his son was born. After the officiating priest offered the incense as the evening sacrifice, it was customary for him to go outside and bless those who were assembled, but because Zacharias was unable to speak after his encounter with Gabriel, the people sensed he had seen a vision.[30]

In the Temple of heaven, the golden altar of incense is located before the throne of God, even as the copy on earth was placed before the Holy of Holies. In both the earthly Temple and in the heavenly Sanctuary, the offerings of incense represented the prayers of the people.

> When the Lamb broke the seventh seal, there was silence in heaven for about half an hour. And I saw the seven angels who stand before God, and seven trumpets were given to them. Another angel came and stood at the altar, holding a golden censer; and much incense was given to him, so that he might add it to the prayers of all the saints on the golden altar which was before the throne.[31]

There is comfort in knowing the prayers of the saints are not only heard and answered at the throne of God, they are also received as worship. King David captured this truth when he said: "O Lord, I call upon You; hasten to me! Give ear to my voice when I call to You. May my prayer be counted as incense before You; the lifting up of my hands as the evening offering."[32] This is also a reminder Christ is our great High Priest and Intercessor, and all the prayers of the saints come before God's throne as a sacrifice of praise and worship.

THE ALTAR OF SACRIFICE

The outer altar, located in front of the sanctuary, was forty-eight feet by forty-eight feet by fifteen feet high. A ramp measuring forty-eight feet long by twenty-four feet wide led to the top where three fires burned continually. The top of the altar platform measured thirty-six feet by thirty-six feet, offering ample room for several priests to function at the same time.

The priests approached the altar by way of the ramp. The largest fire atop the altar was used for offering the sacrifices. In both corners of the altar closest to the sanctuary, two smaller fires burned; one fire produced coals for burning incense on the golden altar, while the other was used to keep the other two fires burning. In the center of the altar platform was a pile of ashes that were discarded daily. Salt was kept close to the sacrificial fire, since each sacrifice had to be salted.

A large laver containing water for the priests to wash themselves stood between the altar and the porch of the Temple. As many as twelve priests could wash at the laver at same time.

Each of the four horns of the altar was one and a half feet high. Two of the horns closest to the sanctuary were hollowed out for drink offerings and for the water libations. A drainage system from the top of the altar passed into the ground below and carried off blood and refuse to the Kidron Valley.

On the north side of the altar of sacrifice, a series of twenty-four rings in six rows were used to hold the animals about to be sacrificed. Eight tables, with three hooks attached to each, were used to prepare the slaughtered animals that would be offered upon the altar. Another drainage system in this area took away the blood and refuse from the animals that were killed.

THE PRIESTHOOD

During the time of the Temple, the Levitical priests were divided into twenty-four groups or courses. Half of the priests lived in Jerusalem, while the other half were scattered throughout the country. The Hebrew word for priest is *cohen,* meaning "one who stands up for another and mediates his cause." After the Babylonian captivity, there was a severe shortage of priests for many years.

Each course of priests served for one week at a time, Sabbath to Sabbath. The priestly duties were chosen daily by drawing four lots. These drawings took place each morning in the Chamber of Hewn Stone. Before drawing lots the priests purified themselves in the mikvah, a pool of naturally collected water. The first lot determined which priests would clear the ashes from the great altar; the second determined which priests would slaughter and prepare the daily sacrifices and which would serve in the Holy Place; the third lot selected the specific priest who would offer the sacrifice of incense. And finally, the fourth lot determined which priests would carry the sacrifices up the ramp and offer them on the altar.[33]

Each priest who came to serve at the Temple had to prove his genealogy before the Sanhedrin. If his father's name was not inscribed in the archives, or if members of the Sanhedrin were unable to verify his credentials, he was disqualified.[34] The Gospel of Luke identified John the Baptist's father, Zacharias, as being descended from the division of Abijah; Luke even included Zacharias' wife, Elizabeth, as being descended from the "daughters of Aaron."[35] This verification process is described in reference to Melchizedek who did not have a supportive genealogy. While Levitical priests were able to serve by virtue of their genealogy, the high priest had to be called by God. "And no one takes the honor to himself, but receives it when he is called by God, even as Aaron was."[36] The Book of Hebrews describes how God chose Christ to be our High Priest and declared His priesthood was superior to the priesthood of Aaron and the Levites.

THE EASTERN GATE

The Eastern Gate, known also as the Golden Gate or the Beautiful Gate, was the main entrance into the Temple from the Mount of Olives. This gate was in direct alignment with the inner gates that led into the sanctuary. Some archaeologists believe a bridge from the Eastern Gate spanned the Kidron Valley and extended to the center of the Mount of Olives. The scapegoat would have been led across this bridge and into the wilderness on the Day of Atonement. Likely Jesus crossed this bridge on Palm Sunday when He entered through the Eastern Gate. Christ will again enter through the Eastern Gate at His second coming.

In an effort to keep the Jewish Messiah from entering through the Eastern Gate, the Muslims sealed it off, perhaps as early as the seventh century. This sealed gate is prophetically described by Ezekiel:

> Then He brought me back by the way of the outer gate of the sanctuary, which faces east; and it was shut. The Lord said to me, "This gate shall be shut; it shall not be opened, and no man shall enter by it, for the Lord God of Israel has entered by it; therefore it shall be shut."[37]

Over the years several attempts were made to open this gate, but each effort ended in failure. The last attempt was in 1967, just prior to the Six-day War, when Jordan planned to open the Eastern Gate in order to support their troops and those who lived inside the Old City. However, one day before the project was scheduled to begin, Israel captured the Old City, and the gate remained closed.

The Muslims constructed a cemetery outside the Eastern Gate to prevent the Jewish Messiah from coming. They reasoned if a priest had to go through a cemetery in order to reach the Temple, he would be rendered unclean and thereby be disqualified from carrying out his duties. Some have suggested the cemetery was placed there because Muslims developed beliefs about their own messiah (the Madhi) who supposedly will enter through the Eastern Gate upon his return. In recent years the cemetery has expanded as Muslims endeavor to increase their claim on the entire Temple area.

King Herod did not disturb the eastern wall when he enlarged the Temple Mount. The present Eastern Gate was likely built in the sixteenth century by Suleiman the Magnificent. A much older gate lies buried below the present gate, but scholars are uncertain as to when the older gate was built. Some believe it dates to the time of Herod, while others suggest it was constructed shortly after the Muslims took control of the Temple Mount, since its design matches other gates located on the Mount. Nevertheless, the older gate lends credibility to the theory the original Eastern Gate was located at the same place during the time of Herod's Temple.[38]

THE COMING TEMPLES

Amillennialists do not hold to any concept of a rebuilt Temple, just as they do not believe the present nation of Israel has any role in biblical prophecy. In his book *The Apocalypse Code*, Hank Hanegraaff ridicules those who interpret ancient prophecies relating to a rebuilt Temple. He states: "Finally, the shekinah glory of God that departed the second temple, thus leaving it desolate, forever dwells within the spiritual temple. The shekinah glory of God will never again descend upon a temple constructed of lifeless stones, for it forever dwells within 'the living Stone—rejected by men, but chosen by God'" (2 Peter 2:4).[39]

Hanegraaff is wrong on two counts: first, the passage from Peter that he quotes here obviously refers to the indwelling of the Holy Spirit in the lives of believers, not to the shekinah glory of God. Secondly, the Bible describes not only the shekinah glory returning to the Temple, but it also makes unambiguous statements that Jesus Christ Himself will return to the Temple at His second coming. You can be certain where Jesus is, there also will be the shekinah glory of God.

In spite of the fact many Jewish and Christian scholars scoff at the idea of rebuilding the Temple, several Jewish groups in Israel are now planning for its construction. An organization called the Temple Mount Institute has crafted nearly all the implements and furnishings required for use in the future Temple. Similar organizations have made musical instruments and garments for the priests. However, the present political situation in Israel does not permit the Jews to conduct even a prayer service atop the Temple Mount, let alone establish a presence or construct a Temple there.

A few years ago, the Sanhedrin was reconstituted in Israel. While this Court is not recognized by leading Jewish rabbis, nevertheless the Sanhedrin is pressing forward with its agenda to reinstitute the system of sacrifices and make ready for the rebuilding of the Temple. Early in 2007 the Sanhedrin voted to resume animal sacrifices relating to Passover; but such sacrifices are not likely to take place as long as the Muslims control the Temple Mount. It is clear from the Book of Revelation the Temple Mount will remain in the hands of the Gentiles until the end of the tribulation period, and portions of Jerusalem will pass from Israel to the Gentiles for a period of forty-two months.[40]

On Sunday July 15, 2007 a delegation of men from the Tribe of Levi and the Cohen clan met in Jerusalem for a conference relating to the rebuilding of the Temple. At the end of the conference, the priests all stood before the Western Wall and declared a priestly blessing over Israel. This gathering was the first of its kind since the time of the Second Temple.[41]

Proving one's genealogy as a priest or a member of the Tribe of Levi is quite different in the twenty-first century than it was in biblical times. Today's priests are identified through DNA testing.

During the tribulation the Jews will either rebuild the Temple or construct some type of structure on the Temple Mount. Likely this will take place through a treaty arranged by the antichrist. While it is impossible to know for certain what events would have to unfold before the Temple or a structure could be erected on the Temple Mount, when God is ready, it will happen, the Dome of the Rock and the al Aqsa Mosque notwithstanding.

Jordan has proposed and the Israeli government has approved the construction of a minaret on the Temple Mount. It will be the first minaret erected there in over 600 years. It is incomprehensible that Prime Minister Olmert's administration granted permission for another archaeological assault on the Temple Mount, but they did. It may be the agreement was given in exchange for Israel's planned construction of a bridge from the Western Wall area to the Mughrabi Gate. If so, it was all for nothing since Israel, bowing to pressure from the Muslims, scraped its original plans in favor of constructing a much smaller bridge. In the meantime, reports coming from Israel in July 2007 indicate Jordan is quietly buying up property close to the Temple Mount. Apparently, they want to assure their continued control of the Temple area.

With the construction of another minaret on the Temple Mount, one is reminded of the prophecy of Jesus, "When you see the ABOMINATION OF DESOLATION which was spoken of through Daniel the prophet, standing in the holy place...."[42] While Jordan's proposed minaret may not be the abomination referred to in Daniel, it will be "standing" in the holy place, and it certainly will be "an abomination."

The Bible speaks of a Temple during the time of the tribulation and another more glorious Temple during the time of the millennial reign of Christ. The former is alluded to by Christ when He spoke of the "abomination of desolation standing in the holy place."[43] Another reference to a tribulation Temple is mention in Revelation: "Get up and measure the temple of God and the altar, and those who worship in it."[44]

Will the tribulation Temple be built by the Jews, by the antichrist or a combination of the two? Will it be built before or during the tribulation? There is really no way to resolve these questions at this time. There are Jews in Israel who are advocating the construction of the Temple soon. Other Jewish groups have proposed erecting a small synagogue on the Temple Mount.

Some Bible scholars maintain a Temple does not need to be constructed at the time of the tribulation in order for these prophecies to be fulfilled. They insist the "abomination which causes desolation" would only have to be placed on the Temple Mount itself, and the antichrist could set himself up there as an object of worship, since the Mount itself is frequently referred to as the holy place.

Where were the first and second Temples located?

One of the more interesting debates regarding the construction of a new Temple concerns the exact location of Herod's Temple. If it stood precisely where the Dome of the Rock now stands, the Dome of the Rock would have to be removed before another Temple could be constructed. There are three prevailing theories among archaeologists regarding the location of the first and second Temples. The first and most commonly held theory places the Temple on the site of the Dome of the Rock. The second theory places Herod's Temple several yards to the south of the Dome of the Rock, while a third theory, put forward by Asher Kaufman, suggested the Temple was located several yards to the north of the Dome of the Rock, with its gates in direct alignment with the existing Eastern Gate.[45]

According to ancient documents, the doors and inner gates leading from the sanctuary to the Eastern Gate were perfectly aligned with one another; one could stand at the entrance of the sanctuary and look through the series of open gates to the Mount of Olives. If the Eastern Gate is located today where it was in the first century, Kaufman's theory about the Temple's location has considerable validity. A small structure known as the Dome of the Tablets now stands in direct alignment with the Eastern Gate. At the base of the Dome of the Tablets, one can see a foundation stone of Mount Moriah protruding. According to ancient Islamic tradition, the Dome of the Tablets marks the spot where the Ark was kept inside the Holy of Holies.

If this third theory regarding the Temple's location is authenticated, some type of structure could be erected on the Temple Mount without tearing down either the Dome of the Rock or disturbing the al Aqsa Mosque. John was instructed, "Get up and measure the temple of God and the altar and those who worship in it. Leave out the court which is outside the temple and do not measure it, for it has been given to the nations; and they will tread under foot the holy city for forty-two months."[46] Considering the ecumenical spirit that prevails today, a place on the Temple Mount for all three religions—Judaism, Christianity and Islam—might be part of a peace plan set forth by the antichrist.

Whatever happens on the world scene, you may be sure Israel and the Temple Mount will be at the center of it all. One day when the situation in Israel ignites into a raging war, a winsome and charismatic figure (the antichrist) will enter the world stage and propose a treaty that will offer both security and peace between Israel and her Muslim neighbors. Most of the world will rejoice, but not for long!

SECTION FOUR

The Lord Still Speaks to His Church

"This is My beloved Son, with whom I am well-pleased; listen to Him!" Matthew 17:5.

"I believe with all my heart that standing up for America means standing up for the God who has so blessed our land. We need God's help to guide our nation through stormy seas. But we can't expect Him to protect America in a crisis if we just leave Him over on the shelf in our day-to-day living."

Ronald Reagan

In a world where everything has turned gray and become a blur, the Scriptures still mark the lines between right and wrong, between good and evil, between blessed and cursed. Teach your children and grandchildren the Scriptures. Stay with the teaching of the Scriptures.

Charles R. Swindoll

"If the church has anything to say, she had better wake up, stand up, speak up or shut up. I hear faintly amidst this moral turpitude and tiredness a faint cry, 'Is there any word from the Lord.'"

Leonard Ravenhill

THE LORD STILL SPEAKS TO HIS CHURCH

INTRODUCTION

Each of the seven churches of Revelation is located in the same geographical area of Turkey (Anatolia in Greek, refers to the portion of Turkey located in Asia). The population of Turkey today is approximately 70 million; this includes 65,000 Armenian Orthodox Christians, 20,000 Roman Catholics, 3500 Protestants, 2000 Greek Orthodox and 23,000 Jews. Turkey is 98 percent Muslim.

Turkey has been an anomaly in the Muslim world since 1923, with its Islamic majority, its secular government and its blend of Western and Islamic cultures. In Istanbul, a city of twelve million residents, it is not unusual to see women wearing the latest Western apparel, with their hair both showing and done up in the latest style; while other women may be seen wearing traditional Muslim dresses and veils. In like manner, men walk about the city in Western suits and ties, even as others wear traditional Islamic attire. The whole country is filled with thousands of mosques, but many Turks do not participate in their services.

Today Turkey is experiencing inner turmoil and struggle as Islamic fundamentalists seek to win control of the government and turn the nation back into an Islamic state. The country's strong military, which has stepped in four times since 1960 to preserve the country's secular government, has warned it will intervene again if the Islamic fundamentalists succeed in taking over.

Four of the cities in which the seven churches of Revelation were located still exist, though with a small Christian presence — Smyrna, Pergamum, Philadelphia and Thyatira. Smyrna is the only city mentioned in Revelation that maintained a significant Christian population into modern times. However, the Christian community at Smyrna nearly disappeared in 1922 when the Turks massacred Greek and Armenian Christians who lived there. Ephesus, Sardis and Laodicea now lie in ruins, as they have for centuries.

Jesus sent letters to the seven churches in Asia Minor through the apostle John. The content of His letters included messages of praise, encouragement and, where needed, a call for repentance. The letters to the seven churches also contain universal messages for the whole church throughout the ages.

Most premillennial scholars interpret the seven letters in Revelation as depicting conditions in the church throughout the entire church age.[1] These scholars maintain the letter to the church in Ephesus describes relevant issues present in the early church, while the letter to the church in Laodicea details the low spiritual condition that will exist in the church at the time of the tribulation.

Premillennial scholars further maintain the church in Philadelphia represents the church at the time of the rapture. The Lord promised they would be spared from the "hour of testing…which is about to come upon the whole world." Smyrna is thought to represent the church during the early centuries when great waves of persecution came upon the church. The church in Pergamum reflects the period in history when the Roman Catholic Church began to promote the papacy and ecclesiastical authority. Thyatira describes the church during the dark ages when immorality and corruption were so prevalent; while Sardis is thought to depict the church at the time of the Reformation. Even though this theological interpretation of the seven churches is somewhat subjective, it accurately reflects the various epochs of church history, as well as the church's present spiritual condition.

IS ANYBODY LISTENING?

Jesus made the following declaration in each of the seven letters: "He who has an ear, let him hear what the Spirit says to the churches." Today vast portions of the church seem deaf to the Word of God. While many have departed from the faith altogether, others cannot seem to get their priorities straight. Sadly, few churches seem to demonstrate any inclination towards repentance or reformation. Thus the primary issue for Christians living in the twenty-first century is not whether the Lord will come (He is coming!), but whether they will be ready to meet Him, whatever the day or hour of His appearing may be.

God has declared His Spirit will not always strive with man. When God speaks we should not harden our hearts or turn from Him. One of the saddest verses in the Bible reflects the limits of God's efforts to persuade the nation of Israel to repent:

> The Lord, the God of their fathers, sent word to them again and again by His messengers, because He had compassion on His people and on His dwelling place; but they continually mocked the messengers of God, despised His words and scoffed at His prophets, until the wrath of the Lord arose against His people, until there was no remedy.[2]

Whether it is an individual who stubbornly refuses to repent or whole denominations that sink into shame and apostasy until there is no remedy, there is for everyone a point of no return. What a tragic day when the God of all grace throws up His hands in exasperation over man's stubborn and rebellious heart. May God help us to faithfully proclaim His truth while there is still time.

A Scripture passage that ought to stir our hearts and prepare us for His coming declares:

For this reason, we must pay much closer attention to what we have heard, so that we do not drift away from it. For if the word spoken through angels proved unalterable, and every transgression and disobedience received a just penalty, how will we escape if we neglect so great a salvation?[3]

One day the age of grace will end. The last sermon will have been preached and the last invitation to repent and come to Christ will have been extended. Those who have spurned the law of God and rejected every opportunity to open their hearts to Christ will weep and mourn over the folly of their actions. Too late they will understand the meaning of God's Word: "It is appointed for men to die once and after this comes judgment."[4]

In these crucial times, God calls each of us to be faithful to the end by gathering in the harvest and extending God's gracious invitation: "The Spirit and the bride say, 'Come.' And let the one who hears say, 'Come.' And let the one who is thirsty come; let the one who wishes take the water of life without cost."[5]

Chapter 16

THE CHURCH IN EPHESUS
"The Church with a Secondhand Faith"

"To the angel of the church in Ephesus write: The One who holds the seven stars in His right hand, the One who walks among the seven golden lampstands, says this: 'I know your deeds and your toil and perseverance, and that you cannot tolerate evil men, and you put to the test those who call themselves apostles, and they are not, and you found them to be false; and you have perseverance and have endured for My name's sake, and have not grown weary. But I have this against you, that you have left your first love. Therefore remember from where you have fallen, and repent and do the deeds you did at first; or else I am coming to you and will remove your lampstand out of its place—unless you repent. Yet this you do have, that you hate the deeds of the Nicolaitans, which I also hate. He who has an ear, let him hear what the Spirit says to the churches. To him who overcomes, I will grant to eat of the tree of life which is in the Paradise of God'" (Revelation 2:1-7).

HISTORICAL PERSPECTIVE

The church in Ephesus disappeared from the scene centuries ago. It did not matter to God that Paul and Timothy had established the church in Ephesus, or the apostle John had ministered there for many years. God had given them time to repent, but when they rejected His pleas, their lampstand was removed.

Ephesus, originally established by Ionian Greek settlers, was conquered in 546 BC by Cyrus of Persia and by Alexander the Great in 334 BC. Ephesus came into the Roman Empire in 129 BC; it later became the chief port of the Roman province of Asia. Under Roman rule the population of Ephesus swelled to over 400,000 in the first century AD.

BIBLICAL PERSPECTIVE

Paul ministered in Ephesus for three years, likely between AD 55 and 58.[1] His experiences in this pagan city are described in Acts 19 and 20. In addition to Jesus' letter to the church in Ephesus, we have Paul's letter to the Ephesians, written while he was imprisoned in Rome.

A riot ensued when Demetrius, a silversmith, attempted to rally the residents of Ephesus against Paul in the city's theater.[2] The theater, which seated 25,000 people, was also a place where gladiators fought and where many Christians faced a cruel death. Alexander the coppersmith, another tradesman, opposed Paul while he was ministering in the city.[3]

Priscilla and Aquila, fellow tentmakers with Paul, came with him to Ephesus.[4] They established one of many home churches there. Years later from his prison cell, Paul urged Timothy to remain in Ephesus in order to contend against those who were teaching false doctrines.[5]

According to the writings of several early church fathers, the apostle John lived in Ephesus with Mary, the mother of Jesus. John led the church in Ephesus until he was exiled to nearby Patmos during the reign of Emperor Domitian. John supposedly returned to Ephesus after Domitian's death in AD 96. According to tradition

John was buried in Ephesus, as was Luke, the author of the third Gospel and the Book of Acts.

Paul summoned the elders of the church in Ephesus to meet with him in nearby Miletus, where he charged them to keep the faith and gave an emotional farewell before setting off for Jerusalem and a long imprisonment that was to follow.[6]

EPHESUS TODAY

Archaeological finds offer but a glimpse into the magnificence and grandeur that once was Ephesus. The ruins include a government center, fountains, public baths, public toilets, a brothel and the beautiful Celsus Library. The city had two impressive temples devoted to emperor worship, the Temple of Augustus and the Temple of Hadrian. Ephesus had its own aqueduct and water system, portions of which are still visible. Water was piped directly into the wealthier homes and public buildings.

Included among the archaeological discoveries from ancient Ephesus are private residences, some of which were very elaborate. In New Testament times, the city was very wealthy and influential, due in large measure to commerce, trade guilds and banking. Money from all over the world was deposited in Ephesus and kept on state property as well as in the Temple of Artemis (the goddess Diana).

One lonely column is all that remains of the Temple of Artemis. Originally it had 127 ionic columns and was listed among the Seven Wonders of the Ancient World. Much of the city's economy was centered on this magnificent temple and the manufacture of the goddess' multi-breasted image by local silversmiths. This lucrative idol trade came under threat through Paul's preaching. Two marble statues of Artemis from the Roman period may be viewed in a nearby museum. The Temple of Artemis and much of Ephesus were destroyed by the Goths in AD 262.

The Magnesian Gate and portions of the walls that once surrounded Ephesus, built by Emperor Vespasian, still remain, as do the ruins of the Church of Mary where the third General Church Council was held in 431. It was this council that declared Mary to be "the mother of God" and condemned the heretic Nestorius.

Today one may walk down the ancient streets of Ephesus and see the remains of buildings known to John, Paul, Timothy and other New Testament personalities. The ruins of the Basilica of St. John, dating to the sixth century, stand on a hill northeast of ancient Ephesus. Inside its walls is the traditional tomb of John. Remnants of a lecture hall were uncovered near the Celsus Library. Some archaeologists believe it may be the same hall where Paul lectured daily in the school of Tyrannus.[7]

HOW DOES THIS LETTER APPLY TO US TODAY?

Every congregation is only one generation from falling away from the truth. The spiritual strength and stability of a fellowship of believers does not guarantee it will remain that way in succeeding generations. Paul said to Timothy, "For I am mindful of the sincere faith within you, which first dwelt in your grandmother Lois and your mother Eunice, and I am sure that it is in you as well."[8]

It is wonderful when a living faith is handed down from generation to generation. However, someone once said, "God has no grandchildren." Just because parents walked with Christ does not mean their children or grandchildren will have the same experience of faith. Each person in each generation must enter into a living relationship with the Savior and be born again. Furthermore, it is up to each generation to keep their congregation's doctrines pure and unalloyed from error. The fact so many denominations and local congregations have failed to guard the faith is the reason why so many have fallen into their present spiritual state.

Years ago most Christian churches in America were established with considerable sacrifice by committed Christians who had a vision for reaching the lost and witnessing God's truth. Because their children do not share the same commitment or vision, the spiritual fires have gone out in many of these churches today. Congregations that once were spiritually alive have been led astray by shepherds who dared to substitute a false gospel for the real thing.

Likewise, many denominations founded on the unchanging Word of God have abandoned their heritage of faith. Though their constitutions and confessions were once grounded upon Scripture, these denominations have exchanged truth for a lie. They permit false teachers to spew their poisonous venom with no threat of discipline whatsoever. Like the false teachers mentioned in Jesus' letter to the church at Ephesus, "they call themselves apostles," but they are not.

Jesus is Lord of His Church! He still walks among His churches and speaks to them through the Word and witness of the Holy Spirit. He knows their strengths, weaknesses and sins, and He understands the struggles and persecutions they face. Where churches remain true to His Word, the Holy Spirit abides in their presence.

Countless churches have had their lampstands removed because they failed to follow the Word and witness of the Holy Spirit. While they may still refer to themselves as "churches," the glory of the Lord has departed from their midst. Many lost souls continue to look for spiritual nourishment in spiritually dead centers of worship, but they do not find it.

LOSING OUR FIRST LOVE

The fires of God's unconditional love burned brightly in the hearts of first-generation Christians at Ephesus. They had heard the proclamation of the gospel from Paul, Timothy, John and other saints. They had received the message of salvation in Jesus Christ with meekness and joy, and they stood fast against false teachers and a pagan culture. Their witness of Christ became so powerful it threatened to undo the very fabric of the pagan culture around them. Some of the citizens of Ephesus reacted with violence as the Christian witness took root in the hearts of many people who lived there, especially when an improved moral climate threatened to disrupt their lucrative idol trade. A near riot took place when the silversmith Demetrius incited the citizens of Ephesus against Paul.

Compare the influence of the church in Ephesus to the diminishing influence of Christian churches today. John Osteen got it right when he stated, "The church has become so worldly, while the world has become so 'churchy,' that one can scarcely tell the difference."[9] Christians have joined themselves to the world by embracing sin and unrighteous living. Having lost their first love, they have forsaken their heritage of faith.

In churches where spiritual compromise is the order of the day, a watered-down gospel has been substituted for the life-changing truth of Christ. Vast numbers of people in mainline churches have never heard the pure gospel of Jesus Christ. They go into their worship services lost, and they come out lost.

The type of love the Ephesian church had lost was not something that could be measured by human feelings; it was the unconditional *agape* love of God, summarized in the commandment, "You shall love the Lord your God with all your heart, soul, mind and strength." The first generation of Christians in Ephesus understood from experience as long as they remained obedient to the Word of God nothing could ever separate them from the love of God. But the second generation of Christians in Ephesus cast aside their heritage of faith when they stopped walking in the truth of God's Word and instead began to walk the road of compromise. As their love for God grew cold, they fell away from the faith of their fathers. Though they were zealous in many things, they were not obedient to God's Word. The Lord directed them to repent or lose their lampstand.

It is no trifling matter when the Lord calls churches to repent and reclaim their true Christian heritage. America's culture and institutions were formed and guided through the influence of her churches. The motto of the American Revolution was "No king but King Jesus." In 1831 French statesman Alexis de Tocqueville toured America; later he wrote about his impressions of the new country:

> Not until I went to the churches of America and heard her pulpits flame with righteousness did I understand the secret of her genius and power...The Americans combine the notion of Christianity and liberty so intimately in their minds, that it is impossible to make them conceive of one without the other.[10]

Our nation desperately needs such godly influence again. Unless the churches of America find their voice and speak a prophetic Word against our nation's mounting sins, we will face the inevitable judgment of God. The only hope for the United States of America lies in the willingness of her churches to repent and return to the established standards of God's Word. The voice of the Spirit of God is still speaking to the churches of America, if only they will heed His voice.

WHEN WE HEED THE SPIRIT OF THE AGE

Our love for God is forever connected with our obedience to His Word. Jesus said, "If you love me, you will keep my commandments."[11] God's love compels us to stand fast and "contend for the faith that was once for all delivered to the saints."[12] In a church where true love for God is diminished, false doctrines and unbiblical practices are sure to follow.

More and more denominations are establishing their doctrines and formulating their positions on social issues by heeding the spirit of the age. The homosexual lobby is more welcome at some church conventions than those who uphold the Word of God. The standard of right and wrong in these Bible-denying denominations is no longer determined by what God has said in His Word, but rather by the perverted values of their leaders and by majority votes in church conventions. The agenda of most mainline churches today is not how to bring the message of Christ to a lost world, but how to get members to accept the ordination of homosexuals and the blessing of same-sex unions.

God will not be mocked! Though church conventions pass resolutions and establish policies that are in violation of God's Word, they will not stand! Bishops and theologians in these apostate churches who were entrusted to guard the doctrines of the church are the very ones who are now denying them and encouraging others to do the same. These masters of deceit write books and go on the speaking circuit, urging people to ignore what the Bible teaches and instead listen to them. One day they will be required to give an account to the Lord of the church.

The Church of England issued a report calling on its clergy to refrain from using biblical texts that included such masculine terms as "He" and "Lord." The report stated that sermons and

hymns containing certain masculine terminology actually encouraged "male oppression." The Archbishop of Canterbury, Rowan
Williams, suggested the continued use of these masculine terms,
even those found in the Bible, contribute to domestic abuse.[13] Psalm
11:3 declares, "If the foundations are destroyed, what can the righteous
do?"

Dr. C. F. W. Walther, in his book *The Proper Distinction
Between Law and Gospel*, described the judgment that awaits every
false teacher. Walther stated:

> On that day every false teacher will wish that he had
> never been born and will curse the day when he was inducted
> into the sacred office of the ministry. On that day we shall
> see that false teaching is not the trifling and harmless matter
> that people in our day think it is.
>
> God requires, not only that we love His Word, but also
> that we tremble at it, that is, that we sincerely dread to deviate
> from a single letter of the divine Word, that we do not dare
> to add anything to it or take anything from it. We are to be
> ready to shed our blood rather than yield a tittle of God's
> Word.[14]

When churches no longer proclaim the whole truth of God's
Word, the damage inflicted on their members is beyond calculation.
Today sermons in mainline churches rarely mention sin, repentance
or commitment to Christ. Missions and evangelism are a mockery
in these dead and dying churches. Liberal clergy no longer seek to
convert the lost because they reason all religions are equally valid in
bringing people to salvation. Someday they will answer to the Lord
for this grievous sin. Truly the light of God has gone out in these
churches.

THE SPIRIT OF THE NICOLAITANS

Jesus commended the Ephesian church for "hating" the deeds
of the Nicolaitans. *Nikao* means to conquer, while *laos* means the
people. Likely the Nicolaitans were a sect that promoted the domi-

nation of the people by the clergy. The acceptance of clergy-dominated churches came swiftly in the latter part of the second century. It ultimately brought about a church with its powerful bishops and popes. Throughout the centuries obedience to bishops and popes was falsely equated with obedience to Christ. In order to successfully carry out this plan, church officials kept the Bible away from the people. They warned the laity no one was permitted to interpret the Bible without the official sanction of the church's clergy. That same mentality still controls vast portions of the nominal church today, even as church members willingly turn over all theological matters to their learned clergy and believe what they are told.

Far too many Christians in the twenty-first century, even in evangelical churches, are ignorant of the Bible's teachings; they neither read nor study it. Sunday Schools and Bible studies are disappearing from our churches. Instead, people turn to their pastors and say, "Tell us what we are supposed to believe, and tell us the position of our denomination on such and such an issue or doctrine." It is little wonder false teachers have such an easy time promoting strange doctrines and perverting the Word of God, when biblically illiterate and apathetic church members permit themselves to be dominated by these apostles of apostasy.

Martin Luther once commented, "A layman armed with Scripture is mightier than any pope." Christians who face a plethora of false teaching need to become like the Bereans who "received the word with great eagerness, examining the Scriptures daily to see whether these things were so."[15] The glory of the Protestant Reformation has long departed from churches that still bear the names and seals of the Reformers. These churches have cast aside foundational doctrines in order to embrace the apostate ecumenical movement. Not long ago nearly all Protestant churches faithfully proclaimed the great Reformation doctrine "sola scriptura," Scripture alone. They understood that true authority rested not in bishops, denominations or position statements but in the Word of God alone.

Today liberal mainline churches are adorning themselves with increasing layers of ecclesiastical authority. They fall all over themselves writing position statements that are in direct contradiction of the Scriptures. Some influential Protestant leaders even advocate the recognition of the Pope of Rome as the supreme head over the whole church, even though Pope Benedict XVI has reaffirmed the ancient doctrine that the Roman Catholic Church is the only true church.

The ecumenical movement has prompted mainline churches and their members to go crawling back to the land of bondage, where powerful authorities are only too willing to control their lives, property and faith. They are returning to a land where clergy and dictatorial denominations control the people and their congregations. Local congregations that once were free to govern their own affairs must now obtain permission from their denominations regarding ministry and property. The spirit of the Nicolaitans lives today!

HEEDING THE SPIRIT'S CALL

Our Lord still walks in the midst of His people. His own hear His voice and follow Him. Across the nation countless Christians are obeying the voice of the Holy Spirit and separating themselves from church bodies that no longer proclaim or follow the Word of God. Congregations, large and small, as well as individual laity and pastors are separating themselves from denominations that have walked away from truth. By doing so they are finding new life and freedom in the Word and Spirit of God. To this end and for this purpose, God is raising up new congregations and faith-based movements that are giving a faithful witness to His unchanging truth.

Every congregation needs to hear and heed the voice of the Spirit of God as He speaks from the pages of Holy Scripture. Congregations which remain under the authority of denominations that have jettisoned the true Word of God for the spirit of the age need to repent and return to the faith upon which they were founded. Christians in these wayward denominations need to flee apostasy as they would flee a contagious plague. Such admonition is not a suggestion, it is a command, "Come out from their midst and be separate," says the Lord.[16] Church members who are waiting for spiritually bankrupt church leaders to bring about reform in their churches will be greatly disappointed. Christians need to stop compromising and stand fast in the faith that was once for all delivered to the saints. Our loyalty must be to Christ, not to a corrupt and rebellious denomination.

RETURNING TO OUR FIRST LOVE
MEANS A SPIRIT-LED REVIVAL

The pathway that will bring about the return of churches and individual Christians to their first love is nothing less than a Spirit-led revival. But any revival or renewal that does not cause people to repent is not Spirit-led. True revival will only come when Christians open their hearts to experience the power of God's Holy Spirit and live in obedience to God's Word. The Holy Spirit is ready to pour down His power upon us; the question is—Are we ready to receive it?

In the presence of the Lord, there is peace. In the presence of the Lord, there is joy. But what is not found in the presence of the Lord is sin or a rejection of His Word. Genuine revival always leads to genuine repentance and a life of sanctification and obedience. A secondhand faith is never sufficient to bring us into a right relationship with God. Those who are living through a secondhand faith need to repent and be converted. The time to come to Jesus is now!

The Lord calls Christians who have fallen away from the joy of their salvation to return to their "first love." We are called to overcome the world and everything that sets itself above God and His Word. One day when the strife is over and the victory is won, Christ will invite His true church, the church of the first-born, to eat of the Tree of Life in the Paradise of God. Until that day, may God help us all to be faithful!

Chapter 17

THE CHURCH IN SMYRNA
"The Suffering Church"

"And to the angel of the church in Smyrna write: The first and the last, who was dead, and has come to life, says this: 'I know your tribulation and your poverty (but you are rich), and the blasphemy by those who say they are Jews and are not, but are a synagogue of Satan. Do not fear what you are about to suffer. Behold, the devil is about to cast some of you into prison, so that you will be tested, and you will have tribulation for ten days. Be faithful until death, and I will give you the crown of life. He who has an ear, let him hear what the Spirit says to the churches. He who overcomes will not be hurt by the second death'" (Revelation 2:8-11).

HISTORICAL PERSPECTIVE

Smyrna of biblical times is known today as Izmir, Turkey. The city's population in the first century has been estimated at 200,000, while the population of modern Izmir is over 3 million. Smyrna was located on a beautiful bay of the Aegean Sea. The trade and commerce generated through its port made Smyrna a very prosperous city in ancient times.

Smyrna may have been established as early as 1500 BC. It claims to be the birth place of the poet Homer who was born in the eighth century BC. The city was destroyed in 600 BC, and lay in ruins for three centuries. It was rebuilt around 290 BC by Lysimachus, a successor to Alexander the Great. However, Smyrna did not come into prominence until the Roman era.

Writers in Roman times described Smyrna as the most beautiful city in the region. The heart of Smyrna was Mount Pagus (Kadifekale), adorned with several temples and beautiful buildings. The summit of the mountain was ringed with stately white columns, causing it to be called "the crown of Smyrna." This may have been the motivation for the Lord's reference to the "crown of life" that awaits believers who are faithful to death.

In AD 26 eleven cities competed with one another for the honor of being selected as the seat for emperor worship in Asia Minor. Smyrna was chosen, and a magnificent temple to Emperor Tiberius was erected atop Mount Pagus. From that time forward, emperor worship became a dominant factor in the lives of the city's residents.

The emperor was considered as being divine throughout the Roman Empire. Caesar was the embodiment of Rome's power, pride, wealth and glory. Although emperor worship was practiced throughout the empire, it was practiced with extreme fervency in Smyrna. A second temple dedicated to Emperor Hadrian was later constructed in the city. Prayers and sacrifices to the emperor were regularly offered in both temples.

As a matter of official policy, Jews were exempted from practicing emperor worship, but Christians had no official exemption or covering. The penalty for Christians who failed to worship or pay homage to the emperor was imprisonment or death.

The confession of the early church "Jesus is Lord" was viewed by Roman officials as being in conflict with the required profession of all who lived in the Roman Empire that "Caesar is Lord." Christians in the early church saw a great deal of difference between praying *for* the emperor and praying *to* the emperor. The penalties and persecution inflicted upon Christians because of their refusal to participate in emperor worship was at the forefront of the Lord's letter to the church in Smyrna.

BIBLICAL PERSPECTIVE

The only mention of Smyrna in the Bible is found in the Book of Revelation. We do not know for certain who organized the church there, but likely it was Paul or someone who traveled with him. Smyrna was only thirty-five miles from Ephesus where Paul resided and ministered for three years. The fact Jesus addressed His second letter to the church in Smyrna indicates its prominence in the region at that time.

SMYRNA TODAY

Today less than two percent of those living in Izmir (Smyrna) are Christians. This is due to a wave of persecution that descended on the city's Christian community in 1922. Little effort has been made to excavate Smyrna's ancient ruins because the modern city of Izmir has grown so quickly and covers such a broad area. Yet significant archaeological discoveries reflect the glory of ancient Smyrna, including the remains of a citadel known as the "Velvet Castle." Originally built by Lysimachus, this castle stood at the summit of Mount Pagus. In addition, remnants of the Roman agora, a government center and a market place have been uncovered. Within the agora are the ruins of store fronts, a street and a two-story basilica.

JESUS SPEAKS WORDS OF COMFORT

Jesus did not have a word of rebuke for the church in Smyrna. He knew about their tribulation and poverty. He was aware of the lies and blasphemies hurled at them by certain Jews who were identified as "a synagogue of Satan." Some of the Jews living in Smyrna had come from Israel when it was destroyed by the Romans in AD 70. In the years that followed, many of Smyrna's Jews became wealthy, influential and decidedly anti-Christian.

Certain Jews living in Smyrna during the first and second centuries demonstrated a deep hostility to Christians, because so many Christians had been converted from their ranks. The Jews of Smyrna sought to separate themselves from any connection with followers of "The Way," as Christianity was called at that time. Some Jews spread lies and blasphemies concerning Christian practices. For example, they claimed Christians engaged in cannibalism, referring to their eating the body and blood of Christ in the Lord's Supper. They also accused Christians of being disloyal to Rome and helped public officials to arrest them.

A large gap existed between the living standards of the average citizens of Smyrna and the Christians who lived there in the first century. Christians often had their property confiscated and found it difficult to obtain employment. Believers who were sent to prison understood it was likely a death sentence. One of the favorite sports in ancient Smyrna was throwing Christians to the wild beasts in the arena, thus they were always looking to replenish their supply.

Jesus comforted the church in Smyrna by telling them "not to fear what they were about to suffer." He assured them their tribulation would last for only ten days. Most Bible scholars interpret the expression *ten days* as meaning "for a limited period of time." The number ten appears several times in Revelation as relating to the fullness of earthly matters. Actually there were ten literal periods of persecution imposed on the church from Nero to Diocletian, during which time an estimated one million Christians were put to death. Interestingly, Emperor Diocletian's wife and daughter became converts to Christianity.

THE MARTYRDOM OF POLYCARP

One can hardly address the subject of Christian persecution in Smyrna without mentioning Polycarp, the city's bishop and a disciple of the apostle John. Polycarp stood steadfastly against a wave of heresy that plagued the church in the second century. Marcion, whose Gnostic heresies seriously threatened the churches, was vigorously opposed by Polycarp. The Epistles of John and

Jude indicate the seriousness of heresies that had invaded the early church.

When Polycarp was an old man, another wave of persecution swept the churches in Asia Minor, and emperor worship was at its very core. To avoid arrest Polycarp left Smyrna and went into seclusion at a country house near Philadelphia. A young servant boy who knew of Polycarp's whereabouts was captured and tortured by the authorities until he revealed the Bishop's location.

When Roman officials arrived at Polycarp's residence to arrest him, he invited them in and gave them something to eat. On the way back to Smyrna, one of the officials pleaded with Polycarp to say the words "Caesar is Lord," even if he did not believe them. He asked, "What would be the harm in saying those little words and offering a small sacrifice to the emperor?" Polycarp assured the official he would never utter those words or offer a sacrifice to the emperor.

Upon arrival in Smyrna, Polycarp was taken to the arena where thousands had gathered to watch him die. The Procounsul (governor) ordered Polycarp to make the declaration "Caesar is Lord" and reproach Christ. Polycarp answered: "For eighty and six years I have served the Lord and He has done me no harm. How can I blaspheme my King who saved me?"

When the Procounsul threatened Polycarp with death by burning, he responded, "You threaten me with the fire that burns for a time, and is quickly quenched, for you do not know the fire which awaits the wicked in the judgment to come and in everlasting punishment."

Thus on February 23, 156, Polycarp was tied to a stake inside the arena in Smyrna. Some who were on hand for the execution hastily arranged the wood for the fire. Initially the flames had little effect on the aged Bishop. When it became apparent the flames would take too long to kill Polycarp, the executioner stabbed him to death in order to spare the old saint additional suffering.

Reflecting on the courage and commitment of Polycarp and other Christian martyrs, one is reminded of the words of the Psalmist: "Precious in the sight of the Lord is the death of His saints." Another commentary regarding such stalwart soldiers of the Cross is found in Hebrews 12:16: "...the world was not worthy of them."

PERSECUTION IN CHURCHES TODAY

More Christians died for the Christian faith in the 20th century than in the previous nineteen centuries combined. There is no reason to believe the situation will change in the twenty-first century. Today an estimated 200 million Christians in at least forty nations are suffering under various degrees of persecution.

The Massacre of Christians in Smyrna in 1922
Perhaps one of the most egregious acts of Christian persecution in history came between 1905 and 1922 when approximately two million Armenian Christians were put to death by the Ottoman Turks. In one day, April 24, 1915, the Ottoman Turks were responsible for killing 600,000 Armenians.[1]

In September 1922, as many as 150,000 Greek and Armenian Christians were put to death in Smyrna; the city was utterly destroyed, except for the Turkish quarter. Twenty-seven Allied ships, including three American destroyers, were in Smyrna's harbor at the time; however, the ship's crews merely watched as the city burned and the massacre took place. Greek and Armenian Christians who sought to escape the slaughter and flames swam to the Allied ships, but most were denied rescue. Some tried climbing up the ropes that moored the ships in the harbor, but they either fell or the ropes were cut to prevent them from boarding.

The Greek Orthodox spiritual leader at that time, Archbishop Chrysostomos, was taken from his church during services and subsequently turned over to a mob by a Turkish official. The mob stabbed and beat him to death before mutilating his body.

Persecution by the Communists
In the Democratic People's Republic of North Korea, there is no religious freedom. North Korea, with a population of nearly 23,000,000, is ruled by a brutal dictatorial regime that has persecuted Christians for years. As recently as 2006, Open Doors International released its annual "Watch List" of nations engaged in the persecution of Christians. For the fourth straight year, North Korea headed the list. Tens of thousands of Christians are locked away in North

Korean prison camps. Open Doors president Dr. Carl Moeller said, "North Korea is suspected of detaining more religious and political prisoners than any other country in the world."

Godless communistic governments persecuted churches and Christians without mercy in the Soviet Union and Eastern Europe throughout much of the twentieth century. Certain state-approved churches were permitted to operate under strict rules, but many underground churches were formed to worship and serve the Lord Jesus Christ. When the Soviet Union fell apart in the early 1990s and enslaved countries in Eastern Europe gained their freedom, people in the West were amazed to discover how much spiritual life and vitality actually existed among their churches.

After the collapse of the Soviet Union, churches appealed to Christians in the West for help. Today numerous evangelical churches and ministries in the United States are working in these countries to establish Bible schools, seminaries and new congregations. Just how long this window of opportunity will remain open is a matter of considerable concern. Russian president Vladimir Putin appears ready to slam the door shut on Russian democracy and freedom.

Persecution in China

The churches in China have experienced horrendous persecution since the country fell to the communists in 1948. But China underwent a significant change in 1979 when the atheistic government, seeking to improve relations with the West, began allowing more religious toleration. Christians in the West were surprised to discover the church in China was alive and well. The number of Christians living in China today is estimated to be between 100 and 200 million.

There are three types of churches in China— the Three-Self Patriotic Movement, the Chinese Patriotic Association and the underground church. The Three-Self movement is comprised of government-recognized Protestant churches. Three-Self stands for self-supporting, self-governance and self-propagation.

The Roman Catholic Churches in China comprise the Chinese Patriotic Association, also a government-recognized church.

However, even in this official church structure, the Chinese government does not permit the Pope to appoint his own bishops without obtaining government approval. Many Roman Catholics are part of the underground church. In 2007 Pope Benedict XVI made overtures to Chinese officials that they recognize his authority to appoint bishops and to allow both the registered and the unregistered Catholic churches to have more freedoms.

The underground church in China has existed since the communists took over the country in 1948. The underground churches are the most spiritually alive and the most persecuted of all the churches in China. Membership in underground churches has been estimated as high as eighty million; however, those affiliated with unregistered churches are constantly being rounded up, imprisoned, tortured and killed. Thousands of Christians in China are serving lengthy prison sentences in labor camps.

Government-sanctioned churches in China are not allowed to evangelize, hold Bible classes or conduct youth meetings. Even so, worship services are well attended and their churches are experiencing significant growth. There is a great hunger in China for the Word of God. While the government of China permits a specific number of Bibles to be printed and distributed by the official Three-Self Patriotic Church, less than half the Christians in China own a Bible. Christian leaders in the underground church have stated they must rely on Bibles being smuggled into China.

Persecution in Islamic Nations

From its inception Islam has sought to extend its influence through forced conversions, a policy still practiced today. Christians in Muslim countries are often forced to convert to Islam or face death. With all the talk about human and religious rights coming from the United Nations and various liberal organizations, few ever mention Christian persecution in Islamic countries.

Most Islamic nations have a burning hatred for Jews. Muslim sects and organizations share a common desire to see Israel destroyed. While Jews have lived in Islamic countries for centuries, they are not permitted to live in Saudi Arabia, nor are Christian churches permitted there.

Only a few years ago, Christianity was the dominant religion in Lebanon; now it comprises less than twenty-two percent of the total population. Hezbollah is making life hard for Christians who live there. Thousands of Christians have left the country, while many more are looking for a way out. Hezbollah wants to make Islam the dominate religion in Lebanon and impose sharia law. Twenty years ago there were 225,000 Armenian Christians in Lebanon; today there are less than 65,000.

More than fifty percent of all Christians in Iraq have fled the country since 2003. Before the war, an estimated 1.2 million Christians lived in Iraq; today there are less than 500,000. Christians in Iraq are constantly being threatened with bodily harm and death. Their churches have been destroyed, and Christian women are being forced to wear veils and observe Islamic law when in public. Dozens of churches in Baghdad have been destroyed or forced to close in the last few years. Death by crucifixion and other barbaric acts are commonly carried out against Christians in Iraq.

Since 2003, approximately 350,000 Iraqi Christians have sought refuge in Syria, but according to Jim Jacobson, president of Christian Freedom International, Christians in Syria are little better off. "For Christians, one of the core tenets is the ability to share your faith, but in Syria, that can lead to arrest and persecution," Jacobson said. "We list Syria as one of the top countries where Christians face real persecution."[2]

Saudi Arabia employs thousands of foreign workers, many of whom are Christians. However, Christians are not permitted to carry Bibles or wear crosses in public. They are not allowed to hold or attend Bible studies in private homes. If a foreigner brings a Bible into Saudi Arabia and it is discovered, the Bible is confiscated. In some cases, foreigners have been arrested and jailed for violating this law.

While not a single Christian church exists in Saudi Arabia, the Saudis have built hundreds of mosques throughout the United States, Canada and Europe. Christian missionaries are not allowed in Saudi Arabia, but hundreds of Muslim clerics are paid by the Saudi government to promote the Islamic religion in cities and towns across America and Europe.

In Indonesia hundreds of churches have been burned to the ground, and tens of thousands of Christians have been put to death by their Muslim neighbors. It is estimated that as many as 3,000 Christians were killed in 1996 in East Timor alone.

The worst persecution of Christians in modern times continues to take place in Sudan, where between two and three million Christians have been put to death by Muslim radicals in recent years. Forced conversion to Islam is official government policy in Sudan. Any preaching or evangelizing by Christians is illegal.[3]

Christian persecution continues unabated throughout the Islamic world, where missionary work and evangelistic efforts are strictly forbidden. Converts to Christianity in most Islamic countries are marked for death. Even in Europe, a growing number of Muslims who converted to Christianity have been murdered.

Christian Persecution in the West Bank and Gaza

Only a few years ago, Bethlehem was ninety percent Christian. Today the Christian population in the city of Christ's birth is estimated at less than twenty percent. A large number of Christians in Bethlehem have been forced to leave their homes and businesses by militant Muslims. One former Christian resident of Bethlehem stated: "There is no life, no jobs, no work and no future in Bethlehem."

Of the 1.4 million residents in the Gaza Strip, less than 2000 are Christians. In Ramallah and the Gaza Strip, Christians are constantly being threatened and intimidated by Islamic militants. Since 1994 more than 900 Christians have fled Ramallah.

When Hamas took over the Gaza Strip in June 2007, one of their first acts was to storm Gaza's Latin Church (Roman Catholic) and the adjacent Rosary Sisters School. According to reports, Hamas thugs destroyed crosses and Bibles before setting the buildings on fire. Christians were ordered not to engage in "missionary activity," and Christian women were warned to cover their heads while in public.

Over the past few years, the Palestine Bible Society Center in Gaza has been targeted several times by Muslim radicals. One flyer read: "Be aware we are watching you closely. You spread a doctrine against Islam and are operating a Crusaders' evangelistic campaign supported by the Crusaders from the West." The Bible Society's bookstore was bombed in April 2007. A group called the Sword of Islam claimed responsibility for the blast.

In September 2006, the YMCA building in the West Bank city of Qalqiliya was set ablaze by Islamic mobs, after preachers in a dozen or more mosques called on their people to revolt against the YMCA. There are fewer than a hundred Christians living in Qalqiliya, a city with a population of over 28,000 Muslims.

Christians in Nazareth comprised sixty percent of the population twenty years ago; today Christians in Jesus' hometown number less than thirty percent. Even though Nazareth is located in Israel proper, Muslims have made life extremely difficult for Christians living there; many have chosen to leave.

As Muslim extremists gain more influence in cities and towns in Israel as well as the West Bank and Gaza, they are forcing Christians out by threats, persecution and boycotts of their businesses. In some areas of the West Bank, it is impossible for Christians to find employment. Many mainline denominations in America have joined Muslims in blaming Israel for persecuting the Christians in Gaza and the West Bank, even though they know the suffering is being caused by Islamic radicals.

HOW DOES THE LETTER APPLY TO US TODAY?

The failure of Christians in America and Europe to identify with their persecuted brethren throughout the world is a great sin that must be confessed with sincere repentance. For whatever reason, the media seldom reports atrocities being committed against Christians in Islamic countries and elsewhere. In July 2007 when four Christians were crucified in Iraq, there was silence from all the major media outlets. The Bible directs Christians to "remember the prisoners, as though in prison with them, and those who are ill-treated, since you yourselves also are in the body."[4]

One does not have to wait for the tribulation to see harsh persecution falling upon those who bear the name of Jesus Christ; it is happening now to thousands of our brethren. As our modern culture here in the West moves away from any acknowledgement of God, and as the new global religion gets a stronger grip on both church and society, the persecution of Bible-believing Christians will continue to grow more intense. If the anti-God movement continues to grow, persecution will take place in America also. Jesus remembered the persecuted church in Smyrna; may God help us to remember our persecuted brethren in the twenty-first century.

Chapter 18

THE CHURCH IN PERGAMUM
"The Church that Needed to Clean House"

"And to the angel of the church in Pergamum write: The One who has the sharp two-edged sword says this: 'I know where you dwell, where Satan's throne is; and you hold fast My name, and did not deny My faith even in the days of Antipas, My witness, My faithful one, who was killed among you, where Satan dwells. But I have a few things against you, because you have there some who hold the teaching of Balaam, who kept teaching Balak to put a stumbling block before the sons of Israel, to eat things sacrificed to idols and to commit acts of immorality. So you also have some who in the same way hold the teaching of the Nicolaitans. Therefore repent; or else I am coming to you quickly, and I will make war against them with the sword of My mouth. He who has an ear, let him hear what the Spirit says to the churches. To him who overcomes, to him I will give some of the hidden manna, and I will give him a white stone, and a new name

written on the stone which no one knows but he who receives it'" (Revelation 2:12-17).

HISTORICAL PERSPECTIVE

Pergamum (Pergamon) is one of Turkey's most impressive archaeological sites. The city did not come into prominence until the era of Alexander the Great. When Alexander died his empire was divided into four parts by four of his generals—Cassander, Lysimachus, Ptolemy and Seleucid. Lysimachus was given the part of the empire known as Thrace (Southeastern Europe and European Turkey). He later expanded his kingdom into portions of Asia Minor, including Pergamum.

Pergamum was only a small settlement when Lysimachus came to power. His control over the area ended abruptly when one of his generals, Philetarios, led a successful revolt against him. Philetarios developed Pergamum into a prominent center of culture and made it the capital of the Seleucid kingdom. Rulers who followed Philetarios continued the development of the city.

Pergamum became part of the Roman Empire around 133 BC. Eventually Rome made it the capital of the Province of Asia. During the Roman period, numerous temples and buildings were erected, including the construction of a 50,000-seat arena.

The word "parchment" (pergamena) is derived from Pergamum. Parchment or vellum made from animal skins was developed in Pergamum during the third century BC, after Ptolemy put an embargo on papyrus coming from Egypt. Soon parchment was considered superior to papyrus. One of the largest libraries in the world was located in Pergamum. Its 200,000 volumes were sent to Alexandria as a wedding gift for Cleopatra by Marcus Antonius (Mark Antony).

BIBLICAL PERSPECTIVE

In the letters addressed to the seven churches, imagery peculiar to each specific place was used. None of the churches had any difficulty recognizing how the imagery in their particular letter related to their location or specific circumstances.

The city of Pergamum, for example, was the seat of governmental authority for the Roman province of Asia. Because the proconsul held the full authority of Caesar, Pergamum used the symbol of a sword to identify itself as the official seat of Roman power in the region.

Jesus revealed Himself to the church in Pergamum as "the One who has the sharp two-edged sword." Such imagery was a vivid reminder to the church in Pergamum that although they lived in a center of Rome's imperial power, their lives were secure through a far greater power—the power of God's Word. Jesus is described in Revelation as having a two-edged sword coming from His mouth. Other passages of the Bible describe the sword of the Lord as the incomparable power of God's Word.[1]

PERGAMUM TODAY

The modern city of Bergama, population 80,000, lies in a valley beneath the ancient acropolis and in an area where portions of ancient Pergamum were located. A small Christian community exists in Bergama today, as it has throughout the centuries.

The ruins on Pergamum's ancient acropolis are both extensive and impressive. A theater on the side of the acropolis seated as many as 10,000 spectators. The theater, one of the steepest in the world, was erected in the third century BC and enlarged during the Roman era. A road in front of the theater led to the Temple of Dionysos, the god of wine.

Atop the acropolis are the ruins of the palace of Eumenes II, a ruler during the Greek period. The ruins of the Temple of Trajan, which was the center of a powerful cult of emperor worship, tower over the acropolis, as do the ruins of the city's famous library. In another area are the remains of the Temple of Athena, dating to the third century BC.

Just below the acropolis are the ruins of the Temple of Zeus with its huge throne-like altar. The altar, discovered in 1871, was taken to Germany and housed in the Museum of Pergamum in Berlin. The government of Turkey has been attempting to get it back, but thus far without success. On the north side of Bergama are the ruins of the Red Hall, built by Emperor Hadrian. It was later turned into a Christian basilica.

In southwest Bergama lie the ruins of the Asklepion, a temple and medical complex dedicated to Askepious, the god of healing. The Asklepion contained its own theater that seated 3500 people. There was also a clinic where people came from near and far to be treated by doctors and priests for various medical conditions. Treatments at the clinic included music and the interpretation of dreams. Images of a serpent associated with Asklepious may be seen among the ruins.

DWELLING WHERE SATAN DWELLS

Not only did Christians at Pergamum dwell in a city that reflected Rome's power, but according to Jesus they also dwelt "where Satan's throne is." Bible scholars have long debated the exact meaning of this statement, since a satanic influence was evidenced in most of Pergamum's cults and institutions. But which specific cult prompted Jesus' description of Pergamum as the place where "Satan dwells?" Most scholars link one of the following three cults to Christ's statement.

The Cult of Emperor Worship

Pergamum was the location of a temple dedicated to Emperor Augustus in 29 BC, one of the first temples promoting emperor worship in the region. During the Christian era, every Roman citizen was required, at least once a year, to offer a pinch of incense in a temple of the emperor and say the words, "Caesar is Lord." For devout believers this edict was impossible to obey, because it contradicted the Christian profession of faith "Jesus is Lord."

The Temple of Zeus

The altar of Zeus, built around 230 BC, commemorated a great victory over the Gauls. The altar appeared as a huge chair in the middle of the acropolis. Smoke from the sacrifices offered on the altar rose to the skies continuously. Zeus was identified by his followers as "Zeus the Savior." The Temple of Zeus stood directly above the temple of the Greek goddess Athena.

The Temple of Asklepious

Asklepious was the serpent-god of healing. The fact that the chief symbol for Asklepious was the serpent and he was called "the Savior" makes the Asklepion a prime candidate to be identified as "the seat of Satan."

Although some scholars endeavor to explain the meaning of Jesus' words "where Satan's throne is" by choosing one of these cults, the term may have been used collectively for all three cults, as well as other satanic rituals practiced in Pergamum.

PRAISE FOR THOSE WHO HAD NOT DENIED HIS NAME

In spite of threats and temptations, most believers at Pergamum remained faithful to the name of Christ. Jesus' reference to Antipas who was killed "where Satan dwells," was certainly not lost on believers at Pergamum. While we have no reliable historic reference as to who Antipas was or just how he died, Jesus linked his death directly to the satanic powers at work in the city. In a Christian context, the word *martyr* means "one who gave up his life for the faith." It also means "witness." Christian martyrs certainly offered up the ultimate witness to Christ by giving up their lives.

Throughout history the church has understood when the laws of man conflict with the law of God, believers ought to obey God rather than man. Though Christians may suffer for disobeying the laws of human governments when they conflict with Scripture, the Lord always has the last word.

In the United States, conflicts between God's law and man's law seldom lead to persecution. However, this may be changing as Christians are being called upon to conform to politically correct forms of religion, and as anti-hate legislation endeavors to silence criticism of immoral behavior. In many parts of the world today, Christians face great peril when they are forced to choose between obeying God and obeying the unjust laws of man.

Because followers of Christ in Pergamum lived "where Satan dwells," they could not avoid daily contact with a pagan culture or the consequences of an oppressive government. Yet the Lord praised them because of their refusal to adopt pagan ways or yield one inch of blood-bought ground.

THE PATH OF COMPROMISE

While Jesus had words of praise for believers who remained faithful to His name in Pergamum, He identified two groups in the church who had chosen the path of compromise. The first group to receive the Lord's stern rebuke had encouraged fellow-believers to compromise with the false religions around them. He compared them to Balaam, an Old Testament seer who attempted to get Israel to commit immorality with false religions.[2] The Epistle of Jude spoke about those in the church who "have gone the way of Cain, and for financial gain, they have rushed into the error of Balaam and perished in the rebellion of Korah."[3]

Jesus' words of rebuke were addressed to the entire church, though He made it clear only *some* in the church at Pergamum had participated in the sins of Balaam. He held the entire church of Pergamum accountable for tolerating the actions of those whose compromises threatened to defile the church. While the letter to the Pergamum church does not specify the precise nature of their shameful behavior, perhaps they had participated in pagan feasts and had eaten meat offered to idols. It is possible they might have performed the required incense offerings in the Temple of the emperor and uttered the words "Caesar is Lord." Whatever their compromises, Jesus was displeased over the fact they had encouraged others to commit the same sins. And it appears they did it for financial gain.

A second group in Pergamum that received a harsh rebuke from the Lord held to the teachings of the Nicolaitans. While the nature of this sect is not known for certain, their name implies an effort to elevate the clergy over the laity. Jesus praised the church in Ephesus for rejecting the Nicolaitans, while He rebuked the church in Pergamum for embracing it.

Dr. Henry A. Ironside, one of America's greatest preachers and Bible scholars, referred to the teaching of the Nicolaitans as "clerisy." According to Dr. Ironside clerisy is the "subjection of those who were contemptuously styled 'the laity' by a hierarchical order who lorded it over them as their own possessions, forgetting that it is written, 'One is your Master, even Christ, and all ye are brethren.'"[4] Perhaps one of the most egregious sins in twenty-first century churches is the ongoing elevation of the clergy over the laity. People in the pews must bear some of the blame for this sin, because they have allowed themselves to be dominated by the clergy. The average church member today is both passive and silent as their leaders guide them into heresy, apostasy and unbiblical practices.

Jesus commanded both groups in Pergamum to repent, or else He would make war against them with the sword of His mouth. The command to repent was addressed to the entire church, since they all needed to repent of their failure to correct and discipline those who were engaged in false teachings and acts of compromise.

WORDS OF PROMISE AND ENCOURAGEMENT

Jesus offered words of encouragement to the faithful: "To him who overcomes, I will give some of the hidden manna, and a white stone, and a new name written on the stone known only to the one who receives it." The white stone is the token that gives its bearer the right to enter the Lord's banquet hall. Most Bible scholars believe the inscription on the stone may refer to a new name for Christ; others suggest it is a new name for each believer. In times past God gave new names to many after they entered into a new relationship with Himself. Abram became Abraham, Jacob became Israel and Simon became Peter (the rock). The color of the stone is also important. White represents purity or holiness, without which no one will see God. In ancient times the white stone represented acquittal in courts of justice.

HOW DOES THE LETTER APPLY TO US TODAY?

The religious climate in America today is not unlike that which existed in Pergamum when the Book of Revelation was written. The belief all religions are equally valid expressions of faith in the same deity is a widely held view by many living in America. It has become politically incorrect to claim otherwise. The biblical teaching Jesus Christ alone is the Savior of the world and the only hope of mankind has been rejected by most of the mainline churches.

The influence of Balaam may be seen in the modern ecumenical movement. The World Council of Churches and the National Council of Churches, along with other local ecumenical organizations, continue to promote a watered-down version of Christianity that accepts all religions as equally valid paths to God. It is increasingly common today for Christian congregations to participate in ecumenical services that include representatives of non-Christian religions. This is nothing less than a sell-out of biblical Christianity.

Today liberal clergy in the mainline churches urge everyone to pray "to the God you choose to worship," as though it makes no difference which god people worship. Many Christians, especially compromising clergy, refuse to pray in the name of Jesus Christ or even mention His name at public gatherings. Yet clerics belonging to other religions are never asked to follow such restrictions. The only person not welcomed at ecumenical services is Jesus Christ.

The Case of Gordon James Klingenschmitt

Gordon James Klingenschmitt graduated from the U.S. Air Force Academy in Colorado; he obtained a Master of Divinity degree from Regent University while serving in the Air Force. Klingenschmitt rose to the rank of Major before sensing a call from God to become a military chaplain. In 2002 he volunteered for a demotion from the rank of Air Force Major to Navy Lieutenant, in order to become a military chaplain. During Operation Iraqi Freedom, Chaplain Klingenschmitt served aboard the USS Anzio where he witnessed a great revival among the ship's crew.

In September 2006, Lt. Gordon James Klingenschmitt was fined $3,000 for praying in Jesus' name in front of the White House while in uniform. Chaplain Klingenschmitt stated he was protesting a newly implemented Navy policy regarding the use of "non-sectarian" prayers outside of officially sponsored worship services. As a result Klingenschmitt was charged with disobeying an order from a superior officer and with quoting John 3:36 during a chapel service. Found guilty at his court-martial, Chaplain Klingenschmitt was dismissed from an otherwise flawless 16-year career in the Navy.

Janet Folger, who sat in the room during Klingenschmitt's hearing, said, "Before I could go through the metal detectors to get to the courtroom, a Navy official had already taken Jesus' name in vain. No trial for that. No penalty. No problem. But the use of the name in reverence, in honor or in prayer, and you'll find yourself looking in the face of a court-martial. Welcome to the criminalization of Christianity."[5]

Praying in Jesus' Name

Christians should be respectful and loving to people of other religions. This does not mean we are to set aside foundational truths of Christianity, however. Respecting the rights of others to practice their religion is the proper course to take in a free and democratic society. But the acknowledgement of this right does not mean we should embrace other religions as being equal with Christianity. For any Christian to deliberately refrain from praying in Jesus' name because someone might be offended is a scandal to the cross! Jesus said, "Whoever denies me before men, I will also deny him before My Father who is in heaven."[6]

Our spiritual identity as Christians should compel us to pray in Jesus' name anytime we are asked to pray, whether it is in church or in public. As we would not expect a Jewish rabbi or a Muslim imam to pray in Jesus' name because ninety-eight percent of those in the assembly are Christians, neither should a Christian pastor be expected to refrain from praying in the name of Jesus Christ, even if he is the only Christian present.

Even some conservative, evangelical pastors try to do an end-run with the name of Jesus when their close their prayers at public gatherings by saying, "and I pray in your name, Amen." While they want to appear to be praying in Jesus' name, they cannot quite get the name of Jesus to roll off their tongues. If people are offended when we pray in the name of Jesus, let them be offended. The One in whose Name we pray was nailed to a cross for our sins. Like Polycarp, we should prefer to die rather than deny our Lord and Savior, Jesus Christ.

The essence of Christianity is Christ. The Bible and the church's confessions affirm Jesus Christ alone is the way to eternal life. He is "one with the Father," and "very God of very God." As Christians we pray in Jesus' name because we believe in Him, and because He instructed us to do so. Paul also writes, "always giving thanks for all things in the name of our Lord Jesus Christ to God, even the Father."[7]

If all religions are equally valid in bringing mankind to salvation, then Jesus' death on the cross was futile, His teachings were bogus, and the Bible is no more holy than any other book. If all religions are equally valid in bringing salvation to all mankind, every Christian who ever died for his or her faith has died in vain. If all religions are equally valid paths to God, every Christian missionary sent out to bring others to Christ was on a fool's errand. Peter said it best, "And there is salvation in no one else; for there is no other name under heaven that has been given among men by which we must be saved."[8]

At the National Interfaith Service at the National Cathedral, September 14, 2001, Nathan Baxter, dean of the Cathedral, opened with a prayer to "the god of Abraham, Mohammad, and Father of our Lord Jesus Christ."[9] But the God of Abraham, Isaac and Jacob, the God of the Bible, the God and Father of our Lord Jesus Christ is not the god of Islam, Buddhism, Hinduism or any other religion. For a Christian to equate Christianity with other world religions is a compromise condemned by the Lord to the church in Pergamum.

One cannot imagine Paul or Peter participating in ecumenical services where other religions were equated with Christianity. The apostles would never have instructed anyone to refrain from praying or speaking in Jesus' name, so as not to offend people of other religions. To the contrary, Paul was bold enough to witness Christ to men in authority. King Agrippa was so moved by Paul's witness he said, "In a short time you will persuade me to become a Christian." To which Paul replied, "I would wish to God, that whether in a short or long time, not only you, but also all who hear me this day, might become such as I am, except for these chains."[10] We will never be effective in our witness to Jesus Christ if we compromise His Word or blush to speak His name.

A few years ago, David W. Cloud reported the World Council of Churches (WCC) joined with the Lutheran World Federation, the World Student Christian Federation and the World Young Women's Christian Association (YWCA) in issuing a booklet entitled *No Longer Strangers*. The booklet encouraged Christians to call God by such names as "Lady of Peace," "Lady of Wisdom," "Lady of love," "Lady of birth," "Mother," "Baker-woman" and "Simplicity." One of the readings stated: "I believe in God, mother-father, spirit, who called the world into being; I believe in God, who because of love for her creation, entered the world to share our humanity, to be rejected, to die and finally to conquer death and to bind the world to herself."[11]

David Cloud remarked: "Each year the World Council of Churches becomes more radical, more openly pagan. Yet the farther this organization moves from the Bible, the more we see evangelical/charismatic leaders attending its meetings and dialogues and speaking well of it. What does this mean? If the WCC is drawing farther and farther from Christ and Scriptures with each passing year, and evangelicals are following the WCC, we see clearly the departure of these evangelicals from the Word of God."[12] How is it possible for Bible-believing Christians to accept their denomination's participation in the apostate World Council of Churches?

The largest Episcopal church in Tucson, Arizona announced they were removing all "power imagery," including the word "Lord" from their worship services. Thomas Lindell, deacon at St. Phillip's in the Hills, told the *Arizona Daily Star,* "Our service has done everything it can to get rid of power imagery. We do not pray as though we expect the big guy in the sky to come and fix everything." The church's associate rector, Susan Anderson-Smith, said: "Jesus was for an egalitarian community. He did not have room for titles or status. And it is recorded that many of the disciples called him Lord.

But they had a different idea about worshipping him. Jesus was a rabbi and teacher. It was a relationship of mentoring, looking up to him for that kind of companionship."[13] It is highly unlikely clergy from St. Phillip's in the Hills or any other church will dare to stand before the Lord on Judgment Day and refer to Him as "the big guy in the sky."

Polycarp and a host of Christian martyrs in the early church yielded their lives to the flames and wild beasts, rather than utter the words "Caesar is Lord." Today there is a great temptation on the part of many to embrace ecumenism and lay aside all exclusive claims that Jesus Christ is the world's only Savior. There is a conscious effort in America to remove the name of Jesus Christ from the public arena. The purveyors of the new global religion want us all to worship the politically correct, government god who leads and heads all of the major world religions, but who never offends anybody. Psalm 138:3 declares, "You have exalted above all things your Name and your Word." The second Commandment instructs us, "You shall not take the Name of the Lord in vain."

We must never yield one inch of blood-bought ground. Christians who stand for the truth of God's Word in these days of political correctness and spiritual compromise must embrace Jesus Christ alone as Savior and Lord! Those who overcome and remain faithful to the end will be numbered with those who will receive the "white stone" inscribed with the glorious Name, and they will feast at the Lord's Table and eat the hidden manna with the world's only Savior.

The old hymn of the church, once sung with such deep conviction, should once again become the battle song of the church. Though written over two hundred years ago, its challenge to every Christian is timeless.

Am I a soldier of the Cross, a follower of the Lamb?
And shall I fear to own His cause or blush to speak His name?

Must I be carried to the skies on flowery beds of ease,
While others fought to win the prize, and sailed through bloody seas?

Are there no foes for me to face? Must I not stem the flood?
Is this vain world a friend to grace to help me on to God?

Sure I must fight if I would reign, increase my courage, Lord,
I'll bear the toil, endure the pain, supported by Thy Word.

Thy saints, in all this glorious war, shall conquer though they die;
They see the triumph from afar, by faith they bring it nigh.

When this illustrious day shall rise, and all thy armies shine
In robes of victory through the skies, the glory shall be Thine.

Isaac Watts (1674-1748)

Chapter 19

THE CHURCH IN THYATIRA
"The Church with a Jezebel Spirit"

"And to the angel of the church in Thyatira write: The Son of God, who has eyes like a flame of fire, and His feet are like burnished bronze, says this: 'I know your deeds, and your love and faith and service and perseverance, and that your deeds of late are greater than at first. But I have this against you, that you tolerate the woman Jezebel, who calls herself a prophetess, and she teaches and leads My bond-servants astray so that they commit acts of immorality and eat things sacrificed to idols. I gave her time to repent, and she does not want to repent of her immorality. Behold I will throw her on a bed of sickness, and those who commit adultery with her into great tribulation, unless they repent of her deeds. And I will kill her children with pestilence, and all the churches will know that I am He who searches the minds and hearts; and I will give to each one of you according to your deeds. But I say to you, the rest who are in Thyatira, who do not hold this teaching, who have not known the deep things

of Satan, as they call them—I place no other burden on you. Nevertheless what you have, hold fast until I come. He who overcomes, and he who keeps My deeds until the end, TO HIM I WILL GIVE AUTHORITY OVER THE NATIONS; AND HE SHALL RULE THEM WITH A ROD OF IRON, AS THE VESSELS OF THE POTTER ARE BROKEN TO PIECES, as I also have received authority from My Father; and I will give him the morning star. He who has an ear, let him hear what the Spirit says to the churches'" (Revelation 2:18-29).

HISTORICAL PERSPECTIVE

Thyatira was strategically located in a fertile valley and on a heavily traveled highway between Pergamum and Sardis. It was founded by Seleucus I around 282 BC as a military outpost to protect the kingdom's eastern region, especially Pergamum. Advancing enemies had to break through military defenses stationed there before they could threaten more populated areas. Thyatira remained an outpost of little significance until it came under Roman control in 133 BC.

As Thyatira developed it became known for various types of trade products—wool, linen, leather, bronze and the dyeing of purple cloth. The manufacture of purple cloth was very costly and associated with the wealthy. The purple dye came from the roots of plants indigenous to the area.

Deities worshiped in Thyatira included Apollo, Artemis, Asklepious and Bacchus. Images of Apollo and other gods were found on coins discovered in the area. There were no magnificent temples in Thyatira to either gods or emperor. A woman of the city named Sambathe was renowned for her fortunetelling abilities.

BIBLICAL PERSPECTIVE

There are only two references to Thyatira in the Bible; one is in Revelation and the other is found in Acts. The longest letter to the seven churches was addressed to Thyatira. Their toleration of sin and their accommodation with the culture reflects both the length and the importance of this letter. While in Philippi, Paul encountered Lydia, a seller of purple cloth from Thyatira. He led her to the Lord and baptized her whole family.[1] It is possible Lydia and her family may have been associated with the Church at Thyatira.

THYATIRA TODAY

The modern city of Akhisar, population 25,000, is built over ancient Thyatira. The only archaeological remains of the ancient city are a few ruins from the Temple of Apollo, a church and a colonnaded street. Everything else lies buried beneath Akhisar. Compared with the archaeological ruins at Ephesus, Pergamum and Sardis, this site is disappointing. The few uncovered ruins serve mostly to identify the place where the city of Thyatira once stood.

THE TRADE GUILDS AT THYATIRA

People who wanted to do business in Thyatira's trades were required to belong to a trade guild. Guild meetings involved social and religious gatherings where meals were shared and formal sacrifices were offered to various gods. Meat sacrificed to the gods was consumed at these meals, and sexual immorality was commonplace.

The general population of Thyatira accepted the idolatry and immorality of the trade guilds as a normal way of life. Because there was so little toleration for those who did not participate in the guild meetings, this likely became a major issue for Christians who needed to make a living through various trades, while wanting to remain faithful to the Lord.

It could have been that the woman referred to as "Jezebel" in Jesus' letter tried to persuade believers in Thyatira they could belong to the guilds and still remain loyal to Christ. She might have reasoned participation in the guilds' idolatrous feasts was a necessary accommodation to the culture. In any event, a pragmatic theology of accommodation developed in the church at Thyatira that was reinforced by this false teacher and her followers. Even though some

Christians living in Thyatira neither participated in guild meetings nor sanctioned this woman's false teachings, the Lord was greatly displeased because they had closed their eyes to her pernicious influence. The practice of accommodation seemed to have worked well for the church in Thyatira until the Son of God came knocking at the door.

THE CHURCH—THEN AND NOW

Messages contained in the letters to the seven churches of Revelation have prophetic significance and application for churches in every age. The message of impending judgment sent by the Lord to the church at Thyatira certainly needs to be heeded by churches in the twenty-first century, especially in America and other Western nations where accommodation and compromise are all too common.

There have been few times in history when churches so blatantly embraced evil or accommodated the world's immoral system as churches are doing in our day. Considering Christ's threat to the church at Thyatira, what makes Christians believe they will get away with similar compromises of the faith?

In many ways the state of the church in the twenty-first century is worse than it was in the first century. Then, the culture was totally pagan and churches had to stand against it. But today mainline churches are actually corrupting the culture by sanctioning evils condemned in the Scriptures, such as their support of abortion, same-sex marriages and the ordination of practicing homosexuals. Many mainline churches have aligned themselves with organizations such as the American Civil Liberties Union or People for the American Way, in order to drive God from all aspects of our nation's life. By turning the nation away from our Judeo-Christian heritage, churches are telling the world the God of the Bible is dead or, if not dead, irrelevant when it comes to establishing moral absolutes. How can such wickedness go unpunished?

If the church in Thyatira was unable to plead ignorance for having entered into alliances with Satan, neither can churches in the twenty-first century. With the Word of God and the Holy Spirit to guide them, Christians in Thyatira were without excuse. How much more will God hold present-day churches accountable when they endeavor to justify sin and sanction evil through official church policy? Denominations and congregations that establish their teachings and practices on majority opinion rather than on Scripture will answer to God. Of what value are position statements if they are not in agreement with the clear teachings of the Bible?

CHRIST REVEALED AS THE SON OF GOD

Jesus identified Himself to the church in Thyatira as the Son of God, with eyes like a flame of fire and feet like burnished bronze. In Revelation 1:14-15, Jesus Christ is described in the same words, and as the Son of Man who walks among the churches. The title *Son of God* is used only once in the Book of Revelation, and it is used here in this letter to the church in Thyatira. Christ presents Himself as the righteous judge who brings the full authority of God against every form of sin within and without the churches.

The god who held the highest honor in Thyatira was Apollo, the son of Zeus and chief of all gods. While the altar of Zeus commanded the center of attention on the acropolis in Pergamum, his son Apollo was ensconced in a burnished-bronze statue in Thyatira. All Roman emperors claimed to be the incarnate sons of Zeus.

Jesus' description of Himself as the Son of God to the church in Thyatira flew in the face of Thyatira's culture and religion. Christ left no doubt He is the Son of the one, true and living God, empowered to execute judgment on all who deny or defy Him. His flaming eyes can see everything, even the intentions of the heart. Every sin will be trampled under His burnished-bronze feet.

Sinners will stand exposed on Judgment Day; they will be without excuse and without defense. As they appear before the Son of God, there will be no debate regarding differing interpretations of morality. On that day the great and small shall stand before the Great White Throne where truth alone shall prevail.

Jesus reminded the church in Thyatira it could not continue to sin or enter into accommodation with the world without facing judgment. Christ gave Thyatira's Jezebel and her followers an opportunity to repent, but they refused. Therefore Jesus said they would be held accountable and bear the consequences. God's messengers need to declare this truth from their pulpits in the twenty-first century — Jesus Christ is coming again! However, at His second coming He will appear not as Savior but as Judge.

Churches today may think they are getting away with false teachings and unbiblical practices, but one day they will be required to render an account to the Lord of the Church! Every church and every Christian must heed the words of Scripture: "For if we go on sinning willfully after receiving the knowledge of the truth, there no longer remains a sacrifice for sins, but a terrifying expectation of judgment, and the fury of a fire which will consume the adversaries."[2]

LOVE AND DOCTRINE CANNOT BE SEPARATED

While the church in Ephesus was praised for its doctrine and reprimanded for its lack of love, the church in Thyatira was praised for its love and service and reprimanded for its failure to honor doctrine. Throughout the ages it has not been unusual to see a disconnection of love and doctrine within the churches. Zeal for correct doctrine while lacking in works of love, or zeal for works of love while lacking in correct doctrine are both rejected by the Lord of the Church.

The diligence of liberal churches to care for the poor is highly commendable. At the same time, their willingness to align themselves with a godless culture while laying aside sound doctrine is intolerable in the sight of God. Similarly, there are Bible-believing churches today that are long on doctrine and short on loving service to those in need. While their passion for correct doctrine is commendable, their concern for the needs of the poor leaves much to be desired. The disconnection of love and doctrine is no less a serious offense today than it was in the first century.

We should note the Lord praised the church in Thyatira regarding their "love, faith, service and perseverance." His praise certainly must have encouraged the faithful few in Thyatira. How lovingly the Lord prompts His church to be faithful in both word and deed. The fact the Lord is slow to chastise and swift to bless reveals the quality of His grace and mercy. We should never put Him to the test in this regard, however.

THE JEZEBEL SPIRIT

The Lord chastised the church in Thyatira for tolerating a woman who was leading people into idolatry and immorality. He compared her to the wife of Israel's wicked King Ahab. Queen Jezebel enticed Israel into idolatrous and immoral practices, but God confronted and ultimately judged Ahab and Jezebel for their many acts of wickedness.

"You tolerate the woman Jezebel who calls herself a prophetess," Jesus said to the church at Thyatira. Though this woman was not anointed to preach or teach, she claimed to have had a special word from God. She did not! Who can imagine how much Scripture she quoted and twisted in order to convince the church her views were correct? Those who followed this Jezebel had elevated her words above the Word of God. They failed to heed the example of the Bereans who first listened to the teachings of Paul, and then "examined the Scriptures daily to see whether these things were so."[3]

There are many in the church today who claim to have a special revelation from God, when, in fact, their "special word" is in total contradiction of the Scriptures. Throughout the ages there have been those with *a Jezebel spirit* who have sought to lead fellow believers into accommodation with the world. Those who follow false teachers have no one to blame but themselves for their sorry spiritual condition or the spiritual condition of their churches.

Accommodation with the world has become routine in our modern churches. Some mainline congregations have adopted the feminist agenda by writing nonsexist versions of the Bible and promoting goddess worship. It is not uncommon for liturgies in mainline churches to prompt worshippers to pray to "the Father/ Mother God," which is both blasphemous and heretical.

The radical feminist influence in today's church is evidenced in the promotion of goddess worship, same-sex marriage, homosexuality, transsexual and bisexual behaviors. Furthermore, radical feminism is behind the mainline church's support of abortion, better known euphemistically as "a woman's right to choose." Perverted teachings about Jesus being a homosexual or being married to Mary Magdalene are frequently espoused by radical feminist theologians. All of these doctrines, teachings and practices come from the same satanic source. They are, as Paul described them, doctrines of demons.

Several mainline denominations are presently engaged in highly questionable studies to determine whether or not they should ordain homosexuals and conduct ceremonies for same-sex couples. The only Book members of these churches need to study in order to determine God's will in all of these matters is the Bible! If mainline churches truly believed in the doctrine of "Scripture alone," their so-called studies regarding homosexual practices would quickly conclude this lifestyle is an abomination before God, and ordaining homosexuals and conducting same-sex ceremonies is a violation of the clear teachings of Scripture. No church can conclude otherwise and remain faithful to the Word of God. Church bodies may arrogantly pass resolutions declaring evil is good, and good is evil, but these resolutions will not stand. One day the Son of God will come knocking on the doors of all who have sanctioned sin and entered into accommodation with the world.

"Love the sinner and hate the sin" is not a hollow slogan; it is the teaching of the Bible. Liberal churches today put down every effort by Bible-believing Christians to minister to homosexuals and help them to be set free from their bondage to sin and enter into a living relationship with Jesus Christ. Christian organizations, such as Exodus International, have had great success in reaching homosexuals for Christ and seeing them released from their bondage to sin. The whole church should be praying for and supporting the work of such ministries.

JUDGMENT IS NOT ALWAYS DELAYED

God gave Thyatira's Jezebel time to repent, but she refused. He declared those who were tolerating her perverted ways would face the same judgment. It is no small matter when Christians promote or sanction sinful practices. As in Thyatira Christians today live in a corrupt culture, but the Lord expects us to live without compromising or selling out the gospel. The Lord's patience in giving sinners renewed opportunities to repent is a gift of grace. But God's Spirit "will not always strive with man." God sets a limit for sin to run its course. He sets a limit for repentance to be made. Then comes the time for judgment.

When I was growing up in Worthington, Pennsylvania, my pastor, A.W. Smith, often closed his sermons by quoting Isaiah 4:12: "Seek ye the Lord, while He may be found. Call upon Him while He is near." Then Pastor Smith would lean over the pulpit, look us all in the eye and add—"and He may never be nearer to you, than He is right now!" God used these words to capture my heart and set me on the path to eternal life.

As the culture in America continues its downward spiral, we may have little time left in which to repent. The signs of the Lord's return are all about us. Accommodation with the world and toleration of sin will not stand—not in the churches and not in our individual lives. Christians must say "no" to the Jezebel spirit, "no" to accommodation with the world, and "no" to entanglements with sin. It is time for churches that have strayed from God's Word to repent and live in full obedience to the infallible Word of God. If they do not, it is the duty of every Bible-believing Christian to flee from their midst and find a church that upholds and lives out the Word of God.

Jesus' words to the church in Thyatira about tolerating false teachers remind us about our responsibility to "earnestly contend for the faith." It is one thing for the church to be about the work of gospel ministry while reaching out to those in need; it is quite another matter when we encourage our members to do "church work" while ignoring the attacks on our homes, our churches and our nation.

What happens when churches and Christians refuse to stand up for the truth of God's Word and to be salt and light in our culture? Just look around at the present spiritual condition of our nation and our churches, and the answer will be clearly evident. Preach the gospel? Yes! Stand for the truth? Yes! Both are essential. And both are biblically mandated.

"HOLD FAST UNTIL I COME"

In spite of the many sins that threatened to destroy the church in Thyatira, Jesus was tenderhearted toward the remnant—"the rest in Thyatira who do not hold to this teaching or have not known the deep things of Satan." The phrase "the deep things of Satan" could be translated "the profundities of Satan." Jesus told them, "I will place no other burden on you, only hold fast until I come."

While the vast majority of those around them were engaged in doctrinal compromises and sin, the godly remnant in Thyatira refused to join them. The saints in Thyatira not only had to fight the forces of their culture, they had to stand against their own church leaders who promoted false doctrines and unbiblical practices. Countless Christians face the same dilemma today. Far too many church members must remain vigilant and guard themselves from their own pastors.

Liberal clergy in the twenty-first century seem more inclined to wink at the works of Satan than they are to warn people about their dangers. The "deep things of Satan" include the obvious—idolatry, the occult and witchcraft, but they also include the higher critical method of biblical study, rewriting the Bible, as well as promoting humanism, moral relativism and ecumenical alliances with those who promote false teachings. One of the most subtle deceptions being promoted within our churches is the substitution of politically correct views for true biblical doctrines. Many clergy and church members are far more concerned about being politically correct than they are being biblically correct.

Many Christians today delight in going in and out of the devil's playground. They think a little compromise with sin will not harm them. Most people who are in bondage to pornography, gambling, drugs and alcohol never dreamed they would one day become addicted, but sin has a way of trapping and ensnaring its victims. Satan's big lie continues to spring the trap—"No one will ever know." But that is not true; God knows!

Our Lord also knows what it is like to live in a hostile and sinful world. He understands the pressures and temptations we face daily. But armed with His Word and enabled by His Spirit, we can "hold fast" to the end. Paul wrote: "No temptation has overtaken you but such as is common to man; and God is faithful, who will not allow you to be tempted beyond what you are able, but with the temptation will provide the way of escape also, so that you will be able to endure it."[4]

Even in the face of satanic attacks, persecution or hardship, we can trust the promises of God for a victorious outcome. As Paul said, "...for I know whom I have believed, and am persuaded that He is able to keep that which I have committed unto Him against that day. Hold fast the form of sound words, which thou hast heard of me, in faith and love which is in Christ Jesus."[5]

OVERCOMERS AND THE MORNING STAR

When the Book of Revelation was written, Christians were threatened daily by many external forces—government officials, Roman soldiers, hostile Jews and the practitioners of false religions. Believers rose from their beds each morning not knowing what the day might bring. Would they be hauled before the magistrates, sent off to jail or sent to the arena? The temptation to compromise was present everyday. Life and death decisions were often required before the setting of the sun. Holding fast was extremely difficult.

The world system that shapes so much of our modern society and demands our conformity is not unlike that which confronted the first-century church. We too can choose the path of compromise, or we can be "overcomers." Holding fast until Jesus comes means we must overcome the world, even as Jesus overcame the world. The Bible defines one who overcomes this way: "And who is he that overcomes the world, but he that believes that Jesus is the Son of God?"[6]

The "morning star" promised to believers refers to Jesus Christ when He comes to rapture His church before the outpouring of God's wrath that will be measured out on this sinful world. The gospel song by Esther Kerr Rusthoi captures this truth so well:

It will be worth it all when we see Jesus,
Life's trials will seem so small when we see Christ;
One glimpse of His dear face all sorrow will erase,
So bravely run the race till we see Christ.

THE CROWN AWAITS THE CONQUEST

Jesus Christ was "faithful unto death, even the death of the cross."[7] By looking to Jesus and relying on the power of the Holy Spirit, we too can be faithful to the very end. The crown of life is not awarded until the last battle is fought and the final victory is won. May we be able to say with Paul, "I have fought the good fight, I have finished the course, I have kept the faith."[8]

Jesus promised the church in Ephesus: "To him that overcomes will I give to eat of the tree of life which is in the Paradise of God." He promised the church in Smyrna: "...be faithful until death and I will give you the crown of life." He promised the church in Pergamum: "To him who overcomes, to him I will give some of the hidden manna, and I will give him a white stone, and a new name written on the stone which no one knows but he who receives it." And to the church in Thyatira, Jesus promised:

He who overcomes, and he who keeps My deeds until the end, TO HIM I WILL GIVE AUTHORITY OVER THE NATIONS; AND HE SHALL RULE THEM WITH A ROD OF IRON, AS THE VESSELS OF THE POTTER ARE BROKEN TO PIECES, as I also have received authority from My Father; and I will give him the morning star.

The joy that awaits those who hold fast until Jesus comes is beyond all telling. Overcoming means we shall reign with Christ over the nations. But surely the greatest joy of all will be when Christ, the Morning Star, comes and receives us unto Himself. The Son of God is coming again—as Judge to the wicked and as the Morning Star and Savior to all who believe in Him. Each of us needs to look deep within our hearts and ask—Is the Lord returning as my Judge or as my Savior? If I died today, where will I spend eternity?

If you are not ready to meet Him, you need to know your relationship with God can change today as you repent of your sins and yield your life to Jesus Christ. God has made this promise to you:

"...that if you confess with your mouth Jesus as Lord, and believe in your heart that God raised Him from the dead, you will be saved; for with the heart a person believes, resulting in righteousness, and with the mouth he confesses, resulting in salvation."[9]

Christ has paid in full the penalty for your sins through His death on the cross. Through His burial and resurrection, He has opened the way to heaven for you. If you believe His Word, repent of your sin, He will save you today. Right now, offer this prayer from your heart:

Lord, I come to you, a sinner in need of a Savior. I believe You died on the cross for me and for all sinners. I believe you rose from the dead, and you are in heaven today interceding for me. I repent of my sins and earnestly seek your forgiveness. Grant me eternal life. Write my name in the Lamb's Book of Life. Fill me with Your Holy Spirit that I may be enabled to live a victorious life and overcome the world. Thank you for hearing my humble prayer. Thank you for saving me! This I pray in Jesus' Name. Amen.

Welcome, friend, to the family of God!

Chapter 20

THE CHURCH IN SARDIS
"Dead Church Walking"

"To the angel of the church in Sardis write: He who has the seven Spirits of God and the seven stars, says this: 'I know your deeds, that you have a name that you are alive, but you are dead. Wake up, and strengthen the things that remain, which were about to die; for I have not found your deeds completed in the sight of My God. So remember therefore what you have received and heard; and keep it, and repent. Therefore if you do not wake up, I will come like a thief, and you will not know at what hour I will come upon you. But you have a few people in Sardis who have not soiled their garments; and they will walk with Me in white; for they are worthy. He who overcomes will thus be clothed in white garments; and I will not erase his name from the book of life, and I will confess his name before My Father and before His angels. He who has an ear, let him hear what the Spirit says to the churches'" (Revelation 3:1-6).

HISTORICAL PERSPECTIVE

The population of Sardis at the time of John the apostle was about 120,000. Sardis was situated at a junction of important highways linking Ephesus, Pergamum and Smyrna. It was located about thirty miles from Thyatira and fifty-six miles east of Smyrna in the fertile Hermus Valley. Built on top of Mt. Tmolus, Sardis stood 1500 feet above the valley floor. The city was surrounded by steep cliffs on three sides and accessible only from the south. Eventually Sardis grew into the valley below, creating an upper and a lower city.

Sardis was the capital of the Lydian empire in the seventh and sixth centuries BC. Croesus, the last Lydian king, is considered to have been the wealthiest person of his time. He accumulated vast quantities of gold, taken from the Pactolus River. Some historians claim King Croesus was the first to mint gold and silver coins.

The city's nearly impregnable location atop a mountain gave its citizens a sense of security. Regardless of its location, Sardis was twice invaded and captured. The first time was in 549 BC when Cyrus of Persia conquered it; the second time was in 214 BC when the city was taken by Antiochus III. During the first invasion, no guards had been posted to keep watch over the city. The Persians discovered a large vertical cleft in the steepest part of the mountain which they scaled under the cover of darkness and gained access to the city. The same strategy was used by Antiochus over 300 years later.

Sardis surrendered to Alexander the Great in 334 BC; it later became an important city in the Greek-Selucid Empire. The city fell to Roman control in 133 BC, and remained affluent throughout the Roman era. When a massive earthquake destroyed Sardis in AD 17, Emperor Tiberias helped to rebuild the city.

In New Testament times, Sardis was known for its commerce, especially the woolen trade. The art of dyeing wool was developed in Sardis. A large and impressive temple dedicated to Artemis (Diana) was erected in lower Sardis in 300 BC, but it was subsequently destroyed. An effort was made in 175 BC to rebuild the temple, but the project was never completed. The half-finished Temple of

Artemis remained a source of embarrassment for the city's residents until it was completed by the Romans in the second century AD.

Sardis was known for its infamous Temple of Cybele, a fertility goddess known as the Great Mother. The Temple of Cybele and the Temple of Artemis were located in the same area of the city. Sex orgies that sometimes included castration and mutilation were practiced among those who worshiped Cybele. William Barclay observed "even on pagan lips Sardis became a term of contempt. Its people were notoriously pleasure loving."[1] Sardis was destroyed in 640 and never rebuilt.

BIBLICAL PERSPECTIVE

The only mention of Sardis in the Scripture is contained in this letter. The history and geographical settings of the cities in which the seven churches were located offer insight into the message contained in each church's respective letter. This was especially true of Sardis. Jesus' command that the church in Sardis should "wake up" or else He would surprise them "like a thief" was a vivid reminder of the city's humiliating history when it was caught off-guard and captured, not once but twice. On both occasions the city fell because the people were asleep and no one was guarding the city. The reference to "uncompleted deeds" was in keeping with the city's reputation for unfinished tasks, such as its Temple of Artemis.

SARDIS TODAY

The modern town of Sart stands today in the general vicinity where ancient Sardis was located. It is a beautiful community situated in an area of green valleys and wooded hills. Locals take great pleasure in decorating their homes and lawns with flowers. Harvard and Cornell universities conducted extensive archaeological excavations in Sardis. Among the discoveries are royal burial mounds, a city wall and a gold-working installation. The ruins from the Temple of Artemis are particularly impressive. Of the original 82 columns, only two Ionian pillars remain, along with portions of thirteen others. In the vicinity of the Temple of Artemis, archaeologists also discovered the remains of a fifth century church, giving the impression Christians in Sardis directly challenged the pagan religions of their neighbors.

Other excavations include a bath-gymnasium complex, constructed in the third century AD, and a beautiful Jewish synagogue with mosaics and colored carved-stone panels. The synagogue was once used as a Christian basilica. Ten Byzantine shops, dating to the fifth century, were discovered near the gymnasium complex. The shops were owned by both Jews and Christians, suggesting that during the Byzantine era Jews and Christians in Sardis had harmonious relations with one another.

IN THE LORD'S HANDS

In His letter to the church in Sardis, Jesus identified Himself as the one who "has the seven spirits of God and the seven stars." The seven spirits of God represent the authority and power of the Holy Spirit; while the seven stars are symbolic of the messengers or leaders of the seven churches. The message is clear—Jesus Christ has full authority over the churches and their leaders. Nothing is hidden from His eyes. Such knowledge offers joy to those who walk in obedience to His Word, but fear of impending judgment for those who do not.

The Lord empowered His church with the fullness of the Holy Spirit to carry out the work of witnessing the gospel to the ends of the earth. Church leaders are anointed to do God's will, not their own. Nothing should be on a congregation's agenda that is not in accordance with His Word.

Congregations do not "hire" pastors, as many are inclined to believe. Pastors are called by God and are ultimately accountable to Him for the stewardship of their ministries. To be sure, pastors are accountable in many ways to their congregations, but their accountability to God always comes first. The Scripture says, "Obey your leaders, and submit to them; for they keep watch over your souls as those who will give an account."[2] Pastors should never use the office of the ministry as a pretext for imposing their own personal desires on their congregations. They certainly should never use their office to promote anything contrary to the Word of God.

Church members should not find it necessary to go searching outside their congregations for the authentic Word and power of God. All the gifts of the Holy Spirit are available to every congregation, so they lack nothing in the spiritual dimension. Churches that do not walk in the truth and power of the Holy Spirit will be held accountable to God.

DEAD CHURCH WALKING

"You have a name that you are alive, but you are dead," the Lord told the church in Sardis. There was no mention of false teaching or compromise as there was in His letters to the previous four churches, though these things would have been present. The main issue regarding the church in Sardis was they were spiritually dead. The Sardis church was not being destroyed from without but from within by indifference and apathy.

The fact they had a reputation for being alive likely meant there was no shortage of activity in the Sardis church. Apparently they fooled those around them regarding their spiritual life and vitality, but the Lord saw their deeds and knew their true spiritual condition.

Only a generation earlier, Christians in Sardis had sat under the ministries of apostolic leaders. But when the next generation tried to live on the reputation of their parents and grandparents, they no longer were able to distinguish the truth from a lie. Like those in the church in Ephesus, members of the Sardis church were trying to live on a reputation they neither owned nor deserved. They seemed to have done quite well at it until the Lord of the Church called them to account.

It is not unusual today for congregations to worship in buildings erected by Christians who had a genuine love for the Lord and a heart for winning lost souls. But those who follow in their steps no longer share the same passion and vision for ministry. There are Sardis-like churches today with beautiful buildings and ambitious programs, but nobody gets saved! They have entertaining worship services, but nobody gets saved! Their preachers know how to make worshippers feel good about themselves by proclaiming what is popular or what the people want to hear, but nobody gets saved! These churches measure success by attendance figures and financial reports. As long as the pews are full or as long as the money comes in, they are satisfied. Like the church in Sardis they have a reputation for being alive, when, in fact, they are spiritually dead. Dead men can only proclaim a dead religion.

Many evangelistic efforts in the twenty-first century are not based on winning the lost to Christ, but rather on finding ways to prompt people to join the church. So often, evangelism is equated with transferring members rather than transforming lives. Years ago a man displayed on television a most impressive engine encased under a clear plastic bubble. It was amazing to watch the parts of the engine move with great precision. There was just one problem—the engine was not connected to anything! It just sat there and ran. This is a picture of spiritually dead churches; they may be running, but they are not plugged into the power of God. Unless churches are connected to the Word and Spirit of God, what possible use are they to the kingdom of Christ? The only reputation that should concern local congregations or Christians is the reputation they have with God.

WAKE UP!

Christ offered no words of praise or commendation to the church in Sardis, as He had in His letters to the previous four churches. Instead He delivered a stern warning to a church dying from apathy. The city of Sardis had a reputation for sleeping while enemies scaled their walls and invaded their city. Centuries later the church in Sardis suffered from the same reputation spiritually. Jesus told them, "Wake up, and strengthen the things that remain, which were about to die; for I have not found your deeds completed in the sight of my God."

So many Christians do not have a clue about what is going on around them; furthermore, they do not want to know! While moral and spiritual conditions in the churches are deteriorating, typical church members are concerned only if a particular issue directly

impacts their personal lives. Every year as mainline denominations continue to depart from biblical absolutes, their membership
declines by the tens of thousands. Yet members of these denominations seem oblivious to what is happening, because they cannot see
substantive changes in their local congregations.

Pastors are usually aware of doctrinal compromises being
promoted by their denominational leadership, but few bother to
inform their people about what is taking place. "Don't rock the boat,"
they reason, and "Don't upset the bishop or endanger the pension."
However, more often than not, the typical pastor is in full agreement
with his or her denomination's teachings and practices.

Christians do not become apathetic overnight. Apathy is a slow
evolving process that grows like a cancer until it consumes the last
measure of spiritual life and vitality. Christians afflicted with apathy
will eventually lose their desire to worship, pray or serve the Lord.
Apathy in a church or in the life of a Christian produces a spiritual
malaise that eventually brings about devastating consequences.

Many Christians know the church where they worship no longer
resembles the church they knew years ago, yet they choose to remain
and do nothing about it. They know their denomination or congregation no longer teaches the pure Word of God and is engaging in practices condemned by the Bible, yet they continue to support it with
their tithes and offerings. These things ought not to be! It is inconceivable how Christians can continue to attend churches and support
denominations that have made a shipwreck of the true Christian
faith. It is even more inconceivable how parents and grandparents
can continue to endanger the spiritual wellbeing of their children.

In far too many churches and denominations the only voices
left to warn wayward churches to turn back to God are silent. The
cosmic battle over spiritual truths and moral values raging in both
church and society will determine the ultimate destiny of America
and her churches. If Christians do not stand up and speak the truth,
there is little likelihood their congregations will ever be renewed.
There is so much for believers to do and so little time left in which
to do it. C. F. W. Walther said, "Woe to the Church which has no
men who stand as watchmen on the walls of Zion, sound the alarm

whenever a foe threatens to rush the walls, and rally to the banner of Jesus Christ for a holy war."[3]

Even though it is difficult to leave a denomination or a congregation that has been important in one's life for years, many are taking this step today in obedience to God's command:

> "Do not be bound together with unbelievers; for what partnership have righteousness and lawlessness, or what fellowship has light with darkness? ...Therefore, come out from their midst and be separate, and do not touch what is unclean; and I will welcome you."[4]

Over the past several years, faithful pastors have walked away from their denominations at great and personal cost to themselves and their families. They have organized new congregations built upon fidelity to the Word of God. Pastors who once preached in beautiful sanctuaries are now preaching in storefront churches or humble structures in order to remain true to their calling from the Lord. In like manner, individual Christians are finding their voices and speaking out for the truth of God's Word. Many who have spoken out, but with little or no response on the part of their church leaders, are stepping out in faith and uniting with a fellowship of believers where the Word of God is both believed and honored.

REMEMBER

"Remember therefore what you have received and heard; and keep it," Jesus appealed to the church at Sardis. One of God's greatest gifts to us is the gift of remembrance. Old Testament prophets often instructed the people of Israel to look back on special times of divine blessing and deliverance, in the hope they would remember and repent! Even the remembrance of trials and adversity helps us to focus on God's faithfulness. The Psalmist declared: "The lines have fallen to me in pleasant places; indeed, my heritage is beautiful to me."[5]

An exit sign at Yad Vashem, Israel's memorial to the six million Jews murdered in the Holocaust, reads: "Forgetfulness leads to exile; while remembrance is the secret of redemption." This simple message is a reminder the Holocaust must be remembered and never be allowed to happen again.

God spoke to Israel through His servant Jeremiah: "Stand by the ways and see and ask for the ancient paths, where the good way is and walk in it; and you shall find rest for your souls." But they said, "We will not walk in it."[6] It is not enough to simply remember; the Lord commands us to "remember what we have received and heard *and keep it.*"

Christians in the twenty-first century need to remember our spiritual heritage and reclaim it. As long as there are still Christians in the pews of our churches who can remember the true proclamation of the Word, there is hope! But what will happen when no one in a congregation is left who remembers hearing the authentic gospel of Christ? Solomon wrote:

> Remember your Creator in the days of your youth, before the evil days come and the years draw near when you will say, "I have no delight in them"...Remember Him before the silver cord is broken and the golden bowl is crushed, the pitcher by the well is shattered and the wheel at the cistern is crushed; then the dust will return to the earth as it was, and the spirit will return to God who gave it.[7]

REPENT

There is only one direction a congregation or an individual Christian can go if they desire to be freed from the sin of apathy, and that is to return to God with sincerity of heart. Those who have allowed themselves to become oblivious to the encroachments of the enemy and no longer sensitive to the Master's voice need to wake up and be stirred to repentance before it is too late. True repentance involves more than just feeling sorry for having sinned. Godly sorrow always leads us to forsake our sin and turn to God.[8]

Paul reminds us we were all dead in trespasses and sins when Jesus found us. The spiritually dead cannot repent unless they are enabled to do so through the energizing power of the Holy Spirit. Thankfully, Jesus not only calls us to repent, He enables us to do so through the Word and Spirit of God.

LIKE A THIEF IN THE NIGHT

"If therefore you will not wake up I will come like a thief, and you will not know the hour I will come upon you." Regardless of God's love, grace and mercy, there are those who stubbornly refuse to repent. However, there is a tremendous price to pay for resisting the Spirit's plea.

Christ's warning to the church in Sardis that He would come upon them as a thief at a time they least expect is reminiscent of the stealth used by forces that captured Sardis. Surely this message was not lost on those living there. The imagery of Christ coming as a thief in the night is also used in connection with His sudden appearing at the end of the age — "...the day of the Lord will come like a thief in the night. While people are saying 'Peace and safety,' destruction will come on them suddenly, as labor pains on a pregnant woman, and they will not escape."[9] It is a loving Savior who calls us to repent, so we will not be ashamed at His appearing.

A FAITHFUL FEW, EVEN IN SARDIS

Though much of the church in Sardis was dead and dying, the Lord identified a faithful few who had "not soiled their garments." These faithful few represented whatever future or hope remained for the Sardis church.

Even in the darkest days of the church's history, there were always a few stalwart men and women who remained faithful to the Word of God and the testimony of Jesus. The Reformation was no accident of history. It began as a few courageous men and women of God stood fast for truth in an age of hostility and deception. John Hus and John Wyclif made their stand for the Lord a hundred years prior to the Protestant Reformation. Martin Luther was but an ordinary man, until God gripped his heart and conscience with

His Word, enabling him to stand before prelates and princes and exclaim: "Here I stand, I can do no other!"

The spiritual condition in mainline churches today is bleak; yet in almost every church body there are a faithful few who are standing against their denomination's efforts to enshrine false teachings and apostasy. Yes, God has a remnant church in the twenty-first century. The question of the hour is this—Are you part of the faithful remnant or are you part of the crowd that would rather compromise than stand upon God's truth?

PROMISES FOR OVERCOMERS

Even in His letters that contained stern words of warning and rebuke, Christ offered to all who would truly repent the promise and hope of deliverance. In contrast to the soiled garments of those who offended God through unrighteous living, Christ promised His saints they would be arrayed in robes of white. Paul wrote: "Husbands, love your wives, just as Christ loved the Church and gave himself up for her to make her holy, cleansing her by the washing with water through the word, and to present her to himself as a radiant church, without stain or wrinkle or any other blemish, but holy and blameless."[10] The white robes describe the righteous attire of martyrs and saints who will come out of the great tribulation.[11]

The Lord of the Church has promised if we confess Him before mankind, He will confess us before the Father in Heaven. What a day that will be when Jesus speaks our names before the throne of God and identifies us as His redeemed children! "Everyone therefore who shall confess Me before men, I will also confess him before My Father who is in heaven."[12]

So many people believe they must wait until they die to find out where they will spend eternity. At that point it will be too late. The time to come to Christ is now! The apostle John wrote: "...these have been written so that you may believe that Jesus is the Christ, the Son of God; and that believing you may have life in His name."[13]

Our Lord also spoke about the Book of Life that contains the names of all who have received the free gift of salvation and have been made righteous through His blood. He also promised when the

Book of Life is opened our names will be written there. The most important question anyone will ever be asked is this—Is your name written in the Lamb's Book of Life?

> Lord, I care not for riches, neither silver nor gold,
> I would make sure of heaven, I would enter the fold.
> In the book of Thy kingdom, with its pages so fair,
> Tell me, Jesus, my Savior, is my name written there?
>
> O that beautiful city, with its mansions of light,
> With its glorified beings, in pure garments of white;
> Where no evil thing cometh to despoil what is fair;
> Where angels are watching, yes, my name's written there.
>
> Yes, my name's written there, on pages white and fair!
> In the book of Thy kingdom, yes, my name's written there.
>
> Mary Kidder

Chapter 21

THE CHURCH IN PHILADELPHIA
"The Church of the Open Door"

"And to the angel of the church in Philadelphia write: He who is holy, who is true, who has the key of David, who opens and no one will shut, and who shuts and no one opens, says this: "I know your deeds. Behold, I have put before you an open door which no one can shut, because you have a little power, and have kept My word, and have not denied My name. Behold, I will cause those of the synagogue of Satan, who say that they are Jews and are not, but lie—behold, I will make them come and bow down at your feet, and know that I have loved you. Because you have kept the word of My perseverance, I will also keep you from the hour of testing, that hour which is about to come upon the whole world, to test those who dwell on the earth. I am coming quickly; hold fast what you have, so that no one will take your crown. He who overcomes, I will make him a pillar in the temple of My God, and he will not go out from it anymore; and I will write upon him the name of My God, and the name of the

city of My God, the new Jerusalem, which comes down out of heaven from My God, and My new name. He who has an ear, let him hear what the Spirit says to the churches'" (Revelation 3:7-13).

A MESSAGE OF HOPE

Jesus' letter to the church in Philadelphia was filled with praise, promise and hope! Not one word of criticism was given to this church of faithful believers. The Lord understood the horrendous opposition they were required to endure. Yet through it all, believers in Philadelphia faithfully kept His Word and honored His name. They would not be forgotten.

Today even though vast portions of the church have denied and betrayed the Word of God, a remnant church still remains faithful to the Lord. His words of comfort and encouragement to the church in Philadelphia are also meant for the remnant church in the twenty-first century. Throughout the world, the remnant church is holding fast to the Word of God. The Lord sees their deeds; they will not be forgotten.

No greater assurance can be given to any believer than this: "I will keep you from the hour of testing...about to come upon the whole world." This is the unbreakable promise of the Lord to His bride, the true church. He will come and receive her unto Himself before the tribulation begins and the wrath of God is poured out upon the earth. The remnant church longs with eager anticipation for the Bridegroom's return. Maranatha, come Lord Jesus is the heart-cry of the bride!

HISTORICAL PERSPECTIVE

Philadelphia was founded by Attalus II who reigned from 159 to 138 BC. His loyalty to his brother Eumenes prompted some to call him "Philadelphus of Pergamum," which means "one who loves his brother."

The city of Philadelphia, located twenty-eight miles east of Sardis, was the newest of the seven cities mentioned in Revelation.

Attalus II established the city as a missionary center, in order to spread the Greek language and the Greek culture in the region. His plan succeeded; it was only a short while until the chief language in Philadelphia and the surrounding districts became Greek, as did their culture and religion.

Philadelphia was located on an earthquake fault line near the northern slopes of Mt. Tmolus overlooking the Cogamus River, a tributary of the Hermus River. A powerful earthquake nearly destroyed Philadelphia and ten other cities in the region in AD 17. Tremors continued for several years, causing inhabitants of the area to live in fear of another major earthquake. After Emperor Tiberias donated money to rebuild the city of Philadelphia, its name was changed to Neocaesarea in his honor. During the reign of Flavius Vespasian, the city's name was changed once more to Flavia, but the locals continued to call it Philadelphia.

In New Testament times, a road passing through Philadelphia linked Troas, Pergamum and Sardis. During the Byzantine era when commerce was moving in and out of Constantinople, Philadelphia played a vital role in the area's economy. When the region passed into the hands of the Ottoman Turks in the fourteenth century, the general population was forced to embrace Islam. Because Christians who lived in Philadelphia resisted Muslim threats to "convert or die," it remained one of the last Christian strongholds in Turkey.

BIBLICAL PERSPECTIVE

The only mention of Philadelphia in the Bible occurs in Revelation. As with the other six churches, Jesus' letter to the church in Philadelphia contained unique references understood by those living there at the time. His reference to the "hour of trial" was likely understood in the context of the cataclysmic earthquake that had earlier destroyed the city. Jesus' promise to give them "the name of My God" may have been understood in reference to the city's name having been changed twice before in honor of Tiberias and Vespasian.

PHILADELPHIA TODAY

The modern city of Philadelphia, known today as Alasehir, has a population of about 25,000 inhabitants. While it is largely an agricultural community, Alasehir has some small industries. The city is comprised mostly of Muslims, but about 2500 Greek Orthodox Christians live in Alasehir today.

THE KEY OF DAVID

Jesus identified Himself to the church in Philadelphia as the one who is "holy and true," and as the one who "holds the key of David." Christ's call to holiness was in stark contrast to the false religions and immorality practiced by the adherents of pagan religions in Philadelphia. This passage reminds us "without holiness no man shall see God." It also reminds us we do not enter the kingdom of God by our personal merits, but only through the merits of Christ who holds the "key of David."

While we are made righteous through the finished work of Christ on the cross, and while our merits add nothing to what Christ has done for us in terms of our salvation, still we are called to live in holiness before the Lord. Today so much of the church looks and acts like the world when it comes to talk, walk, dress and the love of material things.

Paul wrote to the church in Ephesus: "But immorality or any impurity or greed must not even be named among you, as is proper among the saints; and there must be no filthiness and silly talk, or coarse jesting, which are not fitting, but rather giving of thanks."[1] The apostle John implored believers: "Do not love the world nor the things in the world...The world is passing away, and also its lusts; but the one who does the will of God lives forever."[2]

In His letter Jesus instructed the church in Philadelphia to hold fast and remain faithful to the end. By doing so they would receive the crown of life. He also admonished them not to allow anyone to take their crown. It is not enough for us to start out being faithful; faithfulness must continue as long as God gives us life. Paul lamented to Timothy: "Make every effort to come to me soon;

for Demas, having loved this present world, has deserted me and gone to Thessalonica...Only Luke is with me."[3]

Jesus declared as the One who holds the key of David, He opens doors that no man can shut, and shuts doors no man can open. This unique power to grant admission into the presence of the King is described in Isaiah 22:22. The risen Savior who now holds the keys to the Kingdom said, "No one comes to the Father, but through me."[4] Likewise, Peter declared salvation is found in no one other than in Jesus Christ.[5] Yet so many today dare to contradict the Lord of the Church by claiming there are many other roads that lead to God.

INTERFAITH SERVICES
AND SPIRITUAL APOSTASY

Today's nominal church is deliberately ignoring the teachings of Scripture regarding salvation through Christ alone by offering to fellowship with every false religion on the planet. False teachers within the church claim salvation exists for all people regardless of their beliefs. Islam has become the darling of those connected with the ecumenical movement. For them, Allah and the God of the Bible are the same; they further claim Jesus and Muhammad are equal in bringing truth and salvation to mankind. Such teachings are both a denial of Scripture and a betrayal of the Lord Jesus Christ.

In Seattle an Episcopal priest became a Muslim while retaining her relationship with the Episcopal Church. She said she attends the mosque on Fridays, and on Sundays she attends the Episcopal services. "I am both Muslim and Christian, just like I'm both an American of African descent and a woman. I'm 100 percent both," Ann Holmes Redding told the *Seattle Times*. According to the Seattle paper, Redding has been hired to teach New Testament studies at Seattle University, a Roman Catholic school.[6] Her Episcopal bishop, rather than defrock her, asked her to take a year and consider which religion she wants to follow.

In April 2007 the Wiccans won a lawsuit to have a pentacle included on the gravestones of veterans. While the Wiccan religion claims to be based on nature and respect for the earth, their true agenda is to promote the occult, witchcraft and other satanic teachings. Their symbol, the pentacle, has long been associated with Satanism. As soon as the court ruling was made, Barry W. Lynn, director of Americans United for Separation of Church and State, commented: "This settlement has forced the Bush Administration into acknowledging that there are no second class religions in America, including among our nation's veterans."[7] It is truly remarkable the Wiccan symbol can be placed on a veteran's gravestone, but a Christian chaplain is requested not to mention the name of Jesus Christ in a public service.

An Episcopal clergyman prayed at a Memorial Day observance in Minnesota, "in the name of the Great Spirit, in the name of Buddha, in the name of Muhammad and in the name of Yahweh." Since September 11, 2001, an increasing number of Christian clergy have been promoting and participating in interfaith services with leaders of false religions, even though such acts are expressly forbidden by the Scriptures.[8] Many Christian clergy think nothing of inviting Muslims, Buddhists and representatives of other religions to speak and pray from their pulpits, all in the name of tolerance and diversity. Such idolatrous acts should be protested and rejected by all true Christians, but more often than not, such ecumenical services are met with silence, agreement or indifference. It is totally inappropriate for Bible-believing Christians to attend or support such services.

St. Olaf College, located in Northfield, Minnesota and affiliated with the Evangelical Lutheran Church in America (ELCA), has appointed a practicing Hindu as head of its religion department. Anantanand Rambachan, who has taught religion at St. Olaf since 1985, was appointed to head the school's religion department; he is the first non-Christian to hold that post in the school's history.[9]

In an interview with *Hinduism Today*, Rambachan discussed his participation in the Pontifical Council in Rome in 2006. He wrote:

> Last year we met in Rome in a joint consultation with the World Council of Churches to discuss conversion. This was the first meeting of a three-year project to study issues and to develop an acceptable code of conduct. Certain forms of Christian proselytization have given rise to tension and even

violence between some religious communities. We gathered to share our perspectives on this matter and to consider acceptable ways of sharing our faiths in communities.

Our discussion was frank and at times difficult, but we agreed that while everyone has a right to invite others to an understanding of their faiths, no one has the right to violate others' rights and religious sensibilities. At the same time, all should heal themselves from the obsession of converting others.[10]

In an interview with *WorldNetDaily*, Charles Wilson, a professor of religion at St. Olaf, commented favorably on Rambachan's appointment as head of the school's religion department by citing a colleague Harold Ditmanson who endorsed the hiring of Rambachan:

> He argued…St. Olaf is a church college in the Lutheran tradition, and Lutherans believe that studying religion at a college is not the work of the Church but rather the work of a liberal arts education in the religious things of the world.
>
> …Studying religion at St. Olaf, consequently, must be centrally a cognitive, not a spiritual exercise: indeed, in the words of the St. Olaf mission statement, the academic study of religion cultivates 'theological literacy.'[11]

Contrary to Ditmanson's remarks, the only Lutherans who "believe that studying religion at a college is not the work of the Church but rather the work of a liberal arts education *in the religious things of the world*" are leftist liberals who have jettisoned the Word of God as the supreme authority in matters of faith and life. One can only imagine the righteous indignation of Lutheran pioneers who contributed their prayers and sacrificed their resources to help found St. Olaf as a place where young people would obtain a Christian education and where the truth of Jesus Christ would be proclaimed.

THE OPEN DOOR OF SALVATION

The One who holds the key of David places before everyone who believes in Him the open door of salvation. He uses the key of David with absolute authority, because all power in heaven and on earth has been given to Him. As Christ opens doors for believers, so also He shuts doors to protect them from harm. He shuts doors against those who would enter heaven with sin in their lives. Jesus' parable of the Ten Virgins—five wise and five foolish—concluded with the somber warning for all who neglect to prepare for the day of His appearing—"and the door was shut."

God's Spirit will not always strive with man. When the door of salvation is opened, only the most foolish will fail to enter. Every Sunday there are those who listen to the last sermon they will ever hear and spurn the last opportunity they will be given to receive God's free gift of salvation. While God is not willing that one soul should perish, He forces no one to come! One day those who have spurned the Spirit's call will cry out in deepest sorrow: "Harvest is past, summer is ended and we are not saved."[12]

AN OPEN DOOR TO WITNESS THE GOSPEL

The concept of "open and closed doors" contained in Jesus' letter to the church in Philadelphia was also addressed by Paul in reference to reaching the unsaved with the gospel of Christ. Paul wrote: "...for a wide door for effective service has opened to me, and there are many adversaries."[13] He also described an open door he was given in Troas.[14] Paul urged believers in Colossae to pray "God will open up to us a door for the word...."[15] On several occasions the apostle to the Gentiles related how the Lord closed doors, preventing him from going to a specific place.[16]

The open door for Christians in Philadelphia included an opportunity to witness to the Jews. As Paul reminded Christians in Rome, the gospel "is the power of God for salvation to everyone who believes, to the Jew first and also to the Greek."[17] The great commission of Christ as recorded in Acts 1:8 directed the church to take the gospel to the Jews first, and then to the uttermost parts of the earth.

Because Jews in Philadelphia were so antagonistic to Christians, Jesus called them the "synagogue of Satan." Like Saul of Tarsus, the Jews in Philadelphia thought they were serving God when they attacked and persecuted Christians. Had their hearts been open to the truth, they would have recognized Jesus as the Messiah; instead they attacked the true work of God.

There is an open door today for Christians to share the gospel of Jesus Christ with Jewish people. Not since Pentecost have so many Jews been as open to hearing the claims of Christ as they are now. Throughout Israel there continues to be a mighty harvest as Jews embrace Jesus Christ as their personal Savior and Messiah.

Every Christian congregation should include among its ministries an outreach to the Jews. Though Paul was a missionary to the Gentiles, in each of His missionary journeys he always went first to the Jewish synagogues where he witnessed the gospel of Christ; only then did he seek out the Gentiles.

Today there are evangelistic ministries devoted to bringing the gospel to the Jews. One of the most successful in this endeavor is Jews for Jesus. Though this organization has been vilified by the press and others for their aggressive evangelism to Jews, it has an outstanding record of reaching thousands of Jews with the gospel. Years ago when Dwight L. Moody was being criticized for his evangelistic approach, he commented to a detractor, "I like my way of doing it, better than your way of not doing it."

ATTACKING THE TRUE WORK OF GOD

Throughout the world today, the remnant church is making a valiant stand against those who would corrupt the authentic teachings of the Bible and set the church on the path of destruction. In virtually every mainline church there are those who are endeavoring to resist those who are subverting biblical Christianity. However, many are paying a great price for their loyalty to the truth of God's Word.

Over the past several years, Christians by the millions have been forced by conscience to leave their liberal denominations because of false teachings and unbiblical practices. Membership losses in mainline churches are staggering. Small Bible-believing churches, organized and maintained by refugees from various denominations, now dot the landscape of nearly every community. These remnant churches offer people a real choice—to be part of a congregation that upholds the Word of God or to be part of a congregation that walks in the path of compromise and apostasy.

Christians who stand for the Word of God and the testimony of Jesus are often marked for ridicule and scorn by fellow-church members and clergy who see nothing amiss either in their congregations or in their denominations. When these stalwart soldiers of the cross attempt to expose the false teachings of their denominations, they are often vilified and met with derision and hostility.

Attacking the true work of God has been a common occurrence throughout the history of the church. Presently there seems to be an unprecedented attack on Bible-believing Christians by persons both within and without the church. The media portrays Bible-believing Christians as stupid and deluded, while liberal church leaders attack them in order to justify their own departures from truth.

The day Jerry Falwell passed away (May 15, 2007), his critics condemned him on radio and television networks. Atheist Christopher Hitchens, whose book *God is Not Great: How Religion Poisons Everything,* stated during an interview with Anderson Cooper on CNN: "I think it's a pity there isn't a hell for him to go to." Hitchens went on to say:

> The empty life of this ugly little charlatan proves only one thing, that you can get away with the most extraordinary offenses to morality and to truth in this country, if you will just get yourself called reverend. Who would, even at your network, have invited on such a little toad to tell us that the attacks of September 11th were the result of our sinfulness and were God's punishment if they hadn't got some kind of clerical qualification?

> People like that should be out in the street, shouting and hollering with a cardboard sign and selling pencils from a cup. The whole consideration of this—of this horrible little

person is offensive to very, very many of us who have some regard for truth and for morality, and who think that ethics do not require that lies be told to children by evil old men, that we're—we're not told that people who believe like Falwell will be snatched up into heaven, where I'm glad to see he skipped the rapture, just found on the floor of his office, while the rest of us go to hell...Lots of people are going to die and are already leading miserable lives because of the nonsense preached by this man, and because of the absurd way that we credit anyone who can say they're a person of faith."[18]

Whatever may be said of Jerry Falwell, he was a true servant of the Lord. Falwell's legacy includes Liberty University, a school where young people by the tens of thousands have been trained in the Word of God and sent out into the world to make a great impact for Christ. Falwell also founded Thomas Road Baptist Church, a congregation of over 25,000, where multiplied thousands have been brought into a living relationship with Jesus Christ. When America was in danger of losing its moral compass, Jerry Falwell inspired millions of Christians to stand up for the foundational principles of faith that made this nation great. Thankfully, God, not Christopher Hitchens, will have the last word about the life and legacy of each of His children, including Jerry Falwell.

Jesus stated He would make the Jews in Philadelphia bow at the feet of His true church and acknowledge "I have loved you." Paul wrote that one day, "every knee will bow and every tongue will confess Jesus is Lord...."[19] There is coming a day when God will set everything right, a day when truth will forever be separated from falsehood, a day when those who practice false religions will confess the one, true and living God. And there is coming a day when those who say they are Christians, but are not, will endeavor to recite a long list of their works to impress Christ, but He will say to them, "Depart from Me, I never knew you."

In an age when so many within the church treat sin and false teaching so lightly, the message needs to go forth that God's sure and certain judgment awaits all who dare to elevate lies above His revealed truth.

GOD TURNS WEAKNESSES INTO POWER

The Lord was fully aware that although the church in Philadelphia had "little strength," they "had kept His word and had not denied His name." A similar situation existed when Jehoshaphat, king of Judah, heard about an overwhelming force that was advancing against his kingdom. He cried out to God: "We are powerless before this great multitude who are coming against us; nor do we know what to do, but our eyes are on You."[20] Then God sent Jehoshaphat this word— "The battle is not yours but God's...you will not need to fight this battle...stand and see the salvation of the Lord on your behalf."[21]

As Christians living in a hostile world, we need to recognize the battles we face are not ours, but the Lord's. God will give us victory through our Lord, Jesus Christ. Many Christians who are part of the remnant church are often burdened because their fellowship is so small, while neighboring churches are filled to overflowing. They need to remember the words of Christ, "Enter through the narrow gate; for the gate is wide and the way is broad that leads to destruction, and there are many who enter through it. For the gate is small and the way is narrow that leads to life, and there are few who find it."[22] So often we fail to understand just how precious the remnant church is to the Lord.

It is better for Christians to worship with a small handful of people who are faithful to God's Word than to gather with the crowds who believe biblical doctrines are no longer important. It is better to be part of a small church where the Word of God is honored than to worship in a large church where truth is sacrificed on the altar of political correctness. It is better for individuals and families to pray and worship in the privacy of their homes than to attach themselves to a church or denomination that preaches a false gospel or tolerates apostasy. And it is far better for Christians to financially support Bible-based ministries than it is to give their tithes and offerings to apostate denominations or congregations that fail to stand upon God's truth.

"DO NOT DESPISE
THE DAY OF SMALL THINGS."

The prophet Zechariah spoke from the Lord when he said, "For who has despised the day of small things?"[23] In our success-driven society, Christians frequently suffer from "a mega-church syndrome," in which they compare their congregation with churches they see on television. The size of the average church in America today is less than two hundred members. But what matters to God is not the numerical size of a congregation but the size of its vision to reach the lost with the gospel of Christ.

While some congregations are small because they have failed to witness the gospel to the lost, other congregations are small because they are faithful to the Word of God. They are small because they do not offer a watered-down message of accommodation, nor do they augment their worship services with worldly entertainment and gimmicks in order to attract crowds.

Perhaps your Bible-based congregation will never have a large membership, as it seeks to be faithful to God's Word. Yet never forget, every God-anointed fellowship is holy ground! God may have called you into a fellowship teeming with people, or He may have placed you in a fellowship with limited members and limited resources. In either place you can experience the utmost joy knowing you are where God has called you, doing what He wants you to do.

It is time for church members to stop thinking about size and start thinking about souls. It is time for church members to remember their highest call is not to be loyal to a pastor, a church or a denomination, but to be loyal to God. When Jesus comes in glory, He will not take an inventory of church buildings. He will little note most things congregations have allowed to consume their time, money and energies. Instead, He will ask each congregation: "Where are the souls I entrusted to your care?"

Years ago the Southern Baptist pastor and evangelist Adrian Rogers remarked:

It is better to be divided by truth than to be united in error. It is better to speak the truth that hurts and then heals,

411

than falsehood that comforts and then kills. Let me tell you something, friend, it is not love and it is not friendship if we fail to declare the whole counsel of God. It is better to be hated for telling the truth, than to be loved for telling a lie. It is impossible to find anyone in the Bible who was a power for God who did not have enemies and was not hated.

It is better to stand alone with the truth, than to be wrong with the multitude. It is better to ultimately succeed with the truth than to temporarily succeed with a lie. There is only one gospel and Paul said, "If any man preaches any other gospel unto you than that which we have preached unto you, let him be accursed."

"I WILL KEEP YOU"

Christians in Philadelphia must have been overjoyed when they heard Jesus' words — "I will keep you from the hour of testing that is about to come on the whole world." Then, as now, when Bible-believing Christians are required to stand against paganism, apostasy and evil, it is good to know our Lord remembers those who are faithful to His Word. The church in Philadelphia received the promise to be kept from the hour of testing which was coming. This same promise also extends to the remnant church of the last days when an hour of testing will come on the whole world.

We are getting closer to the "hour of testing." Present-day events remind us how quickly a worldwide conflagration could take place. The false teachings in the church and the antagonism of our culture against all that is holy remind us we are living in the last days. The letter to the church in Philadelphia reminds us the Lord is still in charge of the destinies of men and nations. Nothing takes Him by surprise. When the hour of trial comes upon the world, and it will come, the Lord has promised to be a shield and a sure defense to all who put their trust in Him. One day the skies will part over this troubled world, and Jesus shall appear in clouds of glory! The trumpet call of God will sound, and every believer will be summoned heavenward.

CHRISTIANS ARE NOT EXEMPT FROM TRIALS

It is highly probable before Jesus comes to gather His church, most Christians will be required to endure a measure of persecution. Such has been true for the past 2000 years; there is no reason to believe those of us living in these turbulent times will be exempt from the world's hatred.

Jesus calls each believer to "occupy" the blood-bought ground and "hold fast" until He comes. As Christians we should not be looking for a free pass from times of testing or persecution. Jesus warned His disciples they would be put out of the synagogues and even killed by those who thought they would be doing a service for God. Through the centuries, followers of Christ have had to endure severe trials; Christians today should not expect less, especially as the world grows more hostile to the teachings of the Word of God.

"LET GOODS AND KINDRED GO"

Few Christians in the twenty-first century seem willing to stand against false teaching in their churches. Instead, many focus their energies on keeping the church property rather than on holding fast to the Word of God. Far too many church members have a greater sense of loyalty to their denomination than they have to the Lord. In the same manner, some pastors seem to fear their bishops and denominational leaders more than they fear God. Some clergy exhibit more concern over their pensions than they do over the spiritual wellbeing of their flocks.

Church members who sing Luther's hymn "A Mighty Fortress is Our God" often fail to grasp the true meaning of the last verse: "Let goods and kindred go, this mortal life also. The body they may kill, God's truth abideth still...." Do those who sing this hymn think these words, inspired from Psalm 46, applied only to the early church or to those living in Luther's day? What about us? Have we become so blinded by personal interests that we have elevated material things above our duty to God? Are we so arrogant as to believe in this present hour we do not need to bear our cross for Christ? Do we think God does not care when we elevate church property or our personal interests above His truth?

Over the past years, we have watched with deep sorrow as congregations and individual Christians who claimed loyalty to the truth of God's Word refused to leave their apostate denominations because they were afraid they would lose their property. Yet we have rejoiced to see literally thousands of Christians who have dared to walk away from church buildings, friends and family in order to remain true to Scriptures. May God help those who have decided the price of obeying His Word is just too high.

If God twice destroyed His own Temple in Jerusalem and sent His own chosen people into exile, what makes us think He has the slightest concern over church buildings, regardless of their size, shape, location or worth? Who among us will dare to stand before the Redeemer of the world on Judgment Day and say—"Jesus, you will be pleased to know although we may have lost the faith, we kept the property."

Stand fast, remnant church. Stand fast! Find your voice and sing! Lift high the cross and live out the words of the glorious hymn:

> Stand up, stand up for Jesus, as soldiers of the cross,
> Lift high His royal banner, it must not suffer loss.
> From vict'ry unto vict'ry, His army He shall lead,
> Till every foe is vanquished, and Christ is Lord indeed.
>
> Stand up, stand up for Jesus, the strife will not be long;
> This day the noise of battle, the next the victor's song.
> To him that overcometh, a crown of life shall be,
> He with the King of Glory shall reign eternally.
>
> George Duffield (1818-1888)

Chapter 22

THE CHURCH IN LAODICEA
"The Church of the Closed Door"

"To the angel of the church in Laodicea write: The Amen, the faithful and true Witness, the Beginning of the creation of God, says this: 'I know your deeds, that you are neither cold nor hot; I wish that you were cold or hot. So because you are lukewarm, and neither hot nor cold, I will spit you out of My mouth. Because you say, "I am rich, and have become wealthy, and have need of nothing," and you do not know that you are wretched and miserable and poor and blind and naked, I advise you to buy from Me gold refined by fire, so that you may become rich, and white garments so that you may clothe yourself, and that the shame of your nakedness will not be revealed; and eye salve to anoint your eyes so that you may see. Those whom I love, I reprove and discipline; therefore be zealous and repent. Behold, I stand at the door and knock; if anyone hears My voice and opens the door, I will come in to him and will dine with him, and he with Me. He who overcomes, I will grant to him to sit down with Me

on My throne, as I also overcame and sat down with My Father on His throne. He who has an ear, let him hear what the Spirit says to the churches' " (Revelation 3:14-22).

THE CHURCH OF THE CLOSED DOOR

The church in Philadelphia has been called "The Church of the Open Door." One could rightly refer to the church in Laodicea as "The Church of the Closed Door." Imagine the Lord being shut out of His own Church! But that is precisely what happened in Laodicea, and sadly it is happening in churches around the world today.

Jesus' words of warning and rebuke to the church in Laodicea were the most severe addressed to any of the seven churches. However, though not a word of praise was given, this letter concluded with one of the most grace-filled scenes in all the Scriptures. The image of the Savior standing at the door and knocking is a portrait of God's mercy, love and grace for all who will receive Him. "Behold, I stand at the door and knock; if anyone hears My voice and opens the door, I will come in to him and will dine with him, and he with Me." This verse has been the inspiration for countless hymns, paintings and sermons throughout the ages.

While each letter to the seven churches has meaning and application for all churches throughout the course of history, the letter to the church of Laodicea continues to serve as a wake-up call to all self-indulgent and apathetic churches. John B. Kahl, in his book *Illuminating the Closet, A Scriptural Approach to Homosexuality,* wrote about a man who was conducting a door to door survey. The first question on his survey asked, "Which is the more serious problem facing America today—ignorance or apathy?" When he knocked at the door of one house and asked this question, he received this curt reply—"I don't know and I don't care."

When Christ knocked at the door of the church in Laodicea, He received a similar response, and such is the response of countless churches today as Christ seeks to enter their fellowship. Those whose hearts are hardened by apathy and whose ears are deafened by the din of sin and unrighteous living callously keep the Lord of the Church standing outside the door.

In his book *The Screwtape Letters,* C.S. Lewis describes the devil giving advice to his nephew Wormwood on how to best tempt people. He says, "The devil will always see to it that there are bad people. Your job, my dear Wormwood, is to provide me with people who don't care." Without question the devil's tactic is working. The most destructive sin in the twenty-first-century church is apathy!

HISTORICAL PERSPECTIVE

Laodicea was situated in the Lycus River valley, approximately forty-five miles from Philadelphia and eleven miles west of Colossae. The city was originally called Diosopolis. When it was taken over by Antiochus II in 261 BC, he renamed it Laodicea in honor of his wife Laodice. Years later Antiochus divorced Laodice after she tried to poison him.

Laodicea was extremely prosperous, due in large measure to its location at the juncture of three important trade routes. It was an important banking center, a fact confirmed by Cicero who wrote several letters from there. The city was so wealthy that after it was heavily damaged by an earthquake in AD 60, it refused financial assistance from Rome.

Laodicea was famous for its medical school, its medical center and for its much sought-after eye salve. The medical center was dedicated to Asklepious, the Greek god of healing. People came from all over the region in order to obtain treatment for their ailments. Horace, the Roman writer and poet, mentioned traveling to Laodicea and using the eye salve himself. The city was also known for producing a type of black wool, around which it developed several other industries, including the manufacture of woolen goods, clothing and carpets.

One thing Laodicea lacked was water, but this problem was solved through a feat of Roman engineering. An aqueduct was constructed to carry hot mineral water from Hierapolis, located six miles north of Laodicea. Another aqueduct was erected from the cool springs of Denizli, five miles to the south of the city. Both aqueducts emptied into several huge water towers, from which a network of pipes delivered drinking water and mineral water directly to the city's homes. However, by the time the cool water from Denizli and the hot mineral water from Hierapolis arrived at the homes of Laodicea's residents, both were lukewarm.

In His letter to the church in Laodicea, Jesus made reference to their wealth, eye salve, lukewarm water and black clothing industry. Surely the specificity and the application of His words were not lost on those living there.

BIBLICAL PERSPECTIVE

While the primary reference to Laodicea is found in Revelation, Paul mentioned the city in his letter to the church in Colossae. He spoke about the Colossians' concern for the Christians living in Laodicea.[1] He also mentioned the affection which he and his fellow-laborer Epaphras shared for believers in Colossae, Laodicea and Hierapolis — all of which were located in the same general area.

The Scriptures do not reveal who was responsible for organizing the church in Laodicea. Some have conjectured Paul might have established it while he was living in Ephesus, but more likely it was organized by Epaphras who came from nearby Colossae.

In his letter to the church in Colossae, Paul sent greetings to a woman in Laodicea named Nympha and to the church in her house. He requested his letter to the Colossians be sent to the church at Laodicea, and he directed the letter which had been sent to the church in Laodicea be read in the church at Colossae. In his letter to the church in Colossae, Paul included a personal message to a man named Archippus who may have lived in Laodicea: "Take heed to the ministry which you have received in the Lord, that you may fulfill it."[2]

LAODICEA TODAY

Neither the city nor the church of Laodicea exists today. While only a small portion of ancient Laodicea has been uncovered, its excavations are most revealing. Visible among the ruins are the remains of a stadium, a large gymnasium and a theater. One of the most amazing discoveries is a water tower with several protruding pipes that carried the mineral water and the natural spring water into the city's homes. The tower bears witness to the accuracy of the Bible's description of Laodicea and its lukewarm church.

As previously stated, there were two other important biblical sites in the area, Colossae and Hierapolis.[3] The excavated ruins of these two cities are limited. The ruins in Hierapolis include the remains of a street, city walls, a theater, a temple to Apollo and a basilica dating to the sixth century AD. In Hierapolis archaeologists uncovered what is believed to be the tomb of the apostle Philip, who may have been martyred there in AD 80.

Not far from the ruins of Hierapolis are the thermal spas of Pamukkale, a natural wonder of Turkey. The hot mineral-spring waters, which remain at a constant ninety-five degrees Fahrenheit, have left calcium and mineral deposits on the adjacent hills, creating white terraces and uniquely shaped formations. From a distance the hills look as though they are covered in snow. Today Pamukkale has several hotels to accommodate the tourists who come to bathe in the mineral-rich waters, just as they did in Roman times.

JESUS IDENTIFIES HIMSELF AS GOD

Christ identified Himself to the church in Laodicea as the "Amen," God's last and affirming Word on all things, and He declared His witness was faithful and true, in contrast to the faithless witness of the Laodicean church. The Lord further identified Himself as the starting point of God's creation. This is not to say Christ was created, but rather He is the creator God through whom all things came into being.

Paul wrote about the divinity of Christ in his letter to the nearby church at Colossae: "He [Jesus Christ] is the image of the invisible God, the first born of all creation. For by Him all things were created, both in the heavens and on earth, visible and invisible, whether thrones or dominions or rulers or authorities—all things have been created through Him and for Him. He is before all things, and in Him all things hold together."[4]

The Gospel of John also identifies Jesus as the Creator God. "In the beginning was the Word, and the Word was with God, and the Word was God. He was in the beginning with God. All things came into being through Him, and apart from Him nothing came into being that has come into being."[5]

WILL IT STAND ON JUDGMENT DAY?

The church in Laodicea was a church in name and appearance only, according to Jesus. They may have been able to deceive the community and even themselves about their true spiritual condition but the Lord saw through their masquerade. By listening to the introduction to Christ's letter, the church of Laodicea had to have known judgment was looming. Christians living in the twenty-first century also need to realize Christ is coming again "to judge the living and the dead." These words of the Apostles' Creed may mean little now, but one day the unsaved will discover just how important they are.

Pastors, churches and denominations that have promoted false doctrines will be required to give an account for every word. Denominational leaders who felt they were at liberty to define what is or what is not sin will come to realize, to their everlasting dismay, how wrong they were. They will discover their denominations' carefully worded resolutions and position statements that sanctioned sin and evil while condemning the good will not stand in the Judgment. Too late they will understand the prophet's warning, "Woe to those who call evil good and good evil; who substitute darkness for light and light for darkness; who substitute bitter for sweet and sweet for bitter!"[6]

Church members and clergy who sanctioned the ordination of homosexuals and gave their endorsement to same-sex unions will be required to stand before the One who declared these acts to be *abominations* in His sight. Abortionists and their supporters who snuffed out the lives of unborn children while they were still in their mother's womb will be required to account for every life.

Theologians who took it upon themselves to rewrite the Scriptures in order to make them conform to their own perverted theologies will rue the day they neglected to heed the words of the Psalmist: "...for You have exalted above all things your name and your word."[7] They will also come face to face with the Lord's warning that not one word should be added to or taken away from the divine revelation.

Pastors, bishops, archbishops and popes who denied the Word of God will be required to account for all the souls they have misled over the years. They may vainly argue their failure to communicate the pure Word of God was somehow justified, or their efforts to sanction sin and placate evil were done in Jesus' name, but their arguments will not stand!

Church members who remained in their apostate churches in order to fight for truth, but somehow never quite got around to fighting, will be at a loss to explain their inactions to the Judge with the nail-pierced hands. Christians who reasoned their continued association with and financial support of Bible-denying churches will wish they had heeded Jesus' words of warning to the church at Laodicea.

The Lord did not find even a remnant in Laodicea who had remained faithful to Him. All were chastised; all were warned. He began His message to the church in Laodicea as he had to the other six churches, "I know your deeds." The self-indulgent, apathetic church in Laodicea was no exception; Christ saw their nakedness.

The Lord sees us not for what we claim to be but exactly for what we are. The Bible reminds us He is able "to judge the thoughts and intentions of the heart. And there is no creature hidden from His sight, but all things are open and laid bare to the eyes of Him with whom we have to do."[8]

THE LUKEWARM CHURCH

The tepid waters of Laodicea were known far and wide. Thus, when Jesus called the Laodicean church "lukewarm," there was no doubt about His meaning. Isaiah wrote about a similar spiritual condition that existed when the people of Israel pleaded with the prophets who were sent by God: "You must not prophesy to us what is right, Speak to us pleasant words, Prophesy illusions."[9] Those who think being spiritually lukewarm is a trivial matter need to search the Scriptures and discover what God thinks about it. Lukewarm churches filled with lukewarm members, proclaiming a lukewarm gospel will not stand on Judgment Day!

On the day of His ascension, Jesus said to His disciples, "…but you will receive power when the Holy Spirit has come upon you; and you shall be My witnesses both in Jerusalem, and in all Judea and Samaria, and even to the remotest part of the earth."[10] On the day of Pentecost, the Holy Spirit poured out His POWER upon the assembled believers, and three thousand souls were brought into the Kingdom of God.

Through the centuries God has empowered followers of Christ to carry out the witness of the gospel and live in victory! No Christian and no church can function without the unction of the Holy Spirit. Those who try to carry out the Lord's work without the power of the Holy Spirit will fail; moreover, it is an egregious sin. Paul described how certain churches in his day held to a form of godliness, although "they denied its power." He instructed Timothy to "avoid such men as these."[11]

Lukewarm churches are responsible for the sorry spiritual condition of the twenty-first century church. Their leaders constantly have their finger to the wind, trying to find out what is popular and acceptable in the culture. They are more concerned about being politically correct than they are about being faithful to the Word of God.

Lukewarm churches are prone to operate by their own rules: "Don't rock the boat" and "Avoid controversial doctrines and issues at all costs." They also operate on these misguided principles: "Don't say anything that might offend people and cause them to stop attending our church," or worse yet, "Don't do or say anything that might cause them to stop giving." Lukewarm churches find it in their own selfish interest to keep silent about the grievous sins that are destroying our nation.

Lukewarm churches bear little concern for lost souls. Over the past fifty years or more, mainline churches have been replacing the authentic life-changing gospel of Jesus Christ with a message of social justice, peace and equality. Sin and repentance are seldom heard. If sin is mentioned in these churches, it is usually preached in the abstract. But where there is no sin, there is no repentance. Where there is no repentance, there is no forgiveness. Where there is no forgiveness, there is no life or salvation. And where salvation's message is not heard, there is no hope! Tragically lost people wander in and out of lukewarm churches without ever encountering the life-changing message of salvation. If God's response to the lukewarm church in Laodicea was to spew them from His mouth, what will be His response to America's affluent churches that have deliberately cast aside God's truth for a lie?

THE FOLLY OF TRUSTING IN RICHES

Prosperity theology is not something new to the twenty-first century; it is an old heresy with new application. Prosperity theology had captured the hearts of the Laodicean church. The church of Laodicea boasted, "I am rich and have become wealthy and in need of nothing." But, Jesus informed them, "You do not know that you are wretched and miserable and poor and blind and naked."

Christians who possess an abundance of this world's goods should certainly thank God for each and every blessing, but they also need to remember material things cannot be compared to the treasures of heaven. The Bible says, "He who trusts in his riches will fall, but the righteous will flourish like the green leaf."[12]

In these prosperous times and especially in America, many are suffering from the same spiritual blindness and arrogance that plagued the church in Laodicea. Pride and riches can cause the heart to forget one's need for God. Yet in a moment, health can fail and troubles can overwhelm. The material things we cherish can vanish in a heartbeat. "But the lovingkindness of the Lord is from everlasting to everlasting on those who fear Him, and His righteousness to children's children, to those who keep His covenant and remember His precepts to do them."[13]

JESUS IS ALL WE NEED

Christ confronted the church in Laodicea with the truth about their spiritual condition because He wanted them to repent and change. Moreover, He offered them what money could not buy and what may only be purchased by faith. Isaiah spoke about God's grace when he said, "...You who have no money come, buy and eat. Come, buy wine and milk without money and without cost."[14]

The church in Laodicea may have had great material wealth, but Jesus saw their impoverished spiritual condition: "I advise you to buy from me gold refined by fire, so that you may become rich." Peter described true riches: "In this you greatly rejoice, even though now for a little while, if necessary, you have been distressed by various trials, so that the proof of your faith, being more precious than gold which is perishable, even though tested by fire, may be found to result in praise and glory and honor at the revelation of Jesus Christ."[15]

The people who were part of the church in Laodicea may have had expensive garments made of rare black wool, but Jesus offered to clothe them in white garments—the same white garments of righteousness all must have in order to enter heaven. The apostle John inquired of the Lord, "And who are these arrayed in white robes?" And the reply was given: "These are the ones who come out of the great tribulation, and they have washed their robes and made them white in the blood of the Lamb."[16]

The people in Laodicea may have had their own potent brand of eye salve; they may have had 20/20 vision, but Christ knew they were spiritually blind. He offered them His eye salve so they might truly see. They were in the same pitiful condition as the Pharisees who sarcastically asked Jesus, "Are we also blind?" He answered them, "If you were blind, you would have no sin; but since you say, 'We see,' your sin remains."[17] Few people in America today, including many church members, sense much need in their lives for God. They live under the illusion they are fully capable of taking care of themselves. Their eyes are blinded to the reality of their own insufficiencies.

The anointing of our eyes by the Holy Spirit enables us to see our sufficiency comes from God. The testimony of the blind man rings true in the hearts of those who have been redeemed: "All I know is that once I was blind, but now I can see." In Jesus we have everything we will ever need in this life and in the life to come!

THE MAN AT THE DOOR HAS NAIL-PIERCED HANDS

The image of Christ standing at the door knocking is "amazing grace" personified. The same Jesus who denounced the church in Laodicea for their tepid, lifeless religion and threatened to disown them is the same Jesus who held out His nail-pierced hands and offered them a final opportunity to repent and be saved.

Why did He do this? Christ Himself answers: "Those whom I love, I reprove and discipline; therefore be zealous and repent."[18] The slowness of Christ to condemn, and the quickness of Christ to forgive should cause every one of us to run to the waiting arms of our Savior as fast as we can go! Sinners should not waste a moment when the Lord comes knocking at the door of their hearts.

SO WHY WON'T THEY LET HIM IN?

The Man with the nail-pierced hands was shut out of the church in Laodicea. Today many churches and individuals keep Christ standing outside as they carry out the man-made forms of religiosity and "churchianity." Religion is a terrible thing when it is man-centered or the truth of Jesus Christ is not its essence. Forms, rituals and even church membership are no substitute for a personal relationship with Jesus Christ. The Holy Spirit's work is not to cause us to become more religious; His work is not to lead us to blindly follow some denomination or a religious leader; the Holy Spirit's supreme work is to lead us to Jesus Christ and to Him alone!

THE CHURCH WHERE CHRIST IS WELCOMED

Do not assume by the name affixed to the outside of a church it is a dwelling place of the Lord Jesus Christ. Just because religious activities are taking place there does not mean the Holy Spirit is in charge, or the Lord sanctions their agenda. How can you be sure?

The church in which God is present is a Christ-centered church where the Word of God is proclaimed in all its truth and power. Those who enter such a church are never the same again, as the gospel of Christ brings them into fellowship with the One with nail-pierced hands. The church where God is present, Jesus is welcomed and the Holy Spirit is working is a place where everyone is loved, especially sinners. They love what God loves and hate what God hates; and they never confuse the two. They know how to distinguish between the sin and the sinner, because they remember their own sinful state before God found them and crowned their lives with love, forgiveness, life and salvation.

IS CHRIST LIVING IN YOUR HEART?

How may we be certain Christ is truly abiding within our hearts? How can we know for certain we are heirs of heaven? Bill Bright, former head of Campus Crusade for Christ, taught in every heart there is a throne and a cross. Before we are born-again, Christ is on the cross and self is on the throne. After we receive God's free gift of eternal life, self is on the cross and Christ is on the throne. The heart where God is present, Jesus is welcome and the Holy Spirit indwells is a heart where love for Christ is demonstrated by true obedience to His Word. "If anyone loves Me, he will keep my word; and My Father will love him, and We will come to him and make Our abode with him."[19]

No one will ever ask you a more important question than this— If you died today, do you know for certain you will go to heaven? Stop reading for a moment and reflect on whether or not you are truly a child of God. Do not waste a moment if you are not certain about your salvation. God will save you today, as you place your faith and trust in Him. The book in your hands at this moment may be the pathway for you to enter into a living relationship with God. Please go back to the close of Chapter 19 and reread God's personal invitation for you to come to Him. Pray the prayer written there. Then seek out a Bible-believing pastor and share your new-found faith with him. He will help you to grow and develop in your daily walk in Christ. Please write and tell us what Christ has done for you. Our address is included in the front of the book.

HE WHO HAS EARS, LET HIM HEAR!

It is amazing how many people actually heard Jesus speak when He walked this earth, yet they rejected everything He had to say. Many within the seven churches of Revelation also rejected His appeals and warnings. In Jesus' parable of the rich man and Lazarus, the rich man pleaded from Hades for someone to be sent to warn his five brothers of what awaited them if they did not repent. But he was told: "If they do not listen to Moses and the Prophets, they will not be persuaded even if someone rises from the dead."[20]

Jesus said to His disciples, "Blessed are your eyes because they see; and your ears, because they hear. For truly I say to you that many prophets and righteous men desired to see what you see, and did not see it, and to hear what you hear, and did not hear it."[21] That same message can be applied to those living in the twenty-first century, because we are witnesses to an unprecedented measure of the gospel's proclamation and to an array of fulfilled Bible prophecies.

The battle for the church and the nation is being fought today whether we like it or not, or whether we want to be part of it or not. We are either part of the problem or part of the solution. We are either standing for Christ, or we are not! We are either saved or we are lost. There is no in-between ground.

Christ's love for His Church knows no bounds. He still walks among His churches today. He still empowers Christians to stand fast and carry out their assigned mission in the strength and power of the Holy Spirit. The wreckage of disobedient churches lies strewn across the landscape of history. Twenty-first century churches are not immune from the same judgment. Today vast portions of the mainline church are marching headlong into oblivion. Sadly, they are taking so many unsuspecting people with them. The blind are leading the blind.

The Holy Spirit is not the inspiration behind feminist theology or the sanctioning of immorality. The Holy Spirit is not the one leading people to stake their eternity on doctrines of demons. The Holy Spirit does not lead anyone into false teachings or unbiblical practices, nor will He lead them to remain where evil is tolerated or accepted. If these departures from biblical truth are taking place in your place of worship, you are not where God wants you to be. Flee while there is still time. Let the very act of your departure be a witness to your love of God's truth.

Praise God for pastors, laity and whole congregations who are taking a stand for the Word of God and the testimony of Jesus. As long as there are church leaders who will stand up for the truth of God's inerrant Word, there is hope. As long as men and women of faith are ready to be counted in the cause of truth, no matter what the cost, there is hope.

If you are part of a denomination or congregation promoting that which is contrary to Scripture, ask the Holy Spirit to show you within His Word what you should do. Do not allow your heart to be guided by your feelings or personal sentiments. Seek the truth of God and His will for your life in the only place wherein it may be found—in the inspired, infallible and inerrant Word of God. This is the ultimate challenge of our time. Thus says the Lord: "Be faithful unto death, and I will give you the crown of life."[22]

Chapter 23

IN TIMES LIKE THESE

"If…My people who are called by My name humble them-selves and pray and seek My face and turn from their wicked ways, then I will hear from heaven, will forgive their sin and will heal their land" (2 Chronicles 7:14).

PRESENT REALITIES IN THE NATION

Conditions in America and throughout the world are causing even the stoutest hearts to tremble. Wars, rumors of wars, terrorist attacks and the unpredictable actions of godless governments make it difficult to believe peace is about to break out anytime soon. It is unlikely many people today would agree with the postmillennialists who claim "every day in every way things are getting better and better."

The entire Middle East is like a giant powder keg ready to explode at any moment. Israel could be attacked without warning by terrorist groups or by Islamic nations. At whatever point Iran develops its nuclear capability, the doomsday clock will have to be reset to thirty-seconds to midnight.

Our global economy is only one disaster away from sending world markets into a freefall. A nuclear attack by terrorists in any one of our major cities or at a nuclear installation could bring about a depression that would make the 1930s look like economic prosperity. Even a major natural disaster, such as an earthquake, could cause our economy to go into a tailspin. Everyone knows how unstable the world has become, but most people reason there is little they can do to change it.

Such thoughts are quite depressing until you realize there is One who is able to do exceedingly abundantly beyond all we ask or think; there is One who is never taken by surprise or caught off guard; there is One who is never faced with a dilemma greater than His power to subdue or control. His name is Jesus Christ! In times like these, our hearts must learn to turn to Jesus who said, "Peace I leave with you; My peace I give unto you; not as the world gives do I give to you. Do not let your heart be troubled, nor let it be fearful."[1] It is said the words "Fear not" appear in the Bible, in one form or another, 366 times, one for each day of the year and even one for leap year. Isn't it comforting to know God has thought of everything when it comes to the welfare and well-being of His children?

Pay attention!

How many times as you were growing up did your parents or your teachers caution you to "pay attention?" Well, so has God on numerous occasions, and He is still saying it today! Throughout Jesus' earthly ministry and in the seven letters of Revelation, He repeatedly cried out, "He who has ears, let him hear." God told Ezekiel, "Son of man, you live in the midst of the rebellious house, who have eyes to see but do not see, ears to hear but do not hear; for they are a rebellious house."[2] These observations certainly are an apt description of the unregenerate heart of man, and they are an apt description of most people in America today. How God's heart must break as he repeatedly tries to get our nation's attention, and we pay Him no heed whatsoever.

The Bible tells us, "For this reason we must pay much closer attention to what we have heard, so that we do not drift away from it."[3] Unless America wakes up soon and returns to the foundational principles upon which this nation was founded, we will face the future without a prayer.

Admittedly, most of the problems facing our nation today are due to the fact we have not been paying close enough attention to what God has been saying. Like the people of Sardis, too many Americans are asleep while the enemy is breaking into our strongholds and stealing our freedoms out from under us. Every day our country is moving farther and farther away from God. Indeed, we are now living in a post-Christian era. Those who choose to ignore the voice of Almighty God as He speaks to us through His Word do so at their own peril.

Just how low will we go?

Every year our culture's acceptance and toleration of evil is degraded to the next lower level. Just how low this country will go morally is anybody's guess. Music, movies and other forms of entertainment often have to be sanitized before being sent over the public airwaves. However, cable and satellite communications have made it possible for unadulterated garbage and filth to flow freely into millions of homes across the nation. Foul language, profanity, nudity and meanspirited epithets that would not have been tolerated just a few years ago have become standard fare throughout much of the broadcasting industry. Television programs, music and movies that glorify sex, violence, crime and perversion are regular fare in most American households. The entertainment industry regularly mocks God, Judeo-Christian values and biblical morality; it spews its poisonous anti-God messages into our homes, twenty-four hours a day. In so many ways, our times reflect Jesus' description of the last days: "And just as it happened in the days of Noah, so it will be also in the days of the Son of Man."

What parents would stand idle while an intruder breaks into their home to harm their children? Yet so many parents remain passive as the godless entertainment industry accesses their homes and seduces their children's hearts and minds with the most despicable filth and humanistic teachings. Some parents allow their children to view R-rated movies and listen to filth-laden music without the slightest idea of what they are experiencing. Harry Potter books with their witchcraft and occult messages are more widely read in many Christian homes than the Bible.

The American culture in the twenty-first century is based on moral relativism and secular humanism. Same-sex marriages and civil unions are being sanctioned by law in state after state. Heterosexual, homosexual, transsexual, bisexual are all the same to the social engineers. It is no wonder the purveyors of evil can not bear to even look at the Ten Commandments. It is bad enough these immoral practices have to exist in our society, but now they are being taught as virtues to our children. The Bible says, "There is a way which seems right to man, but its end is the way of death."[4]

Legislation now being proposed by several school districts in California will require students to use textbooks that eliminate terms such as "mother and father" and "husband and wife," so children who are being raised by homosexuals and lesbians will not be embarrassed or caused to feel they are in any way inferior. The same legislation will require sports teams and cheerleading to be gender-neutral; gender-neutral bathrooms will be mandatory for those who are confused about their gender identity; and scientific information detailing AIDS rates in the homosexual community will be banned.[5]

Students across America are being indoctrinated in public schools to accept the humanist-worldview, evolution and immoral lifestyles, regardless of the beliefs and teachings of their parents or churches. The National Educators Association (NEA) has adopted as part of its official mission the reeducation of America's children to accept the entire homosexual agenda.

The attacks being waged against Judeo-Christian values by governments, school boards and the judicial system have set our nation on a collision course with God. All that stands between America and divine judgment are the prayers of God's people; the only thing that stands in the way of those who want to remove God from this nation's life and value system is the influence of Bible-believing Christians. Therefore the architects of America's destruction are doing everything in their power to silence Christians.

ANTI-HATE LEGISLATION

There is an erosion of liberties in "the land of the free and the home of the brave." Liberal politicians and leftwing organizations are attempting to pass anti-hate legislation at both the state and national levels. They claim such legislation is meant to protect homosexuals and minority religions from intimidation, harassment or from physical and psychological harm. Yet what they really want to do is to silence Christians from speaking out against false religions and immoral behavior.

Anti-hate laws are being promoted by the homosexual lobby and by organizations such as the American Civil Liberties Union (ACLU) and the Council on American-Islamic Relations (CAIR). When this legislation becomes law, it will effectively silence opposition to homosexual perversions, same-sex marriages and criticisms of Islamic teachings. Proposed hate-crime legislation will prohibit pastors, churches and Christian organizations from publicly reading certain verses of Scripture or speaking out on most moral issues. Those who violate anti-hate laws will be jailed or fined. Christian radio and television broadcasts that say anything against the homosexual lifestyle or criticize Islam will be taken off the air. Christian magazines and newsletters will be denied access to the postal system. Freedoms we have long cherished in the country are being threatened.

Canada, Australia, Scandinavia and several European nations have already passed anti-hate legislation. In each of these countries, pastors have been jailed or fined for the content of their sermons, broadcasts and writings. Social engineers and liberal politicians in America are demanding our government pass laws that give an ultimatum to Christians—conform or we are coming after you.

Anti-hate legislation will eventually impact every church, Christian ministry, pastor and individual church member in America. Some Christians who have already been intimidated by these threats are choosing to keep silent, even though their liberties are being eroded and their rights are being threatened. One day these Christians will wake up to discover even their silence will not protect them. Unless God's people stand up to these attacks now, our religious liberties and our right to freedom of speech will be greatly diminished or curtailed altogether.

Martin Neimoller, a Lutheran pastor who was jailed by the Nazis, is credited with writing the following observation in 1945:

> First they came for the Communists, and I didn't speak up because I wasn't a Communist. Then they came for the Jews, and I didn't speak up because I wasn't a Jew. Then they came for the Catholics, and I didn't speak up because I was a Protestant. Then they came for me, and by that time there was no one left to speak up for me.[6]

PRESENT REALITIES IN THE CHURCHES

Christians may choose to pay little attention to the doctrinal and moral departures being promoted within their denominations and congregations, but sooner or later, they and their children will be impacted by all of these evils. Church members may continue to attend and contribute to churches where the authentic gospel message is no longer preached and where sin is sanctioned, but their decision will ultimately cost them far more than they will be prepared to pay.

Just what will happen to people who attend churches that no longer preach the atonement of Jesus Christ or proclaim the true path to salvation? What will happen to church members when not a person has even a memory of the authentic proclamation of the gospel of Christ? What will happen to their culture? More importantly, what will happen to the children?

How will those who continue to maintain membership in apostate denominations respond when goddess worship, feminist theology, homosexuality and other abominations are being promoted from their pulpits? What will be their response when they are asked to pray to the great Mother/Father in heaven? What will they do when a Muslim imam gives a sermon from their pulpits? How will they respond when their pastor is a woman and so is her mate? At what point will church members draw the line and accept no further departures from biblical Christianity? Sadly, compromising Christians in mainline churches keep moving the line.

Members of mainline churches that have adopted sin and evil into their creeds often say, "Well, it's not happening in my congregation or with my pastor, therefore it does not concern me." They are wrong! Church members can close their eyes and stop up their ears to everything happening within their denomination; they can choose to ignore all the warnings and risk their own souls, but are they willing to risk the souls of their children? Are they willing to place their sons and daughters in the care and nurture of clergy who no longer believe the foundational doctrines of Christianity?

WHAT ABOUT THE CHILDREN?

One day our children and our grandchildren will come face to face with a major crisis unlike anything their parents and grandparents have known before. Will they be ready? Will they possess the spiritual strength to see them through the darkest night? Will they be able to press on with the absolute assurance they have a Savior to whom they can turn? Or will they have become so thoroughly confused by their secular humanistic education and their liberal church training they will reach out to the nothingness they have been trained to embrace? "O God, if there is a God, save my soul, if I have a soul!"

One thing is certain, our children are growing up in perilous times. At this very moment America's youth are being bombarded by a godless culture that has turned evil into good and good into evil. Few parents or grandparents have the ability to comprehend how difficult it is for today's young people to resist peer pressure or society's attempts to reshape their beliefs concerning biblical morals and values.

Other than the entertainment industry, perhaps no institution is working as feverishly to reshape young minds or cause them to embrace secular humanistic values as is America's public school system. Our children's participation in the public school system is like having them walk through a minefield. Textbooks are being rewritten by the humanists so children will not be exposed to our nation's Judeo-Christian heritage. The revisionists are striving to make certain they never find out the truth about the major role Christianity played in the establishment of our nation.

In public schools across America, nationalism is out, globalism is in; Christmas is out, Halloween and witches are in; creationism is out, evolution is in; Christianity is out, Islam and most other religions are in; truth is out, and political correctness is in. The secular humanists who control America's schools know without God there can be no absolutes; traditional values have to give way. Prayer and Bible-reading were but the first installments to force God from the nation's schools.

Sex-education classes now include discussions on safe sex, the use of condoms, birth control and the virtues of homosexuality, and that is in the elementary schools! Sex education in high school is even worse. According to the *Washington Post,* the Maryland State Board of Education issued a ruling in June 2007 supporting a sex-education curriculum in Montgomery middle and high schools, finding nothing illegal in the new lessons on sexual orientation and condom use. In the ruling the state board wrote while parents do have a right to control their children's upbringing, "that right is not absolute. It must bend to the State's duty to educate its citizens."[7] This statement should send a cold chill down the spine of every parent in America. The secular humanists and the homosexual lobby, with the full cooperation of the NEA, are successfully accomplishing their goal of indoctrinating our children into believing immorality and the homosexual lifestyle are both normal and good.

America's public schools are riddled with drugs, violence and promiscuity. Behavioral problems are so bad in some public schools that teachers find it nearly impossible to teach. A CNN report in May 2007 stated thirty-six percent of all public school teachers in America claim to have been bullied or attacked by their students. The situation is so bad policemen are stationed in the hallways and metal detectors are used to check for weapons at the main entrances in many schools throughout the nation.

In spite of governmental efforts to improve the academic standards in our nation's schools, the dropout rate is shocking. Indeed it is a national scandal. An estimated 6,000 students per day are dropping out of America's high schools. Dropout rates in numerous major cities—Baltimore, MD; Detroit, MI; Los Angeles, CA; Columbus, OH; Cleveland, OH; Atlanta, GA—exceed fifty percent. The only reason some school districts boast a smaller dropout rate is because they manipulate the figures. The reason many students can move on to the next grade or graduate is because those in charge of the schools have dummied down the standards so they can pass. Students are permitted to graduate from high schools without the necessary math skills to make change at a store or without the necessary reading skills to fill out a job application.

Most Americans today fail to connect the dots. They cannot see any relationship between kicking God out of our public life and the moral disintegration of our society. Martin Luther observed:

I am much afraid that schools will prove to be great gates of hell unless they diligently labor in explaining the Holy Scriptures, engraving them in the hearts of the youth. I advise no one to place his child where the Scriptures do not reign paramount. Every institution in which men are not increasingly occupied with the Word of God must become corrupt.

Christian Schools

Christian schools are the option of choice for many concerned parents. While this option may be expensive and requires a great deal of sacrifice on the part of families, every parent has an obligation to see their children are trained not only in sound academics, but also in the Word of God. Most Christian schools employ highly skilled and dedicated teachers who have taken a huge cut in pay in order to teach in a Christian setting.

Some Christian schools offer scholarships and grants, while others have a sliding-scale tuition that enables parents with limited incomes or with several children to afford a Christian education for all of their children. Even so, parents need to be certain the Christian school they choose is spiritually and academically sound in every way.

In light of the challenges and dangers directed at our children through our nation's public school system, more Bible-believing churches need to establish Christian schools as part of their ministry and outreach. Many church facilities and educational buildings sit idle throughout the week, when they could be put to use for this most noble purpose.

Homeschools

An excellent option for a growing number of parents is home-schooling. Approximately four million children are currently being homeschooled in the United States, and the number is increasing every year. Homeschooling requires tremendous commitment, discipline and sacrifice on the part of the whole family. It requires a family to live on one income, as one parent, usually the mother, undertakes the task of educating the children. In most homeschool families, however, fathers actively participate in their children's education.

There are numerous Christian educational institutions that supply not only the curricula for homeschools but helpful assistance as well. The computer has revolutionized homeschooling by enabling students to study many subjects, including science and math; also it has allowed students to work according to their abilities and at their own pace. In most communities, parents who homeschool have organized support groups to aid and assist one another in various activities and subjects.

Achievement tests have proven homeschooled children excel academically over their counterparts in public schools. Research has further revealed "homeschool graduates far exceed their public and private school counterparts in college by ranking the highest in forty-two of sixty-three indicators of collegiate success. They were also ranked as being superior in four out of five achievement catego-ries, including socialization, as they were assessed as being the most charismatic and influential."[8]

Colleges and universities eagerly welcome young people who have been homeschooled, not only because of their high scoring academics, but also because they know homeschoolers will be successful in their studies.

Because homeschools are growing in this country and because they are having such a high success rate, there are many liberals who want to make homeschooling illegal or stifle it with excessive regulations. Again, this is another area where Christians must pay attention and stand up for their rights.

Public Schools

All public schools in America without exception are steeped in secular humanism and moral relativism. This is a far cry from the early days of public education when textbooks contained Scripture passages and Judeo-Christian principles; they were viewed as essential elements in all instruction. Today the American Civil Liberties Union lies in wait for any school district that dares to allow the mention of God or Jesus Christ in any of its activities.

Christian parents who believe they have no other option than public schools need to be actively involved in their children's studies and activities. They should examine their textbooks and be aggressive in communicating with teachers and school officials about their concerns. Remedial instruction at home is usually required to counter what is being taught in the public schools. Participation in a Bible-believing church is essential in offsetting humanistic teachings and the influence of a morally deficient culture.

Parents who turn their children over to the public schools without knowing what they are being taught are making a terrible mistake. Yet in some cases, students are not permitted to take their textbooks home with them or tell their parents what they are learning. Parents must stand up for their rights and the rights of their children in these matters. Parents should not roll over and play the victim while their children are being indoctrinated with information that can ultimately cause them great harm.

Thankfully, there are highly skilled and devoted Christian teachers and administrators in many of our public schools who care deeply about what is happening to America's educational system. They are like missionaries who bring the light of Christ into a very dark place. If, however, the trend toward moral relativism and godless secular humanism continues at its present pace in public education, Christian teachers will find it increasingly difficult to carry out their duties without compromising their principles or selling out their integrity. All Christian teachers in our public schools should be upheld in prayer and encouraged by the Christian community as they seek to make a difference in this vital area of our nation's life. The negative influence public schools are having on our children would be many times worse were it not for the positive influence of Christian teachers and school administrators. God bless them all.

AMERICA MUST BE RESTORED

Traditional families — father, mother and children — are becoming a rare commodity in America. The traditional family as defined by Scripture is disintegrating before our eyes. A recent report stated the number of divorces in America is decreasing, but what the report failed to take into consideration is the fact more and more couples are choosing to live together without the benefit of marriage. Single-parent homes in America now outnumber those with two parents. The problem will only get worse as same-sex marriages and same-sex unions are recognized and made legal in numerous states. The strength of America is in her families. As long as the destruction of our families continues, the moral and spiritual strength of the nation will decline in like manner, and there is not enough money in federal or state budgets to stop it.

Where is it written Christians should stand by and allow the atheists, liberals and humanists to control our nation's schools? Where is it written Christians should allow the secularists to define the essence of America? Our forefathers established this nation on Judeo-Christian principles. Our forefathers' recognition of God and Judeo-Christian virtues are what made America great, and they are what will keep America strong!

There is a battle raging for the soul of our nation! There is a battle raging for the minds and hearts of our children. If you are a Christian and do not recognize that fact, you need to start reading your Bible and spending more time on your knees. It is time for Christians to stop playing defense and go on the offense. The other side is not timid about attacking family values and Christian principles; neither should Christians be timid about lifting up the banner of truth! We must not be intimidated by cries for the separation of church and state. Being Christians does not mean we are required to surrender our rights to influence our government. We still have the same rights as anyone else in America! We have the right to be heard and the obligation to speak out. If we do not use our rights to defend our rights, we will have no rights.

Christians must play a vital role in the restoration of America. The fact the Lord may come at any time does not release any of us from being salt and light to the nation. Until the Lord comes, or as long as He gives us breath, we must do everything in our power to lift up the banner of truth and shine the light of Christ on every aspect of the nation's life and culture.

Christians can and should vote! Shame on those who do not! Christians can and should make their voices heard at the local and national levels of government. Christians can and should run for public office; they can and should serve on school boards; they can and should become involved in many areas where they can make a difference.

Christians need to become involved in pro-life organizations and stand against the killing of the unborn. Abortions in America are a national disgrace! Christians need to become active supporters of organizations that are standing for truth and opposing evils in our churches and in our nation. Christians should support ministries that litigate in the nation's courts to preserve and protect our rights and freedoms. (See the appendix for additional information and a partial list of such organizations.)

THE CHURCH MUST BE REVIVED

America cannot be restored unless her churches are restored! We cannot expect God to continue blessing a land that does not want Him or that sees Him as the enemy. We cannot expect God to bless a land that dishonors His Name, mocks His messengers and defies His Word.

Regrettably, revival and reformation in America or in her churches may not occur until our nation experiences a major catastrophe. That is the harsh reality of our times and reflects the hardened condition of our hearts. When a major catastrophic event does take place in this country, people will go flocking to the churches for relief and answers. Anguished cries from hearts that have not reverently mentioned God's name in years will implore His help and mercy. However, if these grief-stricken people do not hear the truth as they enter our churches, or if they are not led to true repentance, the spiritual condition of the nation will not change; indeed it will worsen. After September 11, 2001, the churches of America were filled as people sought comfort and consolation from God. But within a few short weeks, remembrance of that dreadful day faded, and life went back as it was before.

God has given His requirements for revival in the churches and for the restoration of America—"*If...My people who are called by My name humble themselves and pray and seek My face and turn from their wicked ways, then I will hear from heaven, will forgive their sin and will heal their land*" (2 Chronicles 7:14). There is no other way. There are no shortcuts. If America, or any other nation, is to be restored, God's people must follow God's directives. The restoration of America must begin with the redeemed children of God.

"If my people" means *every* Christian must bear responsibility for the spiritual condition of the nation. We can not hope to solve America's social and moral problems until we solve her underlying spiritual problems. America must turn back to God in sincere repentance. This means individual Christians need to repent on behalf of the nation. Both Daniel and Nehemiah went to their knees on behalf of Israel; they prayed earnestly and repented with tears over Israel's many sins. God forgave their sin and healed their land. What God did for Israel, He will do for America.

THE AMERICA WE ONCE KNEW

One of my deepest regrets is my grandchildren will never know or experience the America I knew in my youth. As I grew up in the

1940s and 1950s, America was not a perfect nation by any means, but its foundational values were still based on Judeo-Christian principles. My heart would rejoice if my children and grandchildren could know:

- An America patterned after the vision of our founding Fathers, when "In God We Trust" was not only engraved on our coins, it was also engraved on the hearts of our citizens.
- An America where daily Bible reading and prayer in public schools were viewed as steps to help shape moral character and build a sure foundation for successful living.
- An America where patriotism, honoring the flag and showing respect for those who served in the military were all genuine expressions of gratitude for living in this great and free land.
- An America where respect for parents, teachers, police officers and those in authority was both taught and practiced.
- An America where the Ten Commandments were displayed openly in public places, because they were part of the fabric of our nation's life and law.
- An America where the concept of the family—father, mother, and children—was based on the teachings of Scripture and established in law.
- An America where the unborn were protected by law from abortion; the sick were protected by law from assisted suicide; and where the elderly were protected by law from euthanasia.
- An America where illegal drugs in schools were unheard of; where drugs were prescribed by doctors and distributed by pharmacists, not drug-pushers.
- An America where Christians were at liberty to openly speak in public about their faith and trust in Jesus Christ.
- An America where the airwaves were free of cursing and filth, and the bookshelves were free of pornography.
- An America where children played and walked in their neighborhoods without fear of being kidnapped or molested.
- An America in which pastors and churches were considered a vital part in establishing the nation's culture and values.

THERE IS HOPE!

Unless you are a Christian with a biblical understanding of end-time events and have a genuine sense of God's call upon your life, it is extremely difficult to be optimistic about the future. However, for those who are in Christ Jesus, everyday should be filled with optimism. The sure and certain promises of God offer us strength for today and bright hope for tomorrow. The signs of our times are but reminders our redemption is drawing near.

Christians are often accused of believing in and promoting the return of Christ in order to escape the challenges of this life. Nothing could be further from the truth. Jesus said, "I came that they may have life, and have it abundantly."[9] No one truly understands or experiences the joys of living more than those who have been born anew through the sacrifice of Christ and have the indwelling presence of the Holy Spirit. At the same time, Christians know they are citizens of heaven and nothing in this life can begin to compare with what awaits them in the life to come. Paul said it best: "For to me, to live is Christ and to die is gain."[10] Christians living in the twenty-first century can look at all life's challenges and say with Paul:

> Rejoice in the Lord always; again I will say, rejoice! Let your gentle spirit be known to all men. The Lord is near. Be anxious for nothing, but in everything by prayer and supplication with thanksgiving let your requests be made known to God. And the peace of God, which surpasses all comprehension, will guard your hearts and your minds in Christ Jesus.[11]

THERE IS HOPE FOR AMERICA

God has blessed our nation from its inception. From the Jamestown settlement to the Plymouth Colony, the settlers and their leaders framed their lives and communities around the protective grace of God. The phrase "one nation under God" in our Pledge of Allegiance is there for good reason. The words "In God we trust" were engraved on our coins because the American people understood it was God, and God alone, who gave us victory in battle and prosperity in times of peace. Abraham Lincoln was right when he said:

> It is the duty of nations, as well as of men, to owe their dependence upon the overruling power of God and to recognize the sublime truth announced in the Holy Scriptures and proven by all history, that those nations only are blessed whose God is the Lord.

Throughout the centuries, the Creator God has given America leaders to help us stay on the right path. God helped this nation to purge itself of the evils of slavery during the Civil War. He has chastised the nation many times for our sins and helped us to better understand not only the meaning of the words "all men are created equal" but to put them into practice.

America has been used by God more than any other nation in history to spread the light of Christ throughout the world and to alleviate human suffering. He has used this nation's wealth and might to protect the freedoms of nations around the globe. And without question, God has blessed America because we have stood with the nation of Israel.

Yet little by little, God is being forced out of our nation's life. So many people have forgotten it was God's grace that brought this land into existence; and it is only by His grace we will be sustained. America is treading on dangerous ground as we seek to free ourselves from the source of our sustenance and freedom. But there is hope for America *if* Christians will pray and stand for the cause of truth.

However, let us not assume by treating a few of our nation's symptoms we will have cured the nation's illness. If by some miracle we could once again have the Ten Commandments displayed in every court house and public school in America, and yet America's heart remained hardened against those principles of truth, we will have gained nothing. If we fail to get the nation to return to the Judeo-Christian principles upon which our nation was founded, we will surely fail in our efforts to guard our nation's past or to secure our nation's future.

The only person who can restore our nation is Jesus Christ! It is our duty as Christians to lift Jesus higher by witnessing the gospel of Christ and the truth of His unchanging Word. President Calvin Coolidge saw this clearly when he stated:

"The foundations of our society and our government rest so much on the teachings of the Bible that it would be difficult to support them if these teachings would cease to be practically universal in our country."

THERE IS HOPE FOR THE CHURCHES

Most mainline churches today may have already gone beyond the point of no return when it comes to restoration and revival. Their administrative leadership, schools and seminaries have been taken over by those who long ago abandoned the "one holy Christian and Apostolic faith." This is the harsh reality members of these churches must face. Yet so many Christians today are apathetic to the church's present condition. It is not that God is unable or unwilling to restore our churches and denominations; it is that churches and denominations have abandoned and neglected the truth of His Word. God has not turned His back on us; we have turned our backs on Him.

There is yet hope for our churches *if* God's faithful people will humble themselves, pray, seek His face and repent. There is hope for the churches and for our land *if* we Christians turn from our wicked ways with heartfelt repentance. There is hope for the church *if* Christians come once again to the realization the true church has never had its legitimacy in man-made denominations or organizational structures, but rather in true obedience to God's Word.

There is life and hope for the church as individual Christians withdraw from their denominations and congregations that are teaching false doctrines and embracing evil. There is hope for the church, as dedicated Christians establish new fellowships built on the Word of God. There is hope for the church as local congregations strap-up their courage and affiliate with fellowships upholding biblical standards of truth. Standing for God's truth is the heritage of the Protestant Reformation! If we are to keep faith with the rising generation, then Bible-believing Christians must rise up and lead the church into a new Reformation in order to pass on to the next generation the same glorious heritage of faith we have been privileged to know.

THERE IS HOPE FOR YOU

The struggles of this life cause most of us to be discouraged at times. Add to those struggles the challenges of living in times like these, and many people are easily driven to despair. But discouragement and despair are not what God wants for His redeemed children. Remember His promises; they are life and hope. Remember Jesus is Lord! The message of Christ's birth, life, death and resurrection is a message of hope! The message of His coming again in glory is the ultimate message of triumph.

Why should we live in fear and despair, when we can live in hope and victory? After all, we serve the God of all hope! Paul declared: "For whatever was written in earlier times was written for our instruction, so that through perseverance and the encouragement of the Scriptures we might have hope."[12] We are victors, not victims! Read the Bible and discover for yourself the glorious truth—WE WIN!

"Now may the God of hope fill you with all joy and peace in believing, so that you will abound in hope by the power of the Holy Spirit."[12]

Soli Deo Gloria!

APPENDIX A

THE APOSTLES' CREED

I believe in God the Father Almighty, Maker of heaven and earth; And in Jesus Christ, His only Son, our Lord; Who was conceived by the Holy Ghost; Born of the virgin Mary; Suffered under Pontius Pilate; Was crucified, dead and buried; He descended into hell; The third day He rose again from the dead; He ascended into heaven; And is seated on the right hand of God the Father Almighty; From where He shall come to judge the living and the dead.

I believe in the Holy Ghost; The holy Christian Church, the Communion of Saints; The Forgiveness of sins; The Resurrection of the body, And the Life everlasting. Amen.

THE NICENE CREED

I believe in one God, the Father Almighty, Maker of heaven and earth, And of all things visible and invisible.

And in one Lord Jesus Christ, the only begotten Son of God, Begotten of His Father before all worlds, God of God, Light of Light, Very God of very God, Begotten, not made, Being of one substance with the Father, By whom all things were made: Who for us men, and for our salvation, came down from heaven, And was incarnate by the Holy Ghost of the virgin Mary, And was made man; And was crucified also for us under Pontius Pilate. He suffered and was buried; And the third day He rose again according to the Scriptures, And ascended into heaven, And is seated on the right hand of the Father. And he shall come again with glory to judge both the living and the dead: Whose kingdom shall have no end.

And I believe in the Holy Ghost, The Lord and Giver of Life, Who proceeds from the Father and the Son, Who with the Father and the Son together is worshipped and glorified, Who spoke by the Prophets. And I believe one Holy Christian and apostolic Church. I acknowledge one Baptism for the remission of sins. And I look for the Resurrection of the dead, And the Life of the world to come. Amen.

APPENDIX B

THE BALFOUR DECLARATION

The following letter declared Great Britain's intention of establishing a Jewish state in Palestine following World War I and the defeat of the Ottoman Turks.

Foreign Office
November 2nd, 1917.

Dear Lord Rothschild,

I have much pleasure in conveying to you, on behalf of His Majesty's Government, the following declaration of sympathy with Jewish Zionist aspirations which has been submitted to, and approved by, the Cabinet:

"His Majesty's Government view with favour the establishment in Palestine of a national home for the Jewish people, and will use their best endeavours to facilitate the achievement of this object, it being clearly understood that nothing shall be done which may prejudice the civil and religious rights of existing non-Jewish communities in Palestine, or the rights and political status enjoyed by Jews in any other country."

I should be grateful if you would bring this declaration to the knowledge of the Zionist Federation.

Yours sincerely

Arthur James Balfour

APPENDIX C

ISRAEL'S DECLARATION OF INDEPENDENCE

ERETZ-ISRAEL [(Hebrew) - the Land of Israel, Palestine] was the birthplace of the Jewish people. Here their spiritual, religious and political identity was shaped. Here they first attained to statehood, created cultural values of national and universal significance and gave to the world the eternal Book of Books.

After being forcibly exiled from their land, the people kept faith with it throughout their Dispersion and never ceased to pray and hope for their return to it and for the restoration in it of their political freedom.

Impelled by this historic and traditional attachment, Jews strove in every successive generation to re-establish themselves in their ancient homeland. In recent decades they returned in their masses. Pioneers, ma'pilim [(Hebrew) - immigrants coming to Eretz-Israel in defiance of restrictive legislation] and defenders, they made deserts bloom, revived the Hebrew language, built villages and towns, and created a thriving community controlling its own economy and culture, loving peace but knowing how to defend itself, bringing the blessings of progress to all the country's inhabitants, and aspiring towards independent nationhood.

In the year 5657 (1897), at the summons of the spiritual father of the Jewish State, Theodore Herzl, the First Zionist Congress convened and proclaimed the right of the Jewish people to national rebirth in its own country.

This right was recognized in the Balfour Declaration of the 2nd November, 1917, and re-affirmed in the Mandate of the League of Nations which, in particular, gave international sanction to the historic connection between the Jewish people and Eretz-Israel and to the right of the Jewish people to rebuild its National Home.

The catastrophe which recently befell the Jewish people - the massacre of millions of Jews in Europe - was another clear demonstration of the urgency of solving the problem of its homelessness by re-establishing in Eretz-Israel the Jewish State, which would open the gates of the homeland wide to every Jew and confer upon the Jewish people the status of a fully privileged member of the comity of nations.

Survivors of the Nazi holocaust in Europe, as well as Jews from other parts of the world, continued to migrate to Eretz-Israel, undaunted by difficulties, restrictions and dangers, and never ceased to assert their right to a life of dignity, freedom and honest toil in their national homeland.

In the Second World War, the Jewish community of this country contributed its full share to the struggle of the freedom- and peace-loving nations against the forces of Nazi wickedness and, by the blood of its soldiers and its war effort, gained the right to be reckoned among the peoples who founded the United Nations.

On the 29th November, 1947, the United Nations General Assembly passed a resolution calling for the establishment of a Jewish State in Eretz-Israel; the General Assembly required the inhabitants of Eretz-Israel to take such steps as were necessary on their part for the implementation of that resolution. This recognition by the United Nations of the right of the Jewish people to establish their State is irrevocable.

This right is the natural right of the Jewish people to be masters of their own fate, like all other nations, in their own sovereign State.

ACCORDINGLY WE, MEMBERS OF THE PEOPLE'S COUNCIL,

REPRESENTATIVES OF THE JEWISH COMMUNITY OF ERETZ-ISRAEL AND OF THE ZIONIST MOVEMENT, ARE HERE ASSEMBLED ON THE DAY OF THE TERMINATION OF THE BRITISH MANDATE OVER ERETZ-ISRAEL AND, BY VIRTUE OF OUR NATURAL AND HISTORIC RIGHT AND ON THE STRENGTH OF THE RESOLUTION OF THE UNITED NATIONS GENERAL ASSEMBLY, HEREBY DECLARE THE ESTABLISHMENT OF A JEWISH STATE IN ERETZ-ISRAEL, TO BE KNOWN AS THE STATE OF ISRAEL.

WE DECLARE that, with effect from the moment of the termination of the Mandate being tonight, the eve of Sabbath, the 6th

Iyar, 5708 (15th May, 1948), until the establishment of the elected, regular authorities of the State in accordance with the Constitution which shall be adopted by the Elected Constituent Assembly not later than the 1st October 1948, the People's Council shall act as a Provisional Council of State, and its executive organ, the People's Administration, shall be the Provisional Government of the Jewish State, to be called "Israel".

THE STATE OF ISRAEL will be open for Jewish immigration and for the Ingathering of the Exiles; it will foster the development of the country for the benefit of all its inhabitants; it will be based on freedom, justice and peace as envisaged by the prophets of Israel; it will ensure complete equality of social and political rights to all its inhabitants irrespective of religion, race or sex; it will guarantee freedom of religion, conscience, language, education and culture; it will safeguard the Holy Places of all religions; and it will be faithful to the principles of the Charter of the United Nations.

THE STATE OF ISRAEL is prepared to cooperate with the agencies and representatives of the United Nations in implementing the resolution of the General Assembly of the 29th November, 1947, and will take steps to bring about the economic union of the whole of Eretz-Israel.

WE APPEAL to the United Nations to assist the Jewish people in the building-up of its State and to receive the State of Israel into the comity of nations.

WE APPEAL - in the very midst of the onslaught launched against us now for months - to the Arab inhabitants of the State of Israel to preserve peace and participate in the upbuilding of the State on the basis of full and equal citizenship and due representation in all its provisional and permanent institutions.

WE EXTEND our hand to all neighbouring states and their peoples in an offer of peace and good neighbourliness, and appeal to them to establish bonds of cooperation and mutual help with the sovereign Jewish people settled in its own land. The State of Israel is prepared to do its share in a common effort for the advancement of the entire Middle East.

WE APPEAL to the Jewish people throughout the Diaspora to rally round the Jews of Eretz-Israel in the tasks of immigration and upbuilding and to stand by them in the great struggle for the realization of the age-old dream - the redemption of Israel.

PLACING OUR TRUST IN THE ALMIGHTY, WE AFFIX OUR SIGNATURES TO THIS PROCLAMATION AT THIS SESSION OF THE PROVISIONAL COUNCIL OF STATE, ON THE SOIL OF THE HOMELAND, IN THE CITY OF TEL-AVIV, ON THIS SABBATH EVE, THE 5TH DAY OF IYAR, 5708 (14TH MAY, 1948).

APPENDIX D

CHRISTIAN LEGAL DEFENSE ORGANIZATIONS

Alliance Defense Fund – a legal alliance, organized to defend the right to hear and speak the truth through strategy, training, funding and litigation. Its focus is mainly on sanctity of life, traditional family and religious freedom. Alan Sears, President, CEO and General Counsel; www.alliancedefensefund.org.

American Center for Law and Justice—handles cases before various courts that pertain to the rights and liberties of Christians. It has argued cases before the Supreme Court, Federal Court of Appeals and Federal District Courts. Jay Sekulow, Chief Counsel; www.aclj.org.

Judicial Watch—a conservative, non-partisan educational foundation, promotes transparency, accountability and integrity in government, politics and the law. Through its educational endeavors, Judicial Watch advocates high standards of ethics and morality in our nation's public life and seeks to ensure that political and judicial officials do not abuse the powers entrusted to them by the American people. Judicial Watch fulfills its educational mission through litigation, investigations and public outreach. President: Thomas Fenton; **Publications: The Verdict**; www.judicialwatch.org.

Liberty Counsel—an organization whose agenda includes: litigation, education and issues of policy, particularly in the areas of sanctity of human life, religious freedom and the traditional family. Matthew D. Staver, Founder and Chairman; www.lc.org.

Rutherford Institute—a leading advocate of civil liberties and human rights.
John Whitehead, President and Founder; www.rutherford.org.

APPENDIX E

CHRISTIAN ORGANIZATIONS
THAT TEACH, CHALLENGE AND INFORM

Abiding Word Ministries—is devoted to promoting revival and reformation throughout the church, with special focus on Lutheran churches. AWM produces books, literature and a newsletter to help Christians become informed about conditions in the church as they relate to the teachings of God's Word. The ministry works with congregations, pastors and laity seeking to withdraw from their liberal denominations. AWM also conducts evangelistic meetings and conferences on prophecy.
David R. Barnhart, Founder and Director; **Publication**: *The Vine and Branches;* www.thevineandbranches.org.

American Family Association—is an organization that focuses on cultural, social and Christian issues relating to the church in America. AFA has had a profound and positive influence on our culture by prompting Christians to become active in the restoration of America. Donald E. Wildmon, Founder and Chairman; **Publication: AFA Journal**; www.afa.net.

Answers in Genesis—an organization dedicated to enabling Christians to defend their faith and to proclaim the gospel of Jesus Christ effectively. The organization, which believes in a literal interpretation of Genesis, also produces literature and videos on topics dealing with creation. The organization conducts seminars throughout the country and operates the Creation Science Museum located in Kentucky. Ken Ham, Founder and President; **Publication: Answers;** www.answersingenesis.org.

Concerned Women for America—a public policy organization, with offices in Washington, D.C. The organization is focused on family issues, sanctity of life, education, religious liberty and national sovereignty. Beverly LaHaye, Founder and Chairman; Wendy Wright, President; www.cwfa.org.

Eagle Forum—a pro-family organization that seeks to inform the public regarding issues and legislation that affect our nation, our families and our culture. Phyllis Schlafly Founder; Executive Director: Jessica Echard; **Publication: The Schlafly Report;** www. eagleforum.org.

Family Research Council—champions marriage and family as the foundation of civilization; shapes public debate and formulates public policy that values human life and upholds the institutions of marriage and the family. Founded by Dr. James Dobson in 1980. Executive Director: Tony Perkins; **Publications include: Tony Perkins' Washington Update;** www.frc.org.

Summit Ministries—is a Christian ministry that seeks to ground Christians in their faith; equip them to defend the biblical worldview; prepare tomorrow's servant leaders. This ministry offers seminars and conferences; it produces books, literature and other materials to achieve its stated goals. Executive Director: Dr. David A. Noebel; **Publication: Summit Journal;** www.summit.org.

Through the Bible with Les Feldick—is a national ministry led by Les Feldick, a layman from Oklahoma, who has devoted his life to teaching the Bible from Genesis through Revelation. His teaching sessions are nationally syndicated on television and radio. Les Feldick conducts Bible seminars throughout the country. The ministry offers books, DVDs and tapes from various seminars and broadcasts. Executive Director: Les Feldick; www.lesfeldick.org.

Voice of Martyrs is a non-profit, international organization with a vision for aiding Christians around the world who are being perse-cuted for their faith in Christ, fulfilling the Great Commission, and educating the world about the ongoing persecution of Christians. VOM, founded by Pastor Richard Wurmbrand, is headquartered in

Bartlesville, Oklahoma. **Publication: VOM Newsletter;** Executive Director: Tom White; www.persecution.com.

Wallbuilders—an organization dedicated to presenting America's forgotten history and and heroes, with an emphasis on the moral, religious, and constitutional foundation on which America was built—a foundation which, in recent years, has been seriously attacked and undermined. In accord with what was so accurately stated by George Washington, we believe that "the propitious [favorable] smiles of heaven can never be expected on a nation which disregards the eternal rules of order and right which heaven itself has ordained." Executive Director: David Barton; **Publication: Quarterly newsletter;** www.wallbuilders.com.

CHRISTIAN ORGANIZATIONS WITH A FOCUS ON JEWISH EVANGELISM, PROPHECY AND ISRAEL

Friends of Israel Gospel Ministry—This worldwide Christian Ministry communicates biblical truth about Israel and the Messiah, while fostering solidarity with the Jewish people. Executive Director: William E. Sutter; **Publication: Israel My Glory;** www.foi.org.

Jews for Jesus—an international organization dedicated to bringing the gospel of Christ to the Jews. It seeks to enlist Christians and congregations in evangelizing the Jews. The organization conducts Jewish evangelism in cities and towns across America, as well as in various parts of the world. Founder: Moishe Rosen in 1973. Executive Director: David Brickner; **Publications include: Jews for Jesus Newsletter;** www.jewsforjesus.org.

Olive Tree Ministries—focuses on the prophetic teachings of Scripture as they relate to the return of Christ and to the nation of Israel. The ministry sponsors conferences on prophecy, as well as a nationally syndicated radio broadcast. Founder and Director: Jan Markell; **Publication: Understanding the Times;** www.olivetree-views.org.

Zion's Hope, Inc. — The purpose of Zion's Hope is a simple one, yet also bold, direct, and far-reaching. Zion's Hope seeks to graciously proclaim to the Jewish people their need for personal salvation through Jesus the Messiah and to proclaim the gospel of the Lord Jesus Christ to all men regardless of race, religion, gender, education, or national origin. Accordingly, Zion's Hope seeks to educate the Bible-believing Church concerning the place of Israel in both history and prophecy and assist it in fulfilling its God-given obligation to rightfully include the Jewish people in its program for world evangelism.
Founder and Director: Marvin Rosenthal; **Publication: Zion's Fire;** www.zionshope.org.

Zola Levitt Ministries — a ministry devoted to teaching and evangelistic outreach, with a heart for the Jewish people. Zola Levitt, the founder of this ministry, died in 2006. His wife Sandra is now active in the promotion of Levitt Ministries' goals and objectives. They produce a nationally syndicated TV program called "Zola Levitt Presents." Executive Director: Jeffrey Seif; **Publication: *The Levitt Letter*;** www.levitt.com.

ENDNOTES

Part 1 Introduction

1. Matthew 13:17.
2. Acts 1:11.
3. Zechariah 14:4.
4. Revelation 1:7.
5. 2 Peter 3:4, 8-9.
6. 1 Timothy 2:4.
7. Revelation 19:6-9.
8. Hebrews 1:2.
9. Isaiah 9:6-7.
10. Luke 4:16-21. Jesus read this passage from Isaiah 61:1-2a.
11. Matthew 16:3.
12. R. A. Torrey, *The Return of the Lord Jesus,* (Grand Rapids, MI: Baker Book House, 1913), reprinted 1966, pages 20-21.
13. See Appendix A for the Apostles Creed and Nicene Creed.
14. Luke 24:27.
15. Daniel 12:8-9.
16. Matthew 24:15.
17. John 16:13.
18. Revelation 22:10.
19. 1 Corinthians 13:12.
20. 1 Corinthians 13:2.
21. 2 Timothy 4:1-2.
22. 1 Corinthians 11:26.
23. Hebrews 10:23-25.
24. Charles L. Feinberg, *Millennialism,* (Winona Lake, IN: BMH Books, 1936), reprinted 2006, page 162.

Chapter 1
1. Rick Warren, *The Purpose Driven Life,* (Grand Rapids, MI: Zondervan, 2002), page 285.
2. 2 Timothy 4:1-2.
3. Acts 17:11.
4. Luke 24:27, 32.
5. Irenaeus, *Against Heresies*, Vol. 3, Chapter 4.
6. David Larson, "Some Key Issues in the History of Premillennialism," a study paper obtained at www.pre-trib. org/Larson.
7. Francis Monseth, reference cited is from his doctorial dissertation on millennialism within the Lutheran Church.
8. 1 Peter 5:8.
9. John Walvoord, *The Revelation of Jesus Christ*, (Chicago, IL: Moody Press, 1960), page 19.
10. Walvoord, Ibid., page 19.
11. Acts 1:6.
12. Hanns Lilje, *The Last Book of the Bible*, (Philadelphia, PA: Muhlenberg Press, 1957), page 248.
13. Lilje, Ibid., page 252.
14. Lilje, Ibid.
15. Carl E. Braaten, *Principles of Lutheran Theology*, (Philadelphia, PA: Fortress Press, 1983), page 19.
16. Braaten, Ibid., pages 20-21.
17. John Walvoord, *The Prophecy Knowledge Handbook,* (Wheaton, IL: Victor Books, 1990), page 17.
18. 1 Thessalonians 4:13-18.
19. Ibid.
20. Revelation, chapters 19-22.
21. 1 Thessalonians 3:13.
22. Luke 14:14.
23. John 5:28-29.
24. 1 Corinthians 15:50-57.
25. 1 John 3:2.
26. Revelation 3:10.
27. 1 Thessalonians 1:10.
28. Matthew 24:15; Daniel 9:27.

29. Jeremiah 30:7.

30. Zechariah 13:8; 14.

31. Mark 13:19.

32. Mark 13:20.

33. Zechariah 8:3-5.

34. Zechariah 14:16.

35. Romans 14:11.

36. Romans 8:19-21.

37. Revelation 20:10.

38. Ezekiel 48:35.

39. Revelation 20:5.

40. Revelation 20:15.

41. Romans 8:1.

42. Hank Hanegraaff, *The Apocalypse Code*, (Nashville, TN: Thomas Nelson, Inc., 2007), page 197.

43. Genesis 17:7-8.

44. Genesis 26:3-4; 28:13-15.

45. Jeremiah 31:35-37.

46. Romans 11:1-2.

47. Romans 11: 17, 23, 26, 29.

48. Zechariah 12:10.

49. Romans 11:26.

50. Romans 1:16.

51. Wilbur M. Smith, *Israeli/Arab Conflict and the Bible*, (Glendale, CA: Regal Books, 1967), page 54.

52. Smith, Ibid.

53. Smith, Ibid., page 96.

54. Smith, Ibid., page 53.

55. Isaiah 62:1-5.

56. Malachi 3:1.

57. Ezekiel 36:5.

58. Malachi 3:2.

Chapter 2

1. Ezekiel 37:1-14.

2. Ezekiel 37:12.

3. Luke 19:41-44.

4. Luke 21: 20-21.
5. Leviticus 26:32.
6. Isaiah 5:6.
7. Mark Twain, *Innocents Abroad*, University of Virginia Library, Electronic Text Center, Chapter 46.
8. Ibid., Chapter 47.
9. The Balfour Declaration (see Appendix B).
10. Merle Miller, *Plain Speaking, an oral biography of Harry S. Truman*, (New York, NY: G. P. Putnam's Sons, 1973), page 218.
11. Isaiah 35:1-2, 6.
12. *Israel Today,* Headline News, January 31, 2007.
13. Statistics are from a report by Dan Izenberg for the Israel Ministry of Foreign Affairs, July 1998.
14. *Israel Today,* December 2006, page 26.
15. Information is from a report by Dr. Rachelle Fishman for the Israeli Ministry of Foreign Affairs, August 1999.

Chapter 3

1. Ezekiel 14:14; Matthew 24:15.
2. Alva J. McClain, *Daniel's Prophecy of the Seventy Weeks*, (Grand Rapids, MI: Zondervan, 1940), page 6.
3. Daniel 2:31-35.
4. Deuteronomy 32:15.
5. Exodus 17:1-7.
6. Numbers 20:8-12.
7. Hebrews 9:28.
8. 1 Corinthians 10:1-4.
9. Daniel 2:38-43.
10. Daniel 7.
11. Matthew 24:15.
12. Daniel 9:24-27.
13. Leviticus 25:4.
14. Leviticus 25:8-12.
15. Daniel 9:24-27.
16. Luke 19:40.
17. Romans 1:16.

18. Isaiah 9:6.
19. Luke 4:16-21.
20. Zechariah 12:10.
21. Isaiah 40:1-2.
22. Romans 10:12-13.
23. Ephesians 4:4-6.
24. 2 Thessalonians 2:3.
25. Chuck Missler, *Prophecy 20/20,* (Nashville, TN: Nelson Books, 2006), page 70.
26. Daniel 7:25.
27. Daniel 8:12.
28. Matthew 24:29-30.
29. Jeremiah 29:11-14.
30. Luke 21:31.
31. Jude 24-25.

Chapter 4
1. Revelation 13:16-18.
2. Revelation 14:9-10.
3. D. L. Cuddy, *The New World Order, A Critique and Chronology*, page 18
4. Strobe Talbott, "America Abroad," *Time,* June 24, 2001.
5. James W. Wardner, "The Planned Destruction of America," *News Watch,* January 1994, page 8.
6. www.worldnetdaily.com/news/printer-friendly. asp?ARTICLE_ID=55595.
7. D. L. Cuddy, *Now is the Dawning of the New Age New World Order*, (Oklahoma City, OK: Hearthstone Publishing, 1991), page 248.
8. Wardner, Ibid., page 13.
9. www.worldnetdaily.com/news/printer-friendly. asp?ARTICLE_ID=55584.
10. www.msnbc.com., "Just who owns the U.S. national debt?", March 4, 2007.
11. www.msnbc.com., "Migration and the changing face of Europe," June 18, 2007.

12. This proposal may be found on the web site of the Council on Foreign Relations, in a document entitled "Building a North American Community."

13. www.worldnetdaily.com, "North American Union plan headed to Congress," May 24, 2007.

14. Ibid.

15. Phyllis Schlafly, "CFR's Plan to Integrate the U.S., Mexico and Canada," July 13, 2005.

16. www.worldnetdaily.com, "North American merger topic of secret conflab," September 20, 2006.

17. CNN's "Lou Dobbs Tonight," June 21, 2006.

18. CNN's "Lou Dobbs Tonight," April 8, 2006, report by Christine Romans and commentary by Lou Dobbs.

19. www.worldnetdaily.com, Jerome Corsi, "It's official: Mexican Trucks Coming," ARTICLE_ID=54411.

20. Ibid.

21. Patrick J. Buchannan, "The NAFTA super highway," *www. Townhall.com.*, August 29, 2006.

22. www.thestar.com/printArticle/136744.

23. John 1:12-13.

Chapter 5

1. www.worldnetdaily.com., ARTICLE _ID=56645.

2. www.foxnews.com., "Chairman of Joint Chiefs Calls Homosexuality 'Immoral,'" March 13, 2007.

3. www.worldnetdaily.com., Bob Unrugh, "Diss a 'gay'? Go to jail," February 15, 2007.

4. www.worldnetdaily.com., "Cross-snatching college holds porn show," February 16, 2007.

5. Ibid.

6. Article from Focus on the Family's *Citizen* web site, "The Wall That Never Was."

7. Jim Siegel, "House wants preachers to tone it down," *Columbus Dispatch*, May 18, 2007, page 1.

8. Luke 18:8.

9. Matthew 24:4-5.

10. *Biblical Archaeological Review*, January/February 2007.

11. 1 Timothy 4:1.
12. Rita Nakashima Brock and Rebecca Ann Parker, "The Mask of Violence," *UU World,* March/April, 2002.
13. Ibid.
14. John Shelby Spong, *Rescuing the Bible from Fundamentalism,* (San Francisco, CA: Harper, 1991), page 25.
15. Spong, Ibid., page 117.
16. Spong, Ibid, page 215.
17. John Shelby Spong, *Here I Stand,* (San Francisco, CA: Harper, 2000), pages 453-454.
18. *The Five Gospels,* (New York, NY: Macmillan Publishing Company, 1993), page 5.
19. Spong, Ibid., page 7.
20. John Dominic Crossan, *The Historical Jesus,* (San Francisco, CA: Harper, 1991), pages 392-394.
21. Crossan, Ibid., page 421.
22. Marcus J. Borg, "Me and Jesus," www.westarinstitute.org/perodicals/4R_bio/borg/bio.html.
23. Marcus J. Borg, "Questions of Faith and Doubt," www.explorefaith.org/questions/cross.hmtl.
24. Borg, Ibid.
25. Leonard Ravenhill, *Sodom Had No Bible,* (Minneapolis, MN: Bethany House Publishers, 1971), page11.
26. *Time,* "Does God Want You to be Rich," September 18, 2006.
27. Luke 9:23.
28. Matthew 6:19-21.
29. Morgan Jarema, "Church more spiritual than religious," *Grand Rapids Press,* February 3, 2007.
30. 2 Timothy 4:2.
31. 2 Timothy 4:3-4.
32. Hebrews 13:8.
33. 1 Corinthians 2:2.
34. 1 Corinthians 9:16.
35. Deuteronomy 6:4-6.
36. Ephesians 6:13.

Part 2 Introduction
1. Mark Steyn, *America Alone,* (Washington, DC: Regnery Publishing, Inc., 2006), page 46.
2. 1 John 2:22-23.
3. 1 John 4:1-3.

Chapter 6
1. Robert Spencer, *The Truth About Muhammad,* (Washington, DC: Regnery Publishing, Inc., 2006), page 36.
2. Spencer, Ibid., page 85.
3. Alfred Guillaume, *Islam,* (Baltimore, MD: Penguin Books, 1962), page 12.
4. Guillaume, Ibid., page 130.
5. Ergun and Emir Caner, *Unveiling Islam,* (Grand Rapids, MI: Kregel Publications, 2002), page 135.
6. Dave Hunt, *Judgment Day! Islam, Israel and the Nations,* (Bend, OR: The Berean Call, 2006), page 145.
7. Hunt, Ibid., page 163.
8. Deuteronomy 18:18-19.
9. John 1:19-21 (New International Version).
10. www.islam-guide.com/ch1-3.html.

Chapter 7
1. Paul Sperry, "The Perfect Enemy and How to Defeat It," *Whistleblower,* October 2006.
2. David Bukay, *The Jerusalem Alternative,* (Green Forest, AR: Balfour Books, 2004), page 103.
3. Bukay, Ibid.
4. John 14:16; 16:7.
5. Ergun and Emir Caner, *More Than a Prophet,* (Grand Rapids, MI: Kregel Publications, 2003), page 55.
6. Alvin Schmidt, "Islam, keeping the facts straight," *The Lutheran Witness,* May 2006.
7. Schmidt, Ibid.
8. Ravi Zacharias, *Light in the Shadow of Jihad,* (Sisters, OR: Mulnomah Publisher, 2002), page 39.
9. John 17:3.

10. Bridgette Gabriel, *Why They Hate,* (New York, NY: St Martin's Press, 2006), page 194.
11. Christopher Dickey and Rod Nordland, "The Fire that Won't Die Out," *Newsweek,* July 22, 2002, pages 34-37.
12. www.msnbc.com, "Iran arrests 'insufficiently veiled' women," April 23, 2007.
13. Lisa Beyer, "The Women of Islam," *Time,* November 21, 2001; the article appears in *The Truth About Muhammad* by Robert Spencer.
14. Jody Biehl, "The Whore Lived Like a German," *Spiegel On Line,* March 2, 2005.
15. *The Columbus Dispatch,* "Pregnant Jordanian woman slain in 'honor killing,'" July 10, 2007.
16. *Israel Today,* December 2006, page 10.
17. Carol Schersten LaHurd, "Islam and Christianity," *The Lutheran,* March 2007, page 17.
18. Schersten, Ibid.
19. www.elca.com, "Understanding Our Relations with Islam and Muslims," produced by the Evangelical Lutheran Church in America.
20. John 17:17.

Chapter 8

1. Mark A. Gabriel, *Journey into the Mind of Islamic Terrorist,* (Lake Mary, FL: Front Line, 2006), page 135.
2. Bernard Lewis, *Inside Islam,* (New York, NY: Marlowe and Company, 2002), page 195.
3. Lewis, Ibid., page 194.
4. Ravi Zacharias, *Light in the Shadow of Jihad,* (Sisters, OR: Mulnomah Publishers, 2002), page 41.
5. Emir and Ergun Caner, *Unveiling Islam,* (Grand Rapids, MI: Kregel Publications, 2002), page 49.
6. www.worldnetdaily.com, "PBS Targets Dangerous Muslim Brotherhood," March 31, 2007.
7. www.worldnetdaily.com, "Moderate Islamic charities back terror," April 12, 2007.

8. www.worldnetdaily.com, "Mosques awarded Homeland Security grants," May 25, 2007.
9. Ibid.
10. www.onenewsnow.com, "Watchdog calls for greater scrutiny on Council for American-Islamic Relations," April 13, 2007.
11. www.jihadwatch.org, "CAIR membership plummets," June 11, 2007.
12. "Terrorist Group Profiles," http://nps.navy.mil/home/tgp./qaida.htm.
13. Steven Emerson, *Jihad Incorporated,* (Amherst, NY: Prometheus Books, 2006), page 179.
14. Wikipedia, http://en.wikipedia.org/wiki/Hamas.
15. www.worldnetdaily.com, "Smugglers use cease-fire to stockpile guns," December 27, 2006.
16. Ibid.
17. David Bukay, *The Jerusalem Alternative,* (Green Forest, AR: Balfour Books, 2004), page 166.
18. Emir and Ergun Caner, *More Than a Prophet,* (Grand Rapids, MI: Kregel Publications, 2003), page 147. (Footnoted from another source.)
19. www.jihadwatch.org, "Iran could have nukes in 2009," April 2, 2007.
20. www.worldnetdaily.com October 25, 2006.
21. Brigitte Gabriel, *Why They Hate,* (New York, NY: St. Martin's Press, 2006), page 161.
22. www.msnbc.msn.com/id/13804825/displaymode/1098, Lisa Myers.
23. www.townhall.com, "The gap between Islam and Peace," by Diana West, September 30, 2006.
24. www.campus-watch.org/article/id/1148, by Paul Sperry, May 3, 2004.
25. Sperry, Ibid.
26. www.worldnetdaily.com, "EU Guidebook: Don't link Islam with terror," March 31, 2007.
27. Diana West, "Just Shut Up," *The Washington Times,* September 27, 2006.

28. www.worldnetdaily,com/article/ID=52167.
29. Charles Kruthammer, "Intolerance or Intimidation," *Levitt Letter,* November 2006.
30. *Jerusalem Post,* online edition, September 18, 2006.
31. *Israel Today,* "Palestinian Kids Seek Martyrdom," October 2006, page 9.
32. www.jihadwatch.org/archives/2007/03/015655.
33. Luke 17:1-2.
34. David Kupelian, "The Invisible Jihad," Whistleblower, September 2006.
35. Gabriel, Ibid., page 197.
36. www.worldnetdaily.com, September 27, 2006, ARTICLE ID=52184.
37. Ibid.
38. Dave Hunt, *Judgment Day! Islam, Israel and the Nations,* (Bend, OR: The Berean Call, 2006), page 252.
39. www.worldnetdaily.com, "Chertoff's 'Islam PC' rankles fed officials," February 10, 2007.
40. Ibid.
41. www.jihadwatch.com, "FBI Director predicts terrorists will acquire nukes," June 12, 2007.

Chapter 9
1. David Barton, "An Historical Perspective on a Muslim Being Sworn into Congress on the Koran," January 2007.
2. Barton, Ibid.
3. Barton, Ibid.
4. Robert Spencer, "The Crusade We Must Fight Today," *Whistleblower,* October 2006.
5. Mark Steyn, *America Alone,* (Washington, DC: Regnery Publishing, 2006), page 6.
6. *Jerusalem Post,* "Muslims about to take over Europe," January 29, 2007.
7. www.msnbc.com, "Integration questions stir passions," February 14, 2007.
8. Brigitte Gabriel, *Because They Hate,* (New York, NY: St. Martin's Press, 2006), page 15.

9. *The Christian Post,* "Plans for Western Mega-Mosque Rouse Concerns," January 10, 2007.
10. Gabriel, Ibid., page 76.
11. Steyn, Ibid., page 76.
12. *Telegraph Reporter,* "No Lessons on the Holocaust," March 4, 2007.
13. Phillip Johnston, "Terrorists are recruiting in our schools," *London Telegraph,* November 10, 2006.
14. www.msnbc.com, "Nonviolent but still a threat," February 14, 2007.
15. William Boston, "In Germany, terror suspect's arrest shakes sense of security," *USA Today,* August 21, 2006.
16. Steyn, Ibid., page 16.
17. Arnaud de Borchgrave, "Mini clash of civilization," *The Washington Times,* November 15, 2004.
18. www.Zamanonline?bl=international&alt-hn+37109.
19. *Islam Review,* October 13, 2006.
20. Daniel Pipes, "A Madrassa Grows in Brooklyn," *Israel My Glory,* July/August 2007.
21. www.worldnetdaily.com, "Scholastic joins education industry's campaign for Islam," January 3, 2007.
22. Bob Unruh, "Why Johnny is reading Islamist Propaganda," *Worldnetdaily,* October 26, 2006.
23. Chad Groening, "U.S. Military Academy Should Weigh Muslim Applicants," *Agape Press,* October 30, 2006.
24. *WorldNetDaily,* "Quantico mosque leader promoted," December 14, 2006.
25. Spencer, Ibid., *Whistleblower,* page 39.
26. Gabriel, Ibid., page 134.
27. Steven Emerson, *Jihad Incorporated,* (Amherst, NY: Prometheus Books, 2006), page 182.
28. Emerson, Ibid., pages 184-185.
29. Steyn, Ibid., page 66.
30. *Fox News* Report, January 5, 2006.
31. Robert Spencer, "Why We Must Profile," *Whistleblower,* October 2006, page 14.
32. Spencer, Ibid., page 15.

33. *Jerusalem Post Online Edition,* "IDF Finds Undetectable Bomb Belts," November 16, 2006.
34. Gabriel, Ibid., page xi.
35. www.worldnetdaily.com/news.asp?ArticleID=52644, October 31, 2006.
36. Gabriel, Ibid., page 15.
37. www.aol.com/news, December 3, 2006.
38. Matthew 5:44-45.

Chapter 10

1. *Arutz Sheva,* Israel International News.com, October 12, 2006.
2. Mark Hitchcock, *Iran, The Coming Crisis,* (Sisters, OR: Multnomah Publishers, 2006), page 71.
3. Genesis 14.
4. Daniel 5:28.
5. Ezra 1:1-4.
6. Ezra 4:24.
7. Nehemiah 2:1-8.
8. Daniel 9:27.
9. Ezekiel 38:5-6.
10. Zechariah 14:2; Revelation 16:13-16.
11. Peter Hirschberg, "Netanyahu: It's 1938 and Iran is Germany," *Haaretz.com,* November 14, 2006.
12. Hitchcock, Ibid., page 81.
13. *Zion's Fire,* January/February 2007, from a speech given via satellite from the United States to a conference hosted by the Institute for Policy and Strategy at IDC, Herzliya, Israel in 2006 and reported by *Ynetnews.com.*
14. Joel C. Rosenberg, *Epicenter,* (Carol Stream, IL: Tyndale House Publishers, 2006), page XIV.
15. Rosenberg, Ibid.
16. *International Herald Tribune,* http://www.iht.com/bin/php?id=4172553.
17. www.worldnetdaily.com,Article_ID=53954, January 25, 2007.

18. Reuters, "Bush delays moving U.S. Embassy to Jerusalem," December 18, 2006.
19. Dave Hunt, *Judgment Day,* (Bend, OR: The Berean Call, 2006), page 48.
20. Jerusalem Post, "Russia Confirms Tor-M1 Sale to Iran," January 16, 2007.
21. www.Briebart.com/news/2006/12/03/D8LPFG100.html.
22. www.telegraph.co.uk/"North Korea helping Iran with nuclear testing," January 24, 2007.
23. Mark Steyn, *America Alone,* (Washington, DC: Regnery Publishing, 2006), page 142.
24. worldnetdaily.com, "Iran leader's U.N. finale reveals apocalyptic view," September 21, 2006.
25. Daniel 7:8.
26. Revelation 20:4.
27. Ibid., worldnetdaily.com, "Iran leader's U.N. finale reveals apocalyptic view."
28. Daniel 9:27.
29. Daniel 2:32.
30. Hitchcock, Ibid., page 42.
31. Ibid., pages 84-85.
32. Ibid., page 57, relating to article by Mortimer B. Zucherman, "Moscow's Mad Gamble," in *U.S. News and World Report,* Internet Edition, January 30, 2006.
33. *Jerusalem Post* Online Edition, "Gate's shocking thinking on Iran," December 6, 2006.
34. *Jerusalem Post* Online Edition, "Report: IAEA to help Arabs go nuclear," November 4, 2006.
35. Isaiah 64:1-2.
36. Hebrews 12:2.
37. Luke 21:28.

Part 3 Introduction
1. 1 Peter 1:20.
2. Genesis 3:15.
3. Hebrews 11:19.
4. Luke 19:44.

Chapter 11
1. Ephesians 5:32.
2. Romans 5:14.
3. Genesis 2:24; Ephesians 5:28-31.
4. 1 Corinthians 15:21-22.
5. John 19:34.
6. 1 John 5:7-8.
7. John 3:5.
8. Hebrews 11:17-19.
9. 1 Peter 1:8.
10. John 15:16; Ephesians 1:4.
11. Acts 20:28.
12. Jeremiah 31:32.
13. Revelation 3:20.
14. Matthew 26:27-29.
15. Revelation 19:9.
16. Ephesians 5:26-27.
17. 2 Corinthians 5:17.
18. Text and music by Elisha A. Hoffmann.
19. John 14:2-3.
20. 1 Corinthians 2:9 (King James Version).
21. Matthew 24:36.
22. 2 Timothy 4:4.
23. 1 Thessalonians 4:16-17.
24. Matthew 25: 1-13.
25. John 3:29.
26. Revelation 19:7-9.
27. Hank Hanegraaff, *The Apocalypse Code,* (Nashville, TN: Thomas Nelson, Inc., 2007), pages 64-65.
28. Revelation 21:2, 9-11.

Chapter 12
1. Revelation 6:16.
2. 1 Thessalonians 4:14.
3. Joel 2:1-2, 10.
4. Zephaniah 1:14-18.
5. Joshua 10:12-14; Genesis 19:23-24; Matthew 2:2.

6. Zechariah 14:4.
7. Ezekiel 47.
8. Exodus 14:19; 16:10.
9. Numbers 9:17.
10. Exodus 19:9.
11. Exodus 19:16.
12. Exodus 40:34-35.
13. Leviticus 16:2.
14. 1 Corinthians 10:1-4.
15. 2 Chronicles 5:13-14.
16. 2 Chronicles 6:1.
17. 2 Chronicles 7:1-3.
18. Isaiah 6:1, 4.
19. Daniel 7:13-14.
20. Ezekiel 10:18-19.
21. Ezekiel 11:23; Zechariah 14:4; Malachi 3:1.
22. Ezekiel 43:1-7.
23. Matthew 3:17.
24. Matthew 17:5.
25. John 1:14.
26. Acts 1:9.
27. Matthew 26:64.
28. 1 Thessalonians 3:13.
29. Revelation 11:12.
30. 1 Thessalonians 4:16-17.
31. 1 Corinthians 15:52.

Chapter 13

1. Romans 11:33.
2. Luke 24:32.
3. Exodus 12:11-14.
4. Hebrews 10:4.
5. Hebrews 11:24-26.
6. Isaiah 53.
7. John 1:29.
8. Exodus 12:5.
9. Revelation 5:1-14.

10. John 19:33.
11. Isaiah 53:5.
12. Kevin L. Howard, "Behold the Lamb, The Feast of the Passover," *Zion's Fire*, March/April 1996, pages 4-11.
13. 1 John 1:7.
14. Romans 5:9.
15. Ephesians 1:7.
16. Leviticus 17:11.
17. Hebrews 9:22.
18. Hebrews 13:20.
19. William Cowper 1731-1800.
20. Matthew 16:5-12; 23:28; 1 Corinthians 5.
21. Hebrews 12:1.
22. 1 Corinthians 5:7-8.
23. 2 Corinthians 5:21.
24. John 6:32-35.
25. 1 Corinthians 10:3.
26. Psalm 16:10.
27. William Arndt, *Bible Difficulties& Seeming Contradictions,* (St. Louis, MO: Concordia, 1987), pages 188-190.
28. 1 Corinthians 15:21-23.
29. Colossians 1:18.
30. James 1:18.
31. Romans 8:11.
32. Romans 8:23.
33. Revelation 14:4.
34. John 1:17.
35. Hebrews 12:18-24.
36. Acts 2:47.
37. Matthew 9:37-38.
38. Zola Levitt, *The Seven Feasts of Israel,* (Dallas, TX: published by Zola Levitt Ministries).
39. 1 Thessalonians 4:16-17.
40. 1 Corinthians 15:51-52.
41. Exodus 19:16.
42. Matthew 24:31.
43. Isaiah 1:18.

44. Hebrews 9:11-12.
45. Matthew 27:20.
46. John 11:49-52.
47. Zechariah 13:9.
48. Isaiah 40:2.
49. Revelation 11:12.
50. Jude 20-25.
51. Revelation 21:1-3.
52. Revelation 21:22.
53. Leviticus 23:40.
54. John 7:38.
55. John 9:7.
56. Israel Ariel and Chiam Richman, *Carta's Illustrated Encyclopedia of the Holy Temple in Jerusalem*, (Jerusalem, Israel: The Temple Institute, 2005), page 192.
57. John 8:12.
58. Isaiah 9:2.
59. John 1:9.
60. Revelation 21:23.
61. Zechariah 14:16.
62. Micah 4:1-3.

Chapter 14

1. John 16:13.
2. Romans 5:12-14.
3. 1 Corinthians 15:21-22,45-47.
4. Hebrews 11:7.
5. 1 Peter 3:20.
6. Romans 4:11.
7. Genesis 17:7-8.
8. John 10:3, 27.
9. John 3:16.
10. Romans 8:28.
11. Psalm 126:5.
12. Psalm 30:5.
13. Hebrews 11:17-19.
14. John 19:17.

15. John 10: 17-18.
16. Luke 22:42.
17. Philippians 2:8.
18. 1 Peter 2:24.
19. William Steuart McBirnie, *The Search for the Tomb of Jesus,* (Montrose, CA: 1975), pages 43-44.
20. Lamentations 1:12.
21. Leviticus 1:11.
22. Exodus 26:35.
23. Romans 10:9-10.
24. Daniel 4:32.
25. Luke 1:32.
26. Luke 1:52.
27. Ephesians 2:14:Colossians 1:20.
28. Hebrews 7:3.
29. Nehemiah 7:64.
30. Hebrews 8:5.
31. Hebrews 7:27-28.
32. Hebrews 9:11-15.
33. John 1:17.
34. Hebrews 7:25.
35. Hebrews 4:14-16.
36. Hebrews 7:25.
37. Zechariah 6:13.
38. Zechariah 14:9.
39. John 3: 14-15.
40. John 19:37-39.
41. Zechariah 12:10.
42. Exodus 23:20-21.
43. Numbers 20:12.
44. 1 Corinthians 10:1-4.
45. Hebrews 7:27.
46. John 4:13-14.
47. John 7:37-39.
48. Lamentations 3:22-23.
49. Deuteronomy 32.
50. Matthew 16:18.

51. John 6:32-33, 35, 47-51.
52. Luke 22:19; 1 Corinthians 11:24.

Chapter 15
1. Isaiah 30:13.
2. Exodus 15:17-18.
3. 2 Samuel 24:18-25.
4. Psalm 137:5-6.
5. Exodus 25:9.
6. Hebrews 8:5.
7. Hebrews 9:23-24.
8. Hebrews 8:1-2.
9. Revelation 4:2, 5.
10. Revelation 11:19.
11. Revelation 15:8.
12. 1 Chronicles 28:11,19.
13. Randall Price, *The Temple and Bible Prophecy,* (Eugene, OR: Harvest House Publishers, 2005), page 51.
14. Luke 2:36-38.
15. Luke 2:24.
16. Acts 21: 23-26.
17. Matthew 9:23.
18. Matthew 6:2.
19. Psalm 122:1.
20. Psalm 23:6.
21. Psalm 84:1-4, 10.
22. Revelation 3:12.
23. Isaiah 56:7.
24. 2 Chronicles 6:32-33.
25. Leon Ritmeyer, *The Temple and the Rock,* (Harrogate, England: Ritmeyer, 1996), page 7.
26. Acts 21:27-31.
27. 2 Maccabees 2:3-8.
28. Revelation 4:5.
29. Luke 1:11-25.
30. Luke 1:18-24.
31. Revelation 8:1-3.

32. Psalm 141:1-2.
33. Alfred Edersheim, *The Temple, Its Ministry and Services,* (Peabody, MA: Hendrickson Publishers, 1994), page 114.
34. Edersheim, Ibid., page 66.
35. Luke 1:5.
36. Hebrews 5:4-5.
37. Ezekiel 44:1-2.
38. James Fleming, "The Undiscovered Gate Beneath Jerusalem's Golden Gate," *Biblical Archaeological Review,* January/February 1983, pages 24-37.
39. Hank Hanegraaff, *The Apocalypse Code,* (Nashville, TN: Thomas Nelson, Inc., 2007), page 221.
40. Revelation 11:1-2.
41. www.israeltoday.co.il/default.aspx?tabid=178&nid=13445.
42. Matthew 24:15.
43. Ibid.
44. Revelation 11:1.
45. Asher Kaufman, "Where the Ancient Temple of Jerusalem Stood," *Biblical Archaeological Review,* March/April, 1983.
46. Revelation 11:1-2.

Part 4 Introduction
1. Charles Feinberg, *Millennialism, The Two Major Views,* (Winona Lake, IN: BMH Books, 2006), page 153.
2. 2 Chronicles 36:15-16.
3. Hebrews 2:1-3.
4. Hebrews 9:27.
5. Revelation 22:17.

Chapter 16
1. Acts 20:31.
2. Acts 19.
3. 2 Timothy 4:14.
4. Acts 18:19.
5. 1 Timothy 1:3.
6. Acts 20:17-38.

7. Acts 19:9.
8. 2 Timothy 1:5.
9. John Osteen, *This Awakening Generation,* (Humble, Osteen, 1964).
10. *The Rebirth of America,* published by the Arthur S. DeMoss Foundation, 1986.
11. John 14:15.
12. Jude 3.
13. worldnetdaily.com, October 4, 2006.
14. C. F. W. Walther, *The Proper Distinction Between Law and Gospel,* (St. Louis, MO: Concordia Publishing House), page 89.
15. Acts 17:11.
16. 2 Corinthians 6:17.

Chapter 17

1. Ergun and Emir Caner, *More Than a Prophet,* (Grand Rapids, MI: Kregel Publications, 2003), page 222.
2. www.worldnetdaily.com, "Christians flee Iraq, find Syria 'ruthless,'" December 29, 2006.
3. Ergun and Emir Caner, *Unveiling Islam,* (Grand Rapids, MI: Kregel Publications, 2002), pages 176-177.
4. Hebrews 13:3.

Chapter 18

1. Ephesians 6:17 and Hebrews 4:12.
2. Numbers 22.
3. Jude 11.
4. H. A. Ironside, *Revelation,* (Neptune, NJ: Loizeaux Brothers, 1920), page 48.
5. worldnetdaily.com,news/ARTICLE ID=51979.
6. Matthew 10:33.
7. Ephesians 5:20.
8. Acts 4:12.
9. www.cathedral.org/cathedral/programs/wtc9.11/wtc.shtml, video recording.
10. Acts 26:28-29.

11. David W. Cloud, "World Council of Churches Promotes Female Gods," *O Timothy,* Volume 9, Issue 1, 1992.
12. Cloud, Ibid.
13. www.christianpost.com/ARTICLE ID=27129.

Chapter 19

1. Acts 16:14-15.
2. Hebrews 10:26-27.
3. Acts 17:11.
4. 1 Corinthians 10:13.
5. 2 Timothy 1:12-13. (King James Version)
6. 1 John 5:5.
7. Philippians 2:8.
8. 2 Timothy 4:7-8.
9. Romans 10:9-10.

Chapter 20

1. William Barclay, *The Revelation of John,* Volume 1, (Edinburgh, St. Andrews Press, 1962), page 146.
2. Hebrews 13:17.
3. C. F. W. Walther, *The Proper Distinction Between Law and Gospel,* (St. Louis, MO: Concordia Publishing House).
4. 2 Corinthians 6:14, 17.
5. Psalm 16:6.
6. Jeremiah 6:16.
7. Ecclesiastes 12: 1,6-7.
8. 2 Corinthians 7:10.
9. 1 Thessalonians 5:2-3.
10. Ephesians 5:25-27.
11. Revelation 7:13-17.
12. Matthew 10:32.
13. John 20:31.

Chapter 21

1. Ephesians 5:3-4.
2. 1 John 2:15, 17.
3. 2 Timothy 4:10-11.

4. John 14:6.
5. Acts 4:12.
6. www.worldnetdaily.com/news/printer-friendly.
   asp?ARTICLE_ID=56244.
7. www.aol.news, April 24, 2007.
8. 2 Corinthians 6:14-18.
9. www.worldnetdaily.com/news/ARTICLE-ID=56067.
10. Ibid.
11. Ibid.
12. Jeremiah 8:20.
13. 1 Corinthians 16:9.
14. 2 Corinthians 2:12.
15. Colossians 4:3.
16. Romans 15:22.
17. Romans 1:16.
18. www.worldnetdaily.com,"Hitchens: 'I wish there were a
    hell for Falwell,'" May 16, 2007.
19. Philippians 2:10-11.
20. 2 Chronicles 20:12.
21. 2 Chronicles 20:15, 17.
22. Matthew 7:13-14.
23. Zechariah 4:10.

Chapter 22

1. Colossians 2:1.
2. Colossians 4:17.
3. Colossians 4:13.
4. Colossians 1:15-17.
5. John 1:1-3.
6. Isaiah 5:20.
7. Psalm 138:2. (New International Version)
8. Hebrews 4:12-13.
9. Isaiah 30:10.
10. Acts 1:8.
11. 2 Timothy 3:5.
12. Proverbs 11:28.
13. Psalm 103:17-18.

14. Isaiah 55:1.
15. 1 Peter 1:6-7.
16. Revelation 7:14.
17. John 9:41.
18. Revelation 3:19.
19. John 14:23.
20. Luke 16:31.
21. Matthew 13:16-17.
22. Revelation 2:10.

Chapter 23

1. John 14:27.
2. Ezekiel 12:2.
3. Hebrews 2:1.
4. Proverbs 16:25.
5. www.worldnetdaily.com, "Ban on 'mom' and 'dad' considered again," April 27, 2007.
6. *Time,* August 28, 1989.
7. www.washingtonpost.com/article/2007/07/03/AR2007070200991.
8. www.cnbcnews.com, "Socialization: Homeschooling vs. Schools," May 2, 2007.
9. John 10:10.
10. Philippians 1:21.
11. Philippians 4:4-7.
12. Romans 15:4.
13. Romans 15:13.

BIBLIOGRAPHY

Anderson, Robert, *The Coming Prince*, Grand Rapids, MI: Kregel Publications, 1957.

Ariel, Israel, *The Odyssey of the Third Temple*, Jerusalem, Israel: The Temple Institute, translated and adapted by Chaim Richman, 1992.

Arndt, William, *Bible Difficulties & Seeming Contradictions*, St. Louis, MO: Concordia Publishing, 1987.

Caner, Emir and Ergun, *More Than a Prophet*, Grand Rapids, MI: Kregel Publications, 2003.

Caner, Emir and Ergun, *Unveiling Islam*, Grand Rapids, MI: Kregel Publications, 2002.

Comay, Joan, *The Temple of Jerusalem*, New York, NY: Holt, Rinehart and Winston, 1975.

Dolan, David, *Israel in Crisis*, Grand Rapids, MI: Fleming H. Revell, 2001.

Dolan, David, *Holy War for the Promised Land*, Nashville, TN: Broadman & Holman Publishers, 2003.

Edersheim, Alfred, *The Temple Its Ministry and Services*, Peabody, MA: Hendrickson Publishers, 1994.

Ehlke, Roland, *Christianity, Cults and World Religions*, Milwaukee, WI: Northwestern Publishing, 1999.

Emerson, Steven, *Jihad Incorporated*, Amherst, NY: Prometheus Books, 2006.

Feinberg, Charles, L. *Millennialism*, Winona Lake, IN: BMH Books, 2006, originally published 1936.

Folger, Janet L., *The Criminalization of Christianity*, Sisters, OR: Multnomah Publishers, 2005.

Gabriel, Brigitte, *Because They Hate*, New York, NY: St. Martin's Press, 2006.

Gabriel, Mark, *Journey Into the Mind of an Islamic Terrorist*, Lake Mary, FL: Front Line, 2006.

Geisler, Norman L. and Saleeb, Abdul, *Answering Islam*, Grand Rapids, MI: Baker Books, 1993.

Guillaume, Alfred, *Islam*, Baltimore, MD: Penguin Books, 1962.

Haleem, M. A. S. Abdel, *The Qur'an*, New York, NY: Oxford University Press Inc., 2005.

Hanegraaff, Hank, *The Apocalypse Code*, Nashville, TN: Thomas Nelson, 2007.

Hitchcock, Mark, *Iran: The Coming Crisis*, Sisters, OR: Multnomah Publishers, 2006.

Hunt, Dave, *Judgment Day! Islam, Israel and the Nations*, Bend, OR: The Berean Call, 2006.

Ice, Thomas and Price, Randall, *Ready to Rebuild*, Eugene, OR: Harvest House, 1992.

Intrater, Keith, *From Iraq to Armageddon*, Shippensburg, PA: Destiny Image Publishers, 2003.

Josephus, Flavius, *The Jewish War*, Grand Rapids, MI: Zondervan Publishing House, 1982.

Katz, Samuel, *Battle Ground: Fact and Fantasy in Palestine*, New York, NY: Taylor Productions, 2002.

Kotker, Norman, *The Earthly Jerusalem*, New York: Charles Scribner's Sons, 1969.

Kupelian, David, *The Marketing of Evil*, Nashville, TN: Cumberland House Publishing, 2005.

Levitt, Zola, *In My Father's House*, Dallas, TX: Levitt, 1981.

Levitt, Zola, *A Christian Love Story*, Dallas, TX: Levitt, 1978.

Levitt, Zola, *The Seven Feasts of Israel*, Dallas, TX: Levitt, 1979.

McBirnie, William Steuart, *The Search for the Tomb of Jesus*, Montrose, CA: Acclaimed Books, 1975.

MacArthur, John, *The Second Coming*, Wheaton, IL: Crossway Books, 1999.

Missler, Chuck, *Prophecy 20/20*, Nashville, TN: Nelson Books, 2006.

Price, Randall, *The Battle for the Last Days' Temple*, Eugene, OR: Harvest House, 2004.

Price, Randall, *The Temple and Bible Prophecy*, Eugene, OR: Harvest House, 2005.

Richman, Chaim, Carta's *Encyclopedia of the Holy Temple in Jerusalem,* Jerusalem, Israel: Carta, 2005.

Richman, Chaim, *The Holy Temple of Jerusalem,* Jerusalem, Israel: Carta, 1997.

Ritmeyer, Leen, *The Temple and the Rock,* Harrogate, England: Ritmeyer Archaeological Design, 1996.

Ritmeyer, Leen and Kathleen, *Secrets of Jerusalem's Temple Mount,* Washington, DC: Biblical Archaeology Society, 1998.

Rosenberg, Joel C., *Epicenter,* Carol Stream, IL: Tyndale House Publishing, 2006.

Shoebat, Walid, *Why I Left Jihad,* USA Top Executive Media, 2005.

Spencer, Robert, *The Truth about Muhammad,* Washington, DC: Regnery Publishing, Inc, 2006.

Spong, John Shelby, *Rescuing the Bible from Fundamentalism,* San Francisco, CA: Harper, 1999.

Steyn, Mark, *America Alone,* Washington, DC: Regnery Publishing, 2006.

Tancredo, Tom, *In Mortal Danger,* Nashville, TN: WND Books, 2006.

Zacharias, Ravi, *Light in the Shadow of Jihad,* Sisters, OR: Multnomah Publishers, 2002.

CPSIA information can be obtained at www.ICGtesting.com
Printed in the USA
BVOW061411050312

284460BV00001B/20/A